Forensic Psychology

Forensic Psychology

L.R.C. HAWARD
Professor of Clinical Psychology
University of Surrey

Batsford Academic and Educational Ltd
London

DEDICATED
with respect to
Dr Gerald E. Duggan-Keen
M.B., Ch.B., F.R.C.Psych., D.P.M.
Consultant Psychiatrist
One time Medical Superintendent, Winterton Hospital
Mentor and Friend

First published 1981
© L.R.C. Haward 1981
ISBN 0 7134 24753
Photoset by Photobooks (Bristol) Ltd
28 Midland Road, St Philips, Bristol
and printed and bound by
Billing & Son Ltd
London, Guildford and Worcester
for the publishers
Batsford Academic and Educational Ltd
4 Fitzhardinge Street, London W1H 0AH

Contents

List of Tables and Figures

TABLES

FIGURES

Preface

FORENSIC PSYCHOLOGY, defined in this volume as the application of psychology to the study of evidence for a court of law, is a comparatively new branch of the profession, but one which has developed rapidly during the past two decades. Because, in its development, its professional and theoretical boundaries have fluctuated and expanded, any textbook which attempted to be comprehensive would be premature. Moreover, there is so much that the forensic psychologist needs to know in order to make a fully effective contribution to legal proceedings that no single book could encompass it. The aim has been twofold: first to provide a conceptual scaffold upon which a more detailed knowledge of the subject can be erected by further reading and experience; and second, to provide some detailed guidance and advice on presenting expert evidence in a court of law, for the benefit of those psychologists who are called upon to do so. There are some important omissions which should be made explicit: only the barest minimum of information is given about the law, with which the forensic psychologist should endeavour to become familiar, and this is confined to a brief description of British courts and to a few relevant facts in the law of evidence. The psychometric methods and techniques adopted by the psychologist in solving forensic problems have not been included, but these should be already well-known by all practitioners who wish to employ them.

All the numbered cases have been drawn from the author's own casebook. Only the barest summary could be given here, and discussion of the accompanying legal problems and the many psychological implications in these cases have had to be omitted. The cases have been chosen to exemplify one main point as it occurs in the text, although many single cases would, and have, served as the basis for an introductory course in forensic psychology, and the more notorious cases have received only a brief mention.

This is then, an introduction to the subject as a whole and a practical guide to one particular aspect of it—expert testimony—and the choice of emphasis reflects the personal approach to forensic psychology developed by the author during the past quarter century. The text itself grew out of some of the lectures given as part of a formal course in forensic psychology to postgraduate clinical psychology students since

Preface

1965, formerly as part of the South West Metropolitan Region Training
Scheme, and latterly as a component in the course leading to the degree
of M.Sc. in Clinical Psychology at the University of Surrey.

Although addressed primarily to psychologists, it is hoped that
lawyers, medical practitioners, probation and police officers, and social
workers, who inter-relate with psychologists in court work, will find
this insight into the psychologist's view of forensic problem-solving of
interest and help in their professional work.

PART I

Introduction

1. Psychology and Law

WELL KNOWN to an older generation of psychologists, Dr Hastings Rashdall was one of those academicians whose intellectual brilliance was somewhat divorced from the mundane trivia of everyday life. He could ride a bicycle, but could not understand it. On one occasion, a colleague passing by noted that although he appeared to have a puncture in his front tyre, he was vigorously pumping up the rear one. When this was pointed out to him, he exclaimed in some surprise 'What! Do they not communicate?'[1].

For many decades, law and psychology were like the wheels of Dr Rashdall's bicycle, always pursuing the same course together, but rotating quite independently on their own axes. And certainly not communicating. This is perhaps surprising considering the fact that human behaviour is the *raison d'être* for both law and psychology. Both are concerned with the control of behaviour, although in different ways and at different levels. The jurists' control is explicit, rational and immediate, whereas that of the psychologist is implicit, empirical and ultimate.

Other differences between the two professions arise from the differing views of man held by the lawyer and psychologist respectively. The latter is generally deterministic and sees conduct as being activated primarily from unconscious motivations. The law, in contrast, assumes free will, and judges conduct as if man had complete and rational control of his decisions. The law is based upon commonly accepted beliefs (not necessarily well-founded) and reflects commonly adopted attitudes (however prejudiced). Cowan's detailed analysis of judicial decision-making shows that while the scientist generalizes, the lawyer individuates. He states: 'litigation aims to individuate, and the judicial process is most at home when it disposes of a unique conflict situation uniquely'[2], and believes that the law warps and twists facts to obtain a *just* result. In this view true equality in law consists in the maxim: *no two cases are ever really alike.* Modern psychology's attitudes are those of scientific scepticism, its theories derive from the hypothetico-deductive methods of classical science, and its beliefs rely on public, reproducible facts and the exclusion of at least 95% chance. For criteria the psychologist looks to René Descartes, the jurist to that character of legal fiction, the man

15

on the Clapham omnibus. Thus although the two professions move towards the same goal in a series of successive approximations to society's needs, the law lags behind contemporary social thinking, while psychology tends to anticipate it. Law is a system of regulating man's relations in society and aims at the just resolution of human conflict. Encompassing, as it does, the whole field of human interaction, its underlying processes lean heavily on psychological theory for understanding and clarification. Since the law evolves as society evolves the law is never a static process, although sometimes its rate of change is such that it may appear to have stagnated. Yet despite their differences, law and psychology are indissolubly bound together by their common role in the regulation of human behaviour, their responsibilities in maintaining the fabric of civilized society, and by the mutual use of psycholegal concepts which have existed since man-made law took over from the law of the jungle.

Law existed long before psychology, yet as soon as man became a social animal with time to sit and think, the first roots of jurisprudence and legal psychology began their tentative exploration in the human mind.

It was in the civilization of ancient Greece that psychology and law became closer than they were to remain for the next 2000 years. Plato, especially, showed explicit concern for psycholegal concepts; *The Republic* is devoted to the search for the meaning of justice[3], and related concepts appear in much of his later writings. The intertwining of law and psychology can be traced, with difficulty, in both legal and philosophical writings between then and the present day, but it was not until Wundt founded his famous psychological laboratory at Leipzig exactly a century ago that psychology cut the umbilical cord which had tied it to philosophy, and took its first breath as a lusty infant in the arms of its wet-nurse, Science.

This shift in direction from armchair meditation to laboratory activity was viewed without enthusiasm by the lawyers of the time. They regarded the new science as coming from decidedly dubious parentage, and were suspicious of the statements made by scientists. 'The Law' said that great jurist Jennings, 'walks a respectful distance behind science'. Perhaps this is as it should be; the wisdom of the judicial process has accumulated, slowly and painfully, through every century of human social history. The course of science, on the other hand, is littered with the wrecks and relics of outmoded ideas and of theories espoused too soon. Yet the gap between science and the law is of critical dimensions. Too *little* may do society a disservice, as when dangerous offenders remain in the community because of some fanciful sociological notion and repeat their offence. Too *much*, and the individual suffers injustice, as when a paternity case was settled on the basis of resemblance despite the evidence of incompatible blood groups[4].

For the past century, psychologists have been able to offer the law their explicit skills; lawyers, not unnaturally, remain somewhat sceptical. It is a sad fact that not all of psychology's contributions to the law have been crowned with success, and on occasions its greatest protagonists have been disappointed and disillusioned. One such supporter was Judge David Bazelon, a renowned American jurist who recognized the profession's expertise but believed it to be irrelevant to the needs of the judiciary. This great Appellate judge, who was instrumental in establishing the admissibility of psychologists as expert witnesses in the American Courts[5] once remarked that psychology, in offering its services to the law, reminded him of a certain doctor. A mother had called in the doctor to attend her young child, and explained that he was suffering terribly from fever, nausea and cramps. 'But is he having fits?' the doctor asked. The mother said 'No'. 'That's too bad', replied the doctor. 'I'm terrific on fits.'

Clearly psychology, if it is to make any real contribution to the course of justice, cannot wait until the law has fits. Neither, if its contribution is to be positive and beneficial, should it rush in prematurely with inadequate skills or inappropriate remedies. Bazelon's viewpoint has been influenced to some extent by those clinicians who enter the witness box and expose weaknesses of the same kind and degree as those cogently, validly, and justifiably damned by Szasz[6]. More seriously, Bazelon believes psychology's inability to come to grips with the problem of criminal behaviour is because psychologists use a medical model and theories based on middle-class samples, both of which are inappropriate when applied to offenders from the botton of society's barrel[7].

With great respect to their legal friend and sympathizer, psychologists will probably reply that while what the worthy judge says is to some extent the truth, it is not the whole truth, and presents too restrictive a view of what psychologists are actually doing within the various activities of the law.

This can best be understood by reference to Figure 1, which shows the present relationship between the various branches of psychology and the law. At first glance this may appear over-inclusive, covering as it does every established branch of psychology as a profession, but the fact remains that each specialty within psychology is making a definite if not always direct contribution to the process and development of law and order, with various degrees of utility. The legal process has three clearly defined phases. First, the preparation of a case arising from the notification of a crime or the instigation of civil proceedings by a plaintiff. Secondly, the judicial hearing of the case, and the arriving at a judgement, and finally the supervision of the consequences of the judgement. In criminal proceedings, the constabulary are mainly concerned in Phase I, the law in Phase II, and the prison and probation service in Phase III. This is, however, a rather artificial division of labour, and lawyers are generally concerned from the time of the initial summons to the accused until the last of the appeals or parole boards. In civil actions, of course, the process is entirely a legal one. The triphasic nature of legal process is also reflected in the way some of the specialties in psychology tend to concentrate on one particular phase of this process; for example, Home Office psychologists and those working in criminology concentrate on the nature of the criminal activity[8], whereas prison and correctional psychologists have been concerned primarily with the consequences of it[9]. However, psychologists in all branches of psychology contribute to the three phases in one way or another. Academic psychologists are involved in providing psychology training to the police[10], run courses for magistrates and lawyers[11,12], and are also involved in the retraining of recidivists. Experimental psychologists have examined the validity and reliability of police procedures, such as interrogation[13] and identity parades[14] or police techniques such as the identikit[10,15]. They have looked at Jury room processes[16] and sentencing structure, and examined experimentally the relative effectiveness of alternative correctional measures. Forensic psychologists, too, whether their postgraduate training has been in child or clinical psychology, are concerned in each of the three phases. They will be collecting and examining evidence in Phase I, presenting it in court in Phase II, and preparing and taking part in appeals, parole enquiries, and probation in Phase III. The forensic psychologist is wholly and exclusively concerned with *evidence*—and this will include the methods by which it is collected, presented, examined, and deliberated upon, together with the influence which particular evidence will have on the verdict and decision of the court, including the disposal of the case[17], thus, the forensic psychologist can expect to be interested in a wide variety of activities involving evidence, including many of those enumerated in Table I, since his knowledge of these processes can be used to practical advantage when he himself is collecting, examining or presenting evidence for court. It should be understood, however, that the *raison d'être* of the forensic psychologist, *qua* forensic, is as an expert on evidence pertaining to a particular case. From his primary professional training as a psychologist, and his subsequent experience in legal proceedings, the forensic psychologist will have acquired a fairly extensive knowledge which when co-ordinated, critically examined and synthesized, may make a useful contribution to the subject. His first concern, however, will be the contribution to justice which he can make by applying the existing knowledge of his speciality to any particular case[18].

Figure 1

Psychology and Law

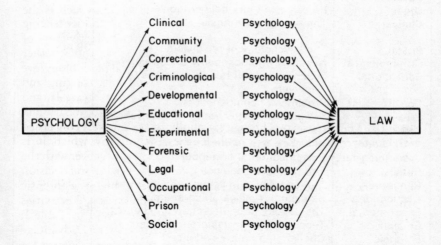

Each professional specialty developing from the mainstream of psychology
has made its own unique contribution to law.

Introduction

Table I

Psychology and Law

Some activities by psychologists which contribute to the processes of law and order.

Psychology Specialty	General field of activity	References
Developmental	Nature of juvenile delinquency	19,20,21,22
Clinical	Psychopathology of crime	23,24
Prison	Prison classificational problems	25
Criminological	Teaching criminology to psychologists	26
Legal	Judicial attitudes to sentencing	27
Educational	Courses in preventive law	12
Experimental	The psychology of identification	28
Social	Processes of jury selection	29,30
Legal	Processes of jury deliberation	31,32,33
Clinical	The nature of amnesia	34,35,36, 37,38
Prison	The psychology of recidivism	39,40
Criminological	Nosology and nosonomy of delinquency	41
Educational	Teaching mental health concepts to lawyers	42,43
Social	Problems of compensation	44,45
Prison	Stigma associated with prison psychology	46
Forensic	Deriving evidence by experiments	47
Correctional	Selection of prisoners for parole	48
Criminological	Classification of criminality	49,50
Clinical	The nature of violence	51
Community	Training police in community intervention	52,53,54
Occupational	Selection of police officers, etc.	55
Experimental	The validity of lie detection procedures	56,57
Educational	Teaching human factors to lawyers	43
Forensic	Challenging police evidence	58
Correctional	The effectiveness of the penal system	59
Clinical	Law regarding the mentally abnormal offender	60,61,62
Criminological	Criminal typology	63,64
Educational	Psychological studies of legal training	65
Experimental	The processes of interrogation	13,66,67
Forensic	Giving expert testimony in court	68,69,70
Occupational	Job effectiveness in law enforcement	71
Correctional	Prediction methods in penal training	72
Clinical	Behaviour therapy for penal inmates	73
Educational	Lawyer-client communications	74

N.B. This list is not intended to be comprehensive, but merely gives a sufficiently wide selection of psychological activities to indicate the diversity of subject and specialty of psychologists with legal interests.

2. Defining Forensic Psychology

FORENSIC PSYCHOLOGY is here defined as that branch of applied psychology which is concerned with the collection, examination and presentation of evidence for judicial purposes. The definition is consistent with that used by English psychologists writing on the subject[75,76,77]. The term forensic comes from the Latin *forensis* meaning 'of the forum'. It is specifically referring to the Roman Forum and therefore to the functions of the court. However, it has an additional meaning, namely 'to argue', often distinguished from the primary meaning by a new adjectival form 'forensical'. In this sense, used especially in the U.S.A., it refers to the presentation of a thesis or dissertation which argues strongly in one direction or another. This derivation from *forensis* comes closer to our use of the word forum, meaning a place for public discussion of important issues. Thus we can see that the term forensic refers directly to arguments in court. It is of Tudor origin[78] and emerged in the context of the English adversary system. Clearly forensic matters concern 'evidence in dispute'. They may be criminal matters, but equally, they will also refer to civil disputes regarding evidence[79].

In this latter respect, a distinction between forensic psychology and forensic psychiatry[80] needs to be made, at least as practised in England. Here the role of forensic psychiatry is taken to refer exclusively to concern with the abnormal offender. Following the recommendations of the Butler Committee[62], special secure units are being established on a regional basis to enable abnormal offenders to be treated and socially rehabilitated in a setting which is unlike either a prison or a mental hospital. It is etymologically unfortunate that these were called forensic psychiatry units, for it not only strengthened the existing role limitation of forensic psychiatry but led to further absurdities. The author, who was involved in the preparation of evidence for the Butler Committee[60,61] attended an important meeting between senior officials of the Home Office, responsible for abnormal offenders in prisons, and those of the Department of Health and Social Security, responsible for their care in mental hospitals, to discuss the detailed organization of the forensic psychiatry units. During the discussion, a serious proposal was made that since forensic psychiatrists were to be employed, the nursing staff should be allowed to call themselves 'forensic nurses'. *Reductio ad absurdum* was reached when the representative for domestic services asked 'Can we have forensic porters?'

The narrowing of the definition to refer only to matters pertaining to crime and criminals seems to have come about because the adjective has been mainly used with reference to the forensic science laboratories set up by the police and Home Office in the U.K., and by the forensic pathologists who work in conjunction with the police. The work of the forensic scientist, by virtue of his employer, is entirely criminal and forensic pathologists, from the nature of their specimens, are concerned primarily with the consequences of crime. The publicity accorded famous pathologists of the past, in the context of their most successful criminal cases, has served to emphasize the relationship between forensic medicine and crime.

In America, the psychiatric profession has explicitly made a stand against such a narrow role. Robey and Bogard in their presentation of the *Compleat Forensic Psychiatrist* remark that 'too often the entire field of forensic psychiatry is thought to consist solely of going into court and testifying on the criminal responsibility of some hapless defendant' and point out that the psychiatrist has a role in the civil courts and in other judicial functions. Similarly the expansion of the horizons of forensic psychiatry is described at some length by Robitscher[81]. The interest of American psychiatrists in civil issues, particularly those concerning involuntary hospital commitment and patients' rights, has led to a healthy increase in professional activities concerned with non-criminal litigants, an increase mirrored by a threefold increase in articles in legal journals indexed under 'psychiatry'.

Elsewhere in Europe, the emphasis remains confined within the role of dealing with the mentally abnormal offender. In Iceland 'the main task of forensic psychiatry is without doubt the psychiatric examination of probable mentally abnormal offenders'[82]. In Scandinavia, forensic psychiatry is virtually criminological psychiatry, a longstanding tradition from almost half a century ago when Professor Kinberg held the chair of Forensic Psychiatry in Stockholm and was an international authority on criminology. His book *Basic Problems of Criminology*[83] expresses clearly his view as a criminologist rather than as a psychiatrist. The identification of forensic psychiatry with criminality has led to attacks on this specialty by lawyers, criminologists, and journalists during the 1970s. In Sweden a newspaper journalist published a book entitled *Abolish Forensic Psychiatry*[84]; in Denmark, the Head of the Forensic Psychiatry Unit of the Ministry of Justice at Copenhagen published a medical paper questioning whether the existence of forensic psychiatry can be justified[85]; in Finland, criminologists have strongly criticized forensic psychiatrists for bringing treatment ideology into the disposal of offenders[86], while in Norway, physicians have argued that the role of the forensic psychiatrist conflicts with that of the physician[87]. Forensic psychiatrists in Scandinavia have aired their own version of the problems[88,89,90,91], but appear to have accepted without question the concept of forensic psychiatry as related exclusively to the disposal of offenders.

It would, of course, be grossly unfair to under-rate the contribution made to criminology by forensic psychiatrists. Professor T. C. N. Gibben, whose own meticulous scientific work has made a substantial contribution to criminological knowledge, makes an excellent example of what the forensic psychiatrist can achieve in this area, and has his own ideas on what should be the task of forensic psychiatry[92]. It could be argued, however, that much of the scientific knowledge produced by the painstaking investigations of such experts is not strictly within the field of psychiatry at all. To bring their whole contribution to criminology under the label of forensic psychiatry implies an acceptance of the belief that all proscribed conduct is a sign of mental illness, and deserves the scathing criticisms which Szasz has made of this viewpoint[93]. Related professions also have their labelling problems *vis à vis* forensic matters[94].

In Scotland, an attempt has been made to find an all-inclusive term which covers all activities embraced jointly by Medicine and the Law. Nagle calls it medico-legalism[95] and elsewhere proposes the establishment of a medico-legal service staffed by so-called medico-legal officers who are trained for the new medical specialty and career structure[96]. Since the Scottish capital created the first British Chair of Forensic Medicine[97] it is particularly appropriate that this new move towards semantic sense should emerge north of the border. Scottish law and legal procedures have sometimes predated and anticipated changes in English law and legal procedures, the concept of diminished responsibility being the most significant recent example, so it would not be surprising to see the establishment of the first fully comprehensive medico-legal service in this ancient kingdom, in which forensic psychiatry, as presently conceived, would be a branch.

British psychologists have been at pains to distinguish between the existence of psychopathology, in the sense of a *medical condition*, and other psychological processes in the criminal offender which contribute to his decisions to commit an unlawful act. In England there has, too, been a clear distinction between those psychologists who make a specific contribution to criminology, such as criminological psychologists, prison psychologists, and Home Office psychologists, and those who contribute to the law generally. This distinction was embodied in the formation of the latest professional division of the British Psychological Society, which became incorporated as the Division of Criminological and Legal Psychology[98]. This title emphasizes and makes explicit the dichotomy of subject. On the one hand are all those psychologists concerned with the criminal mind and criminal behaviour, whether it is before, during or after the *actus reus*, or criminal act. On the other hand are all those psychologists who are concerned with the people (other than criminals) who are brought into the focus of the law. These will include, inter alia, policemen, lawyers, jurors, magistrates, litigants, victims of crimes, and witnesses of events. The psychologists who study such groups will be interested in a variety of processes.

How the police or litigants collect evidence, the legal rules which hold evidence to be admissible, material and relevant, the processes whereby the evidence is presented and examined in court, and the influence that evidence has on the Jury and judiciary, are clearly problems of concern to the forensic psychologist. What happens after a judicial decision has been reached are not. It is here that forensic psychology and forensic psychiatry show their most profound differences, for it is only in the disposal and after-care of the criminal offender that forensic psychiatry comes into its own, whereas these matters are no longer within the bounds of forensic psychology.

By confining the scope of forensic psychology to the 'arguable facts', i.e. the evidence, and the processes whereby it is collected, presented, examined, and deliberated upon in a court of law, psychologists have not only retained etymological purity and semantic clarity for their professional specialty, but have discouraged the proliferation of diverse and meaningless occupational labels like 'forensic porter'.

3. Forensic Psychology in the U.K.

ALTHOUGH IN 1972 there were 41 psychologists in America who checked 'forensic psychology' as their occupational specialty[99], elsewhere the subject has not yet achieved the status of an independent employment category. Indeed, many would argue that for it to do so would be premature and detrimental to the profession. At present, forensic psychologists provide expert testimony from the standing of their own professional specialty, be it clinical, experimental, educational, social, criminological, occupational and so on. The forensic psychologists are admitted to court as experts because their expertise has already been proved in one of the branches of psychology relevant to the case before the court. They are not there as experts on evidence in general. To be so, they would necessarily be that much less the expert in the subject under dispute, and this could reduce both the value of their testimony and the justification for their being in court at all. Until this paradox has been satisfactorily resolved, both psychology as a profession and the ends of justice will be better served by the forensic psychologist being first and foremost a specialist in one of the traditional branches of psychology. Nevertheless, to be such an expert is not enough. Psychologists do law a disservice if they come to legal processes naive, unsophisticated and ignorant of the nature of these problems. They will be required to discuss in court, under vigorous verbal attack, concepts which are not those of their profession, and which they may regard as meaningless or of no utility. They will have to use terms foreign to their science, and with whose meaning they disagree. When in Rome, says the old adage, it is wise to do as the Romans. In court it is imperative to communicate in a way both comprehensible to the plain man and consistent with legal terminology. Knowledge of legal concepts and of the rules of evidence will therefore enable the psychologist to make an optimally effective contribution to the proceedings. Cases in which the psychologist's evidence tips the balance in favour of one side or another may be won or lost purely on the way the psychologist handles the evidence, rather than on the intrinsic value of the evidence itself. Expertise in the law of evidence is a considerable asset to the forensic psychologist, but first and foremost he must be an expert in some recognized field of psychological knowledge.

The number of psychologists who designate their occupational specialty as forensic psychology is consequently no guide to the actual number of psychologists engaged in forensic work. In 1965 a questionnaire was sent to the 477 members of the British Psychological Society who were either educational or clinical psychologists, asking for details of their participation, if any, in forensic work[100]. The response rate was approximately 25%, fairly evenly divided between the two specialties. Follow-up enquiries elicited some evidence suggesting that the non-responders tended to be psychologists who had no connection with court work, and that only those who were interested in this interdisciplinary collaboration had bothered to reply. Almost all respondents (total 113) had submitted written evidence to the Courts, and about half had appeared in court to give oral testimony. There was no significant difference in frequency between the clinical and educational psychologists in these last two activities. Of course, this survey covered only two specialties in psychology, and although these two professional groups probably contributed more to court work than any other psychological specialty, it would be wrong to assume that other specialities did not do so. In *R.* v. *Anderson et al. (1971)*, for example, four psychologists were called to give evidence for the defence, of whom only one was a practising clinician, the remainder being primarily academic psychologists. Extrapolation of this ratio would indicate that a very substantial number of British psychologists were likely to be involved in court cases: while this conclusion would not be justified on such evidence alone, it seems reasonable to believe that the number of psychologists contributing to the work of the courts is significantly higher than that calculated from the survey based solely upon membership of the clinical and educational divisions of the B.P.S.

The 1966 survey was of interest in being the first data source to provide information on the frequency with which psychologists appeared in court, and the types of problems they encountered in this type of professional work. The report shows that while most British psychologists at this date were engaged in forensic activities no more than twice per year, some were preparing reports for court nearly every week, while others were appearing in court as expert witnesses nearly every month. The educational psychologists gave evidence concerning disposal in 53% of their court work, and 40% covered educational standards. Only 7% of the evidence tendered in court by this specialty concerned diagnosis. Among clinical psychologists a reverse trend was noted, with 55% of their legal consultations concerned primarily with diagnosis and clinical assessment, 33% concerned with cognitive functions, and only 12% referring to disposal. The difference between the forensic work of the two specialties at that time was appropriately summarized by

Castell when he said the clinicians were almost entirely concerned with present disablement, whereas the educational psychologists were primarily concerned with future education and care[101]. Further differences existed in the courts to which the two specialties were usually called. Most of the educational psychologists appeared exclusively in the juvenile courts, as would be predicted from the legal procedure appropriate to the age group of their clients. Clinicians, in contrast, appeared mostly in the High Court of Justice or the Assize Courts (now the Crown Courts), with a preponderance of Civil over Criminal cases. Most of the forensic work of the psychologist still lies in the Civil Courts or in the domestic jurisdiction of the Lower Courts, where 'care and protection' orders, 'place of safety' orders, and problems concerning the custody of children following divorce, separation or parental death figure prominently. This preponderance of family law and compensation in tort in the forensic caseload of the psychologist emphasizes the semantic limitation of 'forensic' when used in place of 'criminological'.

The decade following the B.P.S. 1966 survey saw a significant increase in forensic work by British psychologists, and a personal survey conducted at the Annual Conference of the B.P.S. in 1978 showed that the number of psychologists involved in court work at that time was nearly threefold that of the earlier survey. No direct or exact comparison is possible because the sampling procedure was different on the two occasions, and in 1978 included academic psychologists as well as those working in the educational and clinical fields. However, it is clear that a substantial proportion of British psychologists have experience of forensic work and many of them are extremely active in this field. Although at present court work has an irregular ebb and flow for psychologists, and those relying on it for a living would soon develop a streaky bacon constitution, if professionally developed and managed it could offer full-time employment for a significant number of psychologists in the U.K. Recently some clinical psychologists have had as many as six forensic cases active at any one time—a few on occasions twice as many—so the potential work for forensic psychology is clearly manifest.

Table II

Problems in Forensic Psychology

Some idea of the scope of forensic psychology is provided by the following questions put to the author in various cases and answered in the form of evidence, submitted either as a psychological report, a proof of testimony, or as expert parole evidence from the witness box. The numbers refer to case numbers in the text.

1. Is the confession made by the accused likely to be genuine?
2. Did the plaintiff suffer brain damage; if so, to what extent? What degree of mental recovery can be expected over what duration of time?
3. Is the appellant a fit person to have the custody of his child returned to him? What is the present risk of physical assault against his children?
4. What psychological evidence is there to support the claim of the accused that the dazed condition noted by the police at the time of the accident was due to post-concussional confusion and not excess alcohol?
5. Can the recall of the 17 witnesses who have agreed to undergo forensic hypnosis, be improved by this technique to provide a more consistent and detailed description of a motor vehicle which the police wish to trace?
6. Is the person complaining to the police about obscene phone calls and damage to personal property manufacturing the evidence to satisfy psychological needs?
7. Is the suicidal risk present in this patient compulsorily detained in hospital on a Mental Health Order sufficient to justify her continued detention on the grounds of her own health and safety?
8. Is the mental condition of this patient sufficient for him to be detained under the Mental Health Act on the grounds that it is necessary for the protection of others?
9. What evidence can be offered to demonstrate the invalidity or unreliability of an uncorroborated statement by a police officer?
10. What evidence can be offered to demonstrate possible errors in the corroborated statements of two police officers?
11. What steps should the constabulary take to eliminate a weakness in a certain type of evidence?
12. What evidence is there that the physical condition complained of arises from the working conditions of the complainant?
13. What evidence is there to substantiate the statement of the accused that he was unaware of his conduct by reason of drunkenness?
14. What evidence is there that the accident arose from a genuine machinery hazard and not from carelessness?
15. Is there a sufficient *prima facie* case to plead against the carrying out of the death sentence on the grounds of insanity?

16. What evidence is there that customers confuse two different brands of a certain commodity and to what extent does this occur?
17. Are there any psychological factors relevant to the prisoner which would justify bail?
18. What psychological evidence of cruelty can be put forward to justify a plea for divorce on these grounds?
19. What evidence can be offered that the appellant is capable of managing his own financial affairs?
20. Can evidence of the effectiveness of the proposed treatment be sufficient to justify release of the prisoner from his prison sentence in favour of treatment under a probation order?
21. Can the plaintiff's probable future earnings be psychologically assessed?
22. What is the probability of the accused being schizophrenic? What evidence is there that he is insane?
23. What is the probability of the suspect having been a member of a proscribed political party and of arrestable rank?
24. What psychological evidence is available to show how suggestible children and mentally handicapped adults are, when interrogated by police officers.
25. What psychological evidence is available to show the validity of various methods of personal identification?
26. What defects exist in the medical evidence being put forward by the expert witnesses called by the 'other side'?
27. What are the psychological implications for the future of the party concerned in this particular case?
28. To what extent is the plaintiff mentally handicapped? To what extent is this handicap likely to effect his cycling skill? What is his probable loss of earning power, if any, as a result of the accident? What weaknesses, if any, exist in the medical evidence tendered by the witnesses for the defendant?
29. What was the perceptual basis of the Master's misjudgement in docking his ship?
30. Was the testator mentally capable of making a valid will at the time she did so?
31. What evidence can be offered as to the state of mind of the deceased shortly before death.
32. What psychological help can be offered to bring about a rapprochement and out of court settlement between these two litigants?
33. Are there psychological grounds arising from evidence heard at the previous trial and appeal which should be communicated to the House of Lords?

PART II

The Roles of the Forensic Psychologist

4. The Clinical Role in Forensic Psychology

WHEN forensic psychologists are invited to bring their professional expertise to bear upon some problem of evidence, a number of different approaches, or roles, are available[102-116]. Although all psychologists have a primary interest in studying human behaviour, they do so in a variety of different ways. Some do it by entering into a personal relationship with the individual being studied, so that the interactions between psychologist and client, and between the client and his world, can be examined in detail. This could be called the *clinical* approach, since the original model was that of physician and patient. The client, of course, is not necessarily a patient, and in place of problems of health may have, *inter alia*, problems of education, occupation or marriage. Some psychologists study human behaviour not by personal interaction but by experimentation, using a representative sample of human subjects and placing them in an environment where the significant factors can be controlled or varied according to some predetermined plan, which follows the hypothetico-deductive method of classical science. This is the *experimental* approach, and it uses what Allport calls the *nomothetic* method, as distinct from the *idiographic* method which is more appropriate for the clinical approach[117]. In the third approach to the study of human behaviour, the psychologist neither interacts with the subject nor controls the environment in any way. Instead, the method makes use of observation only, but elevates it to a scientific level by using large numbers of observations from which the variations in observation can be analyzed and predictions concerning future observations made. Although this approach follows that adopted in astronomy, its focus on human behaviour, and particularly its mathematical basis in probability theory, makes it more akin to the actuarial process. For this reason, it has been called the *actuarial* approach[118]. The forensic psychologist, therefore, in facing the evidential problem requiring solution, will take on one of these three roles, clinician, experimentalist, or actuary, whichever happens to be the one most appropriate to the problem in hand. These roles are not necessarily exclusive, and the forensic psychologist may adopt more than one role in dealing with a particular court case; however, each problem usually has its own appropriate mode for optimum solution and for this reason, the three roles will be examined independently in a little more detail.

The clinical approach to forensic problems

The clinical role is adopted by the forensic psychologist more frequently than any other. As the B.P.S. Survey (op.cit.) made clear, clinical and educational psychologists represent a substantial proportion of those working in the forensic field. Since their professional practice is generally a client centred one, and since the purpose for which psychologists from these two specialties have been engaged by lawyers usually concerns the mental state and/or capacities of the client, it is to be expected that in most cases the clinical role is the only appropriate one. The clinical techniques themselves, their limitations and their problems, are well known to the practitioners who regularly employ them in their professional duties, and need not be repeated here. The essence of the clinical approach is that the psychologist has to enter into a professional relationship with the client in order to obtain the evidence: this in itself raises professional and ethical issues which have not yet been fully resolved. One problem is the question of who legally is the client. Normally the contract lies between the psychologist and the solicitors. The latter, in the terms of the law of contract, make the offer. Their offer includes what the law calls 'consideration', in this case payment of a fee and expenses in consideration for the psychologists' professional services. Legally then, the psychologists' client is the firm of solicitors who engage his/or her services and guarantee payment for them. It should be noted that, life being what it is and criminals being what they are, a substantial number of the solicitors' clients who escape a prison sentence will vanish into the underworld immediately they are released from court. Thus a depressing number of bills sent out by the solicitor to the last known address of the client are returned marked 'Gone Away'. In such circumstances, the solicitor can do nothing more than muse with the Bard on the sharpness of serpents' teeth, and increase future fees to cover past bad debts. By having his contract with the solicitor and not with the parties of the case, the psychologist avoids this unprofitable side of forensic work. The contract in this form has another advantage, since in theory, at least, the psychologist can provide an impersonal and unbiased report to lawyers who are seeking facts about their client. While hoping the facts will help both the client and their presentation of the case, the solicitors at this stage are more interested in getting the facts right. Opinions, emphases, and re-interpretations can come later.

In practice, however, things tend to work out a little differently. To the professional psychologist, a client is someone with whom he relates for the sole purpose of improving the client's lot. In entering into a professional relationship with the client, he cannot help entering into a human relationship also, for this after all is what psychology is all about. And in this relationship, if it is to be affectively warm, honest and valid, the client will come with expectations that the psychologist is going to help him personally. Not Justice in the abstract, or the golden lady surmounting the Old Bailey's copper-green dome, but this particular individual, embroiled in the processes of the law, and desperately seeking help. Implicit, indeed often explicit, is the client's expectancy that the psychologist is there to provide direct and personal help and succour. Moreover, the client is paying for the privilege. Even if Legal Aid has been granted, the client will normally have to find initial costs of preparing his case, and these may well be more than he can afford, and require some not insubstantial sacrifice on the part of his family. If he has not been granted Legal Aid the whole of the psychologists' remuneration and professional expenses will be coming from the client's own financial resources which may be tied up in a high-interest mortgage, support of an ex-wife and family, or other personal commitments which make the grounds and cut-off level for granting Legal Aid extremely controversial.

Who then, is the psychologists' client? Legally, as noted earlier, it is the engaging solicitors. Professionally, however, forensic psychologists cannot but view the party in the case as their true client. Within the framework of their professional integrity, they normally undertake to do their best in their 'client's' interest. In most cases, the interest of the party as client will not clash with the interests of the solicitors who engage the psychologists' services. After all, if the findings of the psychological investigation are unhelpful to the client, showing perhaps that the effects of a road accident are less severe than the client believes, or that the basis of a defence on the grounds of diminished responsibility cannot be supported on the psychometric evidence available, then they need not be used. In such circumstances, if the lawyers on the other side learned of the existence of such findings they could order a *subpoena duces tecum* to be served on the psychologist, compelling him to bring his findings to court where they would be used against the interests of the psychologists' client. It is for this reason that the utmost confidentiality should be observed in all forensic work. Sometimes, however, the client reveals information to the psychologist which he is unwilling for the solicitor to know. This comes about because of the nature of the relationship as perceived by the client. Frequently the client is seen in a clinic or hospital premises. If in prison he will normally be taken over to the prison hospital, where the psychologist can carry out his examination in appropriate accommodation—usually one of the prison medical officers' consulting rooms. In such settings the client presumes the relationship to be a doctor-patient one, and assumes communication to be privileged. Despite the psychologist making explicit the nature of the relationship as seen from a professional point of view, the very nature of the human interaction, including the development of the necessary rapport, serves to make the relationship a particularly personal one which is clearly different from the one the client has with his legal advisor. If the psychologist has a doctorate qualification, which is more often than not the case, this will only serve to reinforce the belief that medical confidentiality is available. Even if medical confidentiality is denied by the psychologist, the obvious 'clinical' context, and 'clinical' procedures, such as history-taking, will encourage the client to be more forthcoming and self-revealing than he has been in the more formal atmosphere of the lawyer's chambers. This problem will be discussed more fully later: it is raised here in order to make explicit the existence of two possible conflicts; one regarding the use of the evidence collected from the party concerned, and the other emanating from the respective legal and moral responsibilities and duties relating to the two different 'clients'. Generally, the interests of both lie parallel, but this is not always the case, and the forensic psychologist should be prepared for the implications and consequences. The following case exemplifies the problem of who is the psychologist's client, and the conflict of interests which can evolve in this situation.

CASE NO. 1.

A small silver trophy was stolen from the office of a company in which nine people worked. Suspicion fell on a middle-aged lady who had been expressing special interest in it for a long time, and who was always handling it. The suspect had been seen by cleaners returning to the office after the remainder of the clerical staff had gone home. The trophy was discovered at a later date concealed in a locker used by the staff to store their personal chattels. Only the suspect's fingerprints could be identified on the trophy. She was interviewed by the police and although she denied having anything to do with the theft of the trophy, she was told she would be charged. The following day, a male clerk from the same office went to the police and confessed to having removed the trophy, but denied stealing it. His explanation was that he couldn't stand the sight of the thing any longer. The police then dropped the charges against the woman and prepared the case against the man, on the basis of (i) his confession (ii) evidence of opportunity (iii) his statement that he wore gloves whilst removing the trophy, and evidence from the office staff that the woman was always fingering the trophy (iv) evidence that he used the staff locker regularly. He consulted a solicitor, who advised him to plead not guilty on the grounds that the police would have to prove intent to steal, and who referred him to the author in the hope that a psychological examination would support his story of having a special dislike of the trophy. This was not an easy problem to investigate, since most of the obvious methods of measuring his preferences and reactions to the trophy would be contaminated by the fact that it was now the cause of an impending prosecution and possible loss of freedom and pensionable employment. It was decided to probe analytically into the meaning which the trophy had for him using both an anamnesic technique and conceptual analysis based on a Repertory Grid Technique[227] and the Semantic Differential[228]. The latter techniques produced conceptual locations which referred directly to the current situation i.e. to the police, guilt, the woman suspect, and so on. However, in the second long interview, discussing his personal life, the accused broke down and cried, and then confessed that he had entertained feelings of affection for the original suspect over a long period, and had confessed in order to save her from embarrassment. She was supporting an elderly bedfast parent, and apart from the effects of losing her job, she would suffer considerable disgrace in the small community where she had lived all her life and was much respected. He had much less to lose, commuting from a town sufficiently distant to be unaffected by local news even if he was found guilty. He was an intelligent man, and believed that he could present a good story of hating the trophy, unlike the woman whose interest in it was well-known and of longstanding. He pleaded with the author not to reveal his secret to the solicitor, as he genuinely wanted to help his lady friend in her trouble. What does one do with such a latter-day Sidney Carton? If one's duty is to one's legal client, in this case the solicitor, then he should be informed of his client's alleged innocence and the new circumstances of which he was totally unaware. In engaging the psychologist to provide information on the accused, the solicitor is assuming that *all* relevant information will be passed on to him, especially that which would obviously lead to the charges against his client being dropped. On the other hand, the psychologist has now entered into a very special professional relationship with the solicitor's client, and may feel that he has a moral obligation to protect the client's interest. This is the kind of conflict to which reference was made earlier.

It was mentioned that the clinical role is the one most frequently adopted by the forensic psychologist. In these cases, the problem itself is more likely to be a clinical one, and the client is formally a patient who is receiving, or has received, medical treatment for the condition which is relevant to the legal issue. Road traffic accidents form the largest majority of such cases, and the psychologist is engaged on behalf of the plaintiff—the party bringing the action who is usually the victim of the circumstances[104].

CASE NO. 2.

An omnibus overtook a moped rider on his way to college and then swerved into the curb to avoid an oncoming lorry which was passing a car parked on the lorry's nearside. The student was squeezed between the curb and the bus and thrown off his machine, striking his uncovered head on both the vehicle and the road, and sustaining other injuries when the rear wheel of the bus passed over him. The bus company agreed the physical injuries to the lower part of the body but contested the head injuries. Neurologists were called from both sides, and disagreed about the presence of brain damage, the degree of cerebral impairment, and the implications for the future academic progress and earning capacity of the student. The psychologist was called in on behalf of the student, and undertook a thorough psychometric examination of cognitive functioning. As a result of the psychometric test data so obtained, he was able to give evidence of a significant degree of dysmnesia, of cognitive impairment of a degree found only in brain damaged patients, and of a level of intellectual functioning substantially below that appropriate to the plaintiff's scholastic record. In the light of this additional evidence the defendant settled out of court. It should be noted that the psychologists' evidence both complemented and supplemented that of the neurologists. Of the latter, one said there were no memory difficulties apparent, the other said there were, but was unable to quantify these or provide a reasonable explanation of why the memory impairment was more likely than not to be of post-traumatic origin. The quantitative form of the psychologists' findings was convincing evidence of the presence of the dysmnesia and its extent, while the qualitative pattern of defects obtained from the subtest scores could be matched with those obtained in other closed-head injury cases, and contrasted with the patterns obtained from non-injured students of the same background as the plaintiff. Similarly the low Organic Integrity Score could be related directly to the distribution of scores from brain-damaged patients and non-brain-damaged patients: together with other indices of conceptual and other cognitive impairment, the probability of brain damage could be inferred directly and statistically from the available evidence. The opinion of the defendant's neurologist that no closed head injury or brain damage had occurred carried lower substantive weight than that of the psychologist who could display the evidence on which his opinion was based. Finally, the ability to give a quantitative assessment of intelligence, and to demonstrate with figures the disparity between the student's mental efficiency following the accident and that inferred from other evidence originating before the accident, enabled the non-clinical layman to understand the effects of the trauma in simple common sense terms. Of course, the extrapolation of present possibly temporary deficits into future permanent disability requires a knowledge of the rate of change over an adequate time base and experience of the asymptotes produced by post-traumatic recovery. This is an additional problem which will be discussed later.

Alternatively the forensic psychologist may be asked to appear on behalf of the defendant, who is denying any legal responsibility in the matter and may be cross-petitioning on the grounds that he also has suffered physical or financial damage as a result of the accident for which he blames the plaintiff (In Scotland the latter is called the 'Pursuer').

CASE No. 3

A mentally subnormal, epileptic man married to a woman of average intelligence had his two young children removed and put into the care of foster parents by the Local Authority. His wife gave birth to a third child which, when three days old, was forcibly removed from the mother, still recovering from parturition in a maternity unit, and placed into care. The infant, through his legal representative, contested custody by the Local Authority, whose actions were defended on the grounds that the child was at risk from the father, who allegedly had assaulted both his other children and sexually-interfered with his sister-in-law. In defence, it was proven that the single injury to the older child could have occurred as maintained by the father, i.e. by collapsing in an epileptic fit whilst carrying the baby (being subject to frequent grand mal attacks at this time); even medical witnesses called by the council were not prepared to call this an assault. The single incident to the second child involved finger bruising by being held too tightly, the father admitting to shaking the child on being disturbed from sleep; the father worked nightshift in a bakery and was suffering sleep deprivation at the time. Expert psychological evidence had previously been admitted in court when the alleged sexual assault took place: this showed that the father was subject to confusional states after a fit, that the girl concerned was sexually precocious and herself the victim of a long-standing incestuous relationship with a member of her own family (who was subsequently convicted) and that the brother-in-law's denial of conscious intent was commensurate with the facts. The defendant had been under psychological supervision for three years, and repeated psychometric assessments were consistent in showing that he was by nature a mild, passive man with considerable affection for his family and with a strong desire to be a good father, husband and homemaker. He had a good work record, apart from being discharged from one factory on union instructions for working too hard. His epileptic condition had been stabilized by medication on which the author had been conducting research for the past ten years. The psychological opinion on risk of intentional physical injury was given as minimal. A consultant paediatrician estimated it at 60% on the basis of published reports on child battering. The court rescinded the care and custody order, and replaced it with a supervision order, returning the infant to the mother subject to medical examination when required.

Transportation Accidents are big business—even a small car accident may call for six figure sterling damages, while a public transport accident may involve millions of pounds. Damages, as well as costs, naturally reflect the current value of money. In 1675 when James Fford drove his cart over Avigaile King causing the child's death, the court ordered him to pay the father the sum of five pounds: 300 years later a court was examining a similar basis for liability but where the claims exceeded £100,000,000—in the case of the DC10 crash near Paris[94].

Not all road accident cases are confined to the Civil Courts, however. Often, in contributing to the cause of the accident, one of the parties has committed a criminal offence under the Road Traffic Acts, by driving recklessly or without care. If the police decide to prosecute, the accused may seek the help of a forensic psychologist in order to find any mitigating factors which can be taken into account when assessing responsibility and the appropriate sentence.

CASE No. 4

A minor accident occurred when two cars collided at a roundabout. The driver of one appeared to be drunk and dazed, and when the police arrived was found to have an excessive blood alcohol level and charged with an offence under the Road Traffic Acts. The accused was taken to a medical practitioner who recorded severe bruising of the hip and occiput. He was struck by the incongruity between the site and extent of the injuries and the minor nature of the accident, and on closer examination concluded that the discoloration indicated that the bruising must have occurred earlier than the accident. Witnesses were found who testified that the accused had been seen to slip on the ice earlier in the day and had been helped home in a dazed condition. The accused was fairly abstemious but customarily drank a very small portion of brandy each morning. The spouse noted on examining the bottle that on this date more than usual of the contents had disappeared. It was hypothesized that the accused had suffered concussion when the head came into contact with the pavement, and that during the post-concussional confusional state the accused drank a larger than usual measure of brandy. Witnesses testified to the normally abstemious habits of the accused, who claimed to be unable to recall any of the events after leaving the house on foot early in the morning. A psychological examination was undertaken, on the basis of which the psychologist gave as his expert opinion that the pattern of memory defect present was consistent with a post-concussional state and was not typical of drunkenness. The case was dismissed.

At first glance it may be thought that the prosecution side offers no scope for the clinical approach, but there is a special clinical type of service which the forensic psychologist can offer the prosecutor and this relates to the use of hypnosis with witnesses for the prosecution, as in Case No. 5. The psychologist, in the clinical role, also advises the police regarding the validity of complaints, as in Case No. 6. Suffice it here to point out that the forensic psychologist can adopt the clinical role and employ the clinical approach for both parties, and in both civil and criminal law respectively.

Case No. 5

The police wished to trace a car which was reported to have travelled along a certain road on the date of the incident. Conflicting descriptions had been obtained from witnesses present on the road at the significant time. The witnesses all agreed to undergo hypnosis, and the author was asked to determine whether improved recall could be obtained under hypnosis and to interrogate the witnesses in a state of hypermnesia[120]. Over a three-day period 14 witnesses submitted to hypnosis with varying degrees of trance level being achieved. One witness proved resistant to all suggestion. The information obtained under hypnosis provided a more consistent description of the car, which was then positively identified as regards make, model, colour, and additional fittings on the front. The full registration number of the vehicle was not obtained, but this is always the weakest part of car identification under hypnosis and proves more susceptible to error than other characteristics of the vehicle.

Case No. 6

An adolescent girl complained to the police that she was receiving frequent indecent telephone calls. Despite continuous monitoring of her telephone, no such calls were intercepted. The complainant then alleged that her property was being damaged by being smeared with paint, and certain items were shown to the police in proof of this statement. The items, a scarf, duffle bag, etc had clearly been marked with an aerosol paint. The complainant became importunate at the police station and her visits, and the subsequent enquiries undertaken on her behalf, occupied a considerable amount of police time. The psychologist was asked by the police to examine the girl, ostensibly to assess the effect which the events were having upon her, but really to give an expert opinion to the police on whether the girl was manufacturing the evidence in order to satisfy some psychological need. Experienced detectives have more insight and psychological sophistication than the public would credit them with possessing. The result of the clinical assessment served to confirm the police suspicions, and the girl's own medical practitioner was alerted to the situation by the psychologist who provided tentative suggestions regarding the best way the complainant could be helped by the mental health services. Very often, the complainant or alleged victim will not consent to a psychological examination, in which case the psychologist may be approached by the police to advise on the behaviour of the person concerned without actually seeing him or her. This then becomes an advisory role and not a 'clinical' one, as defined for forensic purposes although it may rely on clinical knowledge.

Both civil and criminal law have been mentioned as the two main branches of law with which forensic psychologists are usually concerned. From time to time, however, they will be engaged to assist one of the parties in quasi-judicial proceedings where so-called administrative law is practised. These proceedings involve tribunals and disciplinary committees described in chapter 10. In these proceedings, the three major roles of the forensic psychologist are as appropriate as they are in civil and criminal actions. The clinical approach is used almost exclusively in Mental Health Review Tribunals, constituted under Section 3 of the Mental Health Act (1959), where the psychologist may either be called upon to support the patients' application to be released from a hospital order, or, as is more usual, to support the grounds for detaining the patient for the protection of the community.

CASE No. 7

The patient had been brought into hospital compulsorily under Section 25(2)b of the Mental Health Act 1959 on a '28 day observation order', following an almost successful suicide attempt, rejection of any form of treatment, and evidence of delusional thinking. The medical practitioners approved by law for the purpose of certification had concluded that the patient was too severely depressed and deluded to be capable of making a rational judgement, and required compulsory admission to hospital for her own safety and for the benefit of her family. At the end of the statutory period the order was reviewed but opposed by a relative of the patient, who applied to a Mental Health Review Tribunal under Section 52(b) of the Act for the release from hospital and return home of the patient. The psychologist was asked by his employers, the Hospital Management Committee, to give evidence of (a) the suicidal risk level, and (b) the deluded thinking of the patient, and on the basis of the medical evidence supported by that of the psychological evidence, the patient was detained for a further period.

In more recent years, the attitudes towards hospital committal proceedings have undergone extensive change. Influenced perhaps, by writers such as Laing[121] in England and Szasz[122] in America as well as by a growing sensitivity to the patients' feelings, by ethical considerations, and by the effects of a developing humanism, psychiatrists have been less inclined to continue hospital detention than they were formerly. In the past two decades since the Mental Health Review Tribunals first had their heyday, the need for the psychologist to support or contest the continued detention of a psychiatry patient has diminished considerably. In contrast, the psychologist may be asked by the patient to support his case, against that of the hospital administrators. This puts the psychologist in a difficult situation, in which he may appear to be acting contrary to the interests of his employers, and so may feel disloyal and in an ethical conflict. The conflict is more apparant than real, however, since both parties are concerned to have the significant evidence placed before the Tribunal, and the psychologist's evidence, if relevant, should be welcomed by both sides. At most, the conflict will be one of opinion rather than evidence, and if, in spite of the psychological data, the hospital medical officers still form an opinion that the patient should be detained in hospital, the members of the tribunal will take into account the opinions of both sides, and weigh the respective merits of the witnesses, their evidence, and their responsibilities. What often seems to the psychologist as a simple case in which the freedom of an individual is at stake often has more serious implications, both medical and administrative. Very often the hospital authorities are financially responsible for damage caused by a difficult destructive or aggressive patient, and their liability in this respect can be easily overlooked by the professional worker blinded by his immediate, and sometimes undue emotional, concern to help his patient. Psychiatrists, too, carry a responsibility in law which the clinical psychologist has not yet been forced to shoulder. Whatever evidence the psychologist gives in court, he is not accountable for, except to his own conscience. The decisions of the court or Tribunal, on the other hand, may have a profound effect upon the psychiatrists' professional standing if his opinion turns out to be mistaken. His judgements, therefore, when they are made will tend to err towards caution—both for the safety of the patient and for that of the community. The brash psychologist, lacking both humility and a sensitivity to background pressures, may well on occasions take up a position which is possibly misguided for the patient and which creates an adverse view of himself and his profession which may be of disadvantage later. That said, there are still occasions when the psychologist feels strongly that the patient is paying too high a price by his detention for the caution of those responsible for keeping him in hospital. In such circumstances, the psychologist, with a full awareness of all the implications, and having satisfied himself as to the medical officers' case by personal discussions with them, should have the courage of his convictions and be prepared to take the patients' side against that of his employers.

Although it has been said that, as a matter of principle, the psychologist should not participate in a civil action against his employers, this principle has not won full acceptance by the profession, and in any case should be limited to those falling within civil and not administrative law. The Mental Health Tribunal is examining, not compensation for the allegedly infringed rights of an individual, but his actual freedom, and the professional and ethical considerations attached to such cases are quite different.

CASE No. 8

The patient was admitted to hospital on a compulsory order under Section 26(2) of the Mental Health Act 1959 on the grounds that he was suffering from mental illness and that he should be detained for the protection of other persons. Prior to admission he had invaded a retail shoe shop and amused himself by hurling the stock, one shoe at a time, at the passers by in the busy thoroughfare, to the discomfiture of the populace and the consternation of the female shop assistants. In due course two constables advanced under a barrage of boots and arrested him. His behaviour at the police station led them to believe a mental hospital was the appropriate place for him. On admission the psychologist saw the shoe-thrower for diagnostic assessment, and on the basis of this and a comprehensive psychiatric examination he was diagnosed as suffering from schizophrenia. He was treated with chemotherapy and appeared to regain mental normality. However, the medical officers were reluctant to remove his compulsory detention in the fear that he would make a nuisance of himself in the neighbouring town. The patient then applied to a Mental Health Review Tribunal under Section 31(4) of the Act, and called for psychological evidence to show that he 'was no longer suffering from a mental disorder, or, if he was so suffering, that it was unnecessary in the interests of his own health and safety, or for the protection of other persons that he should be detained in hospital'. The psychologist re-assessed the patient, at the patient's request and with the sanction of the responsible medical officer concerned, and gave evidence that the patient, though showing the residual effects of his previous psychiatric state, was no longer diagnosable as 'psychotic' in psychometric terms, and gave his opinion that the patient was unlikely to repeat his offence in the immediate future, although no guarantee could be given that in a possible subsequent relapse he would not again revert to unlawful behaviour.

5. The Experimental Role in Forensic Psychology

In ENGLAND, all professional psychologists have a thorough grounding in the experimental method of psychology. This scientific training, which owes its origin to the great Wilhelm Wundt, who opened the world's first psychology laboratory at Leipzig exactly a century ago, makes it natural for forensic psychologists to think in scientific terms and to conceptualize the forensic problems encountered in the rigorous scientific way which characterizes their scientific training. As behavioural scientists their role in law is unique. No other profession can bring to the problem the same knowledge, experience and training as the applied psychologist. No other profession can analyze, interpret, explain and predict behaviour in such specific and numerate terms. Whereas psychologists in the clinical role both complement and supplement the contribution made by their medical colleagues, in the experimental role they perform an original and unique function.

It is, therefore, not surprising that the first ever appearance of a psychologist, qua psychologist, in a witness box of a court of law, is believed to be that of Professor Karl Marbe of Wurzburg, himself a pupil of Wundt. Professor Marbe attended the court in defence of an engine driver, who was being held responsible for a railway accident on the grounds that he had not brought his train to a halt in time to avert the disaster. Marbe provided the court with a simple and clear demonstration of the phenomenon of reaction time, and succeeded in convincing the court that it would have been physically impossible for the engine driver to have stopped in time to prevent the accident. The driver was thus exonerated, and Professor Karl Marbe entered legal and psychological history as the first ever forensic psychologist fulfilling the experimental role.

Munsterberg[123], another pupil of Wundt, whom we shall encounter in a later chapter, furthered the history of forensic psychology with a series of famous European cases in which he appeared in the role of experimentalist. When he moved to the United States to develop the forensic psychology he brought with him the traditions of Leipzig which have remained with American and European forensic work ever since. Today, any experimental psychologist who stands in the witness box to give expert testimony does so in the shadow of Wilhelm Wundt. No doubt the Father of Experimental Psychology would regard this as one of the most fitting, as well as perhaps the most important, applications of psychology in the contemporary world.

The scope for experimentation in forensic psychology has been discussed elsewhere[47]. As in the clinical role, the experimentalist can contribute to legal proceedings in civil, criminal and administrative law respectively, in each case finding and presenting solutions to forensic problems for either side. The experimental work may be conducted in the field, that is, in the environment natural to the problem; in the laboratory, either because it is convenient to the particular sample being used or because the experiments require apparatus or equipment, or *in situ*, where they have to be carried out with reference to a particular subject, usually the person accused of a criminal offence.

The latter situation poses a special problem of its own, for frequently the only place available for conducting the experiments is the prison cell itself. Very often, an obliging prison medical officer will allow his consulting room to be turned into a laboratory for this purpose. Sometimes the psychologist, if he is carrying out the experimental work at the weekend, as is so often the case, can use some other room in the prison hospital normally fully utilized during the week for some other purpose. In this way, the author has used, in his time, an EEG room, an eye clinic, and even a dental surgery. Obtaining a venue at all is an achievement in an overcrowded prison with overworked staff, and a special word of praise is due to the prison medical staff, who do so much to help the psychologist perform his forensic functions efficiently. Once suitable accommodation has been obtained for the purpose of forensic experimentation, however, the psychologist has to face a more serious problem, relating to the psychological implications of the experimental milieu. The milieu itself will contain important intervening variables which may have a statistically significant effect upon the experimental results[124], particularly if an electro-physiological recording is being made, or if the assessment involves the reaction of the prisoner to stress[125]. A solicitor's consulting room, a dental surgery, and a much-barred basement cell will possess marked differences in ambience, physical aspects, and psychological cues, and will clearly influence the prisoner's mood, feelings and behaviour, and consequently the experimental data obtained. For this reason the author has developed a special portable booth, composed of telescopic rods (from old fishing gear) and dark green cloth, which can be carried in a small canvas holder, and quickly erected to provide a constant visual environment which enables data obtained in a variety of situations to be validly compared. This has the advantage of providing a sensory cleavage between the prisoner and his immediate prison environment, and so makes his responses correspondingly more natural and less constrained. Occasionally, the prison rules will not permit the prisoner to be out of sight of a custodial prison officer, but the screens can usually be judiciously arranged so that the official is behind the person and can keep him under observation while at the same time keeping out of the prisoner's line of sight. Only once has the author been unable to use the screened booth for psychometric assessment of a prisoner, and this was in the case of Neilson, the so-called Black Panther, whom the prison authorities regarded as so dangerous that for the psychologist's personal safety they insisted on keeping him between two prison officers. On this occasion psychological testing was less affected by the visual aspects of the dungeon in which it was conducted, as by the cacophony emanating from the prison chapel, where the more fervently religious, or less musical, of the inmates were having an ecclesiastical jazz session. If prospects for heaven are measured in decibels, at least some of the prisoners had qualified for wings.

One serious impediment arises in the use of the experimental method and this is that when the appropriate subject for the experiment is on the other side to that of the psychologist, it is virtually impossible to obtain his or her co-operation. The psychologist may question the possibility of the witness performing the visual feats of observation sometimes described in the witness box, but the latter cannot be made to demonstrate those feats experimentally or in conditions similar to the original ones.

Cases exemplifying the experimental approach will be found later in Part III (see cases numbered 16, 29). Some additional examples follow:

CASE NO. 9

This case has been described briefly elsewhere[47]. Three motorcyclists were charged with dangerous driving. In company with a fourth they were out for the day when tragedy occurred. At a country crossroads the leading motorcyclist collided with a young man driving his father's powerful sportscar, and both motorcyclist and his pillion passenger were killed. A constable arrived on the scene and copied down the registration marks of all the vehicles.

Both parties laid the blame for the accident at the door of the other. However the sportscar driver was the well-to-do son of a local councillor, whereas the motorcyclists were from another county, and predictably the motorcyclists were charged but not the car driver. The basis for the charge was that the same policeman had seen the four motorcyclists sometime earlier 'travelling at terrific speed—at least 60 mph'—through a nearby town. In order to obtain a conviction, the prosecution must prove, beyond reasonable doubt, what is called the *actus reus* or guilty act. This has two components. First, it must be proved that an unlawful act took place, secondly, that the person charged with the offence can be identified as the person who actually committed the act. The speed with which a vehicle is driven is an act which the law, in its wisdom, requires to be proved by testimony under oath by one witness and corroborated by a second, although the Road Traffic Acts permit corroboration by a mechanical device, for example, a radar speed detector. In this case, the police officer's opinion on the speed of the motorcyclists was not corroborated; moreover, to prove identity, he had to establish the fact that the motorcyclists seen earlier in the town were the same individuals involved in the accident and then before the court, since other groups of motorcyclists had also travelled along this road at about this time. He attempted to do this by testifying that he had recorded the registration numbers of the motorcycles at the time he observed them exceeding the speed limit. The coincidence that the one number he failed to record was the one obliterated by fire at the time of the accident was noted, as was the fact that he was unable to say what colour the motorcycles were. A psychological opinion was sought as to whether his observation was actually possible. Taking the police constable's evidence as it stood, he had testified that (1) he had recorded the numbers from the *rear* plates during the period elapsing from the time they passed him to the time they passed out of sight round a corner, a distance of less than 120 yards. The registration marks on motorcycle number plates are 2½ inches high—approximately two thirds of those on a motor car number plate. The Chief Constable reported that the average reading distance of car plates by police officers was 65 yards, but that one or two could identify plates at 90 to 100 yards. Since the motorcycle marks were smaller, the reading distance would be proportionately shorter, so that even assuming the police witness had the best reading vision in the constabulary, it was unlikely that he would be able to identify the plates beyond 60 yards; since the number plates on all the cycles concerned were partly obscured by mud and dust, this gives the observer considerable benefit of any doubt. The motorcycles were alleged to be travelling at a speed of at least 60 mph, i.e. approximately 30 yards per second, so that the constable had them within the upper limit of reading distance for only two seconds, and within his vision altogether (unless he had the ability to bend his vision round corners) for only four seconds. To substantiate his statement that he had recorded four registration numbers at this time, he would therefore have to prove that he could see, remember, and record 21 symbols in two seconds (or with unique vision—four seconds) moving, mud-obscured, and in the summer twilight at a few minutes to ten p.m. An experiment was set up in which 100 observers with normal vision on a medical eye-test were asked to identify four registration plates tachistoscopically under conditions of lighting believed to be identical with those existing at the time of the original event, light values for the relevant area being obtained from the meteorological office. Only a few observers could register even one complete number under these conditions. They were instructed to practise registering numbers in the street for 14 days, and were then retested. Even by extending the time until the vehicles would have been out of sight, and increasing the lighting to approximate noon on a sunny day, it proved impossible for any observer to register four complete, hitherto unseen numbers. A cine film made on a similar site showing four motorcyclists driving slowly away, projected with different levels of illumination and varying speeds also failed to reproduce the police witness's testimony. A simple test of the police observer's perceptual efficiency would have been a more relevant and easier way of validating his testimony, and with the inquisitorial system this would have been possible.

Accordingly, the result of this series of experiments was given as expert evidence for the defence. The prosecution who knew in advance that police evidence was to be disputed, countered this in three ways. First, the expert witness was asked to leave court prior to being called, so that he was prevented from hearing the police testimony at first hand. The evidence on which the experiments were based had been taken down in the coroner's court at the time of the inquest. Secondly, the police witness changed his testimony, to the effect that although the motorcyclists were travelling at 60 mph when first seen, they were down to 45 mph by the time they passed the constable, and then slowed further in the traffic, with one actually coming to a stop. This, of course, changed the temporal basis of the perceptual problem, and since the duration of the stationary vehicle was unspecified it made it impossible to compute the range of the observation time, and so invalidated all the research data. Thirdly, the county prosecuting solicitor engaged the services of a children's psychiatrist as medical advisor, who sat by his side armed with a textbook on physiology. She suggested questions for him to put to the psychologist, and which were mostly irrelevant, such as 'what about conditioned reflexes?' or which were unanswerable by this witness, such as: 'what is the strength of the constable's eyesight?'. Finally the witness was asked if he agreed with a sentence read from the textbook which said that the eye can detect moving objects more easily than stationary ones. This was then used to imply that the observer could read moving number plates more easily than stationary ones. The motorcyclists were convicted. Although the psychologist waived his fee in this case, the young lads could not afford to appeal, despite additional evidence in their favour which came to light. The Home Secretary was supplicated by a member of Parliament, the parents of the dead couple, and other interested parties, but no further action was taken.

Police officers are only human, and when they genuinely believe they have apprehended an offender but have insufficient evidence to satisfy a court of law, it must be difficult for them not to fill in the gaps and then come to believe in the completed evidence as a fact. That so few are caught out in extending evidence in this way says much for the professional integrity of the average police officer. It is rare to find an officer whose motivations for success are stronger than his scruples, and who papers over the cracks in his evidence. It is more common to find police witnesses who are honest but mistaken. There is nothing morally wrong in this; we can all be deceived by our senses. Unfortunately, when the psychologist is asked to make explicit the perceptual errors of a police witness in court, it is often interpreted as attempting to prove that the policeman has been lying. The following case, which has been detailed elsewhere[105], is a typical example of this situation, and also complements the previous case as an example of experimental work relevant to the actus reus; whereas Case No. 12 emphasized the proof of *identity*, the following case focuses upon the proof of the *offence*.

CASE NO. 10

Following complaints that indecent behaviour was taking place in a public convenience, two police officers were given the duty of keeping a watch on the interior. To do this effectively, they secreted themselves in a narrow broom cupboard, standing upon a wooden box and peering through a zinc gauze screen partially obscured on the inside by old sacking. After many days of gross discomfort on shift duty in this cubicle, the officers observed two men acting in a manner they regarded as improper, and bursting out of the broom cupboard, arrested both '*in flagrante delicto*', and charged them with committing an act of gross indecency. One of the men, a local citizen of some substance and considerable reputation in the town, denied the charge vehemently and said the policemen were mistaken in what they thought they had seen. The barrister called in for the defence asked for a psychological opinion on the probability that the two policemen could be mistaken, and if so, how. Using volunteer actors, photographs were taken on the site, the positions of the two men having been described in detail in the police statements. The toilet was a subterranean one whose only illumination during daytime was from the daylight which filtered through the glass grill set in the pavement above, lighting conditions at the time and date in question were again obtained from the Meteorological Office. An experiment was set up using W.E.A. students as before, who saw the pictures projected in a range of lighting conditions approximating to those obtaining at the time, and under three levels of expectancy or 'set'. The police statements said that everyone entering the convenience was viewed with suspicion; that is the police observers had a high degree of expectancy that they would see an offence committed. Moreover, they had a high degree of desire to make an arrest and so gain release from their own uncomfortable confinement in the cupboard. The psychological conditions were thus favourable to perceptual error. So too were the physical factors, for the lighting was extremely poor, being eight times darker than the dull day outside, the men were more than ten feet from the policemen, at an angle to them and therefore partly obscured, and the police admitted contact was no more than 'a few seconds' before they burst from their hiding place. Reproducing these factors experimentally provided conditions in which one picture in every eight was 'seen' as indicating an indecent act. A report was prepared detailing the various factors involved, listing relevant studies showing perceptual error from the literature and experimental psychology, and describing the present experimental work. Rather than put this evidence in court directly, the counsel used it as a basis for invalidating the police evidence and so obtained an acquittal.

CASE No. 11

In the experimental role, the forensic psychologist can help the prosecution no less than the defence. In one case, a police car had paced a van along a road running almost parallel with that on which the police car was travelling, noting that in order to keep pace with the van, the police car had to travel at a speed 50% above the permissible limit for that stretch of road. At the part where the two roads joined, the van was stopped and its driver charged with exceeding the speed limit. In court, the defence lawyer obtained an acquittal on the grounds that because the roads were not parallel the police could not accurately assess the speed of the car. To prevent a recurrence of this escape measure the traffic police sought psychological advice on how the speed of a vehicle could be accurately measured in this situation. A special technique was developed using a mark on the car window such that when a second car was kept lined up with the line of sight of the police officer and the passenger seat, the line of sight made an accurate right angle with the longitudinal axis of the police vehicle. If the distance between the two roads was then measured at two points to provide the angle of convergence, and the speedometer reading was taken, the speed of the vehicle on the line of sight could be computed by a simple trigonometrical formula, namely $Vx = Vp \cos \theta$, where Vp is the speed of the police car, Vx the speed of the other vehicle, and θ the angle of convergence of the two roads. Police officers in the traffic division were then given a talk on how and when the formula could be applied, using examples taken from Ordnance Survey maps of the area for which they were responsible. This exercise not only added to the police repertoire of scientific method—it also enabled a useful working relationship to be built up between the constabulary and the psychologist.

Case No. 12

The experimental method is as applicable to quasi-judicial courts as it is to criminal and civil courts of full jurisdiction. In one case, a miner seeking compensation from the National Coal Board at an Industrial Health Tribunal, claimed that his 'miners nystagmus' was due to his working conditions in the pit. Psychological investigation was requested by the NCB to ascertain what conditions, if any, could produce miners nystagmus, medical opinion at the time favouring a psychopathological explanation. Studies were undertaken at the coalface in a large coal mine whose roads run under the hospital where the psychological laboratory was situated, and data was collected of the seam height, illumination, direction of gaze when cutting coal, and other factors possibly relevant to stress upon the visual apparatus. From the factors common among those miners who were suffering from or who had suffered miners' nystagmus, an experimental situation was set up in the laboratory which enabled this type of nystagmus to be experimentally produced. The claim of the appellant was then shown to be valid.

Case No. 13

Another example of experimental work in courts of limited jurisdiction comes from a court-martial study. Here an airman on active service was charged with certain offences contrary to the Air Force Law and the Official Secrets Act. The defence was that the airman was so drunk at the time that he was devoid of criminal responsibility. Psychological help was sought in order to demonstrate this. The airman had been drinking a raw alcoholic concoction illicitly distilled by Polish refugees in a displaced persons compound and evidence was available to show the quantity drunk and the time over which the drinking took place. The still had been constructed out of copper tubing taken from abandoned Wehrmacht vehicles and sealed with birdlime, through which vapour from heated potato peelings, siphoned petrol, and other substances was passed. The still was tracked down and a quantity of the liquor obtained. The accused airman was then asked to imbibe this at an ingestion rate based on independent evidence of the evening in question, and his subsequent behaviour was then recorded systematically and verified by observers from the medical section and from the R.A.F. police. The airman reached a mental state characterized by a clouded sensorium and gross paranoid delusions, and eventually had to be prevented by force from committing an act of arson which could have destroyed an entire operational base. The airman was hospitalized and on the basis of affidavits from all the observers and the psychological report interpreting and explaining this behaviour, the court-martial was cancelled.

CASE NO. 14

Another example of experimental evidence provided for a quasijudicial court comes from a study undertaken for an industrial injuries tribunal.

A workman operating a complex industrial machine seriously injured his left hand. The employer maintained that the workman had inserted his left hand inside the machine against explicit orders to that effect, thus operating the machine incorrectly and circumventing the safety devices installed to prevent this type of accident from happening. The workman made the point that for single operations it was easy enough to follow the operating technique laid down, but that under the pressure to keep up with the production flow line, the left hand was used to clear obstructions in the machine in a purely automatic way and without any conscious intent or awareness. He maintained this risk should have been foreseen and guarded against. Psychological help was sought to provide evidence of this 'automatic' activity for an Industrial Injuries Tribunal.

The Company agreed to train the author on the use of the machine, and to provide facilities for the machine to be used throughout the weekend for research purposes. With the co-operation of the union, workers already trained on the machine volunteered to do shifts under increasing degrees of pressure in terms of specified rates of production. A safety inspector and a member of management were present as observers and a special safety screen was attached to prevent actual entry of the left hand. It was demonstrated that at lower rates of production the machine was cleared of debris correctly, but that the left hand came up to clear the obstruction with increasing frequency as the rate of working was speeded up. Of the sample, 30% attempted to use their left hand at intermediate rates, and 70% at the highest rate. The Company accepted that the risk of left hand injury was a significant one and agreed to an acceptable settlement. The safety screen devised for the psychological experiment was copied and equipped to all similar machines used in the factory. The experiment thus provided the specific data requested and also made a positive contribution to industrial safety. It has been mentioned before that forensic psychology often provides 'spin-off' of general value as well as its value to the particular case.

53

6. The Actuarial Role in Forensic Psychology

PROBABILITY, according to Bertrand Russell, has been the most important concept in science. To the forensic psychologist, as a scientist, the concepts, mathematics, and implications of statistical probability are quite familiar. He answers research questions in terms of probability levels, measures diagnostic accuracy in the same terms, and predicts future behaviour, whether it be absconding, relapsing, becoming violent, or whatever, in an identical measure of likelihood.

The application of probability theory to the law owes most to the Honourable Sir Richard Eggleston, whose name has become synonymous with legal probability theory. He opposes the 'degree of belief' school, saying that one either believes a statement or not, although a great many probability theorists take up the opposite position. Claude Bernard's aphorism: 'one only needs statistics when one doesn't understand causation' is relevant here. As Eggleston points out[126] when probability *is* used for legal purposes, it is often misused. For example, the body of a murdered woman was found outside a Borstal institution, and since it was known to house a large number of violent offenders, the probability of the murderer being one of the inmates was fairly high. One of the victim's breasts had clearly defined teethmarks and these fitted the dental pattern of a particular inmate. The probability of this person being the murderer was thus increased. He was duly charged, tried, and convicted. The weakness of this evidence was that the probability that the teethmarks fitted someone else was not examined, neither was the probability that whoever made the teethmarks actually committed the murder. All that could be proved was a possible biter, not the murderer. In the event, the convicted man was acquitted on appeal, not because of the probability weakness, but because the bite-test had been taken without his permission! In another case, the probability of the accused being the offender rested on the probability of him being a homosexual. This was proved to the satisfaction of the court, but it ignored the probability of other homosexual persons being in the neighbourhood. The hypothetico-deductive method of classical science which the psychologist adopts in his research makes it easy to overlook alternative explanations and external probabilities. Like the accusatorial system of law, which presents evidence concerning only the accused and no other possible suspect, the psychologist is accustomed to testing his working hypothesis by its probability level, and not necessarily examining the probability of alternative hypotheses. Nevertheless, with this caveat in mind, the psychologist is an appropriate expert to make statistical inferences from data on human behaviour. Among the questions which have been put to forensic psychologists are those concerning the probability of earning a living with a given IQ, the probability of two identical cars passing along a road within a given period of time, the probability of finding two persons with a given number of personal characteristics in the same town, the probability of finding two concentration-camp guards who have adopted identical cognitive styles. These and many others have been answered by psychologists using observational data and mathematical analysis.

Unlike the clinical role, where the forensic psychologist enters into an interpersonal relationship with the client, or the experimental role, where the forensic psychologist conducts experiments directly related to the matters in issue in isolation from the parties themselves, the actuarial role requires the psychologist to examine data on specified behaviour (which he either has on file himself, extracts from the scientific literature, or collects himself by direct observation) and then to assess the relative probabilities for the court.

CASE NO. 21

A man driving a van collided with a car at a crossroads and was killed. His 17-year-old son, a passenger in the van at the time, received superficial head injuries and suffered concussion. After discharge from hospital a fortnight later, he was believed to be intellectually impaired and showed a marked memory deficit. Psychological assessment was sought, and the resulting examination showed him to be functioning at IQ 85 on the Wechsler Scale, with evidence of a post traumatic neurosis and memory impairment. The deficits were agreed with the defendant's medical advisor but vocational prospects were disputed. Using published tables of average earnings related to intelligence level, data provided by the National Institute for Industrial Psychology, and by psychologists working in industrial rehabilitation units, a projection on future earnings was calculated, and the discrepancy between this figure and that obtained by extrapolating his pre-injury remuneration provided the basis for a financial settlement. In this latter part of the assessment, the role was actuarial, and the data provided probability figures regarding future earnings. When the forensic psychologist operates in the actuarial role, each case provides sets of data which the psychologist accumulates with experience and can thus refine his probability estimates from case to case.

The actuarial role is as relevant in the criminal court as it is in the civil courts, and indeed the jury seem able to accept probability figures as meaningful and related to their own personal experience, provided they are put to them in the most appropriate way.

CASE NO. 22

A man was accused of attempted murder, having allegedly struck an elderly widow with a poker. Although a psychiatrist testified for the defence as to the mental state of the accused in relation to the M'Naghten Rules, the defence counsel particularly requested psychological evidence of a quantitative kind. The accused was given psychological tests while in prison and expert evidence was given in terms of probabilities. In one diagnostic test, for example, the author was able to say that of every 100 people tested in this way and producing the type of score given by the accused, 95 would have been diagnosed as schizophrenic, and five would have been undiagnosed but presumed to be normal. The probability, it was stated in court, that the accused was schizophrenic, was therefore 19 to one. Although an oversimplification of the case, in view of the sampling variables, this was considered at the time to be a fair representation of the probability, since the more obvious factors were mutually cancelling. Odds of 19 to one are those on which many a punter would be happy to put his shirt; even to the non-betting fraternity it conveys a sense of likelihood that seems satisfyingly precise. It is not 'more likely than not' nor even 'very likely', for these mean different things to different people. The simple figure was immediately convincing to the jury, and although a further and more difficult step had to be made in relating schizophrenia to level of criminal responsibility, the acceptance of the existence of a psychosis by the jury was more than half the battle. Meanwhile, the old reprobate in the dock, who in one of his lucid moments had been calculating his own probabilities, had worked out that he would spend twice as long in Broadmoor if found insane than he would in Wakefield Prison if considered to be normal, and he therefore withdrew the medical evidence for the defence.

CASE NO. 23

During the Allied occupation of Germany, service security units were charged with the duty of seeking out and arresting named Germans and their collaborators whose photographs had been supplied by secret agents and resistance workers and published in a classified document known as the 'blue book'. In addition, persons holding certain ranks in the organizations which made up the N.S.D.A.P. or Nazi party were placed in an 'automatic arrest' category which authorized their detention on proof of identity. Photographs were not generally available for this latter class of fugitive and identification was therefore made on the basis of clues suggesting the former rank and organization. These clues could be given a probability value which the author had calculated from a captured copy of *Das Organisationsbuch der N.S.D.A.P.*, which described in minute detail the badges, uniforms, weapons and official impedimenta issued to the members of the various organizations and differing with rank, area of authority, and function within the specific organization. In one instance, a suspected person denied being the *ortsgruppenleiter* whom the security officers were seeking. However, probability figures were derived from his location, his age, and from an old khaki jacket found in his wardrobe, which although bereft of all insignia, was identified as corresponding to the type issued to *politischenleiters*. This brought the probability figure above 0.5 which the Special Investigation Branch regarded as strong enough to temporarily detain him. On careful examination of the jacket at Police Headquarters, minute traces of blue thread were found, which positively identified the jacket with the *ortsgruppe* and raised the probability figure high enough to justify positive action. His rank was confirmed during the subsequent interrogation and much useful information was obtained. As a result, a few weeks later, William Joyce (the traitor 'Lord Haw-Haw') was arrested in this area.

The prosecution rely on implicit probability in most of the cases where a 'not guilty' plea is entered, since probability forms the only basis for circumstantial evidence. However, explicit probability evidence has been used to secure a conviction in a criminal trial, of which the Collins case[235] is the best example. In this instance, a yellow car drew up to the pavement, and the two occupants alighted, snatched the handbag being carried by a pedestrian, and then drove off. Apart from the yellow car of an identified make, there were a number of witnesses who gave consistent descriptions of the two occupants. The latter were described as a male bearded Negro and a blonde white girl with a ponytail. A couple answering this description and driving a yellow car were picked up by the police in another part of the town sometime after the offence was committed, and the question put to the expert witness was what the probability was of the two arrested suspects being the same two who carried out the bagsnatch. The individual chance probabilities ranged from $p = 0.33$ for finding a blond girl, to p less than 0.001 for finding an inter-racial couple in a car. Using the probability product formula, the odds against finding a couple matching the description, and different from the offenders was put at 12 million. This was good enough for the jury who convicted on the basis of the evidence being beyond reasonable doubt. On Appeal, however, the defence secured a statistician who reworked a lower probability figure and so confused the appellate judges with his mathematical calculations that they concluded that the evidence was not sound enough to justify a conviction, and acquitted the couple, even though it was likely that the jury would still have convicted on the somewhat lower probability value. An interesting sequel to this case, which excited the interest of many mathematicians, was that many of them worked out their own values of p which gave a figure consistently higher than either of the values before the trial court or appellate court. Of special concern was the fact that when the suspects were first arrested, the Negro was cleanshaven, and the police surgeon examined him and reported that his face showed evidence of having a thick beard removed shortly before the arrest. The probability of finding this likely identification evasion was not taken into account by either of the experts in court, but when included in the computation by mathematicians unconnected with the case made a substantial difference to the probability level. Identification by probability calculation was used by the author in Case No. 27.

Probability concepts are similarly useful in quasi-judicial courts. It was mentioned that the advisory role is one frequently required as the psychologists contribution to tribunals: the presentation of data in probability form is particularly appropriate to the type of expert evidence in demand, especially in respect of frequency of accidents occurring with particular machines, or in particular areas of the factory. One of the advantages of giving actuarial evidence to tribunals and official enquiries is that the data is usually required by both sides and is generally non-controversial, so that the setting for providing the evidence approximates more to the inquisitorial system than an adversary one, even though it is one of the parties who actually seeks the psychologists' help. Most of this evidence is given in the form of a report, which is then made available to both sides under the 'Discovery of Documents' Rule, and forms the basis for specific discussions which usually take place before the hearing itself. This is commonly the procedure in civil actions which have been registered for hearing in the High Court. Typically the probability information will be provided to the counsel requesting it, who will use it in out-of-court negotiations, only bringing it into court as expert evidence if the matter cannot otherwise be amicably settled.

An example of the use of probability by a court of enquiry occurred in the Oswald case, following the assassination of President John F. Kennedy. The House Assassination Committee heard evidence from experts on auditory perception, who had analyzed sound tracks made at the time, and testified that the probability that two guns fired almost simultaneously was better than $p = 0.95$.

The police, of course, have used notional, if non-quantitative ideas of probability in their concept of the 'modus operandi' of the criminal for a very long time. This is now being used in a more scientific and quantified way by forensic psychologists, who call the process 'the fingerprinting of the cognitive style'[127].

7. The Advisory Role in Forensic Psychology

A FOURTH ROLE for the forensic psychologist is that of advisor. Often the psychologist can be of more use to counsel sitting with him and interpreting the evidence being given by psychologists of the other side, than he can by going into the witness box as an expert himself. As advisor he may be asked to examine the evidence prepared by the opposing counsel's expert witnesses, both medical and psychological, providing suggestions as to weaknesses in their facts, arguments opinions or their personal experience and qualifications (Case No. 22). Forearmed by the professional and technical insight of the psychological advisor, the counsel can launch a devastating attack during cross-examination. Psychologists who, as expert witnesses, have themselves been victims of a well-prepared attack based on expert guidance, will appreciate how effective this can be, and this role is a particularly useful one when expert evidence involving psychometric data is being given by a member of a profession other than psychology (Case 23).

In the second phase, the forensic psychologist in the role of advisor, will sit in court during the examination-in-chief of the expert witnesses, noting down their evidence and passing on to the counsel questions to put in cross-examination which may reveal weaknesses in the expert's case. In criminal trials, where the defence or prosecution can conceal the greater part of their evidence until the trial itself, counsel will have no warning of what is to come and the professional advisor then becomes especially useful.

Sometimes the parties have to declare their hands, even in a criminal proceeding. This usually comes about where the court is not sure whether the expert evidence which one side or the other wishes to tender is admissible or not. With the jury out of the way, the expert evidence can be presented to the judge, who then decides on its admissibility. If he decides that it is, then the jury are called back, and the experts have to repeat the whole performance. One often feels that the whole palaver is nothing more than a cunning ruse to force the defence to show its hand.

In one case the accused who was conducting his own defence had to battle hard for the admissibility of the expert medical witnesses he wished to call; these included R. D. Laing, the famous philosopher-psychiatrist; a Professor of Psychiatry from one of Englands premier medical schools; and the author, all of whom were likely to be excluded because their evidence was *post-facto* the events, that is, based on examinations undertaken after the alleged *actus reus*. The prosecution arranged to have Dr Peter Scott a leading criminologist and forensic psychiatrist in court as advisor, and then agreed to a dummy run of the defence experts in the absence of the jury. The judge conceded to this course, and all the witnesses gave their evidence. The judge considered the various authorities and precedents and then ruled that the evidence would be admissible. By this time the prosecution's psychiatric advisor had been able to fill the prosecuting counsel in on the strengths and weaknesses of the defence evidence, so that when the jury were brought into court the cross-examination was on *terra cognita* and the witness could be shrewdly guided towards the quicksands of questionable fact or unsupportable theories carefully mapped out by Dr Scott (Case 11).

Fortunately for the peace of mind of the forensic psychologist, the advisor feeding the cross-examiner with verbal ammunition is usually a stranger. When the advisor is recognized as the country's leading expert in the matters in issue, the expert witness may well share with Daniel some of the feelings of being in the lion's den. When going to different parts of the country, it is useful to know who are the 'experts' recognized as such by the legal fraternity. These are usually the Professors of Psychiatry at the local University, and some intimation of their views can be gathered from their writings. On one occasion, the author by some inexplicable prescience, expected Dr Myre Sim to be called as advisor by the prosecution, as indeed he was: his textbook, hailed by the medical press as a distinctive contribution to medical education had just been republished as a new edition. Careful study thus not only afforded an understanding of the author's views (although these were also well-known through the correspondence columns of the Lancet and BMJ) but enabled the author actually to quote from the textbook during the examination-in-chief, hopefully disarming later criticism via the cross-examination.

In administrative law, experts are used as advisors more frequently than as expert witnesses, since the technical context to the industrial injury or labour relations dispute may not be in issue, although some understanding of it by the tribunal is necessary. The psychologist can then give advice on professional matters which are relevant and which come within his province—work capacity, perception, accident proneness, motivation, fatigue, reactive inhibition, and so on. Within this field of forensic work can be included evidence prepared for official enquiries. For example:

CASE NO. 24

Three boys, one of them mentally subnormal, confessed during police interrogation to the murder of a homosexual prostitute, and were duly convicted on the basis of their independently uncorroborated statements, and absence of alibi at the estimated time of death. After a prolonged campaign and search for further evidence, the Court of Appeal declared them to be innocent and ordered their release. An enquiry on how the confessions came to be made was instituted under the Chairmanship of Sir Henry Fisher, an ex-judge and President of an Oxford College. Psychologists drawn from different specialties gave evidence on the psychological factors relating to interrogation, the suggestibility of children, the nature of mental handicap, and the level of reasoning in this condition, the effects of dominance and submission in the behaviour of young persons, and other psychological issues relevant to this case, and this evidence was discussed in the context of the particular crime and the subsequent legal proceedings.

CASE NO. 25

The above enquiry arose from a particular case. Sometimes they arise from more general issues, which themselves arise from a series of particular instances. For many years, psychologists have been carrying out research into the validity of personal identification and of the methods used by the police when asking witnesses for information or identification. Eventually an official enquiry was instituted to examine the validity of methods of identification and to propose changes likely to improve the accuracy of this process in law enforcement. Psychologists, amongst other experts, were called upon to provide the enquiry with psychological information concerning identification procedures and to advise on possible ways of improving the system. Most of the psychologists emphasized the lack of research data on this subject, and as a result research into identification processes has been encouraged and financially supported.

CASE NO. 26

The plaintiff had been examined by two medical practitioners, one a neurologist, the other a psychiatrist. Both diagnosed a closed head injury: the neurologist in the absence of any positive neurological signs, made his diagnosis on the fact that the plaintiff had been concussed in the accident, although even this conclusion was unsupported and relied solely on the plaintiff's own statement; the psychiatrist believed the plaintiff had suffered brain damage, a conclusion reached on the basis of the neurologists' diagnosis of closed head injury and also on the fact that the plaintiff had scored very low on an intelligence test. Psychological advice was sought by the defendant, and the medical evidence was made available for examination. The defendant's legal advisor was furnished with (1) a list of references to articles on closed head injuries which discussed the difficulties of diagnosing this condition and the minimum requirements for validity (which had not been met in this case) (2) some photocopies of papers on concussion which would show up the weakness of the conclusion that it was present in the plaintiff, (3) a critique of the test used by the psychiatrist (viz. the Kent oral norms—abridged emergency scale) in terms of its validity and reliability when used on a middle-aged adult following an alleged head injury, and of the competence of the psychiatrist to administer and interpret the test findings (4) a short résumé on the difficulties of assessing cognitive impairment without adequate quantitative evidence of pre-trauma functioning or an appropriate post-traumatic time-base. No mention was made in the medical reports of the plaintiff's level of functioning before the accident, and his simple manual job could have been undertaken by someone of almost any intelligence above imbecility. At a conference between the Counsel for the two sides, the psychological analysis of the evidence was discussed, and the claim for brain injury was withdrawn.

CASE NO. 27

One other aspect of the advisory role is not uncommonly encountered by forensic psychologists, and this is where one of the members of staff of the psychologist's institution (usually temporarily employed in some unskilled capacity) is charged with a criminal offence, of which theft is the commonest, but which may include offences under the Road Traffic Acts. The latter are not likely to require the psychologist's help, but for forensic psychologists based at University the alleged offence may have been committed by a foreign student possessing a working knowledge of the English language but which is too superficial for an adequate understanding of the nuances of English Law. In such circumstances, the psychologist may be brought in formally by the solicitor, but all too often the accused is pressed to plead guilty because of the prima facie case put forward by the prosecution and the belief that this will give a quick hearing and lower sentence, or the solicitor may be reluctant to complicate the case with an expert, or believe that legal aid would not be granted in the particular circumstances. In such cases, the psychologist may be asked by the appropriate administrator or Departmental Head to attend Court as observer and to report back in case more direct help is required in the students' or staff members' interests or to provide the institution with details of the case which the accused may be unwilling to give. In this case, a postgraduate student from the Middle East was arrested for shoplifting. A search by the police of the student's living quarters revealed a large quantity of stolen goods and it was clear that the student had been involved in fairly regular largescale theft for the duration of her course. During the hearing information was given which not only ruled out any mitigation but which established the fact that the student was morally unfit for the profession for which she was training. This important information would not have been available had the psychologist not been asked to attend court and advise on the proceedings.

Although the four roles adopted by the forensic psychologist—the clinical, experimental, actuarial and advisory— have been described and exemplified individually, often more than one role is involved in any one case. Not infrequently, he will find himself undertaking all four roles in one case. For example:

Case no. 28

A 14-year-old boy turning on to a country road from a farm track was knocked down by a car driven by an elderly man, and received, *inter alia*, a severe head injury. The defendant's counsel sought to minimize the effects of the injury by maintaining that the boy was of low intelligence before the accident, and also claimed contributory negligence on the grounds of the same fact. Considerable argument on these two points took place until psychological help was sought. In the clinical role the boy's pre-traumatic and post traumatic levels of intellectual functioning were evaluated (the former by reference to school and medical records) and the nature of the brain damage assessed. In the experimental role, two groups of cyclists, one of the plaintiff's pre-traumatic intelligence and one of normal intelligence, cycled into a road from a junction similar to the one where the original accident took place and ostensibly delivering a long message they had to remember. The cycle wheels passed through a manufactured puddle to which fluorescein dye had been added, and the tyre tracks showed up on the metalled road as the rider emerged from the lane. The 'area under the curve' between the nearside hedge and the tyre tracks was measured using surveying instruments and used as a measure of road risk.

It was shown that the cyclists with low intelligence were no more at risk by riding into the middle of the road than those of normal intelligence and the actuarial role was undertaken to relate the probability figures obtained in the experiment to the plaintiff's own behaviour. The author was also asked to advise on the validity of the psychological information presented by the defendant's medical witnesses. In this case, therefore, the psychologist undertook, in separate phases, the four different roles which characterize forensic psychology activities[103].

Table III

Table of Cases Cited

Case No.	Page	Court	Role	Party	Exemplifying
1	36	Magistrates	Clinical	Accused	Problem of who is 'client'
2	38	Queen's Bench	Clinical	Plaintiff	Typical compensation case
3	39	Crown	Clinical	Appellant	Claim for return of children in care
4	40	Magistrates	Clinical	Accused	Distinction between post-traumatic and drunken amnesia
5	41	Pre-court	Clinical	Prosecution	Forensic hypnosis of witnesses
6	41	Pre-court	Clinical	Prosecution	Validating complaint to police
7	42	Tribunal	Clinical	Respondent	Opposing appeal of suicidal patient
8	44	Tribunal	Clinical	Appellant	Supporting appeal of psychotic patient
9	47	Magistrates	Experimental	Accused	Challenging uncorroborated police evidence
10	50	Magistrates	Experimental	Accused	Challenging corroborated police evidence
11	51	Pre-court	Experimental	Prosecution	Scientifically closing loophole in law
12	52	Tribunal	Experimental	Appellant	Laboratory production of clinical signs
13	52	Court Martial	Experimental	Accused	Experimental production of unlawful behaviour
14	53	Tribunal	Experimental	Appellant	Experimental production of accident hazard
15	77	Privy Council	Clinical	Appellant	Appeal against death sentence on grounds of insanity
16	78	Commercial	Experimental	Plaintiff	Experimental evidence of infringement of commercial rights

17	94	Magistrates	Clinical	Applicant	Application for bail
18	105	Divorce	Clinical	Appellant	Evidence of mental cruelty
19	76	Protection	Clinical	Appellant	Evidence of capacity to handle own affairs
20	107	Appeal	Clinical	Appellant	Evidence of suitability for treatment
21	55	Queen's Bench	Actuarial	Plaintiff	Assessing probability of future earnings
22	56	Assize	Actuarial	Accused	Assessing probability of accused being psychotic
23	56	War Crimes	Actuarial	Prosecution	Identification of war criminal by probability
24	61	Inquiry	Advisory	Committee	Advising on suggestibility of children
25	61	Inquiry	Advisory	Committee	Advising on psychology of identification
26	61	Queen's Bench	Advisory	Defendant	Advising on defects in medical evidence
27	62	Magistrates	Advisory	Third	Advising institutions on proceedings
28	63	Queen's Bench	All four	Plaintiff	Combination of all roles in one case
29	80	Admiralty	Experimental	Defendant	Experimental evidence on cause of accident
30	83	Probate	Clinical	Defendant	Testamentary capacity
31	98	Coroner's	Clinical	Coroner	Evidence of pre-death state of mind
32	99	County	Clinical	Defendant	Evidence of mental illness
33	109	House of Lords	Clinical	Appellant	Attempt to correct misunderstanding in trial court

Table IV

Cases† exemplifying the four professional roles of the forensic psychologist in each of the main divisions of the law.

DIVISION OF LAW	FORENSIC ROLE: PARTY*	CLINICIAN	EXPERIMENTALIST	ACTUARY	ADVISOR
CIVIL	Plaintiff	2,28	20, 28, 31	17, 28	23, 28
LAW	Defendant	3,10	9	30	22
CRIMINAL	Prosecutor	5	14	27	6
LAW	Accused	1,4,11 19,32	12, 13, 16	26, 33	34
ADMINISTRATIVE	Appellant	7,18	21	‡	24
LAW	Respondent	8	15	‡	25

*   In certain jurisdictions or circumstances other names may be used.

†   The numbers refer to the case numbers as they appear in the text and in Table III.

‡   Un-numbered examples mentioned in text.

PART III

The Courts of Law and the Psychologist

8. Development of the Courts

IN THE Beginning was the Law of the Jungle, where only might was right. As man became a social animal, forming family or tribal groups for support and defence, private law developed on the basis of *Lex talionis*, the law of retaliation—'an eye for an eye and a tooth for a tooth'. This was later supported by the blood-feud, whereby retribution was obtained by combining the help of all the family members down to the sixth cousin, or of all the tribal group, so that eventually private law became public law. When the Romans invaded Britain in the years before Christ, they brought with them their own form of martial law, and later as the Roman occupation became established, some of the elements of Roman law. When they eventually withdrew, every vestige of their law went them, and Britain reverted to the more primitive *lex talionis* of her indigenous population or that of the successive waves of invaders who swept in from Northern Europe and Scandinavia.

It was not until the period of the heptarchy, when England was a collection of separate kingdoms, that the King's 'Court' began to administer man-made laws which developed from Christian missionaries arriving from Rome at the end of the 6th century. These early laws provided a tariff of compensation for wrong-doing which was simple to understand and easy to administer, both judicial desiderata for the kings of those days, whose muscular strength with the broadsword was more obvious than their cerebral activity. Typical tariffs ranged from 2½ Kentish shillings for hairpulling to 100 shillings for murder, with an additional factor if the victim was a churchman—sixfold for a deacon, elevenfold for a bishop[128]. The earliest surviving Anglo-Saxon laws appear to be those of Kent and owe much to King Ethelbert. In Wessex, King Ine developed similar laws and added his own and by the time of Alfred the Great in the 9th century an elaborate tariff of compensation, or *bote*, had developed. Bote for adultery ranged from 40 shillings for a churl to 120 shillings for a 12 hyndeman (a hynde was an area of land). Nonmonetary bote had also been introduced by this time: 'If a theow (servant) rape a female theow he shall give bote with his testicles'[129]. In this period the concept of crimes too serious to be compensated by bote had emerged. These were the 'botless' crimes punishable not only by death but by forfeiture of all the wrongdoer's possessions,

69

and which after the Norman Conquest became recognized as felonies.

These laws were enforced by the community at folk-moots and later at manorial courts as the feudal system developed. Under Alfred, England gradually became one kingdom, and a more organized court system was required. With Germanic administrative thoroughness, the country was divided into *Shires*, each with its own important shire town or estate, and these were subdivided into *Hundreds*, or a hundred hydes, a hyde being an area of land capable of supporting a family. The stewardship of the Chiltern Hundreds still exists as a parliamentary office, and many of the older counties still retain 'shire' in their name.

Local Courts of Common Law

During the Saxon period, therefore, two local courts existed—the Hundred Court which exercised petty civil and criminal jurisdiction in the hundred and met every month under a bailiff, and the Shire Court which met twice a year and was composed of the county land owners presided over by the Shire Reeve. The Shire Court had original jurisdiction in trials of actions concerning property; and the trial of criminal cases, and gradually developed an appellate jurisdiction in hearing appeals from the Hundred Courts. The Bailiff is still a legal figure, although his office in Scotland is closer to the original than it is in England. The Shire Reeve eventually became the 'Sheriff'—the American sheriff and his posse is an indirect descendant of the Sheriff and his Norman soldiers who hunted down such men as Robin Hood. Under the Normans the local courts became known as communal courts and the Shire Court was convened on a monthly basis. Under the feudal system established by the Normans there were also feudal or manor courts which were maintained by the Lord of the Manor and exercised jurisdiction in respect of land and disputes between the serfs and villeins who were attached to the land. At this stage the law was inter-related with land tenure, of which there were two kinds. Military tenure such as knight-tenure and sergeant-tenure demanded personal service from the tenant; sergeants today provide the same kind of service as they did 900 years ago, and senior officers are still made knights. Those who paid rent instead of service enjoyed socage-tenure and this still exists today. The Queen still holds the legal ownership of all land in England, which is leased out by Socage-tenure to the freeholder 'in fee simple'.

The Royal Courts of Law

Under the Normans the old Saxon Witan was replaced by the Curia Regis and through this court the king obtained and exercised judicial, legislative and executive functions. Under Henry I the Royal Justices from the Curia Regis would be sent into the shires to deal with the judicial matters. Gradually during the 12th and 13th centuries the Curia

Regis developed three separate courts known as the Royal or Common Law Courts because they administered the law common to the whole country. The first court to separate from the Curia Regis was the Court of Exchequer which as its name implies exercised jurisdiction in matters concerned with finance. The Court of Common Pleas separated from the Curia Regis about the time of Magna Carta in 1215 and exercised jurisdiction in the common pleas, that is, in ordinary cases of contract and civil wrong between one person and another. The Court of the King's Bench was independent by the reign of Edward I but kept in close touch with the Curia Regis down to the time of Henry IV. Its main jurisdiction was pleas of the Crown, that is, criminal cases. An incentive for the proliferation of Royal Courts was the additional income so gained, judges being paid on a piecework system for each case they heard. This system led them to cast their eyes on other ways of attracting litigants and others to their courts. A big boost to judicial income was achieved when the Royal Courts took over jurisdiction from the Local Courts. This dramatic change in fortune, which made modern Trade Union demands seem very small beer, was obtained by means of a King's Writ which was used to summon the defendant before the Royal Courts instead of one of the Local or Shire Courts. This action was defended by the use of a legal fiction, by which the concept of the *King's Peace* was introduced into the case. An allegation was made that a breach of the King's Peace had occurred and although fictitious, this was considered sufficient to give the Royal Court jurisdiction over the case. Once the case came before the Royal Court, the breach of the King's Peace was conveniently forgotten. This concept of the Sovereign's Peace has continued to the present day and many petty offenders are still brought to court for causing a breach of the Queen's Peace. The work of the Royal Courts was gradually consolidated by later events.

Following complaints about the conduct of the sheriffs, Henry II ordered his famous inquest of sheriffs in 1170 and deprived many of them of their office; this meant that many civil litigants had no alternative but to go to the Royal Courts. Meanwhile Magna Carta itself abolished all criminal jurisdiction of the Shire and Hundred Courts. The civil function of the Local Courts was also superseded by the Statute of Gloucester (1278) under Edward I which limited their jurisdiction to claims not exceeding 40 shillings. The Royal Courts therefore attracted litigants by offering better and more certain justice.

The Manor Courts themselves declined during the upheaval in the manorial system following the Black Death in the 14th century. The introduction of the jury system also meant that since the Manor Courts could not empanel a jury, their jurisdiction became more limited and finally most of the Manor Courts were closed down by Edward I under the Quo Voloto Enquiry.

Once the judiciary of the Royal Courts had obtained the lion's share of the court work itself, they began to compete with each other for the available cases. Considerable imagination and ingenuity was displayed in modifying writs to extend their jurisdiction. For example the Court of Exchequer was primarily concerned with the king's revenue, but not to be outdone in the struggle for power, it resorted to fictions to attract litigants to the court. They therefore claimed that, in cases of debt and also in cases of breach of payment, if the plaintiff did not receive his money he could not pay his taxes to the king. This sufficed to give the Court of Exchequer jurisdiction in cases which legitimately should have gone to the Court of Common Pleas, and so provided extra fees for the Exchequer Judges to the detriment of their judicial colleagues in the neighbouring court.

The King's Bench judges were no less mercenary or imaginative. Although concerned solely with criminal matters, much of their court work concerned barons and other landowners acquiring neighbouring land by intimidation—trespass *vi et armis*—with force of arms, as the indictment put it. This gave those seated on the King's Bench the idea of using this as a fiction for acquiring more litigation. Trespass with force and arms was a criminal matter within the jurisdiction of the King's Bench and irrespective of the precise nature of the claim at issue, the plaintiff could apply to the Court of the King's Bench for a Bill of Middlesex in which he alleged that the defendant had trespassed on his lands *vi et armis*. Although the allegation of trespass was purely fictitious it was sufficient to give the court jurisdiction over the case, and once before the court the plaintiff would pursue his claim without further reference to the trespass. Similarly, the Court of Exchequer would deal with cases intended for King's Bench if by any stretch of the imagination it could find a financial implication.

Originally the Bill of Middlesex could be used only for that county, but later the Writ of Latitat, meaning 'he lurks' was issued if the defendant did not live in Middlesex, and was addressed to the sheriff of the county. ordering the arrest of the defendant. Later a statute of Charles II provided that the defendant when arrested could bail himself from custody for a reasonable sum and required that the true nature of the plaintiff's claim should be stated on the writ. Perhaps the legal fictions reached their acme when the Royal Courts, in filching cases of piracy at sea from the later Court of Admiralty, used the fiction that the piracy had occurred 'in the parish of St Mary le Bow', the initial stages of the hearing conjuring up the picture of two sailing ships locked in deadly combat, gundecks ablaze, somewhere in the local high street.

9. Equity, Mercantile, Maritime and Ecclesiastical Courts

THE WRITS by which a party was called to one of the Royal Courts were limited in number, and at one time the writing of new writs, except on command of the King, was forbidden. If someone had a legal problem for which there was no writ, he could obtain no relief. Even today, the legal maxim is: where there is no remedy, there is no right. Since the King was the 'Fountain of Justice' it was possible for a dissatisfied party to petition the King in a case of special hardship for some kind of relief in the particular circumstances. These were originally dealt with by the King in Council with the help of his chief clerk or Chancellor. As the petitions became more numerous, a statute provided that the petitions should first be presented to the Chancellor who became known as the Keeper of the King's Conscience, and by the middle of the 15th century the Chancellor was acting independently of the Council. Thus originated the Court of Chancery. Because the Chancellor was dealing with iniquitous cases and provided equitable jurisdiction this system of law became known as equity. Originally the Chancellors had no common principles upon which to act. They gave equitable relief according to the circumstances of each case, and the saying common at the time was that 'equity varied with the length of the Chancellor's foot'. By the 18th century, however, sufficient case law had been built up to enable the Chancellors to follow legal precedents. Under the Law of Equity damages could not be granted by the Chancellor but any party who disregarded his judicial orders could be imprisoned for contempt of court. Jurisdiction of the Court of Chancery increased rapidly during the reign of Henry IV and especially under the chancellorship of Cardinal Wolsey in the reign of Henry VIII.

Under James I a quarrel between Lord Ellesmere, the Chancellor, and Chief Justice Coke of the Court of Common Pleas was referred to the King. In deciding the dispute in favour of the Chancellor the superiority of the Court of Chancery was established and maintained from that time onward.

There are two consequences from the development of the law of equity of direct relevance to the forensic psychologist. The first is the subpoena which could not be issued under Common Law; until the development of the Court of Chancery there was no way in which a witness could be forced to come forward and give evidence, but now under the jurisdiction of Equity the subpoena of witnesses is possible. The second implication for forensic psychologists is the 'discovery of documents'. This is an order for each party to disclose all the relevant documents in his possession to the party on the other side before the trial of the case. The authority for this process derived from Equity may be used to acquire for the court the psychometric data and other case notes belonging to the psychologist or his employing authority.

Because the common law was administered in the Common Law Courts and Equity was administered in the Court of Chancery the position was unsatisfactory for litigants who suffered the additional time and expense involved in going to two separate courts. The Judicature Acts of 1873 to 1875 not only reformed the system of courts and established the modern High Court of Justice but also provided that common law and Equity should be administered concurrently in all courts. Furthermore, it ordered that where there was a conflict between the two systems, that of Equity should prevail thus making statutorily explicit the superiority of Equity established by James I. Many of the early chancellors were ecclesiastics, and were well versed in Roman Law. It is therefore easy to appreciate how the development of Equity reflected the nuances of the old Roman *jus gentium* rather than the Anglo-Saxon and Norman elements of the English Common Law.

The Court of Chancery has always been associated with the mentally ill and the mentally retarded. As early as Henry II, the Royal Prerogative included looking after 'the lands and possessions of lunatics until they recovered, and the lands and possessions of natural idiots until they died', and this implicit trusteeship would naturally be delegated to the Lord Chancellor. Later, it was in the Court of Chancery that the concept of trusts or 'uses' appeared, validated under the Law of Equity, and this enabled lands belonging to the mentally ill to be placed in trust before the Sovereign could get his hands upon them. With the coming of the Victorian lunacy acts providing the first statutory protection of pauper lunatics and the advent of non-private asylums exclusively for lunatics, the Lord Chancellor supervised the application of these statutes. Older psychologists will still remember the Lord Chancellor's Visitors in Lunacy, as they were called, silk-hatted gentlemen who visited the asylums regularly but unfortunately not unexpectedly, and inspected the wards and the statutory records showing the use made of padded cells and mechanical restraints, such as strait-jackets. The Mental Health Act (1959) cleared away most of the vestiges of the Victorian approach to lunacy, but the Court of Protection, which has taken over the Royal Prerogative of acting as Trustee to the lands and possessions of those mentally incapable of managing them, still preserves the tradition which has extended over the past 800 years.

Court of Protection

The Court of Protection is administered by the Supreme Court of Judicature and administers the estates of the mentally ill. In an acute psychosis, patients often give away large sums of money or other valuable property in the false belief that they are millionaires or members of royalty and that their funds are limitless or replaceable. To protect such people, power of attorney is often sought by relatives who look after the patients' affairs until they have recovered, the relative being held responsible in law for any misuse of the patients' funds or property. Where there is no individual to take on this duty, the Court of Protection will on request of the hospital authorities or other interested parties, assume legal control of the patients' affairs until such time as he is capable of resuming control for himself. The Court of Protection functions in some ways like the Public Trustee, but has full overall control, not only of investment of funds, but over *all* disbursements. It is relatively easy to put the patients' affairs in the hands of the Court of Protection. What is not so easy is for the patient to regain control of his own affairs. The court is, of course, responsible for the patients' estate, and if control is passed back to the patient before he is fully recovered, and as a result the estate is diminished or lost by reason of impaired judgement due to his illness, the Court of Protection would be liable. To safeguard both itself and the patient, therefore, the court will not relinquish control until it can be assured by the production of satisfactory evidence, that the patient is, in fact, recovered from his illness, is now capable of handling his own affairs *adequately*, and is unlikely to relapse suddenly before the necessary steps could be taken to safeguard his financial interests. It will be apparent from a knowledge of the psychoses that it is extremely difficult to predict the future course of the illness, neither is it altogether easy to determine when the patient is 'recovered', since some theorists hold that certain mental illnesses such as the schizophrenias are progressive and that no recovery is possible from them, and in the affective group of disorders recurrences of acute phases of the illness are the rule rather than the exception. Most professional workers in the mental health field would therefore regard any statement of recovery as distinctly temerous if not outright erroneous. Moreover, many people are not particularly good 'managers' of their personal affairs, even without the handicap of a mental illness: to what extent could one certify them capable of resuming control, when they already have a history of excessive impulse of buying of trumpery chattels? Nevertheless, patients when they recover, apply to the Court of Protection for release from its control, and the psychologist is often brought in to support their claim.

CASE NO. 19

A man aged 70 who had been in a mental hospital for many years, suffering from a schizophrenic illness, but who had been living at home looked after by a daily visiting housekeeper, applied to the Court of Protection for restitution of control of his own affairs. The psychiatrist who had supervised his care and treatment for the past 20 years was prepared to certify that no relapse was expected, and psychological evidence was sought to support the claim that he was mentally capable of looking after his own estate. Careful examination showed that his level of intellectual functioning was substantially below that appropriate to his academic qualifications and the likelihood of a progressive intellectual deterioration had to be considered. A series of tasks was then applied, in which the appellant had to go shopping in company with the psychologist, while ability to check change, compare prices, and judge values was noted. A questionnaire was prepared on the basis of his property, surviving relations, and current investment, and this was administered in a formal interview situation in which his capacity to understand the nature and extent of his estatement, and the implications for himself and others was fully explored. He showed only a limited understanding of the latter, but proved competent in all the applied tasks. A recommendation was made that control be maintained but that his personal allowance be increased.

The Conciliar Courts

It will be remembered that the Court of Chancery developed from the King in Council. During the 15th and 16th centuries other Royal functions were also delegated within this council from time to time. They included that Court of Inequity, the terrifying Court of Star Chamber introduced to enforce control after the chaos brought about by the War of the Roses; the Court of High Commission established by Elizabeth I to enforce religious dogma and stamp out heresy, and Cardinal Wolsey's Court of Requests—'the poor man's equity'. The present day Cabinet also developed in this way, and from medieval times the privileged members of the inner council became known as the Privy Council, who also exercised a judicial function in parallel to that of the Royal Courts and which exists today as the Judicial Committee of the Privy Council, sitting at No. 11 Downing Street. In earlier days it heard matters concerning aliens, ecclesiastical issues referred from the church courts and especially matters affecting the king's interests. In 1641 the Long Parliament abolished its jurisdiction as a court of first instance, although retaining its appellate functions which by then had crystallized into four sources. These were the Plantations (i.e. the overseas possessions), the Court of Admiralty, the Ecclesiastical Courts, and matters of lunacy. Since 1875 Admiralty appeals to the Court of Appeal and matters of lunacy to the High Court, but the Privy Council Judicial Committee is still the final court of appeal for medical practitioners, clergymen and the subjects of the ever decreasing number of British Possessions overseas. It was to this Appellate Court that the author's evidence was presented in the case of Michael X who was eventually executed in Trinidad.

Case No. 15

A man convicted of murder in Trinidad was sentenced to be hanged, the death penalty having been retained by this Commonwealth country. After the trial, and whilst imprisoned in Death Row at the Royal Jail, Port of Spain, the condemned man became withdrawn and acutely paranoid, refusing to see his legal advisors who were preparing his appeals, and rejecting all visitors except a nun. An appeal to the Privy Council having been rejected, Members of Parliament at Westminster with pro-abolitionist views appealed to both the Prime Minister and the Foreign Secretary to intervene and to supplicate for mercy and to have the sentence commuted to life imprisonment. The nun became the only means of communicating with the prisoner and from her account there was reason to believe that his mental state was abnormal. In Britain it is a tradition that an insane prisoner is never executed, and it was hoped that if satisfactory evidence of insanity could be obtained, a Royal Reprieve would be granted. Plans were made for a psychological examination to be undertaken by a psychologist flown out from the U.K., but to justify this step, it was decided to have a psychological analysis made of a series of cassette tapes which had been clandestinely made by the nun at each interview. After a weekend of analyzing the tapes and examining other relevant material being accumulated in London, the author concluded that there was sufficient prima facie evidence of a paranoid illness to justify the time and expense of visiting the prisoner in Trinidad, if he would permit contact. The Trinidad authorities, aware of what was afoot, brought forward the date of execution. An affidavit was immediately prepared, detailing the results of the psychological analyses and the expert opinion, for presentation to Her Majesty the Queen. The document had just been signed in the office of a Public Notary when news arrived that the execution had taken place.

Mercantile Courts

In addition to the Royal Courts which administered common law and the Court of Chancery which administered Equity there developed in the early Middle Ages the Courts Merchant which administered the Law Merchant. The Law Merchant existed in recognizable form from the 10th century onwards. It was an international law, in as much as

Courts Merchant in, for example, Bristol would be administering the same laws as those administered in Marseilles, Venice, and the Hanseatic cities. Since in early times the chief towns were on the coast, maritime law which came to be administered by the Court of Admiralty developed contemporaneously with the Law Merchant. The latter was identical with the Merchant Law of the Continent and owed much to Roman Law; it was therefore very similar to Equity which as we have seen also had strong flavourings of Roman Law in it.

The Law Merchant was administered in a number of courts. There were the Courts Merchant found at various sea port towns such as Yarmouth, Newcastle and the Cinque Ports. Merchants themselves acted as judges and the object was to secure a speedy settlement of the matter in dispute. Courts were also attached to fairs and markets under the bailiff or steward of the grounds and were known as Courts of Pied Poudre (later Pie Powder!) after the 'dusty feet' of those attending them. By a statute of Edward III certain towns which dealt with special commodities of commerce were allowed to maintain courts merchant, and these were known as Courts of Staple. The same statute established that where the litigants were foreign merchants two nationals of their country had to be associated with the Court and if the trial was by jury the jury itself must be foreigners. The Law Merchant itself was incorporated into Common Law by Lord Mansfield in 1669. The Courts Merchant gradually declined during the 17th and 18th centuries and were finally rendered obsolete by the action of the Admiralty taking over the sea port jurisdiction and the Court of Common Pleas taking over most of the other jurisdiction as transport facilities improved: until very recently there were two surviving Courts Merchant, namely the Bristol Tolzey Court and the Liverpool Court of Passage. Today the last of the Courts Merchant is embodied in the 'Commercial' part of the High Court. The Commercial Court hears relevant 'Commercial' cases which are tried under a particular judge specializing in Commercial Law and lengthy pleadings are not used. Law Merchant and its special court thus live on in function if not in name. Psychologists who are involved in cases of a commercial nature—such as disputes over trademarks—will find themselves before the mercantile experts of the Commercial List.

CASE NO. 16

A dispute arose between two food manufacturers concerning the labelling of their products. The older-established company maintained that the labels were sufficiently alike to confuse the purchaser into thinking that both brands were the same, while the defendants pointed out that the trademarks were different and that clearly no infringement of commercial rights had occurred, and that they had every right to show a picture of the contents of the tin on the label. To demonstrate whether or not customers were actually confused or not by the similarity of labels a a psychological experiment was set up with the co-operation of a supermarket. Tins of both products were placed adjacently upon shelves near an inconspicuous viewing window of darkened glass used by the security officer for watching shoplifters. Shoppers were filmed as they selected one or other of the products, and their selection time recorded. At the checkout counter, another psychologist alerted to the 'special' customers, interviewed each one as they left the checkout point and asked them which brand of the goods in question they had purchased. They were asked to examine their purchases and confirm the accuracy of their choice by showing them to the psychologist. Vouchers for further free supplies of the older-established product, subsidized by the manufacturer were then given to them for their trouble. This study established that a statistically significant number of shoppers mistook one brand for another, and a settlement was reached by the two manufacturers out of court. Although unreported, this case has some elements in common with *Coca Cola Company* v. *Chero-cola Company* (1921) which was the first reported case in which studies of mental imagery and associations were used in trademark litigation.

Court of Admiralty

As with all medieval courts, the Admiralty Courts developed wherever lucre seemed likely. To gain some of the financial spin-off from dispute over the cargo of wrecks, and prizes from war and piracy, local Admiralty Courts were set up at seven sea ports, the Admiralty of the Cinque Ports being the most important. The British victory over the French fleet at the Battle of Sluys created so much legitimate loot or spoils of war that it encouraged the establishment of a Central Court of Admiralty between AD 1340 and 1351.

At first the Admiralty Courts were presided over by three admirals, but subsequent jurisdiction was conferred on the Lord High Admiral only, and the method of trial was without a jury. The Court had criminal jurisdiction over crimes committed on the high seas and later, under a statute by Richard II, extended this to cases of death and dangerous wounding occurring on ships in the mouths of rivers. The jurisdiction of the Court of Admiralty was gradually eroded: under Henry VIII all treasons, felonies and murders were transferred to common law jurisdiction. Later, when the Central Criminal Court, was established in London in 1834 the criminal jurisdiction of the Admiralty was transferred to it by the Admiralty Act of 1840. From earliest times, in civil jurisdiction there were conflicts between the Admiralty Court and the Courts Merchant and also the Common Law Courts, and these conflicts persisted through the ages. The Common Law Courts practised common law, as their name implies, while the Courts Merchant practised Mercantile Law—an international law which had absorbed rules of fair trading from the Phoenicians onwards. Similarly, the Admiralty Courts practised Maritime Law, also international in scope, and therefore owing much to Roman Law and its continental development. As trade with both orient and occident developed, especially in the East and West Indies, Maritime Law developed with it, reaching its peak in the 18th century with marine insurance centred in Lloyds Coffee House from 1774. Some important principles of mutual liability in tort were introduced from Maritime Law into Common Law as recently as 1945. Conflict persisted, not so much between the three forms of law but because of the overlapping jurisdiction and the financial and administrative consequences. These inter-Court differences were not settled until the Admiralty Act of 1840. This Act compensated for the loss of criminal jurisdiction by extending the civil jurisdiction of the Admiralty, but its newly created scope was short lived and eventually the Admiralty Court was fused with the High Court as part of the Probate, Divorce and Admiralty Division by the Judicature Act of 1883. Because of the distinctive importance of Maritime Law, cases involving maritime matters are still heard by the special Admiralty branch of the High Court. Maritime matters pose special problems for the forensic psychologist because they usually entail nautical knowledge unfamiliar to those who pursue their vocation on terra firma. However, once the problem can be translated into non-nautical terms, the solution can be sought by methods identical to those used for other forensic problems, as the following example shows.

CASE NO. 29

A small ship engaged in day trips in the summer season was delayed by mechanical trouble and returned after dark. In attempting to come alongside the pier and pick up moorings, the ship collided with the pier, and both ship and pier sustained damage. The master of the vessel, who had not approached the pier for mooring after dark during the current season, was at a loss to understand the cause of his apparent misjudgement. The owners of the pier took legal action in the Admiralty Division of the High Court, and the shipping company also instituted an enquiry. The author was consulted to advise on whether anything could be done to explain the cause of the misjudgement. Detailed discussions with the master made it clear that he believed something was different about the moorings; he insisted that some change had been made of which he was unaware. Reference to the plans and to the Borough Surveyor indicated that there had been no structural changes to the pier or associated structures since the end of the war, when the Royal Navy, then in possession of the area, had withdrawn and returned the pier to its owners. The master was taken out in a boat after dark and asked to describe the situation as he approached the pier. At one point he remarked that everything looked different but could not explain in what way. The position was marked by compass sightings, and photographs taken in daylight the next day from the approximate position. The master then said everything looked normal. His vision, night vision and colour vision was tested and all three were found to be satisfactory. Further enquiries were then made at the offices of both Borough and County Surveyors, regarding any building, demolition or landscaping which had taken place in the area and which would be visible from the seaward approach to the pier. The only likely change reported was the installation of a row of sodium street lamps in a road some way back from the pier. This suggested the possibility of a parallax error, and when the master was next taken out to sea, to the 'significant point', and asked to examine the lights carefully it was apparent that they coincided with certain pier lights, and at some angles of approach, gave the impression that the boat was moving in the *opposite* direction to that in which it was, in fact, going. A model of the area, with battery-powered lights was constructed, and used to demonstrate the nature of parallax error and its relevance and validity in the present case. These circumstances were taken to absolve the Master from full responsibility and he retained his ticket.

Ecclesiastical Courts

Another component of English Law is the Ecclesiastical or Canon Law, a body of church law brought over from Rome by the early church and originally founded upon Roman civil law. The aim of Canon Law was to reduce to a minimum the divergence between law and morals and to provide a legal system which resembled as closely as possible the formalized ideal of Christian conduct. In addition to the elements of Roman law, which comprise the body of ecclesiastical law, additional material came from the opinions of various popes, ancient fathers, cardinals and papal legates. At the time of the Reformation a statute was passed authorizing a review of the Canon Law of England. More importantly, it explicitly ordered that until this revision was completed all existing Canons should remain binding. Since the contemplated review never materialized the result is that the Canons of Ecclesiastical Law, in force prior to the statute of Henry VIII directing the review, remain as valid today as they did in Tudor times. Modern Church Law governs the Church of England and its clergy and in theory the laity as well. It is composed of elements of three types of law; namely, the old civil law of Rome, the Canon Law of ecclesiastic origin and statute law relating to church affairs which has been passed by Parliament and is secular in origin and outlook.

The ecclesiastical courts were unknown until the Norman Conquest when William the Conqueror separated the civil and ecclesiastical jurisdiction in this country and set up a system of church courts. Two provincial courts, Canterbury and York, were created under the jurisdiction of the archbishops. In Canterbury, the court is called the Court of Arches and in York the Court of Chancery of York, and both courts hear appeals from the lower ecclesiastical courts. The jurisdiction over matters of wills and the administration of property, possessed by the ecclesiastical courts was transferred when the Court of Probate was established in 1857. The Diocesan Courts, or as they are also known, the Consistory Courts, were courts of the bishops. There is one for each diocese, presided over by a chancellor who is a skilled lawyer. The Diocesen Courts hear matters concerning the clergy within the diocese and also various cases within the diocese which were formerly heard by the so-called Peculiar Courts which have now been abolished. The Diocesan Court itself was abolished in 1840 but restored in 1892. The Archdeacon Courts originally heard matters concerning the Church buildings and fabrics and are now obsolete. The Court of High Commission was established under Elizabeth I with very wide powers, and heard matters of heresy, schism and contempts brought before it. It was abolished by the Long Parliament in 1641 and although revived again by James II under the Court of the Ecclesiastical Commission it was declared illegal by the Bill of Rights (1689). The Church Courts had considerable jurisdiction in former times, for in addition to dealing with church matters, matrimonial cases and nullity suits also came within their perview.

The Divorce Court and Probate Court took over the jurisdiction of much of the lay function of the church courts, but they still regulate the morals of the clergy. In law they still possess sufficient jurisdiction over the laity that they have power to imprison lay members for up to six months. Fortunately for the general public, if not for the moral standards of the country the exercise of this particular sanction is obsolete in practice. Ecclesiastical Courts, like the Royal Courts, were not without fictions used to extend their jurisdiction, and when the ecclesiastical and secular courts had become separated, the clergy claimed that all Clerks in Holy Orders should be exempt from secular jurisdiction, and should be tried by the Bishop's Courts. In order to increase their jurisdiction in this matter, the latter gradually extended it to lay members of the church on the fiction that they were 'eligible for ordination'. This move was immensely popular by the literate miscreants, since most crimes were punished in secular courts by hanging, whereas the Consistory Courts could only imprison. The accused when brought to the Assize Courts, would plead 'Benefit of Clergy' and ask for his case to be transferred to an Ecclesiastical Court. In order to prove that he was eligible for ordination, he would then be required to read, without prompting, the first verse of Psalm 51: 'Have mercy upon me, O God, according to Thy Loving Kindness; according unto the multitude of Thy tender mercies blot out my transgressions'. Because it saved the accused from hanging, this became known as the 'Neck Verse', and many an illiterate old scoundrel with a literate friend and a good memory saved his life by this means. When the courts realized how many persistent offenders were using Benefit of Clergy on a repeat basis, a statute of 1490 provided that those not ordained should have the benefit only once, and the courts branded such beneficiaries on the thumb. The Benefit remained valid in England until 1827 when it was abolished, but continued overseas where English law prevailed until much later. In the United States of America Benefit of Clergy was being successfully claimed at least until 1855.

As far as can be determined, no psychologist has yet been invited to provide evidence before an Ecclesiastical Court. Psychology so far has not contributed to the unfrocking of a priest or the dismissal of a deacon. However, the Canon Law has had considerable influence on the English Legal System because in earlier days the Church Courts used to deal with such matters as incest, inheritance, intestacy, wills, matrimonial contracts defamation and other matters which today come before the ordinary courts.

In those cases where a psychologist has been called in to provide evidence of testamentary capacity the judgment may well have rested upon the ideas and ideals furnished by ecclesiastical law many centuries ago.

CASE NO. 30

An elderly female patient died in the mental hospital in which she had been nursed for many decades. Her registered next-of-kin had long since died, and she had not been visited by any relations for as long as the ward nursing staff could remember. She left a will, in which she bequeathed her remaining property to an animal charity. Some months after her death, but before probate had been granted, a remote relation appeared and contested the will, on the grounds that the testator had been *non compos mentis* at the time of making the will, and thus lacked testamentary capacity. The author had carried out a routine psychological assessment of the testator some years after the will had been signed. From his records he was thus able to testify that at the time of his examination the testator was, in his opinion, clear in her mind, and fully capable of knowing what she was doing, what property she possessed, and the possible beneficiaries of her will. (These are the three essential criteria to establish testamentary capacity). Under the presumption of continuance (q.v.) the court could presume that her condition when tested could be validly extrapolated retrospectively to the date on which she signed her will. This was supported by the testimony of the ward sister that the patient's mental condition had remained apparently unchanged for many years. There being no evidence provided by the alleged next-of-kin to rebut this presumption, the claim failed.

10. Quasi-Judicial Courts

The Law Courts

FOR A FULLER understanding of the organization of English Courts of Law, the reader cannot do better than consult Archer[103] who provides an excellent introduction to the English Legal System, his diagrams being particularly helpful. In this section, a brief outline of the development of the various courts will be given, the main purpose being to create a feeling for the long history and development underlying the existence of any court in which the forensic psychologist may find himself. These will be of three kinds:

(i) Courts of Criminal Jurisdiction

These are courts where offences deemed to be against the public interest, that is, criminal offences are heard. They include the Courts of Petty Session, commonly called the Magistrates' or Police Courts, the Crown Courts, which since 1972 replaced the Assizes, the Central Criminal Court, known more familiarly as the 'Old Bailey', and the Criminal Division of the Court of Appeal.

(ii) Courts of Civil Jurisdiction

Private wrongs, as between one person and another, and which pose no threat to the safety and welfare of the general public, are not criminal but civil offences. Such wrongs are heard in the Civil Courts; these include the so-called domestic courts held by the magistrates, the County Courts, the High Court in the Strand, London, and the Court of Appeal, Civil Division.

(iii) Courts of Special Jurisdiction

In some cases an official enquiry is required into some matters which are manifestly neither public nor private, or where there is no *prima facie* evidence as yet that a criminal act has been committed. These enquiries take place in courts of Special Jurisdiction, which include the Coroner's Courts (concerned with the *cause* of death and not who encompassed it, but which also deal with treasure trove), Courts-Martial, where the offences considered are confined to those contrary to the Navy, Army and Air Force Acts, and apply only to those enlisted or commissioned in the appropriate armed force, and Ecclesiastical Courts, concerned primarily with the conduct of ordained churchmen, but with valid powers over the laity. The Admiralty and Commercial Courts, although having jurisdiction within these special areas of Maritime and Mercantile Law respectively, are actually courts of Civil Jurisdiction within the High Court of Queen's Bench. From the point of view of Evidence, the various Administrative Tribunals, Disciplinary Courts, and Courts of Arbitration can be subsumed under this heading, although some legal writers prefer to include them under the Courts of Civil Jurisdiction.

Superior and Inferior Courts

In addition to classifying courts according to the nature of their jurisdiction, they can also be separated into two hierarchical divisions. The Superior Courts are those which have gradually evolved from the King in Council and which were at one time presided over by persons of the nobility. These include the House of Lords, the Appeal Court, the High Court of Justice, and the Crown Courts. Although the latter are of recent statutory origin, they replace, and have taken over the jurisdiction of the old Assize Courts, which originated from the Royal Courts. The Inferior Courts are those which owe their origin to local rather than Royal needs. They include the County Courts, the Courts of Justices of the Peace, the Coroner's Courts, and all the many courts of special jurisdiction. Some of these courts are of recent creation, such as the Industrial Relations Tribunals, others predate the Norman Conquest such as the Court of the Cinque Ports and the Court of Husting.

The following brief description of the principal courts, commences with the quasi-judicial courts and Tribunals, and proceeds through the Inferior Courts of record and up the court hierarchy to the Superior Courts and ending with the House of Lords, which once enjoyed worldwide jurisdiction over the whole of the British Empire, and still retains an important, though geographically more restricted, jurisdiction.

Quasi-judicial Courts

With the development of what has become known as administrative law has also come a plethora of quasi-judicial courts and tribunals in which the president or chairman of the court may or may not be legally qualified. In addition to the Mental Health Review Tribunals, in which the psychologist is more frequently engaged, there exists today a wide range of quasi-judicial proceedings such as Rent Tribunals, Land Tribunals, Social Security Appeal Tribunals, and so on. Even Appeals against the rejection of planning applications under the Town and

Country Planning Act (1962) may fall within the province of the psychologist especially where aesthetic judgments or perceptual processes are involved. At the time of writing there are over 1000 independent administrative tribunals in existence. These quasi-judicial Courts, as they are called, fall into two groups, namely Administrative Courts, whose appeal generally has to be to a 'Judge in Chambers', and the domestic tribunals or disciplinary courts, where the sanctions are more severe, and where appeal therefore lies to the High Court. Some Courts of Enquiry are prevented by the statute which created them from having any appeal to a Judicial Court.

The Administrative Courts include the Tribunals concerned with mental health (described in more detail below), national insurance, income tax, rent, pension appeals, local valuation, gas and electricity arbitration, transport, agricultural land, legal aid, together with a vast variety of industrial courts. Although most of the quasi-judicial courts of administrative law came into existence with modern administrative law, and particularly with socialist legislation designed to protect the worker and consumer, a few are of historical interest. Among these will be found the Courts of Survey, responsible for the investigation of a ship for unseaworthiness under a Wreck Commissioner and a judge appointed by the Home Secretary, and the Court of Claims, which sits before each coronation to determine claims to occupy certain places or perform the various acts of pageantry and service to the monarch which make the British coronation such a unique spectacle. There are always more members of the nobility willing to carry the banner, than there are banners to go round, and although many of the services are hereditary and generally beyond dispute, the orders of precedence and the family trees of long-dead noblemen are sufficiently complex and obscure as to ensure the need for arbitration and judgment by this ancient court for many years to come. One other court deserves mention in this section and that is the Court of Chivalry, which is said to be the oldest secular court in the world. Originating as a medieval military court dealing with disputes between knights and criminal offences by knights, for which the procedure was appropriately Trial by Battle, the court lost its criminal jurisdiction under Henry VIII, who employed the instantly effective method of having the Lord Constable, who presided over the Court, beheaded.

The domestic or disciplinary tribunals are quasi-judicial courts which 'discipline' the members of special organizations, and enjoy jurisdiction only over the members of these organizations. The disciplinary committee of the General Medical Council is perhaps the best known of these, its proceedings providing material for the less refined newspapers when a medical practitioner is 'struck off' the register for professional misconduct. Most of the other disciplinary tribunals follow a similar pattern, lacking perhaps the more newsworthy sexual excesses which

87

become less easy to indulge in as the member-client relationship becomes less personal. These other tribunals will include the Bar Council, controlling the professional conduct of Barristers, the General Dental Council, General Nursing Council, Central Midwives Board, and similar professional bodies concerned with chartered accountants, chartered surveyors, opticians and so on. Trade Unions each have their own disciplinary tribunal, and eventually, following registration, so will psychologists. Although the High Court is the Appellate Court for Disciplinary Tribunals, the G.M.C. is an exception because of the special nature of this profession and appeal from the Disciplinary Committee of the G.M.C. lies with the Judicial Committee of the Privy Council.

The tribunals have the advantage of providing a simple and informal hearing, specialized knowledge and low costs. They have serious disadvantages in that they are not subject to the Rules of Evidence used in Common Law (since they function under Administrative Law), often exclude the public, can refuse to hear oral testimony or allow the applicant legal representation, and often have built-in bias, as when the commissioner hearing the appeal is a member of a government department charged with a responsibility relevant to the question at issue but contrary to the interests of the appellant. Some improvement was effected by the creation of a Council of Tribunals under the Tribunals and Enquiries Act (1958), which supervises the functioning of tribunals and provides recourse to the Court of Law on points of law even when the statute creating the tribunal specifically prevents or limits this right.

Although the forensic psychologist may find himself giving evidence on the basis of facts in mitigation and or even of *actus reus*—in any of the quasi judicial courts, it is in the Mental Health Tribunals that most of the evidence given by psychologists has been considered.

Mental Health Review Tribunals

The Mental Health Act (1959) established Mental Health Tribunals created to protect patients from the abuse of compulsory powers. The Mental Health Act enables over 90% of patients to be admitted to and discharged from mental hospitals entirely without formality. There are three main methods of compulsory admission, emergency observation, and treatment. In the case of an emergency any relative or mental health officer can apply for an unwilling patient's admission into hospital with only one medical recommendation and authority for detaining the patient in this way lasts for three days. Admission for observation requires two medical certificates and authorizes detention for 28 days. A treatment order is valid for one year and may be renewed at the end of that period if the patient is still unfit for discharge. Patients who have committed punishable offences may also be detained in the hospital on a court order and these orders made by a magistrate require the recommendations of two doctors. Those found guilty of serious offences by higher courts may also be subject to a restriction on their discharge and in such cases the Secretary of State is the only person in England who can order the patient's release from the hospital. Patients on restriction orders represent less than $\frac{1}{2}$% of all compulsory admissions. Even these patients have access to Mental Health Review Tribunals although these can only act in an advisory capacity to the Secretary of State. Tribunals consist of three panels of lawyers, doctors and lay members and one member of each panel is detailed to hear the application under the chairman who would be the lawyer. The proceedings of a tribunal are governed by the Mental Health Tribunal Rules (1960) made by the Lord Chancellor and the tribunals themselves are also supervised by the Council on Tribunals.

The powers of the Mental Health Review Tribunals are limited. They have no option but to discharge the applicant if, after the hearing, they find that he is not then suffering from mental illness or that it is not necessary for the patient's health or safety or for the protection of others that he should continue to be detained. The Mental Health Review Tribunals are not empowered to consider either the legality of the initial commitment or whether psychiatric treatment is necessary or indeed adequate. Many commentators consider this a weakness of the system, since these factors may well deserve looking into, a proceeding which could possibly reduce the incidence of future appeals. The reorganization of the N.H.S. in 1973 provided a forum at which the patients' complaints could be discussed and further enquiries initiated, namely the Community Health Council. The Mental Health Tribunal, however, is concerned solely with the release or continued detention of the patient at the present time. It is the freedom of the patient which is at issue here, not his treatment. However, one other weakness in the present system is pointed out by Fennel[130]. It has been noticed that there is a disproportionately large number of paranoid patients presented as appellants at Mental Health Review Tribunals, and Fennel draws attention to the implications of the 'disease model' which provides the context for the Mental Health Review Tribunals' deliberations. The imposition of the disease model upon the thinking and arguments of the hospital authorities and medical practitioners opposing the appellants' request to be discharged from hospital implies that the disease may be present although *latent.* The patient's own statements contradicting those of the professional staff opposing his appeal may be. and often are, interpreted as 'symptoms' of mental disorder, and specifically of paranoid thinking. By the very existence of this distorting frame of reference, the patient's own testimony, which should have as much *prima facie* validity as that of his opponents, becomes the very evidence used by the latter to defeat the appeal. If the patient admits his symptoms he is mentally ill. If he denies his illness, he is lacking in insight and therefore psychotic and *ipso facto* mentally ill. This catch 22 situation is also seen in the committal problems of forensic psychiatry especially in the U.S.A., where humanistic trail blazers have done so much to bring to the public awareness the plight of the incarcerated 'state patient'.

About 20 appeals are heard each week at the Mental Health Review Tribunals in England and Wales and in the first five years of operation 5,423 applications were determined and 12.6% of patients were discharged. Statistics on tribunal reviews are published annually by the Ministry of Health. Greenland, in a follow-up study, found that the majority of tribunal applicants suffered from chronic forms of mental illness for whom good after-care support was not always available. About half of the patients discharged made satisfactory adjustments; the other half were readmitted to hospital and some to prison within a year or less. There were a number of suicides but no acts of violence involving others had been reported at the time of his survey[131]. In Scotland the situation is rather different since residents of that country are governed by the Mental Health (Scotland) Act (1960). Here an independent Mental Welfare Commission is appointed to exercise protective functions of persons who may be incapable of protecting themselves or their interests by reason of mental disorder. The commissioners consist of three medical practitioners, a lawyer and three or four lay people including at least one woman, and have wide powers to visit patients at home or in hospital. As in England and Wales, they are able to order the discharge of patients from detention but in fact they rarely do so and in a five year period between 1962 and 1967 only six out of 810 applications considered by the commission were successful. However in Scotland a patient in addition to his right of appeal to the Mental Welfare Commission may also appeal to the sheriff for a discharge. Such appeals are heard in private in the sheriff's court and the patient and the hospital are legally represented and both parties are able to call witnesses. It is here that psychological evidence may well be relevant. This method of appeal is used far less than that to the Mental Welfare Commission. In the same five year period there have been 67 appeals to the sheriff from patients with only two discharges, in addition to 152 appeals with five discharges from the State maximum security hospital at Carstairs. Case Nos. 7 and 8 have already described the role of the forensic psychologist in Mental Health Tribunals.

11. Magistrates Courts

THE LOWEST DEGREE of judicial power is that possessed by those residents in a local community appointed by the Lord Chancellor to act as Justices of the Peace[132]. The Courts of Justices of the Peace, as they were formerly known, were established under Edward I by the Statute of Winchester which authorized the issue of Commissions of the Peace to selected persons.

The Courts of the Justices of the Peace later became known as the Courts of Petty Sessions. They are more popularly known as the Magistrates' Court or the Police Courts, and today 98% of the criminal cases in England reaching court are prosecuted in these courts. The Court is presided over by the Justices of the Peace, who, in addition to trying all summary or petty offences, have jurisdiction to try summarily certain indictable crimes which are serious crimes normally requiring jury, for example, those crimes formerly referred to as treason, felony or misdemeanour. In the case of children under the age of 14 *all* crimes except homicide must be heard summarily. In the case of young persons between the ages of 14 and 16 years inclusive the magistrates may try them summarily for any crime except homicide but the young person has the right to a trial before a jury. In the case of adults aged 17 years or over certain indictable crimes including theft, deception, assault, battery and criminal damage may be dealt with summarily, although the accused had the right to trial by jury. The advantage of being tried by magistrates is that the maximum sentence is six months, whereas if the same offence is tried in a higher court more severe sentences may apply. On the other hand, juries tend to be more in sympathy with the accused than do magistrates, so that the chances of acquittal are somewhat higher in jury trials. Magistrates also have a small jurisdiction in civil cases dealing with affiliation proceedings, separation orders, custody of children, wife's maintenance, consent to marriage, orders under the Mental Health Act, Care and Protection Orders, disputes between master and servant not exceeding £10, and certain matters involving landlord and tenant. Magistrates also have certain administrative functions in connection with the licencing laws, the sale of intoxicants, some civil debts including Income Tax below £30, and some supervision of the local police force.

The inter-judicial reliability of magistrates has been found to be about 17% when tested during special courses for Justices of the Peace and this low prediction of outcome in summary proceedings adds spice to plea-bargaining and considerable anxiety to the accused, whose future often depends less on the nature of his alleged offence than the selection of magistrates he draws for his *jugement de trois*.

Under the Children and Young Persons Act 1933, juvenile courts were established which are also courts of summary jurisdiction, being petty sessions which deal with children or young persons under the age of 17.

The Public are not admitted to juvenile court sittings and although the press is admitted they are not permitted to publish the name of the accused. Special magistrates are selected for these sittings of the Juvenile Courts one at least must be a woman.

More than 90% of criminal cases are tried in Magistrates Courts, and much of the forensic psychologists' work will be found there[106,107].

Magistrates

Certain persons are made magistrates ex officio such as the mayor of the boroughs, and the chairman of urban district and county councils, but normally the magistrates are appointed by the Lord Chancellor on the recommendation of the Lord Lieutenant of the County. Magistrates are generally unpaid, being laymen and not lawyers, but in certain boroughs there are stipendary magistrates who are barristers or solicitors of at least seven years standing. Under the Justices of the Peace Act (1949) magistrates who reach the age of 75 and those who are unfitted to exercise judicial functions because of infirmity are placed on a supplementary list and may only exercise non-judicial duties, such as the signing of warrants.

Preliminary Enquiry

At first the jurisdiction of Magistrates' Courts was simply to deal with breaches of the peace. However, in 1330 the Statute of Edward III provided for Justices of the Peace to hold preliminary enquiries into serious crimes beyond their own jurisdiction to determine whether the evidence was sufficient to send the accused person to trial at a higher court. This practice has continued to the present day. It possesses the merit of preventing an expensive trial which would inevitably lead to an acquittal, but has the disadvantage, since the preliminary enquiry is often well publicized in the newspapers, of giving prospective jurors a journalistic viewpoint of the matters being considered. The prejudicial effects of a preliminary hearing received much unfavourable comment in the case of *R. v. Jeremy Thorpe and others* (1979).

When a party accused of a serious offence is brought before the justice of the peace for preliminary enquiry the prosecution call their witnesses who give their evidence on oath. The evidence given by each witness for the prosecution is taken down in writing and must be signed by the witness and the magistrate, when it becomes known as the deposition. Although the witnesses for the prosecution must be present in person in order to give their evidence again at the trial at the High Court, their deposition may be read as evidence should they be dead, insane, or too ill to attend the trial, or if in the opinion of the magistrate their evidence is immaterial. When the depositions are made the accused must be present and must have an opportunity to cross-examine a witness if he so desires. He may call witnesses in his own defence if he wishes although it is frequently the case that he is advised not to call his witnesses at this stage but to reserve them until the hearing in the High Court. The magistrate will then decide whether the evidence tendered by the prosecution is sufficient to justify him in committing the accused for trial. He makes no decision whether he considers him guilty but merely whether there is sufficient evidence upon which a reasonable jury might find him guilty. If he thinks the evidence is insufficient then he must dismiss the charge against the accused. When the magistrate commits the accused for trial he binds over the prosecutor and his witnesses in their own recognizance to attend the trial. In certain cases, criminal proceedings cannot be initiated without permission of a higher authority. For example, to prosecute under the Official Secrets Act leave of the Attorney General must first be obtained; to prosecute an express trustee for fraudulent conversion the permission from a judge in chambers is required, and the permission of the Public Prosecutor is necessary to prefer a charge of being a persistent offender. In most cases however no further permission is required before the magistrate can institute criminal proceedings and the accused after the preliminary hearing can then be committed to the appropriate court. At this stage the magistrates are exercising the function of the Grand Jury, now abolished, who formerly had the responsibility of deciding whether the evidence was sufficient to justify validating the Bill of Indictment as a 'True Bill'. Since the passing of the Courts Act (1971), all committals go direct to the Crown Courts. At this stage the question of bail will arise. Except for cases of treason, where bail cannot be granted by the magistrate but only by the Home Secretary or a judge in chambers, the magistrate will base his decision on whether the accused will turn up for the trial and whether he is likely to commit more crime between the release from custody and the summons to the High Court. The gravity of the offence is obviously relevant here and for this reason they are seldom granted in the charge of murder. If the accused is refused bail he has the right to appeal to a judge in chambers and if the judge refuses his bail then the accused may bring up the matter before a High Court by means of *habeas corpus* proceedings.

In *R. v. Stonehouse* (1975), for example, John Stonehouse, M.P. was refused bail on six occasions and it was not until after the author had made a comprehensive psychometric assessment of the prisoner in Brixton Prison that bail was secured on the seventh appeal. The question of bail and the prisoner's likelihood of presenting himself in court for the later trial rest upon a number of factors, including his domestic ties, his social mobility, and financial resources. The risk of absconding will also relate to psychological factors, which will include most of the personal and social ones, so that the forensic psychologist can often provide evidence relevant to the question 'What are the risks that this particular prisoner will abscond?

Case No. 17

The prisoner, who had consented of his own freewill to return to the U.K. from Australia was taken direct to Bow Street from London Airport so that bail could be granted the same day. To the surprise of the Australian lawyers, who had flown to England at their own expense in order to defend the prisoner, bail was not granted because of an objection by the D.P.P., despite the fact that the prisoner had been granted bail in Australia and had returned voluntarily to the U.K. An appeal was lodged to a judge in chambers but the application was rejected and the prisoner remained in Her Majesty's Prison, Brixton, pending trial. Meanwhile, people from all over Britain offered support, including one wealthy person who personally offered one quarter of a million pounds surety for the prisoner's bail. The prisoner made a third application for bail without success, and in successive weeks abortive applications by various legal advisors were made. Each time new grounds for requesting bail were put forward—the need for the prisoner to have ready access to an office full of his financial files, the need for the various medical, psychiatric and psychological experts to have adequate facilities for consultation and examination, the fact that in previous cases, prominent figures facing far more serious charges had been granted bail immediately, and so on. A psychological examination of the prisoner while in prison was undertaken and a report submitted on the current state of his mental health, in the context of medical evidence of severe depression existing sometime previously, with an opinion on the possible effects of continued imprisonment upon any psychopathology then present. The psychological evidence was used, *inter alia*, to support the next application for bail, but this was again refused. Finally, when the House of Commons, which the prisoner had applied to address, but had been prevented from doing so by his detention, rose for its summer recess and was no longer available, bail was suddenly granted without any application being made or explanation given.

Although most criminals are brought to the High Court via the preliminary hearing of a magistrates court, in certain cases they may be brought to trial in the High Court in other ways; for example, the witness committing a perjury may, under the Perjury Act (1911), be committed for trial by the judge trying the particular case at which the witness has given perjured testimony. Where criminal information of public importance is laid before the Attorney General he may prosecute in the Queen's Bench direct without a preliminary hearing. The accused may also be brought to trial following a coroner's inquest.

The preliminary hearing presents a special problem to the forensic psychologist appearing as expert witness. Although when asked to appear in the High Court, the depositions obtained in the preliminary hearing can be of inestimable benefit in furnishing him with much of the evidence of both sides in advance, the manner in which the depositions are recorded makes them a two-edged weapon, in that the psychologist's own evidence may be verbally maltreated and convey views contrary to those actually expressed in court at the time by the psychologist. This situation arises because, despite the availability of automatic electronic methods of recording and printing out human speech, magistrates courts still rely on the presence of a scribe, whose only concession to modern technology is the replacement of the quill for the ballpoint pen. Apart from this change of writing instrument, and occasionally the use of a typewriter, the process has remained unchanged through the centuries. This would not matter so much if the scribe was one of those high speed stenographers employed in the High Courts to record accurately at more than 200 words per minute every word spoken in them (averaging 36,000 words each day). On the contrary, the transcript is made by a clerk who has other responsible duties, and who is neither trained nor skilled in taking down evidence verbatim. Even when a typewriter is used, it often provides more of an obstacle than a facilitator, since the testimony is slowed down to the modest ability of the typist to type direct from dictation, and the frequent interruptions of a witness' statement, and requests for repetition, serve to impair the train of thought and often change the nuance of what is being said. On one occasion the author as expert witness in a preliminary hearing had to contend, not only with an abnormally slow typist who could hardly complete a sentence without repetition and correction, but who suffered the misfortune of being saddled with a typewriter of such age and ancient design that it was fit only for a museum, and emphasized the fact by continually breaking down. During this particular case the author spent long periods in the witness box whilst the court twiddled its thumbs and the unhappy typist staggered off with his machine to obtain emergency repairs somewhere in the locality. It is therefore not surprising that the deposition, which has to be presented to and signed by the witness before leaving the box, often turns out to be a very rough approximation of what the witness believes was said. By this time the witness may have been interrupted and asked to repeat himself so often that he can no longer remember clearly what he *did* say. There is usually an uneasy feeling that he didn't say quite what the deposition reports. The problem is further compounded by the fact that the alternating question and answer sequence of the examinations are condensed into one statement allegedly made by the witness. In the examination-in-chief this is usually unimportant, since the questions themselves will be based upon the witnesses' own proof of evidence, but in the cross-examination this may be of significance, and this problem will be considered further in a later chapter.

12. Coroners' Courts and Crown Courts

Coroners' Courts

THE FORENSIC psychologist is not commonly concerned with the Coroner's Court although in cases of suspected suicide he may be called to give evidence as to the state of mind of the patient whom he had tested within a reasonable time of the death. More often he is asked to provide a report for the medical practitioner responsible for the care of the deceased person. The office of coroner appeared as early as Richard I, a coroner being appointed in A.D. 1194 to look after certain financial interests of the king. The word coroner comes from the Latin word for crown. The coroner was concerned with revenue and his particular role was to supervise the sheriff who had formerly been entrusted with this function. Once again we see a court being created out of financial considerations. The coroner's responsibilities in the matter of royal finance explains the connection between the coroner's court—where ownership of discovered valuables are decided—and treasure trove, and in a less obvious way to the inquest held in cases of death. The purpose of the coroner's court originally was not so much to protect citizens from unsuspected foul play as to see whether a crime had been committed; if so the goods of the murderer would be forfeit to the king, and thus became a matter of royal revenue.

The source of the coroner's concern with violent death also arose from the mortality rate among Normans as they settled into the occupation of English territory after the Conquest of 1066. The impossibility of finding the perpetrators among a hostile community led the King to impose fines on all the residents of the Hundred for every violent death unless the victims could be proved to be English. While more humane than the widespread extermination of hostages by the Germans in occupied territories during World War II, it not only appears to have produced a useful source of royal revenue, but was so effective in increasing Norman life expectancy that the principle of punishing local people for undetected crimes persisted into the 19th century. The coroner may call an inquest at his discretion in any case of death, but he has an obligation to do so when there are reasonable

97

grounds for suspecting that the person has died a violent death, by murder, manslaughter, infanticide, transportation accident, or notifiable disease, also when a person dies suddenly and the cause of death is unknown, or when a prisoner has died in custody. Some inquests may be held without a jury but there must always be a jury of seven persons in the case of suspected homicide, infanticide or death in a street accident in which some vehicle is involved. In cases where the coroner's verdict or the verdict of the coroner's jury is murder, manslaughter or infanticide against a known person the coroner is bound to issue a warrant under which the known person is arrested, and committed to the Crown Court for trial. If the accused is subsequently brought before a magistrate for the preliminary enquiry he must still go to the High Court on the coroner's warrant even if the magistrate finds there is insufficient evidence to send him for trial. The coroner also has the power to grant bail to an accused person pending trial, but his powers concerning non-fatal offences were gradually taken over as the Justices of the Peace were created. The coroner may be either a lawyer or a medical practitioner being of five years standing, and is appointed by the County Council. The procedure and jurisdiction of Coroner's Courts today is governed by the Coroner's Acts of 1887 and 1954.

Case No. 31

A female in-patient suffering from recurrent depression was referred for psychological testing. She was actively suicidal at the time, and transferred to and from the psychologist's responsibility on a 'suicidal caution card'—a system used to alert and give explicit responsibility to one person for the safe supervision of the patient whilst considered to be at risk. She was discharged home shortly afterwards and immediately committed suicide. The psychologist was called on to give evidence to the Coroner regarding her mental state at the time of her psychological assessment.

County Courts

As the name suggests, the County Courts have much in common with the old Shire Courts, although they do not have the criminal jurisdiction of the former, and their civil jurisdiction is considerably more limited. They are, however, a relatively local court, visited by a circuit judge or Recorder, and deal with similar problems—namely, money and land matters. They also deal with some of the family matters of the High Court, such as the supervision of adoption and tenancy problems; since the passing of the Matrimonial Causes Act (1967) designed to shed the load of the Divorce Courts imposed by the rapid increase of marriage breakdown, the County Courts have been given jurisdiction to hear any undefended pleas for divorce.

Unlike the Shire Courts, the County Courts are not limited to one per county, and some 400 County Courts were established by the County Courts Acts (1846). The work of these Courts saves considerable time and expense in the case of minor pleas which would otherwise occupy the attention of the High Court in London. They have functioned so well during the first century of their existence that their jurisdiction was consolidated and enlarged by the County Courts Act (1959). Although the number of cases brought to the County Courts exceeds one and a half million annually, the greater number are actually settled out of court before the hearing. Taking a person to the County Court is seen as a serious threat that the aggrieved party means business, and many a trader accused of sharp practice, landlord overstating his rights, or customer bilking his supplier, has settled quietly rather than suffer the adverse publicity which the public hearing would provide. Some of the cases which come before the County Court emanate from quarrels within the family, or from quarrels between neighbours, and since very often such interpersonal strife derives from an unstable personality, the forensic psychologist is sometimes involved, especially when he is primarily a clinician. One of the rewarding aspects of this area of work is that once the psychological evidence is before the antagonists, it is often possible to achieve both sympathy and understanding and to effect a reconciliation. The forensic psychologist can often use the opportunity to perform a counselling service so that some positive good can come from his intervention. Psychological evidence in the preparation of cases for the County Courts leads almost always to a settlement out of court, and this is usually a more satisfactory and certainly a less expensive solution to the dispute.

CASE NO. 32

Bickering and acrimonious relations had existed between a shopkeeper and a customer, whose longstanding and increasing debts led the former to take the matter to the County Court. The defendant's solicitor learned that the customer had previously been treated for a psychiatric illness in a mental hospital, and invited psychological help, as a result of which, the action was withdrawn and relations between the two parties improved leading to the eventual settlement of the debt by instalments and the complete satisfaction of all concerned.

The Crown Courts

Although after the Norman Conquest, the King's Court travelled around the country with him, its main location was in London, where he spent most of his time. While in residence in the capital, the sovereign would send out officials into the shires every few years to deal with administrative, and particularly financial matters. These officials would deal among other things with legal cases reserved for them by the sheriff; since increasing the King's revenue was always the first item in the job description of these officials, they developed a system of fines which were levied on virtually everyone connected with the legal proceedings —jurors for forgetting items of knowledge, litigants for errors in their writs, lawyers for every minor mistake, and offenders for being offenders, irrespective of the punishment awarded by the court for the offence committed. As late as 1670, for example, two men accused merely of being Quakers, had hats put forcibly on their heads, and were then fined 40 marks each—a sizeable sum—for wearing them in contempt of court. By the 13th century the arrival of the King's official to hear and determine the more difficult or serious legal cases was looked on with as much favour as a farmer viewing a swarm of locusts. Indeed the financial depredations of the former left the shire citizenry in a similar state of nihilation. Not surprisingly, those likely to be concerned took a long holiday to distant parts whenever an official visit became imminent, and on one occasion, in 1233, the inhabitants of Cornwall took to the woods *en bloc*[133]. By the time of Henry I the shire-visiting officials began to take on a division of labour, those concentrating on the legal aspects becoming known as Justiciars. It was Henry II who developed this procedure into a system of Assizes (from the French *s'asseoir*, to sit) in which justices from London visited the provinces at regular and relatively frequent intervals 'to sit, hear and determine' the cases which formerly were brought, together with their respective juries all the way to London. The Assizes had complete jurisdiction in Common Law, and existed until 1971 when, together with their traditions, pomp and circumstance, they were abolished in favour of the Crown Courts. The first Crown Courts actually co-existed with the Assize Courts, being created by the Criminal Justice Act of 1956 and established in Manchester and Liverpool. They originated from the inadequacy of the Assize, which met periodically, and then only in the county towns, to deal with the rapidly increasing crime rate in these two populous areas of England, and by having no less than 11 sittings per annum they proved to be effective in reducing the backlog of cases queueing up at the bottle neck of the Assizes. With the increasing population, partly due to immigrants from the many British possessions which had gained post war independence, the need for further Crown Courts was manifest, and since by the 1956 Act, Crown Courts already enjoyed Assize criminal jurisdiction, it was decided to abolish the Assizes altogether and establish Crown Courts in all major cities of the kingdom. This was achieved by the Courts Act 1971, which also abolished the Borough and County Courts of Quarter Session; the time-honoured division of crimes into treason, felony, misdemeanour and petty offence had previously been abolished by the Criminal Law Act 1967. The new Crown Courts, as from December 1971, also absorbed the jurisdiction and functions of the Quarter Sessions. This meant that a lot of minor offences came before the Crown Courts which would not have to take up the time of a High Court Judge had he still been sitting at Assizes. To make the disposition of judiciary time more efficient, offences are now grouped into four classes. Class 1 contains the very serious offences, such as treason, murder, espionage, etc., compulsorily triable by a High Court Judge only. Class II offences are those serious offences, such as manslaughter, abortion, sexual offences, mutiny and piracy, which are in principle triable by a High Court Judge only, but which may be released to a judiciary of lower level i.e. Circuit Judge or Recorder, at the discretion of a High Court Judge. Class III offences may be tried by all three types of judiciary operating in the Crown Court, while the Class IV offences are too minor to engage the time of a High Court Judge and are tried only by a Circuit Judge or Recorder.

It is the High Court Judge who represents the continuing role of the Judge of the former Assizes. He is known as a puisne (pronounced 'puny') Judge of the Queen's Bench Division of the High Court of Justice. The Circuit Judges were introduced to staff the new Crown Courts, as well as the County Courts, and were selected in 1972 from existing County Court recorders and chairmen of Quarter Sessions. The recorders are part-time judges, selected almost entirely from barristers, although solicitors of over ten years standing are now eligible. It is in the Crown Courts that most forensic psychologists provide evidence relating to criminal offences. The Crown Courts are not concerned with civil actions except in a minor appellate way, and the psychologist concerned with civil litigation now usually finds himself in the Law Courts of the Strand where the High Court of Justice exercises its civil jurisdiction, e.g. Case No. 18 above.

The Old Bailey

A description of the English Courts of Law would not be complete without mention of the Old Bailey, the most famous criminal court in the world, and most forensic psychologists interested in criminal work will find themselves giving evidence there sooner or later. Although renamed the 'Central Criminal Court' by Act of Parliament in 1934 it is still popularly known by the name of the street in which it stands, the 'olde bayley of London Wall'[134]. Part of this Roman Wall, which encompassed the old city of Londinium in the second century A.D. during the Roman occupation of Britain, was uncovered during the rebuilding of part of the court after damage by German Air Raids in 1941. Originally criminal trials were held in the infamous Newgate prison, but the mortality amongst court officials due to gaol fever, that is, typhus, caused a new court to be built adjacent to the New Gate in 1539. Of course, the prisoners still brought their gaol fever in with them. In one trial, in 1750, over 50 people in the court succumbed to the infection and died, including the Lord Mayor, the two trial judges, the Alderman and Undersheriff. Two years later, another Lord Mayor caught gaol fever and died, and this led to the rebuilding of the Old Bailey in 1774. At the turn of the last century, when Newgate Prison was finally demolished, the Old Bailey was rebuilt, and extended over the site of the old prison, and the original stonework of Newgate can be seen in the outer walls of the present building. Both the interior, with its Marble and Murals, and the exterior with its dome and the famous figure of 'Justice' are architecturally impressive. Wherever in the world lawyers and forensic experts meet, sooner or later bets will be taken over whether the figure of justice, known locally as 'The Lady' is, or is not, blindfold. The most serious and important cases are heard in No. 1 Court, one of the four original courts, and reconstructions of this court figure in most films and plays about major trials. It was No. 1 Court that was copied for the scenery of both the play and the musical production of the *Trial of OZ*, in which the author was caricatured as one of the many expert witnesses. Until the end of World War II, these four courts were adequate for the annual list of 700 or so cases which remained more or less constant between 1907 and 1937. Since the war the number of persons brought to trial here has trebled, and although nine new courts have been added, it is still necessary also to transfer some cases to the High Court of Justice in the Strand. Since 1972 the Old Bailey has also been a Crown Court and in addition to the familiar 'Red Judges' of the High Court, the new Circuit Judges also hear less serious cases here. There are also two resident judges who retain the ancient and historic titles of Recorder of London and Common Sergeant respectively. The notorious Judge Jeffreys, best-known for his 'Bloody Assizes' when he sentenced men to death in batches of 20 after the Monmouth Rebellion was both Common Sergeant and later Recorder at the Old Bailey. He lies buried in an ancient churchyard close to the court following his death in the Tower of London after the abdication of James II.

13. High Court of Justice

ALTHOUGH through the centuries some courts were abolished because of the misuse of power which occurred within them—the courts of Star Chamber and High Commission, for example—the other courts lived on, either independently in their original form or as part of a court with wider-embracing jurisdiction. Unlike continental law, where laws and legal procedure become void with disuse, English law and procedure remains valid even though latent and inactive. Thus the Court of Chivalry, which heard its penultimate case in 1737 was resurrected to hear a case brought by the Corporation of Manchester in 1954. Similarly, in the case of *Ashford* v. *Thorton* (1818), in an appeal against alleged murder, the appellor claimed the right of Trial by Battle, introduced by the Normans in the 11th Century. His request had to be granted, because this form of trial, though obsolete for 600 years, had never been repealed. With visions of the whole of the English litigious society opting to take each other on *vi et armis*, parliament hastily rushed through an Act of Parliament to repeal this form of trial.

So it was that by the middle of the last century the law was being administered in a bewildering variety of courts, all possessing mutually-exclusive jurisdiction and employing different legal procedures. It was a system which, in the words of Archer 'enjoyed all the advantages of venerability but paid for them with all the penalties of senility'[135]. There were the Common Law Courts of the Queen's Bench, Common Pleas, and Exchequer. There were the Courts of Common Pleas of Lancaster, and of Durham—both preserved as independent courts by the power of the Palatine Bishops. There were the Courts of Probate and Divorce, which had taken over some of the jurisdiction of the Ecclesiastical Courts, and the Court of Admiralty. There were the Courts of Staple, the Courts of the Stanneries (with jurisdiction over tin-mining in Devon and Cornwall), the Commercial Court, the Court of Exchequer Chamber, the Courts of Shapway, of Brotherhood, of Guestling, of Survey and many others too numerous to mention here. Some were in almost daily use, others were convened only a few times each century. The Court of Claims, for example, meets only once during the reign of each sovereign.

By the Victorian era the system was ripe for reform and in 1867 a

103

Royal Commission investigated the working of the Courts. As a result the Judicature Acts were passed which came into effect on 1 November 1875. At that time there were no less than ten different higher courts administering civil law, as well as the Courts of Assize and the High Court of the Queen's Bench administering criminal law. The reforms were directed mainly to these higher courts, which were fused into one High Court of Justice having five divisions, viz. Exchequer, Common Pleas, Queen's Bench, Chancery and the triumvirate of the former Probate, Divorces and Admiralty Courts which became a Division called by A. P. Herbert the Division of Wills, Wives and Wrecks. In 1881 by an Order in Council the first three Divisions were united leaving only three Divisions in the High Court—Queen's Bench, Chancery and the 'three Ws'. During the reshuffling and amalgamations, Durham and Lancaster still retained their Courts of Chancery. In 1970, by the Administration of Justice Act, the Admiralty jurisdiction was transferred to the Queen's Bench Division and the old Mercantile Court, existing in latent form as the Commercial List, was resurrected manifestly as the Commercial Court of the Queen's Bench Division. At the same time a new Family Division was created which absorbed the jurisdiction of both the Probate and Divorce Courts and also included any other matters directly affecting the family—adoption, legitimacy, guardianship, conjugal rights, and so on.

At the time of writing, the High Court still consists of three divisions, as it has done since 1881, but these have changed in title of jurisdiction and now consist of the Chancery Division, concerned with partnerships, mortgages, trusts, companies, etc., the Family Division, dealing with problems of wills and intestacy, marriage, divorce and separation, and the protection of children's interests; and the Queen's Bench Division with three branches, namely, the Admiralty Branch concerned with Maritime Law, the Commercial Branch concerned with Mercantile Law, and the Queen's Bench Branch, dealing with any other matters not especially the province of the other courts.

Psychologists have been concerned with cases in all Divisions of the High Court. Admiralty Courts, which are mainly concerned with disputes over the rights of ownership of salvage, wrecks, and cargo, sometimes have cases in which the responsibility of a Master for a collision is at issue. This creates the same situation as forensic psychology's very first case, that of Professor Karl Marbe and the railway accident mentioned earlier, so it is not surprising that similar maritime cases have potential for the forensic psychologist to contribute his expertise, as in Case No. 29. Similarly the Mercantile disputes may have psychological implications which create the need for psychological evidence, as described earlier in Case No. 16, while the Queen's Bench Branch of the Queen's Bench Division, which embodies the old Court of Common Pleas, is particularly busy in cases of compensation arising from transportation accidents, and this is the scene of most of the clinical psychologists' forensic work, as exemplified by Case No. 2. The new Family Division is the one Division where educational psychologists rub forensic shoulders with their clinical colleagues, for the future care and custody of children displaced from their home by the separation, divorce, cruelty or neglect of their parents have important implications for both psychological specialties. Although contested divorce suits continue to make use of psychological evidence, the Divorce Reform Act (1969), which accepts as satisfactory grounds for divorce the living apart of man and wife for a period of five years, has reduced the demands made upon the psychologist to give evidence of cruelty, and evidence relevant to the disposal of the children has become a more prominent part of the psychologist's contribution to these unhappy situations.

There are still a sufficient number of contested suits to keep him in these courts regularly. The mental state of the spouse has been grounds for divorce for many years, and the clinical psychologist can expect to be involved in the provision of this kind of evidence from time to time. Another aspect is the effect upon the appellant of the respondent's behaviour. The law does not recognize so-called 'mental cruelty' as a ground for divorce, but if the mental suffering of the appellant is sufficient to be accepted as evidence of 'cruelty' then it is admissible. Sometimes the mental suffering is severe without the presence of a mental illness, in which case the psychologist has a unique role as expert witness, since medical evidence *per se* would be inappropriate. In one case evidence was given of adverse changes in the *status psychologicus* of the appellant over an appreciable period of time, with a clear relationship showing between marked changes and the behaviour of the respondent as noted from independent sources, and the judge accepted this as evidence of cruelty (Case No. 18).

In addition the High Courts of the Queen's Bench Division hear appeals from the Lower Courts much as the old Shire Court heard appeals from the court of the Hundreds. The divisions enable the judiciary to specialize in certain matters and so has improved considerably the quality of judicial decision. Although specific matters are delegated to various divisions, each division of the High Court has complete power to deal with all matters and the result is that although a plaintiff is at liberty to commence his action in whichever division of the High Court he chooses he can always transfer to another division at his own expense.

The Court of Appeal

Appeals in criminal cases were most unsatisfactory until modern times. In earlier days, the King's Bench by a Writ of Error could quash a conviction, but could only do so where there was some error in the record or judgement of the trial court. The fact that for practically all felonies the sentence was the death penalty made it impracticable to quash the conviction, change the sentence, or hold new trials, since the sentence would normally already have been carried out. During the 17th century however it did become possible to order a new trial in the case of a misdemeanour. When difficult points of law were involved it became the practice during the 18th century for judges to reserve their judgment and to discuss the problem at an informal meeting of their colleagues. In 1848 these informal meetings were made by Statute into the Court of Crown Cases Reserved but only matters of law could be reserved for this Court and the referral of cases was entirely at the discretion of the trial judge. It was not until a public outcry arose over the fact that an innocent man, Adolf Beck, had undergone two terms of imprisonment for crimes committed by a remarkable double that the whole system of criminal appeals was reorganized and the Court of Criminal Appeal established in 1907.

Civil appeals fared better. Before the Judicature Acts of 1873 to 1875 appeals from the Court of Common Pleas and the Court of Exchequer went to the Court of King's Bench, although again appeal only lay where there was an error in the record of the court. In 1338 the first Court of Exchequer Chamber was set up to hear appeals by error from the Court of Exchequer and in 1558 the second Court of Exchequer Chamber was established and took, in addition, appeals from the Court of the King's Bench. In 1830 the third Court of Exchequer Chamber came to take appeals from all three common law courts. The Court of Appeal which was established in the re-organization of the courts in 1875 included the Exchequer Chamber, the Court of Appeal in Chancery, and the Court of the Lord Warden of the Stanneries. When the Court of Criminal Appeal was established in 1907, the two Appellate Courts ran side by side, one dealing with Civil Appeals, the other with criminal appeals, until 1966. The Criminal Appeal Act of that year abolished the Court of Criminal Appeal and transferred its function to the Court of Appeal as one of two divisions, a Civil Division and a Criminal Division.

It is extremely rare for expert witnesses to be called to the Court of Appeal: the famous forensic pathologist, Dr Keith Simpson, reported that in 30 years of forensic medicine only once had he presented evidence in the Court of Criminal Appeal[136]. This was in the case of *R. v. Jordan* (1956), where the defendant had been convicted of murder at Leeds Assizes, and had appealed on the grounds that certain medical evidence had not been produced at the trial. Lord Justice Hallet allowed evidence of clinical and post mortem findings, not presented at the trial, to be heard in the Court of Criminal Appeal. Once Dr Simpson's evidence had been presented to the Court, Lord Justice Hallet questioned the conviction on the grounds that, had the jury heard the evidence, their verdict may have been different. The author was called to give expert evidence in the Criminal Division of the Court of Appeal in the case of *Relph* v. *D.P.P.* (1971) and this case, which created several legal precedents is discussed below.

CASE NO. 20

A man of 27 was charged with taking and driving a motor vehicle without the permission of the owner. This was his 32nd conviction, and from the age of 12 years he had received so many years of disqualification from driving that even Methuselah would not have lived long enough to have been allowed to drive. He had been sentenced to Approved School, Borstal Training, Detention and over 27 years imprisonment (some of it concurrently), all without effect. On this occasion, the magistrate with more psychological insight than those who had judged him in the past, called for a medical report, in the preparation of which psychological assessment was requested. This showed him to have deepseated problems of sexual inferiority which could have explained the persistent need to drive large high speed cars despite the longterm consequences. The court nevertheless sentenced the man to prison. The author was convinced that the vicious cycle obtaining in this prisoner's life could only be broken by psychological intervention, and prevailed upon the defence solicitors to appeal. At the Crown Court, the psychologist gave his evidence and offered treatment in the form of aversion therapy for the taking and driving away behaviour, and psychotherapy for the sexual psychopathology. The judge confirmed the sentence of the Lower Court and the man went back to prison. By this time the psychological picture had been filled in by more extensive assessment, and the author pressed for a further appeal, and eventually was called before the Lords of Appeal in Ordinary in the Criminal Division of the Court of Appeal to describe the treatment offered and its rationale. Fortunately his psychiatric colleagues had co-operated by making a bed available in the acute treatment ward should it be required. The Appeal Court listened carefully to the psychological evidence (which was the only evidence presented) and agreed to release the prisoner into the author's care there and then. The prisoner, who had been brought to the Appeal Court direct from Wormwood Scrubs Prison, then had to be conveyed by the psychologist 80 miles by public transport to the hospital, an unexpected circumstance of some embarrassment to the psychologist's post-hearing plans[111].

Other Appellate Courts
In addition to the Court of Appeal, other courts have an appellate function. As a general principle of legal procedure, each aggrieved party after judgment can normally take his case to the next higher court, subject to leave to do so being given. In some cases permission to appeal

can only be granted if certain conditions obtain, for example, that the matter of dispute involves an important point of law, and is a matter of public inportance. Thus before 1966 civil cases could go on appeal from Magistrates Courts to County Courts, thence to the High Court, and Court of Appeal, and finally to the House of Lords. Similarly criminal cases could go from the Court of Petty Sessions to the Quarter Sessions, thence to the Assizes and Court of Criminal Appeal and finally to the Lords. There are a number of exceptions to the general rule, and since 1972 the appellate system has been modified with the abolition of the Assize Courts and Quarter Sessions, appeal from criminals in the Magistrates Court goes direct to the Crown Court and thence to the Court of Appeal, Criminal Division. On the civil side it is possible for appeals to go direct to the High Court (Queen's Bench) by way of case stated from the Magistrates Court. A number of changes have occurred during the preparation of this book and at the time of writing one of the best guides to the existing appellate system can be found in Padfield[137]. In theory, the Sovereign is still the Fountain of Justice and therefore hears supplications from her people. The monarch no longer interferes with the due process of law as in days gone by, but can still grant an absolute pardon. The Queen does so rarely, in very special cases, and then only on the recommendation of the Home Secretary. Appeals from overseas go to the Privy Council as do those from the General Medical Council and Ecclesiastical Courts. See Case No. 15 Page 52.

Court of Peers

The House of Lords is part of the high Court of Parliament, which itself stands above the Supreme Court of Judicature. It is, therefore, the higher judicial court of the sovereign state. Although from time to time it has been proposed to abolish the appellate jurisdiction of the House of Lords this has never been carried into effect and the House of Lords, deriving originally from the Barons and the Royal Council of the 14th century, remains the ultimate appellate court. In civil cases the Lords hear appeals from the Court of Appeal on matters of the law, but not until permission to appeal has been obtained either from the Appeal Court or from the Lords themselves, and the appellant must deposit £500 as security for costs. The Lords also hear appeals from the Criminal Division of the Court of Appeal, although not without a certificate from the Attorney General declaring that there is a matter of law of public importance for the Lords to decide. They also continue to deal with matters of privilege and those concerning peerages. In addition to its appellate function the House of Lords originally tried peers for felony or treason as a court of first instance, but this privilege was abolished in 1948. At one time the upper house also heard cases as part of its original jurisdiction that were more appropriate to the Court of Common Pleas. However in the case of *Skinner* v. *The East India*

Company (1668) the Commons made such a violent protest that Parliament had to be dissolved and from this date original jurisdiction between individuals has not been exercised by the House of Lords, being finally abolished by the Criminal Justice Act (1948). The House of Lords also has the jurisdiction to try peers for political offences by Act of Impeachment, a device for removing awkward members of the Upper House who insist on throwing political spanners into the parliamentary works. Despite its obvious usefulness, the practice has fallen into disuse and the last case of impeachment heard by the Lords was that of Lord Melville in 1805. The Act of Attainder was the method whereby peers were punished and this has also fallen into disuse along with impeachment. Although in theory all members of the Upper House are entitled to sit when the Upper House exercises its appellate function, in practice cases are heard by the Law Lords only. These are the Lord Chancellor, the nine Lords of Appeal in Ordinary appointed from Judges and senior barristers, and those members of the Upper House who have held high judicial office.

The Lords do not come to a judgment, but the Lord Chancellor makes a speech on the appellate case in the form of a 'motion', and the individual members then each make a speech which, while not specifically a 'vote' nevertheless conveys their concurrence with or dissent from, the Chancellor's presented point of view. The House of Lords do not receive witnesses, being concerned with the 'point of law of public importance' which justified the appeal going to the Upper House. The point of law is believed to be satisfactorily investigated by examining the transcripts of the hearing by the Court of Appeal, and if necessary, of those from the High Court. The question to be decided is one of law and not one of fact, so witnesses are deemed to be irrelevant, the law lords representing the country's most eminent legal brains. However, in one case involving the present writer the point of law came from facts which in the writer's opinion, as expert witness, had not been adequately communicated[138,139].

CASE NO. 33

Under the Obscene Publications Act (1957) Section 4 the accused is permitted to call expert evidence to show that the material alleged to be obscene has some merit of a scientific, educational or artistic nature, or of some other object of public concern. Psychologists had been called as experts in obscenity cases following the success of the Lady Chatterley Trial, in which over 30 experts had given evidence, and their role was generally an actuarial and experimental one in that their main contribution was to interpret the findings of experimental psychology with respect to the effects on behaviour of pornographic books and films and to provide the court with the statistical results of the various relevant surveys, particularly those in the U.S.A. and Scandinavia. In this instance the judge, trying his first obscenity case, ruled that the psychological evidence should be excluded, on the grounds that it did not refer to the particular books in court, but to pornography in general, and therefore was attempting to rebut the presumption of the Act that obscene literature was harmful *per se*. The author disagreed with the description of his intended evidence given to the trial court by the defence counsel, and asked to give evidence to the Court of Appeal in order to explain the difference between what he intended to say and what the defence counsel said he intended to say. The court refused permission for the psychologist to appear, and the counsel failed to make the point clearly in his appellate address. The Appeal Court confirmed the trial court's verdict, and refused appeal to the House of Lords. However, the House of Lords agreed to over-ride this refusal since an important point of law was involved, and considered the papers sent to them from the Appeal Court. The evidence they had before them still failed to correct the misapprehension that the psychologist's evidence was of a general nature, and the author wrote to the Lords pointing out that he had in the past refused to defend allegedly obscene material and that his defence was a particular one and not general. However his letter was returned with the explanation that the Court could not receive evidence extrinsic to the case, and the verdict was again confirmed. Since this watershed in the history of obscenity trials, psychologists have been precluded from giving evidence as to the general or therapeutic effects of pornographic materials, although they are still permitted to give expert evidence under Section 4 in regard to specific merits falling under the categories enumerated in that Section.

14. Court Layout

APART from the courts at both extremes of the hierarchy, that is, the House of Lords and most of the Quasi-judicial Courts, all English courts follow a similar layout, differing only in minor details of decor and arrangement. As the expert witness gains familiarity with the court surroundings, he also gains assurance and presents his evidence free from the impediments of anxiety and tension. It is important that those psychologists interested in developing a practice in forensic psychology should familiarize themselves with the work of the courts, and spend at least a few periods in the public gallery of their local County, Crown and Magistrates Courts. To assist orientation, a brief description of court layout and the activities of those persons normally seen in the court itself follows.

At one end of the courtroom will be a dais or raised platform on which the Bench is set, and behind this sits the judiciary. This can be one person, such as a stipendiary magistrate, who is a qualified lawyer, a Recorder or a Judge. If the court is exercising its appellate function, it will have more than one member of the judiciary. A Crown Court, for example, will have the Judge sitting in the central high-backed chair, flanked by the justices from the Magistrates Court who heard the original case now on appeal. In the Court of Appeal will be three or more Lords Justice of Appeal, and in the House of Lords three or more Lords of Appeal in Ordinary, together with judicial lords. Traditionally the Appellate Bench sits with odd numbers to ensure a majority opinion, and this also applies to the Magistrates Courts exercising a non-appellate jurisdiction when lay magistrates are sitting. The Chairman or President of the court always occupies the centre seat. In the Old Bailey, which belonged to the City of London and still provides the venue for the City of London Court, the centre seat is reserved for the Lord Mayor of London, the Judge of the High Court being seated on his right in the chair with the second highest back. The other chairs are used on ceremonial occasions by other officials of the Lord Mayor's entourage, such as the Alderman and the Sheriff. Behind the Lord Mayor hangs the great Sword of Justice, and above that is the carved and embossed Royal Coat of Arms, which is seen in every judicial court in the country, except in Scotland where the courts have the Scottish Coat of Arms. In

111

front of the judiciary sits a man in wig and gown who acts as Clerk to the Court. In the lower courts he will be an experienced lawyer, whose principal duty is to advise the lay magistrates on points of law as well as record the evidence, deal with the exhibits and handle the court paperwork. He also ensures the person named on the summons is actually the one before the court, and calls the witnesses in the correct order. In the High Court he may be called the Associate and is not necessarily a lawyer, but may be a senior clerical official of the court. Like the Clerks to the Justices and the Clerks to the Crown Court, he follows the legal arguments with the help of the law textbooks and the law reports, and reminds the judge from time to time of the appropriate Rules of Procedure.

To one side of the clerk in Superior Courts will be the Court Writer, who copies all the oral evidence verbatim. The court writer has exceptional shorthand speeds well in excess of 200 words per minute (the minimum for new entrants) and may write up to 50,000 words per day. The records at the Central Criminal Court alone average 120 million words each year. In important cases, the accused or civil parties concerned sometimes employ their own stenographer to record and transcribe the evidence from day to day so that they can discuss the progress of the case with counsel each evening. In the famous OZ trial, the court quite exceptionally gave permission for a complete tape-recording to be made of the whole proceedings and this was later transcribed and formed the basis for Tony Palmer's book of the trial[140].

In front of the Bench itself are the lawyers' benches. The barristers, who traditionally are the only lawyers allowed to speak to the court on behalf of the parties, occupy the front bench. They wear a black Tudor gown adopted about A.D. 1500, which over the centuries has gained some curious appendages, the origins of which have been long since lost. In more serious cases each side will be represented by two barristers, a Junior (who may in fact be nearing retirement age) known as a stuff gownsman because his gown is made of 'stuff', and a Leader, who will be a Queen's Counsel. The Q.C. is popularly known as a 'silk'; originally they were favoured by the King and his Court, and in hobnobbing with the nobility came to wear the gowns of black silk by which they can be recognized today.

Behind the barristers sit the solicitors and their clerks. They act as an intermediary between the barristers and the witnesses, and also do most of the negotiations with the client. It is the solicitor who chooses the barristers to represent his client in court. In the inferior courts, the solicitors can be advocates in their own right, and usually represent the client before the magistrates. For preliminary hearings, it is common for barristers to appear in Magistrates Courts, however, and even in petty sessions if the offence is likely to have serious consequences for the accused, the solicitor may recommend the more experienced and impressive advocacy of a barrister. During the examination of witnesses, any question which the accused or other party believes ought to be put, or any other point which he feels should be drawn to the attention of the counsel, is conveyed to him via the solicitor, either by means of a note sent from the dock, or by whispered instructions from the party sitting adjacent to his solicitor either beside or behind him. The solicitor's clerk is usually kept on the run summoning or cancelling witnesses as the pace of the proceedings changes, retrieving documents from the office or law reports from the library, and generally contributing to the smooth running of the case.

Facing the Bench, and usually behind the lawyers will be the dock, containing two or more chairs, one each for the accused persons and one each for the police officers or prison warders responsible for their safe custody. In the older courts used for the Assize, a staircase leads directly from the dock down to the cells below, and the dock itself is well barred. The newer courts have a much more notional dock consisting only of a handrail round three or four sides. The accused stands to make his plea and to hear his sentence, and also to answer any questions put to him by the Court. Apart from his plea, he may remain silent throughout the proceedings, on the principle that he is presumed innocent unless and until the prosecutor proves him guilty, and so is not required to offer any defence unless he chooses to do so. If he refuses even to plead, the court will empanel a special jury charged to discover whether he is 'mute by malice, or mute by visitation of God', the alternatives referring to an act of stubborn will in one case and a medical or psychological inability to speak in the other. At this point medical evidence may be proferred to prove that the mutism is unintentional. The author has experienced one case where hysterical mutism occurred just as the accused, an adolescent girl, was about to plead, but usually the medical or psychological circumstances have arisen before the trial and the appropriate examinations can be carried out and reports prepared. *Mute of malice* is not often experienced these days, but in 1972 a 26-year-old street busker of no fixed abode was charged with theft in the precincts of Soho and refused to plead by remaining silent. A jury was specially empanelled for the purpose and declared him to be 'mute of malice'. He was then tried by a separate jury and found guilty, and sentenced to 18 months imprisonment, still without uttering a word[141].

On one side of the court will be the jury box, consisting of two benches or 12 seats in two rows of six. Until 1972 jurors had to be property owners, but this qualification was abolished by the Criminal Justice Act of that year. Now anyone aged between 18 and 65 resident in the area for five years can be called, although peers, lawyers, medical practitioners, servicemen, policemen and mental patients plus certain other categories are exempt. The removal of the property qualification inevitably altered the quality of juries, and by random selection many jurors will be found to be illiterate or intellectually subnormal. The Old Bailey sends out 18,000 jury summonses each year, so that one can expect a substantial proportion to be drawn from the lower end of the distribution in that court alone. A frightening picture of the bias and incompetence in some juries is well documented by Barber & Gordon[142].

Unlike the proceedings in the U.S.A. where the inclusion of a juror can be objected to on a variety of grounds, the jury cannot be challenged on the basis of their fitness for the task. However, both the defence and prosecution can reject jurors, with the permission of the judge if a substantial reason can be offered, for example, if the juror is known to be related to the accused. The defence is also allowed to make a peremptory challenge and reject three jurors without reason, although this can only be made on the basis of visual inspection and not from interviewing or examining the prospective jurors. Until recently the defence was allowed to peremptorily challenge seven jurors for each of the accused, and this did afford some leeway for the defence to exclude the more obvious misfits to their case. In the OZ trial, for example, the presence of three accused persons in the box permitted 21 jurors to be challenged. In obscenity cases generally, the defence find it preferable to exclude women from the jury, on the grounds that they are likely to be less familiar, and therefore more shocked, by the material presented by the prosecution than would be male jurors. Sometimes, however, it works the other way round, as when the defending counsel recognized a well-known prostitute from Soho and was glad to welcome her to the jury.

In complicated cases it may be disadvantageous to have persons of low intelligence on the jury, and although the psychologist is aware of the low correlation between physiognomy and intelligence, he has usually had more experience than any one else in court in testing the mentally and educationally subnormal, and can advise on this aspect of the peremptory challenge where the opportunity permits. Sometimes, in criminal cases where complex financial transactions have occurred, it is to the advantage of the accused to have as intellectually impoverished a jury as possible, in which case the challenges will go to those bright of eye and smart of appearance, especially if wearing a University tie or Rotary lapel badge. Psychologists have been experimenting with mock juries for some years, and knowledge about their behaviour is accumulating all the time. Some very relevant findings, for example that the damages assessed by jurors are negatively correlated with their body weight, are not sufficiently powerful to justify challenging all the obese jurors in a compensation case, but undoubtedly the psychologists' data are more valid than the hunches on which counsel at present relies.

Until recently a unanimous verdict was required, but now a majority verdict of at least ten is accepted after 130 minutes. In civil cases, no minimum time limit is imposed before a majority verdict is receivable, but these days juries rarely figure in civil proceedings except those involving libel or slander. A coroners' jury consists of seven only, and their possible verdicts include death by murder, manslaughter, justifiable homicide, infanticide, suicide, misadventure, accident, industrial disease or natural causes. If in doubt about the cause of death they can return an open verdict.

The jury's lot is considerably better today than it was in the past, when judges could fine, and even commit to prison, juries who brought in a verdict contrary to their wishes. Forensic psychologists appearing at the Old Bailey will not have failed to notice the memorial to Edward Bushell and his fellow jurors, outside No. 5 court, which records the case of *R.* v. *Penn & Mead* (1670) when the jury were locked up for 48 hours without food, drink or chamberpot until they brought in a verdict of guilty. They brought in a verdict of acquittal and were imprisoned in Newgate for many months until released by a writ of Habeas Corpus.

Opposite the jury is the witness box on a raised stand, where the witnesses take their oath and give their testimony. Most witness boxes have a seat—the modern courts a folding one—and after taking the oath, the witness may, with the court's permission, be seated. Expert witnesses usually prefer to stand to give their evidence because they can deliver their evidence to the jury better in this position. The witness box has a ledge upon which the books and papers the expert witness has taken into court with him can be placed, it is normally used for the copy of the New Testament used for swearing the oath. If the witness is not a Christian, he may ask for the appropriate book of his faith on which to swear, most of the common bibles, such as the Koran, being available in the court. In the case of witnesses denying any religious faith, a form of affirmation is used. England being, by law, a Christian country, and the judiciary being generally of conventional religious upbringing, expert witnesses who affirm rather than take the oath may have this fact pointed out to the jury in the summing up by the Judge. Psychologists who have studied the phenomenon of religious experience will perhaps agree with those judges who imply that an oath made on the basis of religious belief offers a marginally higher probability that the evidence following is true, than an affirmation from someone without any religious pretensions. It does not, of course, guarantee any higher degree of accuracy. In *R.* v. *Anderson et al.* (1971), the jury was reminded by the judge of the psychologist who affirmed.

It is usually convenient to place the press gallery on the same side as the witness box, thus balancing the jury box on the opposite side of the court. Behind the dock, and beside or before the public seats, there will be seating accommodation for others who have a professional or personal interest in the case, the probation officer, for example, possibly the spouse of the accused, and the witnesses who have already given evidence and are not allowed to leave court until officially dismissed. When the death sentence is likely to be pronounced (and it is still operative for certain treasonable crimes) the chaplain to the court will also be seated here. When the jury give their verdict, he either leaves the court immediately following an acquittal or moves behind the Bench to the side of the Judge. When the latter pronounces sentence of death, his one duty is to follow the words 'and may the Lord have mercy upon your soul' with 'Amen'.

This only leaves the public gallery, usually arranged along the rear of the court facing the Bench and close to the entrance doors of the Court, where the coming and going of public visitors will lessen the disturbance to the court. There is usually ample room for those members of the public who want to watch the proceedings, and in the winter months many retired or unemployed people find it a free and absorbing performance, with all the drama of a BBC soap opera and no Television Licence to pay. Sometimes the public galleries are taken up by visiting children from the schools or students taking law at college, and when a case of public interest hits the headlines, the queues for a seat in the public gallery outdo any scene for a first-night theatre performance. The accompanying illustration (Fig. 2) portrays the general layout of the court, but psychologists called to court are advised to arrive early and enter the court before the officials assemble, so that they can see where to go, the speaking distances involved and so on. Exceptions to the general plan will always be found. In the Old Bailey, the four older courts have the public gallery high above the court and approached by a completely separate entrance. The jury is tucked away behind the witness as he faces the counsel examining him to listen to the next question, and the judge sits at a different angle entirely; unless the witness speaks in a fairly clear and commanding voice one or other of his main auditors will miss hearing what he has to say. In some country districts, there is no special court building as such, and one used for some other purpose may be employed. The author once gave evidence before a Court of Petty Sessions convened in a village hall which was normally used as a gymnasium. In addition to the difficulties of the peculiar acoustics produced by all the sports paraphernalia lining the walls, the presence of the latter proved distracting to all those unfamiliar with this particular environment.

Figure 2

The general layout of an English Court of Law

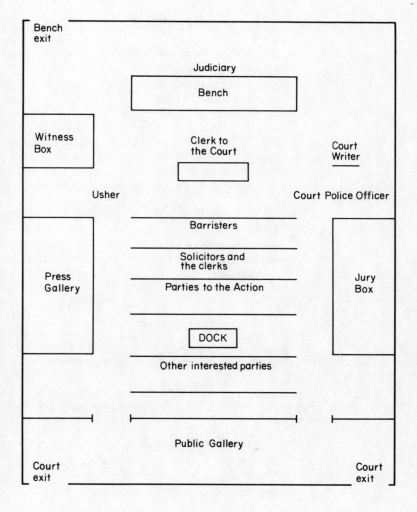

Figure 3

Structure of the English Court System

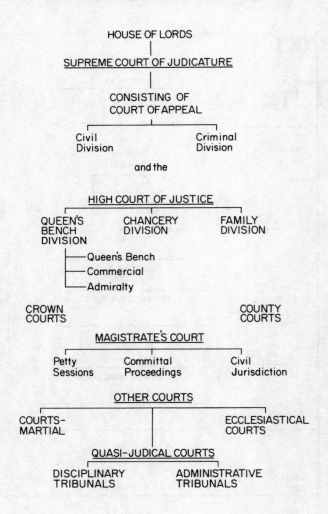

HOUSE OF LORDS

SUPREME COURT OF JUDICATURE

CONSISTING OF
COURT OF APPEAL

Civil
Division

Criminal
Division

and the

HIGH COURT OF JUSTICE

QUEEN'S
BENCH
DIVISION

CHANCERY
DIVISION

FAMILY
DIVISION

— Queen's Bench
— Commercial
— Admiralty

CROWN
COURTS

COUNTY
COURTS

MAGISTRATE'S COURT

Petty
Sessions

Committal
Proceedings

Civil
Jurisdiction

OTHER COURTS

COURTS-
MARTIAL

ECCLESIASTICAL
COURTS

QUASI-JUDICAL COURTS

DISCIPLINARY
TRIBUNALS

ADMINISTRATIVE
TRIBUNALS

PART IV

The Law of Evidence

15. Evidence and Proof

A CLEAR understanding of the law of evidence is a necessary requirement for the forensic psychologist. Even for those who are called to give expert testimony but once in their professional lives, a knowledge of the main tenets of the Law of Evidence is helpful. For a handy *vade mecum* the reader is referred to the excellent pocket book by Ryan[143] but for serious study one of the standard texts, e.g.[229], is essential reading. In this chapter a brief outline of the subject will be given, in order to provide a framework upon which the more essential details can later be constructed. At the same time, the opportunity will be taken to elaborate those areas which have particular significance for the psychologist.

Definition of Evidence

In law, the word 'evidence' has two distinct meanings. The first of these refers to the actual facts of the case, the second to the methods and rules of court which govern the presentation of the former. When there is talk about the evidence being insufficient, or irrelevant, or inadmissible, the first meaning of the term is being used; but when reference is made to the 'Law of Evidence' the second meaning is being used. In earlier legal textbooks on evidence only the first meaning was employed, as in Blackstone 'That which demonstrates, makes clear, or ascertains the truth of the very fact or point in issue'. Even some recent authors such as Taylor[144] confine themselves to this use of the term, e.g. 'All legal means, exclusive of mere argument, which tend to prove or disprove any matter of fact, the truth of which is submitted to judicial investigation.' Phipson[145], however, does cover both meanings in his definition: 'The two main senses of the word are: firstly, the means, apart from argument and inference, whereby the court is informed as to the issues of fact as ascertained by the pleadings; secondly the subject-matter of such means . . . Evidence in the first sense, means the testimony, whether oral, documentary or real, which may be legally received in order to prove or disprove some fact in dispute'.

Types of Evidence

Evidence, whether circumstantial or direct, is of three kinds, namely, parole (or oral), documentary or real. *Parole evidence* (from the Latin 'word') as its name implies, consists of words spoken from the witness box. It is subdivided into *testimony* or what the witness knows through his own perception or thought processes, and *hearsay*, or what he knows through another person's statements. Hearsay will be discussed in more detail later, but it is important to note that the statements made by a third party may be repeated by the witness in the box as either testimony or hearsay. They are testimony as to the truth that the words were uttered, but hearsay as to the content of the utterance. The court will not accept hearsay, as a general rule, although certain exceptions exist. A not infrequent example of the distinction between hearsay and testimony in which the clinical psychologist is involved occurs in Mental Health Review Tribunals when considering cases of actively suicidal patients detained in hospital under the provisions of the Mental Health Act. Here, the psychologist may give evidence that at interviews the patient said she would kill herself. This is direct evidence of a suicidal threat and is therefore testimony: it is not proof that the patient was *suicidal*: in this sense it is hearsay and only circumstantial evidence. The psychologist *knows* that the patient is uttering suicidal threats, but he does not *know* the state of mind of the patient at the time. Her statements relevant to her mental condition are only hearsay and unless the psychologist can provide strong supportive evidence of facts not in issue from which her state of mind can be inferred, then the direct evidence of the patient (to the effect that she is no longer suicidal) would carry greater weight. Problems such as these are particularly acute when the appellant at a Mental Health Review Tribunal is both paranoid and dangerous, because his own testimony that he is both sane and harmless will legally carry greater weight than statements by other witnesses to the contrary. Such cases therefore stand or fall by the weight of circumstantial evidence provided by the psychologist and other professional workers who can testify as to the behaviour of the appellant.

Documentary evidence is that pertaining to a document before the court. As with parole evidence, the document is evidence of its own existence and of its own contents but is not evidence that what is inscribed on the document is necessarily true, except in civil cases where hearsay is more readily accepted, following the Civil Evidence Acts of 1968 and 1972. The rules of hearsay apply to the written word no less than to the spoken word. A psychologist who enters the medical casenotes of his patient into evidence, in order to support his case, (by referring to entries made by previous psychologists, for example) can therefore usually only rely upon the acceptance of the court that this proves such statements were made, and not that they were true. However, if the case notes are public documents, i.e. belong to a government institution, as in the case of a N.H.S. hospital, and have been kept in a secure place for 20 years, the content of such documents is also accepted as proved.

Real evidence originally referred to material objects, such as the murder weapon, but the term has been extended in recent years to cover any kind of evidence, other than parole or documentary, which is acceptable to the court as a means of proof. It thus includes, in addition to objects, such evidence as photographs and even a landscape e.g. *Buckingham* v. *Daily News* (1956). Since psychologists have become interested in what is called 'witness psychology' it is important to note that the demeanor of a witness is now considered to be real evidence.

Best Evidence Rule

Since A.D. 1700 a rule of evidence has existed that only the best evidence of which the nature of the case permits could be received in courts. This rule was so firmly enforced that it led to cases where, for example, a tombstone had to be dug up and brought into court as the best evidence of family relations. Over the years the Best Evidence Rule has been relaxed and evidence which is not the best available is now admissible. However, whenever evidence is submitted which is less cogent than other evidence which may have been tendered, it is a matter for the court to comment on, and obviously such a comment would be adverse to the party tendering the evidence. For this reason it is important for the forensic psychologist when submitting documentary evidence to the court, to ensure so far as it is within his power, that it complies with the Best Evidence Rule. In other words, the best evidence is still the best. Irrespective of the cogency of the documentary evidence, strict proof of contents is of course still required.

Facts Probantia

The facts probantia are the facts in issue. In a civil suit, these are all those facts which the party making the allegation must prove in order to win his case, and these can be determined by examining the pleadings. In criminal proceedings, when a plea of 'Not Guilty' is entered, everything relating to the case is in issue. The prosecution therefore has to prove the whole of their case—the nature of the act, identity of the accused and the existence of any necessary knowledge or intent.

Evidence in court extends beyond the facts in issue, however, for the facts not in issue are often of significance. Their evidential value lies in the inferences which can be drawn from them, and sometimes a point can be established more effectively by inference from facts not in issue than directly from facts in issue. In a hearing before the Mental Health Review Tribunal, for example, the fact in issue is the mental state of the appellant. Facts not in issue may include the destruction of hospital property, but acts of arson may provide very striking examples of pyromania from which inferences as to the mental state of the appellant may be drawn. Facts not in issue are commonly called circumstantial evidence. The strength of circumstantial evidence is exemplified by the fact that accused persons have been convicted of murder even in the absence of the body of their victim and any trace of the manner of death; in such cases, the evidence has led logically to only one possible conclusion—that the victim is dead and that it was the accused who killed him, as in *R.* v. *Onufrejezyk* (1955).

Another aspect of circumstantial evidence is that as the number of facts established in evidence increases, the conclusions drawn from them become more limited, whilst at the same time the possibility of fabrication is progressively reduced. Direct evidence of a fact in issue, such as a statement by the plaintiff in a compensation case that she can no longer use her arm properly is less telling than indirect evidence from unbiased sources, from which impairment of motor function can be inferred. When the clinical psychologist is called in to give expert testimony, it is usually of both kinds. He gives expert opinion on facts probantia, e.g. that the plaintiff *is* brain damaged and that this was a consequence of the accident, and in supporting his opinion, gives evidence of facts not in issue e.g. the performance of the plaintiff on psychometric tests.

Province of Judge and Jury

The general principle is that the judge decides the law and the jury decides the facts: however in civil cases the jury is fast disappearing and is rarely seen except in defamation and personal injury actions. For example, the judge decides whether there is *any* evidence of a fact, and the jury decides whether there is *sufficient* evidence of that fact. Similarly, the judge decides questions on the *production* and *admissibility* of evidence, and the jury decides questions as to its *credibility* and *weight*. In those cases where the judge rules that the available evidence is inadmissible or for other reasons not worth introducing, it is his duty to withdraw the case from the jury. Apart from the *admission* of evidence, the judge rules on *capability*—i.e. whether something *can be* as distinct from whether it *is*, or ought to be, which is a matter for the jury to decide. Thus, in *Metropolitan Railway* v. *Jackson* (1877) the judge had to direct whether negligence *could be* inferred from the evidence as given, whereas the jury had to decide whether negligence *ought* to be inferred. Similarly, the judge decides whether certain words are *capable* of being an alleged defamatory meaning, as in *Nevill* v. *Fine Art Company* (1897), while the jury decides whether the words *do in fact* bear the alleged defamatory meaning e.g. *Broome* v. *Agar* (1928).

An exception to the general rule, is that the judge also decides what is reasonable, for example reasonable suspicion (under the Pawnbrokers Act (1872)), reasonableness of a bargain (under the Moneylenders Acts (1900–1927)), and reasonable cause in cases of malicious prosecution or false imprisonment. The latter is a not uncommon sequel in shoplifting cases where the detention of the suspect by members of the Company's staff may be taken as the basis for an action of unlawful arrest or imprisonment. The judge also decides whether objects are dangerous, for example, a shock box, used for aversion therapy and possessing a defective electric circuit.

The function of the judge in ruling upon foreign law is of special relevance at the present time, when the increase in foreign students, visitors, and workers brings an increasing number before the courts. The psychologist is most likely to experience cases involving this type of judicial decision in the Divorce Division of the High Court. In one important precedent—*R.* v. *Hammer*—a conviction for bigamy was quashed because the judge left the question of the validity of a foreign marriage to be decided by the jury. But all law except English Law is foreign in the eyes of English Courts so that Scottish Law, together with Irish, Manx, Channel Islands, Dominion and Colonial Law are all 'foreign' for this purpose. Foreign Law must be proved by expert witnesses, who as a general rule must have practised the particular law in question. Latterly, however, the court has exercised some discretion in the selection of witnesses, and non-practising experts admitted as experts to speak on particular aspects of foreign law, have included a colonial governor, an embassy official, a banker, a university reader in law, and a Roman Catholic bishop, among others.

Cogency
The cogency of evidence, or what is sometimes called its probative value, rests on two factors:
  (i) whether it is *sufficient*, the judgement of which lies entirely with the province of the judge, and
  (ii) whether it is *satisfactory*, the judgement of which is the responsibility of the jury.
Where no jury is sitting, both aspects of the probative value of evidence lie with the judge or magistrate.

In a civil court satisfactory evidence would be the same as the sufficient evidence provided by the plaintiff unless counter-evidence was called by the defendant, in which case the *preponderance* of evidence would be considered satisfactory. In a criminal trial, to be satisfactory the evidence must be beyond reasonable doubt.

Proving the case
The standard of proof required to succeed in a case depends in part upon whether the case is a civil or criminal action, whether the onus of proof is on the plaintiff/prosecutor or upon the defendant/accused, and the nature of the case itself.

As a general principle the standard of proof in criminal cases is higher than in civil cases. In the former the guilt of the accused must be proved 'beyond reasonable doubt'—*Woolmington* v. *D.P.P.* (1935)—whereas in civil action the party wins the case when the mere preponderance of probability lies in his favour. However, the court demands differing degrees of preponderance depending upon the nature and seriousness of the case. In statistical terms the value of preponderance required is a function of the seriousness of the action: thus loss by fraud is regarded as more serious than loss by breach of contract e.g. *Hornal* v. *Neuberger Products Ltd.* (1957). This also applies where the defence in a civil case bears the burden of proving a particular issue. Where the defence in a criminal case has a burden of proof—as for example, under a statutory provision or on a plea of insanity, (*R.* v. *Carr-Briant* (1943)), the standard of proof required is no higher than that required in a civil case, namely the preponderance of probabilities. For the psychologist this is important since much of his involvement in criminal proceedings will be related to the mental state of the accused; when the patient is suffering from a mental disorder whose characteristics are not obviously those which the lay jury would ascribe to insanity especially in a nonpsychotic condition it is not always easy to prove the existence of 'disease of the mind' beyond reasonable doubt. In one case, *R.* v. *Trotter* (1958), the author tried to avoid the use of this term in order to emphasize the degree of abnormality proven statistically and psychometrically. However the learned judge directed from the bench during cross-examination that he should give an opinion explicitly stating that this was disease of the mind. Such a judical direction would not normally be given in this way in criminal proceedings.

Burden of Proof
The general rule is that 'he who asserts must prove'. There are two kinds of burden—a general burden and a particular burden. In a criminal case the general burden of establishing the guilt of the accused rests entirely on the prosecution, since they commenced the proceedings with an assertion of guilt. Likewise in a civil case the general burden of proof lies on the plaintiff who first brought the suit to court.

The particular burden of proof, unlike the general burden of proof which does not shift from the side bringing the action, will move from side to side according to the nature of the evidence. Thus, in a criminal trial, the prosecution have a particular burden to prove three things (*R.* v. *Simms* (1946)) viz. first, that a criminal act was carried out (known as proof of *actus reus*); secondly, that the accused was the perpetrator of this act (proof of identity), and finally, that the accused possessed guilty knowledge or intent (proof of *mens rea*). Although the latter burden of particular proof was explicitly reaffirmed in *Woolmington* v. *D.P.P.* (1935) inroads into this cornerstone of legal, moral and personal freedom have been made, particularly by the introduction into Statute Law of the concepts of strict and vicarious liability. These enable a person to be convicted on proof of *actus reus* and identity alone. It applies for example, in various cases of food handling, when the principle is legally liable for the criminal acts of his employees (e.g. in watering down milk or alcohol) and is also found in offences contrary to the Road Traffic Acts, where only in the most serious offences is the motorist allowed to plead lack of intent. Thus driving a car after forgetting to renew one's driving licence by one day makes one liable to conviction for the same offence as the driving of a vehicle by someone who has never held a licence, passed a driving test or even learned to drive! However innocent and law-abiding one may feel, proof that one did drive absent-mindedly, without due care and attention, or commit any one of the multitude of offences created by an over zealous legislating authority, makes one potentially as much a criminal in the eyes of the law as those who deliberately set out to flout, and to continue flouting, the law for their own profit or enjoyment. Many people feel that this trend towards eliminating the concept of intent from the burden of proof is an undesirable one, but such critics must face the problem of whether any prosecutions at all would be possible in these cases if *mens rea* had to be proved.

In addition to the proof of *mens rea* required by common law, a number of statutes which have created or codified various crimes have made explicit the statutory requirement of some form of intent. Various words or phrases are used in this connection which signify guilty knowledge—such as 'loitering *with intent*', '*maliciously* wounding' ('maliciously' having the specialized meaning of *intentionally* in criminal law) with malice aforethought, handling goods, knowing them to be stolen, etc. However, despite this basic common law right to have criminal intent an essential ingredient of every crime, the development of statute law has whittled away this right by the use of legal presumptions and by the creation of vicarious and strict liability. In addition, certain statutes place the particular burden of proof regarding *mens rea* explicitly upon the accused: the Bankruptcy Act (1914) for example requires the defendant to prove absence of fraudulent intent. Other exceptions where the burden of proof rests on the accused include those cases where their defence is insanity, or when a special Plea in Bar is raised.

Psychologists will, of course, recognize the profound difficulty facing the prosecutor in attempting to establish criminal intent in many cases, especially in petty offences, and may have some sympathy with legislators whose primary aim is to discourage criminal offences and attempt to do so by attempting to make conviction easier. In doing so, however, legislators inevitably cause a widespread sense of injustice which may have effects contrary to those expected. Diminution of respect for the law leads to contempt for the law, and less moral concern over disregard for the law.

In civil cases, the particular burden of proof rests, at the beginning of the hearing, on the party asserting the issue i.e. the party whose case would fail if no evidence was submitted. Once the hearing is underway, the particular burden of proof will shift from side to side. An exception to the above rule is that where one party involves a *presumptio juris* (explained later), the other side shoulders the burden of proof in rebuttal (e.g. *Joseph Constantine SS Line* v. *Imperial Smelting Corporation* (1942)).

16. Further Concepts in Evidence

Judicial Notice

NOT INFREQUENTLY, a learned judge will ask a question of counsel or of the witness, which appears to reveal an appalling ignorance on the part of the judge of every day affairs. 'Who is Marilyn Monroe?' or 'What is Bingo?' are typical of the questions asked in this way. Such questions are asked not because the judge is really unaware of sexually notorious filmstars or of community pastimes, but merely because these are facts which have to be 'proved'. Every day in court precedents may be created which will be referred to centuries hence, and it is important that the record clearly shows the context of the evidence. A case in which the defendant was said to have the attributes of Miss Monroe may well become meaningless in a future age when such transitory phenomena as cinema idols are unknown to all but specialist historians. By asking such questions, the judge enables the response to go on record.

Some matters are so well known, however, that they do not require proof. These are said to be 'judicially noticed', and the judge and jury are bound to recognize or assume the existence and nature of such matters without further proof. These matters include national laws and procedures (but not by-laws, which must be proved in court), the existence and title of foreign sovereigns, wars in which the U.K. is engaged (other wars must be proved by the Foreign Office), official seals, British territorial jurisdiction, and similar facts effecting nationality and government. A number of statutes have also afforded judicial notice to certain types of document, which no longer have to be proved. The Statutes in question include the Evidence Acts of 1845 and 1933, the Documentary Evidence Acts of 1868 and 1882 and the Commissioners for Oaths Act of 1889. The documents receiving such judicial notice include Public Statutes, Private Acts of Parliament since 1850, Official Gazettes, Royal Proclamations, Orders in Council, Official Regulations, Army and Navy lists, official registers and documents kept in proper custody.

Other matters which receive judicial notice are facts which are so notorious that one is presumed to know them—coins of the realm, weights and measures, public feasts and festivals—the rule of the road and the period of human gestation (e.g. *R. v. Luffe*, (1807)).

Formal Admissions
Presumptions and matters receiving judicial notice do not require proof in court. A third class of evidence not requiring proof are formal admissions in civil actions. Formal admissions are evidence only in the proceedings in which they are made. In other cases, admissions made earlier require strict proof. There are five ways of making a formal admission:

(i)   In the Pleading, where the party explicitly admits an action alleged by the other side (e.g. dropping an iron bar from the window).

(ii) In default of Pleading. When a fact is alleged in a Pleading, the other party must either admit or deny it explicitly: if he neither admits the fact, nor expressly denies it, his absence of denial is taken to be an admission.

(iii) By answer to Interrogation.

(iv) In reply to a notice to Admit.

(v)   By the party's legal representative before or during the trial.

It will be appreciated that Formal admissions save considerable time and expense, but lawyers will not want to admit to facts damaging to their client's case unless there are no possible grounds for doubt. The forensic psychologist will find himself consulted from time to time regarding the point at which facts in issue can be formally admitted. A case of the author's which is *sub-judice* at the time of writing involves the question of whether formal admission can be made that the defendant's action caused a head injury, without prejudicing the issue of whether this led to brain damage and/or subsequent disability. If a line can be drawn between these two consequences, a considerable amount of evidence from casualty officers, surgeons, and other physicians can be dispensed with, so effecting a substantial saving of the court's time and the client's expenses.

Inadmissible Evidence
Certain kinds of material, though factual and true, cannot be admitted under the rules of evidence. These will include irrelevant matters and estoppels (discussed separately) and matters of public policy. Under the latter heading will fall state documents considered to be prejudicial to the public interest (usually involving defence as in *Duncan* v. *Cammell Laird* (1942)), judicial matters (judges, counsel and jurors are under a duty not to disclose evidence concerning previous court proceedings), disclosures made in order to detect crime, such as revenue frauds (*Marks* v. *Beyfus* (1890)) and negotiations in civil proceedings marked 'without

prejudice'. When parties involved in litigation are attempting to arrange a settlement out of court, any correspondence marked 'without prejudice' cannot be admitted as evidence without the express permission of the party making the statement. A presumption that the communication is without prejudice is raised even in the absence of explicit wording provided the context makes it clear the negotiations without prejudice were intended, for example in reply to a 'without prejudice' communication when there has been no break in the correspondence *(India Rubber Works* v. *Chapman* (1926)).

On the same principle, evidence is inadmissible from a probation officer as to what was said by spouses effecting a reconciliation in his presence *(McTaggart* v. *McTaggart* (1949)), but in criminal proceedings there is no similar protection and anything said to prosecutors or their representatives may be admitted in evidence against the accused.

Under the Medical Evidence Act (1978) judicial findings in respect of a plaintiff injured in an accident cannot be admitted in a case brought by another plaintiff injured in the same accident.

Corroboration

Evidence of just one witness is normally admissible as proof, although the weight ascribed to such evidence will naturally depend to some extent upon the behaviour of the witness himself. However, two witnesses are required in cases involving blasphemy or the impersonation of an elector. In certain other cases, the evidence of a single witness is not by itself sufficient to be admitted as proof without independent corroboration. Such corroborative evidence need not be given by an additional witness, but can take the form of a document or any form of material evidence. In some instances corroboration is required by case law, in others by statute law. In the latter case, any conviction obtained without corroboration would be quashed, but in the former the conviction would stand. It is the duty of the judge, however, to warn the jury of the need for corroboration, even though they may choose to disregard this warning.

Some examples of statutory requirement for corroboration of evidence are:

(i) The Evidence (Further Amendment) Act (1869) requires corroboration by material evidence of a promise of marriage in any Breach of Promise action.

(ii) The Sexual Offences Act (1956) requires corroboration in the case of charges for certain offences against women or girls, e.g. procuring the defilement of a female by threats, fraud or drugs.

(iii) The Children and Young Persons Act (1933) requires corroboration of unsworn testimony in court provided the court has been satisfied that the child understands the seriousness of the occasion, and the importance of speaking the truth. The corroborating evidence, if parole evidence, must of course, be sworn, since unsworn testimony cannot be corroborated by other unsworn testimony—by another child, for example. The evidence of children raises many problems relevant to the forensic psychologist and forms an important part of witness psychology[146].

(iv) The Road Traffic Acts require the opinion of more than one person concerning the speed of a vehicle before conviction on a charge involving speed can succeed, a requirement first introduced in The Motor Car Act (1909).

(v) The Evidence Act (1938) requires the corroboration of parole evidence to be more than a document written by the same witness.

(vi) The Representation of the People Act (1949) requires two witnesses of good standing before any prosecution for impersonation at an election can succeed.

(vii) The Affiliation Proceedings Act (1957) requires the child's mother to produce evidence of the paternity of the alleged father other than her own parole evidence.

(viii) The Criminal Appeal Act (1968), following the Court of Criminal Appeal Act (1907) Section 4 (i) provides for the upholding of a conviction even in the absence of corroboration if the court is of the belief that no serious miscarriage of justice has occurred.

Examples of corroboration required by case law are:

a) The evidence of the petitioner in a divorce suit (*Curtiss* v. *Curtiss*, (1905)).

b) The evidence of the co-respondent in adultery when known to be of loose character (*Giner* v. *Giner* (1865)).

c) The evidence of a claimant against the estate of a deceased person (*Rawlinson* v. *Scholes* (1898)).

d) The evidence of a solicitor concerning his unwritten retainer (*Bird* v, *Harris* (1880)).

e) The evidence of an accomplice (*R.* v. *Noaks* (1832)).

f) The evidence of a complainant in sexual cases (*R.* v. *Baskerville* (1916)).

Estoppels

The rule of estoppel prevents a party, in certain circumstances, from denying the existence of some previously asserted fact. It can only be used in defence and not in a plaintiff's formal pleadings. There are five types of estoppel, by Record, Deed, Statute, Agreement, and Conduct.

(i) *Estoppel by Record* is operated by a judgment in Court (e.g.

divorce, probate, bankruptcy, etc.). There are certain exceptions, in that it does not estop a stranger to the action making a formal assertion to the contrary, neither can it estop a court when it has a duty to consider the matter afresh e.g. in transfer from a family court to the Divorce Court (*Hudson* v. *Hudson* (1948)) or when the estoppel would produce a contradiction in law (*Griffiths* v. *Davis* (1943)).

(ii) *Estoppel by Deed* prevents parties to the deed from denying its statements.

(iii) *Estoppel by Agreement* prevents a party from presenting evidence contrary to the validity of the agreement, for instance a receipt stating that the goods were received in good condition estops the receiver from claiming that they were damaged.

(iv) *Estoppel by statute* is created by e.g. the Bills of Exchange Act (1882), Partnership Act (1890) and the Sale of Goods Act (1893).

(v) *Estoppel by Conduct*, otherwise known as *Estoppel in Pais* originates when a party intentionally represents (either by conduct or by words) to the other party that certain facts exist, and where the other party acts upon the presumed facts and suffers damage as a result. In such circumstances the party initiating the conduct is estopped from denying the existence of the facts. For example, a minor who pretends to have reached his majority in order to enter into an agreement is estopped from asserting later that he was under age should he wish to renounce the agreement. Note, however, that estoppels can be over-ruled by a positive law to the contrary. In the case of a contract, for example, the contractual incapacity of a minor under the law of contract prevents this estoppel being applied even if he misrepresents his age, *Leslie* v. *Sheill*, (1914).

Relevancy

Relevancy is the relationship between facts. There are two sets of facts which may be admissible as evidence in a court of law, namely the facts in issue (the Civil Pleadings or the Criminal Indictment and Plea) and the facts relevant to the facts in issue. The former are usually direct and the latter circumstantial. It has been said that the Rules of Evidence are really rules for the exclusion of evidence, and although logical relevancy is frequently identical with legal admissibility, the two do not always go together. Some facts, such as the bad character of the accused, are logically relevant but inadmissible; other facts such as that the witness is dead, are admissible but logically irrelevant to the facts in issue. There are certain categories of relevant evidence all of which have constraints or limitations, and some of which are more clearly defined than others. Apart from the qualifying limitations, all have exceptions, but the list of relevant evidence includes:

   (i)   Proof of initial conditions
  (ii)   *Res Gestae*, that is, facts which explain a fact in issue.
 (iii)   Complaints
 (iv)   Conduct other than at the time of the crime
  (v)   Opinions
 (vi)   Reputation
(vii)   Character.

Relevancy of Initial Conditions

Strict proof of initial conditions is not often required (although strict proof of infancy i.e. that the accused is not an adult, is required). This is why the presumptions of continuance and regularity are important in proving initial conditions.

Relevance of Res Gestae

The *res gestae* are those facts in issue or which accompany and explain a fact in issue. They may be facts of direct perception or cumulative instances to show usage, frequencies, etc. In the case of statements there are strict constraints regarding the relevancy, related particularly to how *material* the statements were (as opposed to being incidental). Statements must also be contemporaneous within very narrow limits. The difficulty in getting statements admitted in the *res gestae* is well exemplified in the case of *R. v. Bedingfield* (1879) where the victim emerged from a building bleeding severely from injuries and saying 'Look what . . . has done', yet this statement was not admitted because it was not made contemporaneously with the crime. Statements forming part of the *res gestae* must be made either by the person committing the act, the person against whom the act was executed, or persons actually present at the time. The modern view casts some doubt on Bedingfield's case, and although in theory the statement must be contemporaneous with the events in issue, in recent years this has been interpreted more liberally in some courts, e.g. *Ratten v. R.* (1972).

Cunningham[127], a military forensic psychologist, gives some vivid illustrations of his investigations of Chinese and North Korean guards accused of crimes against British prisoners of war, using what he terms 'fingerprinting of cognitive style'. A more detailed account of his work is given later; here it is sufficient to note that 'fingerprints of cognitive style' would be admitted as relevant evidence of similarity as part of the *res gestae*.

Statements made by a person as to his mental state at any particular time are admissible as relevant under the *res gestae* rule, and for this reason the patient's description of his symptoms recorded by the psychologist during his interview with the patient may well become part of the *res gestae*. In contradistinction, the 'signs' recorded by the psychologist have a different level of relevancy, and although the mental state of the patient can only be inferred from such signs, and is not direct evidence, nevertheless its weight and probity may be considerably higher than the latter.

Complaints

Complaints are only relevant in the prosecution of sexual crimes, and apply equally to both male and female victims (*R.* v. *Camelleri* (1922)). They form one of the exceptions to the hearsay rule, in that the person to whom the complaint was made is permitted to answer questions, not only as to the circumstances in which the complaint was made, but also concerning what was actually said by the complainant at the time. The psychologist may find himself involved in cases of this nature, since the reasons for making the complaint do not necessarily stem from a criminal offence against the complainant but from the psychology of the situation obtaining at the time. The personality of the complainant sometimes reveals complex processes which have led to the complaint out of revenge, regret, or from unconscious motivations. A patient reported to the police that a clinical psychologist had shown her obscene pictures. Investigation showed that the alleged obscene material was the Rorschach blots! Another psychologist hypnotized a female patient who afterwards complained that she had been sexually assaulted, despite the presence, fortunately, of a chaperone. The complaint itself, when admitted as evidence, is not evidence of the *truth* of the complaint but nevertheless serves two functions. In the first place it is said to negate consent, in those cases where consent would be in issue, *R.* v. *Lillyman* (1896). Secondly, it corroborates other aspects of the parole evidence provided by the complainant in the witness box. Complaints, in order to be admitted, must have been made at the first reasonable opportunity (*R.* v. *Cummings* (1948)) and must have been made purely voluntarily and spontaneously (*R.* v. *Osborne* (1905)). When a child is too young to give sworn testimony a complaint cannot be admitted in corroboration of unsworn statements (*R.* v. *Evans* (1924), Children and Young Persons Act (1933)).

Informal Admissions

Formal admissions have already been discussed under evidence for which proof is not required (q.v.). Informal admissions are more suitably dealt with as exceptions to the Hearsay Rule. An informal admission is an acknowledgment of fact in issue in a civil proceeding. One theory regards its admissibility as evidence as a waiver of requisite proof, but the more generally accepted theory is that an admission against one's own interests must represent the truth. Formal admissions are not conclusive evidence, but merely a presumption (q.v.) of truth; they may, however, operate in the form of an estoppel (q.v.).

There are four types of admission, viz.:

(i) Statements made by a party in litigation against his own interests. Exceptionally, statements made in his own interest are admissible only in questions of domicile.

(ii) Admissions against a party's interest by privies (i.e. those who stand in a legal relationship to the party) e.g. business partners, principal and agent, husband and wife, client and lawyer (unless the former explicitly forbids an admission) parties with a joint interest and predecessors in title. Both the Partnership Act (1890) and the Limitation Act (1939) have relevant sections. Exceptions to this category are that infants are not bound by admissions made by their guardian or next friend; and under the Workmans Compensation Act (1925) and Fatal Accidents Act (1846) the admissions of injured workmen are not binding upon their relatives or dependants. Note too that an admission of adultery is receivable by and against the respondent, but is not binding on the co-respondent who, for legal purposes, may be found non-adulterous (*Crawford* v, *Crawford* (1886)).

(iii) A statement made by a second party in the presence and against the interest of the first party, and not denied by the latter, is in some cases regarded as admissible hearsay. Silence is an admission only in those cases where a denial would be expected, but the law not unreasonably expects and presumes that the normal person will deny any untrue accusation made in his presence. When the accusation has been made in writing, failure to reply to the letter is not construed as silence for the purpose of an informal admission.

(iv) Informal admissions in documents which have been acted upon are also admissible as an exception to the Rule of Hearsay. However, any document marked 'without prejudice' or qualified by a later letter so marked, or answering a previous letter marked without prejudice, even though the reply is not so marked, are inadmissible, except with the consent of both parties, or to prove bankruptcy or compromise, or if the matter therein is criminal e.g. blackmail.

Confessions

A confession is an admission of guilt in a criminal case, and like admissions in civil proceedings may be admissible as evidence as an exception to the Rule of Hearsay. When made in court a confession is called a plea of guilty, and is an admission only of the offence, with which the accused is charged. It is *not* an admission of the truth of the prosecutor's case, and may be withdrawn if the *actus reus* is not proved. A confession differs from an admission in a civil case in that the confession is admissible only if made by, and against, the accused (except in the case of conspiracy etc.) and that if made to or before, authority, it must have been made voluntarily. The voluntary nature of confessions has been a source of much judicial discussion and is not without professional interest to the psychologist. By 'voluntary' is meant without hope or promise of leniency or forgiveness, and without threat of punishment relating to the charge. What does the law mean by authority in this context? Persons in authority include the prosecutor, his spouse or his solicitor, a police officer, a magistrate or his clerk, a prison warder, and a person holding a rank senior to that of the accused if they are both in the Armed Forces.

Where some promise or threat has been uttered by another person (e.g. a social worker or the accused's father) in the presence of a person in authority, that promise or threat might be treated as endorsed by the person in authority unless he gainsays it.

Persons who have been held to be not in authority include the accused person's employer (unless he is the prosecutor or the charge concerns the employment of the accused), a police officer's wife, ship's captain, a prison chaplain.

The test of admissibility for a confession was laid down anew by the House of Lords in *DPP* v. *Ping Lin* in 1975.

A confession may be excluded at the discretion of the judge if the state of mind of the accused, at the time of making the confession, was such as to render it unreliable. Although one or two early English cases exemplified this principle, such as *R.* v. *Spilsbury* (1835) and *R.* v. *Treacy* (1944), the practice appears to have developed mainly in the British Commonwealth Courts, and it is only within the last year or two that the mental state of the confessor has become a more frequent issue in England, e.g. in *R.* v. *Isequilla* (1975), *R.* v. *Kilber* (1976) and *R.* v. *Davis* (1979).

The mental state need not be so disturbed as to require proof of insanity, and a state of post-syncope *R.* v. *Burnett* (1944) or following a suicidal attempt *R.* v. *Williams* (1959) has been enough to exclude a confession. The effects of shock, psychiatric treatment, and other factors influencing cerebral functioning may affect the admissibility of a confession, and in this area of the criminal law there is obviously a useful role for the clinical psychologist. While Cross[229], that Master of Evidential Law, believes it difficult to formulate any governing principle in this matter, he suggests it could well be embodied in the statement of a New Zealand Court in *R.* v. *Williams* (1959), which said: 'Any circumstance which robs a confession of the quality described by the word voluntary will render the confession inadmissible'.

There is also a wider judicial discretion to exclude evidence which has been unfairly obtained from the accused. It was to indicate how this discretion would be exercised that the Judges' Rules were originally drawn up.

The Judges' Rules, which have been formulated to ensure that the police act fairly towards a suspect when taking statements from him, are no longer a good guide to the practice of either the police or the courts.

Hearsay Documentary Evidence

Statements contained in public documents, although hearsay are admitted on three grounds. In the first place they are made by public servants making such statements as part of their official duty. Secondly the facts so recorded are of public interest or importance and thirdly facts of this nature are not normally provable by means of witness. By public documents is meant statutes, official gazettes, public registers and records, official certificates, reports on public enquiries, surveys, etc., as well as standard references such as maps, dictionaries and almanacs. Other examples of documentary evidence which comprise admissible hearsay are discussed later.

Character in Evidence

The general rule is that evidence of character is inadmissible, but exceptions to the Hearsay Rule are embodied in various statutes, some examples being:

1. In civil actions evidence of general character is admissible under S.9 of the Civil Evidence Act (1968) if it would also have been admissible under the rules of common law.
2. In cases of rape or indecency the character of the prosecutrix may be admissible under S.2 of the Sexual Offences Act (1976).
3. The Criminal Evidence Act (1898) permits the character of the accused to be admitted if he himself enters evidence of his own character, or if he impugns the character of the prosecutor or witnesses, or if he accuses another person.
4. The Larceny Acts (1861/1916) admitted evidence of convictions during the past five years if the charge is one of receiving stolen goods. Now re-enacted in S.27(3) of the Theft Act (1968), convictions are limited to theft or handling stolen goods and seven days notice must be given to the accused.

Depending upon the circumstances, character is sometimes taken to mean reputation (as in a libel action) and sometimes disposition (as in most criminal proceedings). The unreliability of a witness, and similar aspects of personality likely to make the validity of his evidence questionable may be the subject of expert testimony, cf. *Toohey* v. *Metropolitan Police Commissioner* (1965) and *R.* v. *Eades* (1972).

Opinions

The general rule is that the opinions of ordinary people who are not experts are irrelevant. Apart from the fact that opinions may be quite worthless, it is the role of the court to form opinions on the facts presented to it. For this reason the general rule allows experts to give opinions as evidence only when the facts to be presented are so technical, scientific or professional that the court would be incompetent to form an opinion on them. Psychological evidence is of this kind. However, there are special exceptions to the opinion rule, and these include opinions on identity (as in an identity parade, for example, or by the use of identikit, photofit, or photographic portraits), libel (to prove that the libel was understood to refer to a particular person or to bear a particular meaning) handwriting, age, value, speed of a vehicle (see, for example, the psychological evidence in Case No. 9) and the *apparent* physical condition of others (note that a witness may not testify that another person *was* drunk, but the fact that he *appeared* to be drunk is admissible).

Witnesses may testify as to their own mental processes, but may not give an opinion on their own sanity. Only an expert witness may give an opinion as to the mental processes of another.

Competency

With certain exceptions, all persons are competent to be called as witnesses. Originally a substantial proportion of the population were not allowed to give evidence, and included convicts and atheists, and those connected with the case. Today the exceptions are generally only those of unsound mind and those who will not swear on oath or affirm. Additional exceptions are the Queen, who may not give evidence on her own behalf, young children in civil cases, the accused and his spouse. Although the Evidence Act (1851) makes the accused an incompetent witness for the prosecution, the Criminal Evidence Act (1898) provided for the accused to be called for the defence, but only if he wishes to do so. Generally, a witness who is competent to give evidence is also compellable to do so. However the spouse of the accused is competent to give evidence for the defence if the accused makes application, but cannot be compelled to do so. In certain statutory offences the spouse is held to be a competent but non-compellable witness for the prosecution (e.g. bigamy, cruelty to children, child destruction, immorality with a mentally subnormal person, incest, neglect to maintain wife and family, offences against females and personal injury by the accused).

Documentary Evidence

Documentary evidence is said to be primary when it is the original document, or one of a number of mass produced copies, e.g. a printed or duplicated sheet. Secondary documentary evidence would be a copy of the original (e.g. by photography, carbon paper or manuscript copying, but secondary parole evidence can also be given by introducing a witness who states under oath that he has written or read the original and who then repeats the contents. Such secondary evidence is, of course, hearsay (q.v.) In civil cases, the refusal of one party to comply with a Notice to Produce a document often leads to the admission of secondary evidence of this sort, which then acts in the form of an estoppel: this is because the possesser of a document who refuses to produce it in court, cannot afterwards tender the document in evidence to use for his own case (*Collins* v. *Geshon* (1860) for example) to contradict secondary parole evidence which has unintentionally misrepresented its contents. The forensic psychologist may have occasion to use secondary parole evidence of this kind when he cannot get the original document entered as evidence. Situations may occur where the plaintiff in a compensation for injury case is unwilling to admit as evidence documents which indicate a below-average level of functioning prior to the injury, such as school reports. In such cases, the psychologist, if he knows of the existence and nature of such reports, may arrange for the plaintiff's school teacher to come to court as a witness to fact and give evidence of what was contained in the school report. Frequently, of course, such evidence is primary parole evidence in its own right, but sometimes school reports, vocational guidance reports and so on, which may be critical to the evaluation of premorbid *status psychologicus* have been lost or mislaid and secondary evidence of their contents required.

The clinical psychologist will need no reminding of the importance of any evidence on the patients' pre-morbid condition. Although it is perfectly justifiable in civil actions, where merely the *preponderance* of the weight of evidence wins the day, for retrospective extrapolations to be made from post-traumatic test data, the psychologist is on much firmer ground if he has some tangible rather than theoretical evidence regarding the patients' level of cognitive functioning before the accident.

For this reason, forensic psychologists are rarely content to rely only on their psychometric skills, but go into the patient's past environment seeking direct evidence regarding his level of efficiency. A surprising number of parents keep school reports for sentimental reasons long after their children are grown up and married, and on several occasions the author has unearthed such sound documentary evidence when the plaintiff himself was quite unaware that such evidence still existed. Schools, even small private ones, tend to keep records for as long as they are in existence, and there are numerous sources of assessments undertaken for vocational guidance, recruitment and selection, promotion, and so on. Remembering the Presumption of Continuance, a good intelligence test administered 40 years before the accident is as valid in law as if administered the day before, until the other side produces evidence to the contrary.

Photographs may be used in evidence, for example, to demonstrate the existence of a phobia allegedly produced by the defendant's negligence, e.g. in a road traffic accident, by changes in the cardio vascular system. The validity of photographs may be challenged if the colour or tonal rendition is suspect, however. The defence will not be slow to point out that various filters can be used to exaggerate certain phenomena (e.g. blushing and blanching) and to refute this charge special test strips should be obtained from Kodak which, if included in the photograph, enable one to assess the filelity of the shades, tones, or colour rendition.

17. Presumptions

PRESUMPTIONS play an important part in evidence. An examination of the full scope of legal rebuttable presumptions makes it clear that their main value and usage lies in civil rather than criminal law. Because of this, the burden of proof is intimately related to the nature of the presumptions being introduced. Ryan[143] describes a classification of this relation, as follows:

Burdens	Presumptions
Legal	Provisional
Provisional	Compelling
Ultimate	Conclusive

Whoever alleges a given fact has the *legal* burden of establishing this fact. Having proved the fact he may rely upon a provisional resumption, e.g. *res ipsa loquitur.* This means 'the things speak for themselves': e.g. a man waves an iron bar out of a window, and drops it accidentally upon a passer-by causing brain damage; the injured party, as plaintiff, brings a case in tort, and proves that the defendant did actually drop the bar, and he as a result did incur a head injury. The *provisional* presumption of *res ipsa loquitur* would then be raised since the circumstances are so clear that there is no obvious way in which the plaintiff could have contributed to the accident, other than walking innocently and lawfully into the path of the iron bar. If the court then draws an inference in favour of the plaintiff from this provisional presumption, the provisional burden of proof moves over to the defendant. Alternatively, the plaintiff may be able to raise a *compelling* presumption, such as the presumption of legitimacy introduced in a testacy case, which the court *must* accept in his favour unless strict proof to the contrary by negative blood tests, for instance is tendered by the defendant. Another alternative is where a party proves sufficient facts to enable the court to accept a *conclusive* presumption which is then incapable of contradiction.

Proof is normally required of all evidential matter whether facts probantia or circumstantial. There are, nevertheless, three classes of evidence for which proof is not required. These are those matters which are presumed, judically noticed, or formally admitted by the opposite side.

142

Presumptions

A presumption is an inference drawn in law in favour of or against a party. Presumptions arise from common law, equity and statute, and fall into two classes: *presumptio juris* or rebuttable presumptions and *presumptio juris et de jure* or irrebuttable presumptions. Examples of the latter would be:

(i)   (a) A child below the age of seven cannot form criminal intention (common law).

      (b) A child below the age of ten years cannot form a criminal intention (Children and Young Persons Act (1933)), amended (1963).

(ii) A boy under the age of 14 years is incapable of having carnal knowledge (*R.* v. *Waite* (1892)).

(iii) A man marrying a woman knowing her to be pregnant is the father (Poulett Peerage Case).

(iv) A person in possession of a marriage licence and for whom the banns have been called, has resided in the district for the requisite period (Marriage Act (1823)).

(v) Everyone knows the Law (Common Law: the true rule is that 'Ignorance cannot excuse the crime').

(vi) A bribe favours the donor (*Industries and General Mortgage Co.* v. *Lewis* (1949)).

(vii) Production of a *London Gazette* containing a notice of a receiving order, or an order adjudging a debtor bankrupt shall be conclusive evidence of the date and validity of such orders (Bankruptcy Act (1914)).

Statute Law, as well as *explicitly* raising presumptions, also raises them implicitly. This applies especially to the irrebuttable *presumptio juris et de jure* raised by the Obscene Publications Act (1957). This was brought to light in the case of *R.* v. *Staniforth* (1976). Until Staniforth, forensic psychologists had been invited to court frequently to defend the accused charged under one of several acts used to control pornography, the justification for their presence in the court as expert witnesses being the so called 'public good' qualification in Section 4 of the Obscene Publications Act. Under this heading, psychologists would present to the court the available experimental evidence on the lack of detrimental effects of pornography upon sexual behaviour, negating the charge made by the prosecution that the material before the court was likely to deprave and corrupt.

In the Staniforth case, the prosecuting counsel pointed out that if the court heard the evidence of the psychologists, which had been outlined in the defence counsel's opening address, it was admitting evidence which clearly negated the intention of parliament, since the Obscene Publications Act was based on the presumption that obscene publications were detrimental to the reader. The judge decided that the implied presumption in the Act made inadmissible any evidence which would rebut that presumption, even though that same Act specifically and explicitly provided for experts to testify in court as to the public good and other merits of otherwise obscene publications. The judge's ruling was confirmed in a following case *R.* v *Jordan* (1977) and later at the Court of Appeal and House of Lords. Although psychological evidence had been of various kinds, not all of which could be held to be a rebuttal of the statutory assumption, it effectively stopped lawyers from engaging the services of forensic psychologists in this kind of case, although sporadic use is still made of them in obscenity trials, when their expert testimony refers to some other aspect of 'public good'.

Examples of *presumptio juris* would be:

(i) A child between the ages of ten and 14 years cannot form a criminal intent (*R.* v. *Lockley* (1902)). When prosecuted, his 'mischievous discretion' must be proved.

Note that the psychologist can be called upon to rebut this presumption if the child is aged ten, but not if the child is aged seven, since he or she then is covered by an irrebuttable presumption.

The author has often found it useful to remind the court of this presumption when giving evidence of a *mental* age between eight and 12 in a mentally handicapped or intellectually deteriorated person. If the law can presume absence of criminal responsibility at the early end of the I.Q. curve, it is logical for it to consider the possibility of doing so at the later end. The weakness of this argument is, of course, that in the case of the deteriorated adult, he has had a chance to acquire responsibility by learning.

(ii) *Presumption of death*:

    (a) A person not heard of for seven years by those who might be expected to have heard is presumed dead. Rule in *Nepean* v. *Doe* (1837).

    (b) A person unheard of for seven years is presumed dead (Matrimonial Causes Act (1950) developed from Bigamy Act 1603 —N.B. irrespective of the expectancy of hearing).

(iii) *Presumption of innocence:* this applies not only to criminal charges but in all cases in which an allegation of criminal acts is made. (*Williams* v. *East India Company* (1802)).

(iv) *Presumption of Commorientes:* when two people die in the same disaster but have not been proved to die simultaneously it is presumed that the older died first (Law of Property Act (1925))—originally in Common Law the presumption was that the weaker, e.g. wife or child, died first. This presumption is of extreme importance in the Law of Testacy and circumstances when psychological evidence could be offered to rebut this presumption e.g. in the case of a highly nervous person vulnerable to shock, will no doubt come to mind. The Intestates Estates Act (1952) negated this presumption in the case of husband and wife who die intestate. This presumption is commonly raised in air disasters, despite the fact that death often occurs differentially, different passengers dying of different causes (impact, asphyxiation, shock) at different times.

(v) *Presumption of marriage:* proof of cohabitation by two people who are treated by those who know them as if they were married, raises the presumption that they are lawfully married. (*Sastry Aronegary* v. *Sembecutty Vaigolic*, 1881). This presumption cannot be raised in proceedings for bigamy or divorce (In re Shepherd, (1902); in re Haynes, (1904)).

(vi) *Presumption of legitimacy:* where a child is conceived in lawful wedlock, the husband not being separated by a court order, the child is presumed to be legitimate (Banbury Peerage Case 1881). Section 26 of the Family Law Reform Act (1969) did much to make rebuttal easier, the illogicality of the presumption reaching its acme in *A. G. Chuk* v. *Needham* (1933) when a court ruled that the chinese child of a white couple was legitimate despite evidence that the mother had a chinese paramour.

(vii) *Presumption of continuance:* human conditions (common law marriage, sanity or insanity, character, behaviour, etc.) are presumed to continue. Their existence at a given time—e.g. at the moment of committing a crime or making a contract—are thereby inferred from their existence at a previous or subsequent time. This is one of the most important of all presumptions for the forensic psychologist, since he can use this presumption to extrapolate a *status psychologicus* at the critical time from his psychometric investigations made subsequently or even from case notes made a considerable time before the event in question. Like Newton's first law of motion, such an extrapolation continues in a straight line until altered by impressed forces. The value of the presumption lies not so much in its cogency, since common sense will dictate to most jurors the implausibility of citing a 20-year-old psychiatric diagnosis as evidence of present mental state, as in its effect of putting the onus upon the prosecution to prove otherwise. It will be seen that in general the value of the presumption to the psychologist lies in (a) excusing him from furnishing proof of something unless the presumption is to be rebutted by the other side, and more importantly, (b) shifting the burden of proof from himself to the experts called by the other party. Of course, in making use of presumptions, it is important for the forensic psychologist to anticipate methods of rebuttal and to prepare for this contingency. It should also be mentioned that in the lower courts solicitors are not always *au fait* with the subtleties of evidential law, and it may be necessary to draw their attention to any special presumptions upon which the forensic psychologist intends to rely. Presumptions, especially the presumption of continuance, are usually very effective in the Magistrates Courts Session. Suitably briefed, the defence solicitor will go into court with the appropriate authority for the presumption earmarked in his lawbooks. In normal circumstances, the defence lawyer does not have to reveal his line of defence to the prosecution. The use of the presumption will therefore probably come as a surprise to the police solicitor no less than to the Bench; a hurried consultation with the clerk of the court will confirm the validity of the presumption, and with luck the prosecution will have no time to devise a suitable riposte.

(viii) *Presumptions of documentary validity:* written documents, such as wills, case notes, etc. more than 20 years old and produced from proper custody are presumed to be what they purport to and to have been duly signed, etc. (Evidence Act (1938)). The content of documents more than 20 years old are also presumed to be correct (Law of Property Act (1925)). Note that this presumption does not cover recent medical case notes or records from the psychology department: these have to be formally proved, both in regard to what they are, and also to their content.

(ix) *Omnia praesumuntur contra spoliatorem:* everything is presumed against a wrongdoer e.g. lost or stolen property was the best of its kind, evidence which has been concealed or destroyed was contrary to the concealer's interests, and so on. The prosecution may make use of this presumption when cross-examining the forensic psychologist appearing for the defence, and the defendant's counsel may also make use of it when cross-examining expert witnesses for the plaintiff in a civil suit. The presumption recognizes the bias on the part of the accused or party in a civil action in respect of the evidence to be submitted. It is therefore presumed that the accused will 'make the most' of his alleged insanity if he is pleading guilty but insane, and of his alleged disabilities if he is suing the person he deems responsible for them. This is not always an easy presumption for the forensic psychologist to rebut, but his task becomes easier the more he confines his technique to strictly objective methods. So long as his client is free to express bias (e.g. in exaggerated symptoms or test responses) so the psychologist makes himself vulnerable to attack by this presumption. By the use of tests with objective scoring, built in lie detection methods and ways of assessing social conformity and bias, and especially by the use of psychophysiological tests outside the control of the client, the forensic psychologist will be well-armed to defend himself against the use of this presumption.

(x) *Omnia praesumuntur rite esse acta:* all presumptions favour the validity of acts. This presumption supports a wide variety of inferences e.g. that official acts and duties have been regularly and properly performed (such as locking the medical records filing cabinets), that persons acting in a public capacity have been regularly and properly appointed (e.g. that a clinical psychologist in a NHS appointment is eligible for membership of the British Psychological Society), and that rights exercised for such a length of time without interruption that they are believed to be lawful are lawful. Most uses of this presumption are drawn from case law, but the Road Traffic Act (1934) Section 36 makes explicit the presumption that traffic signs are presumed to be of the prescribed size, colour and type and to have been lawfully placed in position. Readers will no doubt be aware of a number of interesting recent cases in which this presumption has been rebutted by perceptive if pedantic drivers charged with a driving offence who have obtained an acquittal by proving the contrary.

(xi) *Presumption of Negligence:* where a plaintiff suffers damage from something under the conclusive control of the defendant or his servants, the maxim *res ipsa loquitor* (the thing speaks for itself) applies and negligence may be presumed without further evidence (*Scott* v. *London Dock Co.* (1865) 3 H. & C. 596). This is one of the most important presumptions in the law of tort, and one which the psychologist will have encountered in his study of medico-legal issues and professional liability. The maxim has been cited in innumerable cases, and the presumption has stood the test of time, e.g. *Henderson* v. *Jenkins & Evans* (1970).

There are numerous other rebuttable presumptions, many of which refer to the Laws of Trusts and Contracts. These are unlikely to come within the purview of the psychologist and need not be elaborated here; it is nevertheless useful for the forensic psychologist to familiarize himself with all the presumptions in a comprehensive textbook on evidence.

Makin's Rule

An interesting facet of evidential law which has some logical connection with the presumptions of continuance is the principle known as Makin's Rule. It will be remembered that states of people, mind or things at a given time may be proved by showing their previous or subsequent existence in the same state. This is based on the probability that certain conditions or relationships are likely to continue until changed by events which interfere with their continuance. Although the presumption of continuance weakens with time, it continues to exist as a fact and will prevail in court until the contrary is shown, or until it becomes incompatible with another presumption which may arise from the case. Thus the question of whether Mrs Durham was insane at the time of her marriage in October was settled by admitting as evidence the fact that she was received everywhere without comment and treated as an ordinary person at the time of her engagement in August (*Durham* v. *Durham*, (1885)). This leads on to the question of whether criminal conduct, which frequently shows a continuing pattern, could be admissible. While it may be unfair to reinterpret the presumption of continuance as 'once a crook, always a crook'—and to do so would be to conflict with the presumption of innocence—clearly the probability of the accused being guilty increases if he has been found guilty of the same type of crime before. As a general rule of evidence, previous convictions are not admissible as evidence, although exceptions exist and have been discussed elsewhere. The convictions are, of course, made available to the Bench before sentencing. However a single act, which is proximate in time and method, or, even better, a system of such acts may be proved if showing a striking similarity which goes well beyond the possibility of coincidence. The discussion by Cross[229] of *R.* v. *Straffen* (1952) is relevant to this discussion.

This kind of evidence is particularly relevant to sexual offences and since cases of this kind commonly make use of psychological evidence, the forensic psychologist soon becomes aware of the relevance to him of Makin's Rule. The principle has had some problems of application in court, but the psychologist should be forearmed on this issue, and whenever he is asked to see a client who is making a plea of accident, mistake or innocent intent, he should try and obtain either from the client or from elsewhere, details of similar incidents in the past which may, under one presumption or another, negate the innocent interpretation which the psychologist may otherwise give to the latest incident in question in the light of negative findings of psychopathology.

In *R.* v. *King* (1967) the appellant had been convicted of various acts of indecency with two young boys. It was admitted in evidence that he had met the boys at a public lavatory and had invited them to sleep at his flat, although he denied that any indecent acts had taken place. In the course of cross examination he was asked 'Are you a homosexual?' and he gave the answer 'yes'. One of his grounds of appeal was that this question should not have been allowed. The appeal was dismissed by the Chief Justice Lord Parker who delivered the judgment of the court that in his opinion evidence of the appellant's homosexuality was admissible under what is commonly called Makin's Rule after its well known formulation by Lord Herschell in *Makin* v. *Attorney General for New South Wales* (1894). In this case the bodies of 13 babies had been discovered in a variety of premises occupied at one time or another by the accused, who received lump sum payments for fostering unwanted babies. The evidential problem centred upon the role of coincidence and its admissibility. The most famous statement of this rule was made by Lord Sumner in *Thomson* v. *R.* (1918) 'no one doubts that it does not tend to prove a man guilty of a particular crime to show that he is the kind of man who would commit a crime or that he is generally disposed to crime and even to a particular crime but sometimes for one reason and sometimes for another evidence is admissible notwithstanding that its general character is to show that the accused had in him the making of a criminal. For example, in proving guilty knowledge or intent or system or in rebutting an appearance of innocence which unexplained the facts might wear.

The application of Makin's Rule has always been a matter of some difficulty and the test is whether the evidence is sufficiently relevant to an issue before the jury. The evidence of King's homosexuality could be said to be relevant to the issue of whether he took the boys home out of kindness and hospitality or in order to commit indecent acts. And a comparison of this case with that of Simms (1946) is invited. The difficulties of this aspect of evidence are exemplified by comparing the case of King with that of another decision of the Court of Criminal Appeal in *R.* v. *Cole* (1941). There the appellant had admitted to taking a young man back to his room and sleeping in the same bed but also denied that the alleged indecent acts had taken place. The conviction was quashed because the prosecution had been allowed to adduce evidence of old letters found in the room which showed that, at least when they were written 15 years before, Cole had been a homosexual. Makin's Rule goes contrary to Section 1(f) of the Criminal Evidence Act 1898 which provides that a person charged and called as a witness shall not be asked and if asked shall not be required to answer any question tending to show that he has committed or been convicted of or been charged with any offence other than that where with he is then charged or as a bad character. There are three exceptions to this section which are not material to the Makin Rule. In contrast at Common Law evidence may be admissible under the Makin Rule notwithstanding that it shows the commission of other offences, and this was particularly relevant in *R.* v. *Straffen* (1952).

The case of *R.* v. *King* is now seen as exceptional and atypical, and its precedential authority rendered dubious after *DPP* v. *Boardman* (1975). The starting point for a modern interpretation comes from the decision of the House of Lords in this latter case, but recent decisions have rendered this area of the law even more complex and overlaid with a tangle of complicated distinctions. Until the law becomes clarified in the fullness of time, forensic psychologists will have to rely on counsel's interpretation of the rules of evidence in this matter as they obtain at the particular time.

18. Rule of Hearsay

A LONGSTANDING bone of contention between psychologists and their psychiatric colleagues has been the inclusion of some or all of the psychologist's report in that of the psychiatrist. At the 1964 Annual Conference of the British Psychological Society the author pointed out that the inclusion of psychological data in the testimony of a psychiatrist could infringe the Rule of Hearsay and render such evidence inadmissible[108]. The subsequent lively discussion of this point of law aroused considerable interest, particularly among educational psychologists who suffered most from what they regarded as barefaced plagiarism. Medical practitioners have their own views on this particular practice, and before looking at the merits of both sides of the arguments, some explanation of the Rule of Hearsay will be briefly given and some implications for forensic psychologists preparing 'expert evidence' for judicial purposes examined. Although the admission of psychological data presented by psychiatrists has been explicitly challenged in the High Court, the relevant aspects of the Law of Evidence apply equally to the lower courts; indeed, it is in the Magistrates' Courts that unwitting infringement of the Rule of Hearsay more often takes place. Blom-Cooper has criticized the archaic rules which disallow cogent, trustworthy hearsay[230] and there is clearly a need for discussion regarding their reform.

The Hearsay Rule has never been stated judicially in a complete and explicit form although all authorities agree that the basic principle is that 'assertions of persons other than the witness testifying are inadmissible as evidence of the truth of that which is asserted'. The basis of the rule is of Anglo-Saxon origin and legal historians generally agree that after trial by jury the Rule against Hearsay is the greatest contribution to the world's jurisprudence made by the Anglo-Saxons. The rule is *res inter alios actae alteri nocere non debent* and it has been explicitly enforced on a large number of occasions (e.g. *Beare* v. *Garrod* (1915); *Sharpe* v. *Loddington Ironstone Co.* (1924); *R.* v. *Treacy* (1944)) and is supported by a substantial body of case law. Hearsay evidence was being admitted between 1600 and 1750 because of the widespread social effects of the Wars of the Roses. The courts gradually reacted against the admissibility of hearsay and this in turn led to rigid rules for exclusion, some of these rules have since been modified, but others are with us today. The main reasons put forward by different authorities for the existence of the Rule of Hearsay are as follows[147]:

(i) The original statement was not on oath and because of this is less likely to be true.

(ii) The person originally making the statement is not available to corroborate making the statement.

(iii) The court cannot see the demeanour of the party making the statement. Non-verbal behaviour is an important part of the communication process and in addition to the importance of communicating non-verbal messages, it modifies in various ways the meaning of verbal messages. In the exclamation 'you fool', the noun has two different meanings which can only be judged by whether the exclamation is accompanied by a laugh or a frown. This 'meta-communication' which parallels the verbal communication means that words may take on a different and sometimes contrary meaning, to their accepted one, depending upon the context and manner in which they are uttered. In the absence of those aspects of behaviour which qualify or determine the meaning of any given statement, the court therefore cannot assess the relevance of the latter.

(iv) The process of repetition as Bartlett so clearly showed[148] is likely to change the content, and therefore the truth, of any statement.

(v) The party making the statement originally is not subject to examination and cross-examination and therefore the implications and qualifications which may be latent in the statement cannot be made manifest.

(vi) Admission of hearsay would afford undesirable opportunities for fraud. Although the law regarding perjury would offer some sanction against this, as well as the effects of oath-taking, the prejudicial effects of untrue statements which could not be disproved would be immense.

(vii) Hearsay evidence would tend to prolong legal proceedings and would also encourage the substitution of weaker for stronger proof. Hearsay evidence could therefore be seen as offending the Best Evidence Rule.

Other reasons have been put forward but have not received general agreement. Those above are not listed in order of importance and the only really serious objections to hearsay, according to some authorities, is the absence of oath and cross-examination. The presence of the witness is normally required to secure these and where in the past statute law has provided an exception to the Hearsay Rule (e.g. in the Criminal Law Amendment Act (1867); Criminal Justice Act (1925); Coroner's (Amendment) Act (1926); Children and Young Persons Act

(1933); Evidence Act (1938); Magistrates' Courts Act (1952); and the Summons for Directions, R.S.C. Ord. 30 r.3 and Ord. 37 rr. 1A and 1B) stress has usually been laid on the opportunity for cross-examination provided at the time the statement was made.

When the statement itself, as a unit of verbal behaviour, is part of the transaction or relevant to the matter in hand it is said to form part of the *res gestae* and is then admissible. What a person says when he is called as witness may therefore be admitted when the *truth* of the statement is not in question. This situation not uncommonly occurs in such quasi-judicial proceedings as Mental Health Tribunals, for example, a patient who says she intended to take her own life may be quoted in the absence of the patient, not as evidence that she *was* suicidal but as a piece of knowledge about her behaviour which the psychologist used as evidence on which he recommended her detention for her own protection under the Mental Health Act. Her statement would be an essential part of the matter in hand; it cannot be admitted in the absence of the patient to prove that she was truly suicidal but it is admissible as evidence of why the psychologist thought she was suicidal. It can be admitted even if the truth of the statement is irrelevant to the matter in hand provided the statement itself is *de facto* a part of the *res gestae*. To support his case the psychologist is not using the truth of the statement but the fact that the statement was made and that he believed it to be true. The actual truth or falsity of the statement is irrelevant to the belief and subsequent decision.

Under the Rules of Hearsay the following examples are deemed to be original and not hearsay:

(i) Statements made by the party's agent, provided he had authority direct or implied, to make them.

(ii) Statements in furtherance of a common purpose made by a conspirator are admissible against the other conspirators.

(iii) Documents over 20 years old produced from proper custody, for example, from the hospital archives or medical records department, may be admitted as original evidence.

(iv) In matters of probate and disposition of property under the terms of a will, the written statements made by a person since deceased may be admitted as original evidence to show their state of mind at the time. The statements to be admitted must be relevant to the act of making the will, or its contents or the interpretation of its terms. This rule may prove useful to psychologists if the question of testamentary capacity is raised at a later date and the psychologist is called in to give an opinion. It will be appreciated that in civil actions of this kind the lack of *mens sana* is always claimed by the plaintiff contesting the will, who is invariably an excluded and disappointed relative and the psychologists' case notes may contain documents written for the psychologist by the patient, possibly as part of the psychometric examination. The Sentence Completion Test would be an appropriate example. Such a document could be entered as evidence under this Rule, and would also be supported by the Presumption of Continuance even if it was distant in time from the date on which the will was signed.

Apart from these examples, the law recognizes certain exceptions to the Rule of Hearsay, and the Civil Evidence Acts 1968–1972 have revolutionized hearsay in civil proceedings.

Some Exceptions to the Hearsay Rule
  (i)   Declarations made by persons since deceased are admissible in certain instances.
  (ii) Evidence given in previous trials, subject to certain qualifications.
  (iii) Depositions, in certain cases.
  (iv) Informal admissions and confessions see p. 190, 195 (for the position of Formal Admissions see page 130).
  (v)   Statements in public documents.
  (vi) Written statements admissible under the Evidence Act (1958).
  (vii) Evidence by certificate in criminal proceedings.

(i) *Declarations of Persons since Deceased*
Death is a regular and not infrequent visitor to the mental hospital, where the majority of beds are occupied by those in the second half of their lives. Indeed, with the creation of acute psychiatric wards, in the district hospital, the formerly autonomous county asylums are gradually becoming large geriatric departments of the community health service. Not infrequently, legal proceedings will arise in relation to some patient whom the clinical psychologist has seen for assessment and/or treatment and who has since died. The most common cause of litigation in such circumstances will relate to testamentary capacity, but occasionally civil actions for tort or even prosecutions for criminal negligence may arise in which statements made to the psychologist by the patient concerned become relevant and of evidential value. Although as a general rule statements by persons since deceased are not admissible under the Rule of Hearsay, the following exceptions exist:
(a) Statements made *ante litem motam* by persons competent to speak on the subject are admissible to prove ancient or public rights. This situation not infrequently occurs because the deceased patient's house is sold and the new owners wish to rebuild or modify the premises in such a way that public or private rights, e.g. 'ancient lights' are infringed.
(b) Statements made by persons related by blood or marriage to parties in litigation are admissible to prove matters of pedigree

(e.g. Berkeley Peerage Case (1811)). For this purpose Family Bibles are accepted judicially as Family Registers and entries in such Bibles are admissible in the same way (*Hubbard* v. *Lees* (1866)). Many elderly mental patients die without possessing any traceable relative. Should the patient have left any letters or other documents with the psychologist for safe-keeping (some patients having a distrust of nursing or administrative staff perhaps by virtue of their paranoid illness), these should be passed to the Chief Administrator with the reminder that they might be called for under this particular Rule. Statements from deceased persons not legally related to the party in issue are still admissible in proceedings under the Legitimacy Act (1926) in anticipation of being legitimized by the findings of the court. Equity is not always easy to find in the fine differentiations made in law. Note that the declaration of a deceased clergyman that he legally married the Duke of Sussex to Lady Murray was held to be inadmissible because the clergyman was not related to the parties in litigation (Sussex Peerage case).

(c) Declarations against interest are admissible as proof of the facts stated. Although this usually refers to pecuniary or proprietary interests (e.g. that the deceased person's bills have been settled by his debtors, and that his house really belongs to another member of the family) there are extensions of this principle which may be of importance to the clinical psychologist. An example of such an extension would be the case of a patient injured during treatment who wrote to a correspondent saying that the injury was his own fault (e.g. by turning the current control of a shock box when the psychologist's attention was distracted elsewhere).

(d) Oral or written statements made in the course of duty by a person since deceased (e.g. by a charge nurse, duty medical officer, casualty officer, etc.) are admissible as proof of the facts stated provided the statements were made contemporaneously with events described and within the personal knowledge of the person making the statements. Thus a casualty officer since deceased who said to the clinical psychologist 'I've just admitted an "attempted suicide" who acts as if she's brain damaged', may have his statement quoted by the psychologist in evidence should he be called upon later to testify regarding organic cerebral pathology. Note that, had the casualty officer told the psychologist at a later date that the patient appeared to be brain damaged, this would not have been admissible since it lacked contemporaneity. It will be obvious that as situations develop the possibility of future litigation also opens up the possibility of anticipating appropriate evidence, and the requirement of contemporaneity, is therefore a wise one. This point highlights the importance of keeping a contemporaneous record of everything that happens concerning patients under the psychologist's care. Not all hospitals or psychology departments keep separate record cards or case-history folders for the psychologists' use, and it is a useful medico-legal protection for the psychologist to keep his own 'personal occurrence records' for each patient on his list so that all events can be dated and recorded as they occur. Statements made by the deceased person which are not relevant to his particular duty are not admissible, but those which it is the declarant's duty to record are admissible in both civil and criminal cases (e.g. *Chambers* v. *Bernasconi* (1831)).

(e)   In trials of homicide, but in no other, dying declarations are admitted as exceptions to the Rule of Hearsay provided that the declarant has since died and that at the time of making the statement he was in a hopeless expectation of death. The statement must be relevant to the circumstances surrounding the declarant's death e.g. related to his assailant, and may even be non verbal (i.e. by signs, as in *Chandrasekera* v.*R.* (1937). For a forensic psychologist's review of the reasons why a dying person's accusation may be credible, malicious or mistaken, see Altavilla [149].

(ii)   *Evidence given in previous trials*

Hearsay evidence is exceptionally admissible when it forms part of the evidence of a previous trial (or a previous stage of the same trial) provided the issues and the parties are the same, full opportunity to cross examine the witness at this time was afforded the other party, and the witness himself is either dead, insane, physically incapable of attending court, is out of the jurisdiction or has been kept out of the way by the other side (the last two conditions applying to civil cases only).

(iii)   *Depositions*

A number of statutes provide for depositions taken on oath before an examining magistrate or coroner. The Criminal Law Amendment Act (1867), the Merchant Shipping Act (1894), the Coroners (amendment) Act (1926), the Magistrates Courts Act (1952), the Criminal Justice Act (1967) *inter alia* allow such depositions to be admitted as hearsay evidence in criminal trials provided the deposition was taken in the presence of the accused and opportunity for cross-examination was afforded, and the evidence is merely formal or the accused has admitted the charge.

The Criminal Justice Act (1925) as amended by the Criminal Procedure (Attendance of Witnesses) Act (1965) provides for the admission of a deposition proved by oath if the witness is dead, insane, medically unfit to travel, or is not available to the prosecution.

The Children and Young Person's Act (1933) permits the reading of a deposition by a child or young person as evidence at a trial in the cases of certain offences against children provided the attendance of the child in court would create a serious medical risk (by which is meant a psychiatric risk), and that the deposition has been signed by a magistrate or the accused has had opportunity to cross examine the witness. For this purpose the clinical or educational psychologist may be called in to give preliminary evidence as to the likely effect of court proceedings upon a young child's mental health. This is, of course, not an easy matter to decide upon; the testimony of children is often unreliable[146] and when placed in a psychologically threatening situation there is a tendency for them to become obdurate and to stand by their original statements whatever their degree of falsity or inaccuracy. In these circumstances psychologists can not only assist the court in deciding whether or not to admit a deposition in lieu of direct testimony, but he can use his knowledge of child-adult interactions to arrange the situation in the way which is most likely to produce honest testimony. However, the forensic psychologist is cautioned against putting too much reliance upon the testimony of a child, especially below the age of ten years, and the lawyers involved in the case should be acquainted by the psychologist with the facts relating to the low reliability of this source of evidence.

The Criminal Law Amendment Act (1867) and the Magistrates Courts Acts (1952) allows the deposition of a witness who is seriously ill and unlikely to recover to be admitted in a criminal trial under the same circumstances as above.

In civil cases the situation is much easier and depositions *de bene esse* may be read at the trial if the witness is unable to attend the hearing on medical grounds or is out of the country. Such depositions are also admitted by consent of both parties.

Research Data as Hearsay

Clearly, much of a psychologists' data are drawn from an experimental population, and in many experiments the data itself would be considered hearsay. Depending upon the nature of the experiment, there will be some subtle distinctions to be made as to when the response of a subject is, or is not, hearsay. In sociological surveys the problem is more acute because the data are concerned generally with the verbal response of the subject, and social psychology surveys will obviously present the same problems.

Until a decade ago survey research data were inadmissible in court because of the Rule of Hearsay. The justification for their exclusion was that in the conditions in which social surveys are conducted the court cannot be given primary or first degree facts relating to the respondents. However, the American courts have gradually relaxed the rules of evidence relating to hearsay and now survey data and opinion poll results are generally admissible in the U.S.A. Doubts have been expressed in European jurisdictions concerning the admissibility of social survey data, and on occasions the author has been warned by counsel not to present certain data which was thought to be likely to be refused admission by the judge.

Clearly, the forensic psychologist, in carrying out his preparations for the collection of psychological data will need to bear in mind the future admissibility of his results. The admissibility will greatly depend upon the nature of the response. The psychologist can testify as to the fact that his subjects responded in one way rather than another, or that a given percentage of them responded in one way, because this is evidence within his own perceptual experience. What he is normally prevented from doing is testifying as to the validity of the response in so far as it relies only on the content of the response itself and has no external validation. Thus in Case No. 9 the court accepted the author's statement that only a small proportion of the sample produced an identification of the vehicle number plates. However, the fact that the remainder were unable to identify the numberplates was, in theory, not admissible, because the author did not himself know directly that the subjects could not identify the plates, only that they said they could not. The subjects would really have needed to be brought into court to make this statement directly under oath. It would then be accepted as a fact. Nevertheless, in this instance, the court was prepared to allow the author to enlarge upon his experimental findings and admitted the hearsay evidence. In contrast, the counsel in Case No. 9 was not prepared to allow the author to present his experimental findings in their direct form for fear of antagonizing the court. As discussed earlier, the distinction to be made is that it is admissible for the psychologist to testify that his subjects made certain responses, but not as to the *truth* of those responses. That a patient responded to a questionnaire item or MMPI card by marking it TRUE is admissible in his absence if the psychologist saw him do just this. The fact that the item said 'I can hear voices when I am alone' is not admissible in his absence as evidence that he was aurally hallucinating. If an experimental psychologist finds 100 people who are unable to repeat the perception of a police witness under identical conditions, as in Case No. 10 he may testify to the fact that he arranged the experiment and the entire sample *did* not do so. He cannot say they *could* not do so, no matter how vehemently and convincingly they said so to the psychologist at the time. In practice, many courts have accepted such evidence because the court was unable to discern the subtle distinctions in a form of expert testimony which was completely new to them. However, one aspect of the Law of Evidence has enabled the Rule of Hearsay to be relaxed for the forensic psychology and that is the question of *opinion* evidence. As discussed on page 138, the expert witness, unlike the witness to fact, is allowed to express an opinion (but only upon facts before the court) so that he can give a confident opinion, assuming he possesses one, on the findings of his experimental studies, which gives them greater cogency than they would otherwise possess.

In the last decade the courts have shown more willingness to admit as evidence the results of psychological surveys and experiments. The admission in the Central Criminal Court of the various surveys into attitudes towards sex crimes by Professor Kutchinsky[231], the famous Danish criminologist, was followed by the acceptance of similar data presented by the author in courts in many parts of the U.K.

Hearsay in Psychiatric Reports

It was mentioned earlier that difficulties have occurred from time to time regarding the use made of the psychologists' report by the psychiatrist. Psychologists naturally prefer to make their own report to the court, or to the probation officer, or to the client's solicitor independently of other professional reports.

However, they often find that their reports are embodied into those of medical practitioners with whom they work, sometimes without their consent, sometimes against their wishes, and sometimes even without their knowledge.

The situation arises because the psychologist often has a duty, as part of his N.H.S. contact either explicitly or implicitly, to provide the psychiatrists or other medical practitioners with whom he works with reports on patients referred to him for this purpose. In the decade following the introduction of a career structure for clinical psychology in the Health Service, this was virtually the psychologist's only task, apart from some research and teaching, and it is only in the latter half of the post-war period that the role has widened and therapy of one kind or another became the predominant activity. In a virtually unquestioning way, therefore, the psychologist has furnished his medical colleagues with reports on patients, without necessarily knowing the use to which such information will be put. The psychiatrist, for his part, has accepted this particular aspect of his information-gathering as part of his taught medical routine. Thus, when asked to provide a report on one of his patients for court purposes, he has naturally referred the patient for evaluation by whatever hospital departments seem appropriate. Thus the surgeon in charge of a patient injured in a road accident and claiming compensation from the second party, asked to report on the patient's condition to the patient's solicitor, would refer the patient to the radiology department for X rays, and would include information derived from the radiologist's report in his final report to the lawyers. Similarly, physicians report on their medical patients in terms of the analyses provided by the pathology laboratory. Similarly neurologists and psychiatrists would normally include statements in their reports based upon the psychologists' findings if these were deemed to be relevant. They would do this in the firm belief that they are profession-ally entitled to do so, and be unlikely to understand why psychologists should object to this practice when other hospital departments do not. When challenged about this practice, psychiatrists have pointed out that as part of their medical training they have worked in various medical departments to acquire first-hand experience in the preparation of pathology specimens, X-ray photographs, and so on, and have had training in the analysis of reports based on such evidence. Similarly, psychiatrists will point out that psychology, including the basis of psychological tests forms part of their professional postgraduate training, and therefore qualifies them to use psychological reports in the same way as they use any other form of medical report.

Psychologists, however, argue that they are not part of a medical 'service' department in the same way as pathology laboratory technicians or radiographers. Indeed this fact was formally established by the Zuckermann Committee which examined in the early 1950s the professional structure of the scientists working within the Health Service. Moreover, psychologists point out that the interpretation of psychometric test data calls for extensive specialized training which in the case of clinical tests extends over five or six years, and includes an honours course in psychology and a two or three-year postgraduate clinical course of training. They maintain that the modest course in psychology provided for the membership of the Royal College of Psychiatry or its equivalent does not qualify the psychiatrist to interpret test data, although this is not to say that individual psychiatrists who have made a special study and with considerable experience in a particular psychometric technique are not more proficient in its use than the clinical psychologist working with him. Ryle, with his extensive work on the Repertory Grid Technique[150] is one example. Hamilton, who has made a major contribution to quantifying behavioural assessment, and who eventually became president of the psychologists' own learned society[151], is also one of the medical psychometric giants who, with one foot in each profession has done so much to bring about a rapprochement between the two. However, such figures as these are exceptional and the average psychiatrist would not claim to be competent in assessing the validity of the tests used by the psychologist as his basis for his report.

It should be noted too that the laboratory reports used by the medical practitioner contain factual data such as the concentration of certain chemicals in the blood, the position and extent of fractures and similar data. Such data have direct meaning for the physician in contradistinction to the data from psychological tests. Few psychiatrists would understand what the code of the Minnesota Multiphasic Personality Inventory is, or what the code of the Kahn Test of Symbol Arrangement implies, so such symbolic statements have to be interpreted by the psychologist himself. When the psychiatrist discusses the psychologist's report in his own evidence he is thus not talking about the facts within his knowledge of the test, not even about facts within his own knowledge, but about another expert's interpretation of facts (for example, that the patient put the Kahn Y-piece over the red heart) which are not before the court, and not even known to himself. Even if presented with all the basic data, the psychiatrist is usually neither competent nor qualified to comment upon them as an expert. His qualification as an expert in psychological testing has not been proved to the court, as discussed in the next chapter. Obviously anyone can obtain an IQ of sorts given the test material and the appropriate handbook with instructions for administering and scoring the test, but only a psychologist trained in the theory, construction and use of psychometric instruments is qualified to determine how valid and reliable the measure is, how relevant it is to the person being tested, whether it reflects special or general intellectual functions and the meaning it possesses relative to the norm of the population from which the standardizing scores were obtained. The most simple datum in psychometric tests has no real meaning until interpreted in the context of the test, the person being tested, and the testing situation itself. The fact that the medical practitioner has received special training in a particular test, such as that provided for school medical officers in connection with the Terman-Merrill revision of the Stanford-Binet Test, qualifies them only for the purpose for which the training was provided, namely the formal ascertainment of school children for educability within the terms of the Education Act (1944).

The law is explicit in stating that the opinion of the expert witness must be based upon facts within his direct knowledge. In *Daine* v. *Edinburgh Magistrates* (1953) Lord President Cooper said: 'The duty of the expert is to furnish judge and jury with the necessary scientific criteria for testing the accuracy of their conclusions, and so enable the judge and jury to form their own independent judgment by the application of these criteria to *the facts proved in evidence*'. An expert is 'proved' in court, both by his belonging to a profession specializing in a particular branch of knowledge, and by his own personal training, and experience. An expert who is testifying may not give an opinion on matters outside his own field of expertise, even though the matters are generally within the field of his own profession[152]. In *R.* v. *Kusmack* (1955), for example, a physician was held to be incompetent to give an opinion on the cause of a wound on the hand. Having offered such an opinion spontaneously, his evidence was ruled inadmissible retrospectively, and a completely new trial became necessary. The limitation upon the expert's opinion has also been defined by saying that when the expert's opinion is based upon reports of facts, those facts, unless within the experts' own knowledge, must be proved *independently*[153]. The position is made clear in all textbooks on the Law of Evidence that the opinion of an expert must be upon facts admitted, proved by himself or by other witnesses in his hearing at the trial, or be matters of common knowledge. Case law, while supporting this position, does have some exceptions which require legal training to properly evaluate. The most relevant English case for the forensic psychologist is that of *R.* v. *Trotter* (1957) where a psychiatrist called for the defence was explicitly prevented from presenting to the court evidence which the author had specially prepared for this purpose. As a result, the author was called to court to present his own evidence as an expert in his own right. The reason for rejecting the psychiatrist's presentation of this evidence was stated categorically as being an infringement of the Rule of Hearsay, and having established the precedent in case law psychologists have had no difficulty, at least vis-à-vis lawyers, in presenting their own expert testimony since. The situation remains unsatisfactory for some psychologists, however; usually the difficulties are personal ones relating to the personalities of the parties involved, although often they stem from ignorance of the legal issues or misconceptions about the precise role of the psychologist and the status of the psychological tests. The supply of psychometric tests used professionally is now carefully controlled in the U.K. and only qualified users may have legitimate access to them. The fact that medical practitioners are not, *ipso facto*, qualified users is itself evidence supporting the difference between psychological test reports and those from other medical departments. In general, the situation is one which could be resolved by better communication between psychology, psychiatry and law and sufficient goodwill on everybody's part. Professional jealousies, a desire to avoid fee-splitting, and similar less than laudable motives will continue to promote the occasional conflict between interprofessional colleagues. More serious are those cases which psychologists bring before their professional body, in which the psychologists claim their report was being misused. The most frequent complainants regarding this practice are educational psychologists but clinical psychologists have not been immune from it. In a number of cases the psychologist's report has been included *en bloc* in the report provided to the court by the medical officer who requested the psychologist's report in the first place. This is not only flagrant plagiarism, but may also be an infringement of copyright, since the presentation of a report in a court of law is 'publication', although it may be protected by qualified privilege. More seriously, and more commonly, it has been alleged that selected pieces from the psychologist's report have been embodied in that of the medical practitioner in such a way as to support, validate and give additional credence to the opinions expressed in the medical report and which lead to different or even contrary conclusions from those which would follow had the same information been read in its original context. In such circumstances psychologists have naturally been concerned that their findings have been distorted in this way. Generally psychologists who complain of these practices are not seeking any form of redress, but merely request advice on how to deal with this situation should it recur. They are concerned, not so much with what many regard as medical malpractice, as with the consequences for the person on whose behalf the report has been prepared. They feel that it can be scarcely in the best interest of patient or offender if their *status psychologicus* is misrepresented. The psychiatrist may well reply that since the psychologist's findings and opinions did not coincide with his own, and that both could not be right, he was entitled to use his professional discretion and use only those parts of the psychologist's report which were consistent with his own findings and opinions, thus providing a measure of consistency in the information presented to court which, in terms of probability, was more likely to be correct than the conclusions upon which they differed. This argument has a certain plausibility especially when, as is often the case, the psychiatrist has more professional experience than the psychologist, but it does not stand up to logical analysis and the ethical considerations also deserve examination. The problem is unlikely to concern clinical psychologists, who are gradually moving out from under the medical umbrella and achieving autonomy within the National Health Service. For psychologists in other government service, especially those such as some educational and prison psychologists who occupy a clearly defined subordinate role under medical practitioners, the situation may continue to be unsatisfactory for some time, and any individual psychologist finding his reporting being misused will need to consult his conscience and weigh up the balance between the consequences to the patient or client if he remains silent, and the consequences to his own personal working relationships and professional development if he raises objections. When in doubt, the clerk to the court is the best person with whom to discuss the problem. Knowing both sides of the case from the deposition already in hand, he will be the person best able to appraise the significance of the psychologist's findings, given that these have been explained to him by the psychologist concerned. Should he deem the information to be important, he can arrange for the psychologist to be called by the court, and not by either side, and will do this in a way which causes least embarrassment to any party.

In summary, while there are certain arguments which can be put forward to support the inclusion of the psychologist's findings and opinions within the report of a medical colleague, there are good professional ethical and legal reasons why they should be kept separate and the psychologist called if required to give evidence as an expert in his own right. To do otherwise infringes not only the Rule of Hearsay but the Best Evidence Rule as well, and Ward expresses the hope that the learned societies representing psychology and psychiatry will reach a working agreement on this problem[154].

PART V

The Psychologist in Court

19. Expert Evidence

Common Witness to Fact

THE LAW OF EVIDENCE recognizes two types of witness, both of which apply to the forensic psychologist. The first type is known as a *common witness to fact*, the fact concerned being personally perceived, that is, within the direct knowledge of the witness. The witness recounts to the court matters that are within his immediate personal knowledge. The professional psychologist, if he has knowledge of this kind, is a skilled common witness to fact, and may be summoned to court to convey relevant information to the court. In this particular role, the correct attitude is that of the patriarch Job: 'I shall see for myself, and mine own eyes shall behold, and not another's'. As a common witness to fact, the psychologist functions in the capacity of an ordinary citizen. He is not in court *by reason* of his professional expertise, although his evidence may be more cogent because of the use he has made of his professional knowledge in trying to minimize distortion in the recall of events. Apart from his role as common witness to fact occasioned purely by circumstances, for instance, by observing an accident or crime, the psychologist is not uncommonly required to give evidence in this role by virtue of his professional duties. The educational psychologist may be asked to testify as to bruises seen on a child under treatment at the child guidance clinic, in the case of a 'place of safety' or 'care and custody' order. The clinical psychologist may be summonsed to appear at court, to give evidence as a common witness to fact, concerning for example, the continued relapse of a patient in a divorce suit after weekend leave from hospital, or the behaviour of the patient at or about the time a will was signed. In this role the psychologist does not, and must not, spontaneously express an opinion. To do so could put before the court prejudicial evidence which is inadmissible, and this could involve the stopping of the trial, discharge of jury, and the convening of a completely new trial which has to start again from the beginning. If the psychologist *is* asked to express an opinion, he immediately changes his category from common witness to expert witness, discussed in the next section. A whole new set of rules then come into operation, and the psychologist should, therefore, be alert to this change of status. It may occur in a number of ways, for example, by a solicitor who mistakenly believes the psychologist has been called as an expert (this usually happens, when it does, by the solicitor for the other side); sometimes it appears to be used when the witness has shown reluctance to appear as an expert, and has been brought to court by subpoena; once having got the psychologist in the box, the lawyer converts him into an expert witness by this subtle change of status, which in a rural magistrates court may well go unnoticed and unchecked. The courts are so used to medical witnesses being present as experts and giving their opinions, that it would be difficult for them to notice exceptions to the general rule. Sometimes, of course, the psychologist is summonsed to court as a witness to fact, to testify in respect to certain clinical facts relating to one of his patients whom he has examined or treated. In the course of the enquiry it may suddenly be appreciated by counsel that the psychologist is in a position to give expert opinion of value to the court, and may then effect a change of status of the witness from common witness to fact to expert witness. Appearance in court as common witness provides a good introductory experience for the would be forensic psychologist. It gives him the full experience of examination and cross-examination in the witness box, yet will probably be on non-controversial matters which require nothing more than a statement of knowledge. Interpretations cannot be ridiculed, nor opinions shown to be contrary to those of other experts. In most cases it is an interesting, non-threatening experience and an excellent preparation for giving expert evidence.

Expert Witness

The common witness to fact is said to state the *minor premiss* of the forensic argument. The expert witness, in contradistinction, states the major premiss of the syllogism, whose conclusion is found in the verdict of the jury. The expert witness is one who by his training, knowledge and experience, is qualified to express a professional opinion. Most commonly, the experts invited to give an opinion in court are medical witnesses. English courts recognized expert medical witnesses long before the law of evidence reached a comprehensive formulation or legal procedure became standardized, even before the office of magistrate was introduced. One of the earliest examples on record dates from 1290 when the court was advised by physicians regarding the legitimacy of a posthumous child[155]. By 1345 a writ was available to bring '*medicos, chirugicos de melioribus Londinii ad informandum . . .*' and by 1571 Plowden was reporting that Saunders J. said it was customary for judges to call surgeons to advise 'whether it be maihem or not, because their knowledge and skill can best discern it'[155]—probably the first regularization of forensic pathology. Medical experts were also used in early times in cases of alleged pregnancy, when a woman 'pleaded her belly'. The first statute to bring the expert witness from Common Law to Statute

Law was the Regulation of Railways Act (1868) which introduced the medical referee or assessor. This was followed by numerous Victorian Statutes which authorized the use of experts in judicial proceedings, such as the Regulation of Railways Act (1871) which brought the expert to the Coroner's Court, the Judicature Act, 1873, Patents Act 1883, Arbitration Act (1889), and the Workman's Compensation Acts of 1897 and 1956. Statutory recognition has continued during the present century and the diversity of experts now recognized by the courts is perhaps best exemplified in the Obscene Publications Act (1959) which under Section 4, enables a wide variety of experts to be called.

McCormick has given one of the best definitions of expert testimony. He states: 'To warrant the use of expert testimony, then, two elements are required. First the subject of the inference must be so distinctively related to some science, profession, business or occupation, as to be beyond the ken of the average layman, and second, the witness must have such skill, knowledge or experience in that field or calling as to make it appear that his opinion or inference will probably aid the seeker in his search for truth. The knowledge in some fields may be derived from reading alone, or in some from practice alone, or as is more commonly the case, from both'[156].

The qualification of an alleged expert to express an opinion in court on a given topic is decided by the judge alone, but the weight given to an opinion by an expert witness is exclusively for the jury to decide.

Opinion

The essential difference between a common witness to fact and an expert witness is that the latter is called to court to express an opinion. True, he has 'qualified' himself to the court as an expert in the relevant matters, but his *raison d'être* as an expert witness is because the court requires his expert opinion upon the matters before it. The witness to fact may also be highly qualified in the matters before the court—the professor of medicine who encounters a road accident whilst driving along is called to give evidence of what he found in the wreckage, for example—but he is there to give information to the court on facts within his direct knowledge. The court jealously guards the privilege of opinion to the expert. In *R.* v. *Davies* (1962) the accused was convicted of driving when under the influence of drink, and evidence was given by another driver that the accused was drunk and unfit to drive. The appellate court declared that the statement that the accused was unfit to drive was an opinion and inadmissible.

Even when the witness is testifying as an expert, he must not give an opinion outside his own field of expertise, and in criminal trials the court will impose stringent boundaries to this. Thus, in *R.* v. *Kusmack* (1955) a medical practitioner was held to be incompetent to give an opinion on the cause of wounds of the hand, and his spontaneously given opinion rendered a completely new trial necessary. The court regarded his opinion as purely conjectural and out of order.

Opinion, which in logic means a subjective and possibly irrational conviction, in law means any statement not expressing a direct perception. The court thus rejects all opinions except those of the appropriate expert. Expert opinion, in law, is deemed to be a fully-reasoned conclusion from scientific facts, although frequently counsel will insist on an expression of opinion which falls far short of this ideal. Originally, the law required the expert to form his opinion only on the facts directly perceived by him—and conveyed to the court by direct evidence—or on facts proved to both the court and the expert by other witnesses. Recently the courts have admitted survey data in the absence of the witnesses who actually collected the data. The expert witness, therefore, presents his data to the court, and then states what inferences he draws from them: the court then appraises its cogency. In contrast, the common witness to fact presents the facts and the court draws the inferences.

The opinion of an expert is admissible whenever the subject is one upon which the competency to form an opinion can only be acquired by a course of special training or experience[157]. In addition to giving opinions on facts, either known directly to the expert or proved by others, the expert may also be asked to give an opinion on hypothetical questions, which can be particularly potent weapons in the cross-examiner's armoury. Psychologists being pressed *in extremis* under cross-examination will eventually reach the conclusion that if marriages are made in Heaven, the hypothetical question almost certainly emanates from the Other Place.

Whenever the opinion of the witness is deemed to be relevant, the grounds upon which that opinion is based are also deemed to be relevant. An expert may therefore give the court an account of an experiment performed by him for the purpose of forming an opinion[158]. See e.g. Cases 9 and 10. An expert witness may also be called to court to explain special terms which have been used—in a contract between a therapist and a private patient, for example—and may make reference to accredited dictionaries. This use of the expert occurs mainly in civil actions, and is more common in the early days of a new technical development, (e.g. *North Eastern Railway* v. *Hastings* (1900) and *Van Dieman Land Company* v. *Table Cape Board* (1906)). The expert may also be asked to express an opinion on the *opinion* of other experts. The opinions referred to do not become evidence of their truth, but it *is* evidence of their existence, and this serves to bring to the jury's attention the fact that opinions exist contrary to those of the expert being cross-examined.

The Psychologist as Medical Witness

An expert witness can be defined as someone who has the requisite specialist knowledge, skill, experience, and learning in matters before the court which the layman cannot fully understand without expert help. Other forms of the definition are available in the standard textbooks on evidence and elsewhere[157,158]. The psychologist is presented in court as one of two forms of expert—either as a scientific witness or as a medical witness. He will be presented as a 'medical witness' whenever the matter before the court is deemed to be a 'medical' one. To be presented as a medical witness does not imply that the witness is a medical practitioner. In the past, unqualified medical practitioners, medical students, pharmacists, and the manufacturer of pharmaceutical preparations have appeared in court as medical witnesses. The expert need not be qualified in the sense of possessing academic certificates of scholastic proficiency. He could have acquired his knowledge by home study or merely by experience of doing the job. The courts are more concerned with the *effective* knowledge of the expert than with his theoretical knowledge. Thus on a question of test findings, a psychometric technician working on a fulltime assessment in a psychiatric hospital would probably be regarded as better qualified to give an opinion on the test responses of a psychiatric patient than would a university lecturer responsible for a course on psychometrics.

It has been argued by some psychiatrists that the psychologist has no place in court as 'medical witness', on the grounds that there is no matter on which he can assist the court which is not more closely within the province of the psychiatrist. The assessment of the psychiatrist's contribution to court proceedings by members of their own profession does not always reflect credit upon their efforts in this respect, so there is perhaps room for another profession to try to do better; however, psychology needs no plea for its *raison d'être* in court. This has already been established in a long succession of cases in which the psychologists' contribution has been both unique and useful. As a medical witness, the psychologist is bound to overlap the evidence of medical witnesses drawn from other professions. Nevertheless the psychological evidence can usefully supplement and complement that of the physician, neurologist, psychiatrist and should, indeed, if the psychologist has done his work well, make it easier for the court to appraise the validity and the cogency of that of the other expert witnesses.

As a complement to other medical evidence, the clinical psychologist is obviously in a position to supply evidence to court. He can add to the *weight* of evidence by giving an opinion of the facts from a different viewpoint to that of the other witnesses. The psychiatrist, for example, interprets the symptoms of a mental illness in the context of *pathology*, the psychologist, on the other hand, approaches them as deviations from *normality*. Thus, a psychiatrist and a psychologist called together for one side can offer two different sides to the same set of facts. The facts themselves are not understandable to the court without help. By helping from two different positions the court can come to understand more fully the full meaning and implications of the facts.

Secondly, the clinical psychologist generally has had a sounder training in psychiatry than a psychiatrist has had in psychology. In addition to a full year's course in abnormal psychology as a special subject of his undergraduate honours course, the clinical psychologist will have had two or three years specialized postgraduate clinical training in which, in addition to formal academic teaching in psychiatric subjects, he will have worked in a variety of psychiatric settings in close contact with mental patients of all sorts and conditions. He is thus well-qualified to *supplement* the psychiatrists' evidence with his own observations and inferences, speaking as a biological or social scientist rather than as a medical scientist (though still as a medical witness). Because clinical psychology is a comparatively new profession with many young members, many clinical psychologists asked to give expert evidence will have more recent and perhaps more technical knowledge than their possibly much older psychiatric colleagues. Again, by joining forces they can bring to the client a combination of knowledge and expertise, the young psychologist bringing to court the fruits of recent learning and technical advances, to supplement the experience and wisdom of their senior psychiatric colleagues.

In addition to supplementary information and a complementary viewpoint, a third justification for using the psychologist as a medical witness is that he is taught, above all his skills, the art of measurement. Following the famous scientific dictum: 'To measure is to know', psychologists in their clinical work can be differentiated by their use of measurement from other professional workers. Indeed, where their activities do not include measurement, it will probably be found that they are being professionally misused, and that the work they are doing could be done better, or more cheaply, by someone more appropriately trained for the task. In giving expert testimony in court, therefore, their evidence should differ from that of their medical colleagues by its numerate character and the fact that it is obtained by special methods or skills of behavioural analysis and measurement that are particularly the province of psychology. Thus, by his quantitative evidence, the forensic psychologist both complements and supplements the evidence of the medical practitioner (Case No. 2).

A fourth justification for expert medical evidence given by the psychologist is that some medical signs and symptoms have been of special interest and concern to psychologists, who through a century of learning and experimenting, have accumulated a vast store of knowledge on the subject far beyond the scope of the medical practitioner. The dysmnesias, or disorders of memory, would be one such example. Well-known to the medical profession long before psychology became a profession in its own right, the dysmnesias and amnesias are described by neurologists and psychiatrists in qualitative terms, and noted as being absent or present, consistent or fluctuating, and possibly of a given duration and intensity. Learned books which have made a major advance in medical knowledge, have been written on aphasia, without using a single number except to refer to duration or incidence. In contrast, memory is a fundamental subject for the psychologist, and data from experiments on its processes have filled the textbooks and journals of scientific psychology ever since Victorian times. Sensation and perception are similar basic subjects for the psychologist, who can thus draw on a considerable data bank for evidence relevant to disturbances of the visual, auditory, olfactory and other functions of the senses. Pain, a common ingredient in claims for compensation in tort, has been studied and measured by psychologists for many years. Locomotor efficiency, often impaired in orthopaedic patients following a road accident, is also an aspect of behaviour of special interest to psychologists.

Fifthly and finally, a professional training in psychology provides a diversity of scientific skills (in statistics, computor-usage, probability theory and research methodology to name but a few) which can be applied to clinical problems to yield additional information of potential value to the court. Mindful of the immaturity of his profession, and the limitations of his science, the psychologist can nevertheless feel justly confident that he has a place in court as a medical witness, and belongs to a profession that can make a unique, positive and substantial contribution to evidence in cases of a medical nature.

The Psychologist as Scientific Witness

When the facts in issue are not medical ones, the forensic psychologist will be presented, not as a medical witness, but as a scientist, of course. Even as a medical witness he is also a scientist, since the nature of both his training and his profession is a scientific one. As a scientific witness, however, he enjoys a freedom from unfortunate comparisons which are frequently used to discredit his evidence when he appears as a medical witness. In forensic discussions, lawyers frequently express the need for scientific witnesses who are ready to come forward and give evidence in courts of law. As contemporary society becomes more technological, so the disputes which come into court become, in their turn more technological. To apportion blame, and thereby legal and financial responsibility in tort, in the case of a commercial aircraft accident, requires the court to consider evidence based on metallurgical, crystal-radiographic, electromagnetic, radio-electronic, medical and psychological facts. A whole platoon of experts, drawn from the many fields from which the complex operations of air transport develops, is required to bring to the awareness of the court the critical factors, ranging from metal-fatigue to pilot-fatigue. However, it is axiomatic that scientific facts by themselves are of little everyday significance unless interpreted and explained by someone who can appreciate their full significance. The role of the forensic psychologist as experimentalist and actuary have been described earlier, and the cases cited would be examples of where the psychologist has been admitted to court as a scientific witness. The non-medical expert witness, while of more recent origin than the medical expert, has nevertheless been recognized since the middle of the 16th century[155]. Mr Justice Saunders in *Buckley* v. *Rice-Thomas* (1554) stated 'If matters arise in our law which concern other sciences or faculties, we commonly apply for the aid of that science or faculty which it concerns: this is a commendable thing in our laws'. The status of the scientific witness in court, and the rules of the procedure which govern the admission of his testimony, are now soundly formulated by custom and precedent.

Admissibility of psychologists as expert witnesses
Psychologists have a well-established role as expert witnesses in England, and in some other European countries. In the USA the position of the psychologist as expert witness differs between states, but the trend is towards increasing admissibility. Hugo Munsterberg, the father of forensic psychology, established the role of the psychologist in the American courts in 1908[123] although not without criticism from the legal diehards. Moore, his chief critic, said 'Experimental psychologists are no more welcome in the court room than Sherlock Holmes'[160] and on a later occasion said of experimental psychology that he could 'imagine nothing better designed to distract attention from the real tests of credibility, based on the experience of mankind . . .'[161] The main development towards acceptance of psychologists as expert witnesses in America started with *People* v. *Hawthorne* (1940) in which a Michigan court rejected the argument that insanity is a purely medical matter upon which only a qualified physician can testify. The progress of psychologists' testimony since then have been reviewed[162,163,164]; the most important precedent occurred in the case of *Jenkins* v. *United States* (1962), which has been well documented[166,165,164]. In this case, the U.S. Court of Appeals voted seven to two in favour of admitting the evidence of properly qualified psychologists in cases involving the determination and meanings of mental disease and defect as productive of criminal acts. By 1973 Pacht and his colleagues following Bock[168], had analyzed the American Law Reports over the relevant period[169] and were able to list the states which had admitted psychologists as experts by that date. Only 19 of the 50 states had established precedents in case law supporting the admissibility of psychologists. Three states, Arkansas, Nebraska and New Jersey have rejected the introduction of

psychological testimony by psychologists. However the picture is by no means clear, since a number of cases have imposed limitations on the scope of the psychologists' evidence, and many are somewhat contradictory or have reversed earlier trends. In Alabama, for example, the courts have said that only physicians can testify on the question of insanity, although in *Odem* v. *State* (1911) a witness not medically qualified was admitted to give expert evidence on this issue. Similarly, New Jersey Courts have rejected psychological evidence but in one exceptional case allowed a psychologist to give expert testimony as to whether the idiocy of a child resulted from prenatal radiotherapy (*Stemner* v. *Kline* 1942). Such cases as *Roberts* v. *State (1969)* and *Sandour* v. *Weyerhaeuser C.* (1969) present a formidable body of case law favouring and justifying the admissibility of psychologists to give expert evidence. It should be remembered, further, that the difficulties experienced by forensic psychologists in getting their evidence admitted have usually been because their assumed role of 'medical' witness clashed with that of qualified medical practitioners who were also appearing as experts in the same case. In the case of the role of the scientific witness, the position is likely to be very different.

In the U.K. and U.S.A., forensic psychologists qualify as experts by virtue of their academic and professional qualifications, and their experience, but in many countries the courts have lists of 'approved' experts in the relevant disciplines. Czechoslovakia, France and Mexico were among the first to adopt this system, which has much to commend it, the list itself being drawn up with the aid of the appropriate professional organization. Holland uses an unofficial list, while in many European countries the various professional organizations are asked to provide names of suitable experts. In the U.K. the British Psychological Society performs this function, which is not an exclusive one, but some solicitors prefer to seek out a local psychologist for this purpose. The advantages of having a 'recognized' expert, especially where psychology is concerned, is fairly obvious. Lawyers are generally unaware of the difference in training between members of one branch of applied psychology and those of another. They may prefer a psychologist with a PhD degree to testify on a medical matter, (even if his doctoral thesis was concerned with circadian rhythms in the woodlouse and he has had no clinical training whatsoever), to a well-trained and clinically-qualified Master, merely because the former is called 'doctor'. This leads to situations in court which are detrimental to the profession and to the ill-chosen 'expert' alike. For example, in a recent case involving a complex issue concerning brain damage, the plaintiff supported his plea by evidence from a very senior clinical psychologist of many years experience, whose opinion was contested by a prison psychologist devoid of clinical qualifications or training, and whose own professional background and experience were quite inappropriate to the matters in issue. Faced with his very first case of this type, he could not but make himself appear inept and incompetent, and brought discredit to himself and to his own specialty. On a criminological issue he no doubt would have done credit to his specialty by utilizing his expertise, here his client suffered through the mistake in selecting him. The use of approved lists of experts and recommendations avoids such situations. British lawyers not uncommonly adopt a blunderbuss approach, sending a circular round to the psychology department of universities and to other psychologists recommended to them, indicating briefly the nature of the indictment and soliciting help from any one prepared to support their client's case. This again has the disadvantage of catching a variety of unsuitable fish in the net, although the more careful solicitors check up on the status and credentials of their volunteer forensic army before short-listing them for final casting as experts. The short-listing is necessary, because although English law imposes no limit on the number of experts called by either party, the courts have discretionary power to limit or exclude repetitive or irrelevant expert evidence. In some countries, a maximum number of experts admissible is laid down varying from two in Norway to five in Canada, although the latter may be increased with the leave of the court.

The role of the psychologist as expert witness has also extended into the quasi-judicial proceedings by Government bodies created by statute, for example, Mental Health Tribunals, although here again the American scene reveals a significant degree of advancement in comparison with other countries. In the United States, psychologists give expert testimony in a wide range of administrative agency settings, and Kolasa emphasizes the fact that the quasi-judicial agencies are becoming more active and important in determining individual and social outcomes than ever before[170].

The use of experts by international tribunals has also become well-established in the present century. It has been common practice to confer upon international tribunals express power to call upon independent experts and to order enquiries and investigations of various kinds, and this practice is reflected in provisions in the Hague Convention of 1907. Similar provisions appear in instruments setting up the various tribunals and mixed commissions in the period since the end of World War II to the present day.

The Bias of the Expert Witness
Many psychologists dislike the idea of giving evidence in court. Some dislike the adverse publicity which usually follows, irrespective of whether one is defending the saints or sinners. Others dislike the thought of public exposure of some aspect of their professional incompetence—we all have our Achilles heel. The case of *U.S.* v. *Kent* (1964) is a dreadful confirmation of the fears of many psychologists that

their mumbling efforts under cross-examination will be placarded in ego-disintegrating detail in some journal of international reputation and world-wide circulation. Others again fight shy of court work because of the excessive amount of time wasted. It is not uncommon in a long-drawn out case to travel to court by appointment on one day but not be called until the next, or even the day after that. Court work spells death to any professional appointments system. However, it could be argued that the psychologist like every other citizen, has a moral duty to assist the course of justice, and if he possesses knowledge, experience and skills which can contribute to the processes of the law he should be prepared to make them available to those in most need of them. Where some are reluctant to become expert witnesses, others rush in with gay abandon, venturing on ground where even angels fear to tread, only too anxious to savour yet another professional experience, to receive a little transitory limelight, or to save one more far-from-innocent head from today's well-padded and non-lethal block. Szasz[122] asks why a physician wishes to testify in a court of law at all: 'What prompts him in his desire to testify, and what conscious and unconscious gratification does he receive from doing so'? Szasz feels this to be a very important question for scientific psychiatry and it is clearly one that the forensic psychologist must face, since the same considerations may well apply. Bertrand Russell's concept of social power may possibly be relevant here; Szasz at least believes the desire to gain power over man is an unquestionably relevant consideration. Psychologists, especially clinicians who habitually haunt the humanistic or 'soft' end of their professional continuum—the 'brass-knob psychologists' being at the other, will probably ask themselves different questions and proffer different answers. This is of more than passing importance, because the motivation of the expert witness determines to some extent the degree of bias he shows towards the party who calls him, and away from the opposing party. Functioning purely as a scientist, of course, the question of bias should be irrelevant, for the expert is examining facts and giving an opinion on them. Yet we know from our professional studies that freedom from bias is impossible, even in a scientific laboratory situation. The human brain, teleologically motivated, consciously and unconsciously sifts and selects the sensory inputs that will give it most satisfaction. The emergence of the 'double-blind' technique in drug research is evidence enough of our inability to be as impersonal as automata. We cannot always be as skilful as the psychiatrist whose objectivity was challenged by prosecuting counsel when he was asked 'Would you tell the court if there is any chance because the defendant has paid your fee that your testimony may be biased'. The expert witness, instead of denying possible bias as so many do on similar occasions replied: 'Certainly. It is impossible not to be biased in some way about most things. It has been written: "Whose bread I eat, his songs I sing". Being very much aware of this I try to be even more cautious than usual and do my best to be sure that my bias is not interfering with my clinical judgement"[171]. Despite his protestation to the contrary, his clinical judgment would be affected by his bias, albeit in very subtle ways which would not be readily apparent. Nevertheless, it is a good answer which strengthens his case and gives the court confidence in his opinions. The fact that virtually every writer on the subject of expert testimony cautions against bias shows how ubiquitous this tendency must be (see Bib 171–74). Bias has at least two detrimental effects. Firstly it produces an ego-involvement with the outcome, so that the success or failure of the client's case becomes in some way reflected upon the psychologist. In order to defend his ego, therefore, the expert is under some pressure to make the best of what evidence he has—prompted at times by the lawyers engaging him whose duty it is to do their best in the client's interests. One case arose after a schoolboy was injured while playing on a railway line. For the purposes of litigation the child was psychologically tested shortly after the accident by psychologists for both plaintiff and defendant, and found to be intellectually very low and well below that predicted from the school history and records. On retesting 15 months later by the psychologist called for the plaintiff, the boy's intelligence was found to be normal. The plaintiff's lawyer asked the psychologist to suppress the report of the second psychological examination, and went to the length of suggesting that the psychologist should write a letter saying she would be out of the country on the date set for the hearing, in order to avoid having to communicate to the court the substantial improvement in the child's intelligence. With such overt encouragement towards partisanship, the psychologist can be faced with an embarrassing and almost impossible task of trying to avoid bias. As a result, he ends up in grave danger of overplaying his hand, and producing in court a strong unequivocal opinion which cannot be validly supported and under cross-examination breaks down to reveal the facts for the poor creatures they are. In Sirham's case, for example, the jury was cautioned that the psychologist's theory was 'an absurd, preposterous story, unlikely and incredible' which raised 'the gravest problems of clinical proof and credibility'. Fortunately for the reputation of forensic psychology, the prosecutor aimed at the wrong target when he said in his closing address: 'I have heard that Charles Dickens wrote in a book that the law is an ass. I think the law became an ass when it let the psychiatrist (*sic*) get his hand on it. It would be a frightening thing for justice to decide a case of this magnitude on whether he saw clowns playing pattycake or kicking each other in an inkblot test'[176].

A second consequence of bias is that alternative interpretations on the data become ego-threatening and lead to entrenched positions which move away from centre in order to make their position explicit.

So is born the battle of the experts, said to be one of the most unedifying aspects of forensic psychiatry in which two or more psychiatrists on opposing sides present testimony which appears to be biased to the side on which the expert has been called. Psychiatrists on both sides give contrary interpretations of virtually the same evidence. Sometimes these contradictions arise from the application of the rules of evidence. For example, by the use of the hypothetical question which encourages the development of adversary positions. Often the differences arise from the conscious or unconscious identification on the part of the psychologist or psychiatrist with the party which employs him. The expert should be alert to this natural tendency and most realize their role is that of an impartial expert presenting objective opinions and conclusions irrespective of the party for whom he appears. The natural tendency arises because of the normal relationship between the clinician who is always doing his best for his patient or client. Although psychologists themselves have in England rarely been involved in this battle of the experts, psychologists have been involved in some battles where psychiatrists have been on either side. Sometimes the battle arises from theoretical obscurities and obfuscations. Psychiatry, particularly of the psychodynamic orientation, lends itself to alternative interpretations. The Freudian theory of reaction-formation whereby a person can supposedly be shown to hate a parent either by overt displays of hate or by its disguise as affection, is tailormade for those theoretical disputes in court which at times have reached esoteric heights and left the court feeling like the citizens of Babel after God had bestowed on them 'the confusion of tongues'. Judge Bazelon, that most patient and psychophilic jurist, regards psychiatry as the ultimate wizardry[177]. 'My experience', he writes 'has shown that in no case is it more difficult to elicit productive and reliable testimony than in cases that call on the knowledge and practice of psychiatry'. Even when more than one psychiatrist appears for the same side there is no guarantee of consensus. The old Chinese proverb: 'when in doubt, call in three doctors' does not seem to apply to forensic testimony. Mrs Sofaer, in *Sofaer* v. *Sofaer* (1960), called in three doctors. The question was not whether she knew the nature and quality of her acts, in the terms of the M'Naughton-Rules, but whether she knew that what she was doing was wrong. The psychiatrist called by one side was quite certain she did. He based his opinion on the fact that her expression of regret and promise to behave in future implied knowledge that it was wrong. In came Mrs Sofaer's three doctors. The first one gave as his opinion that her expression of regret merely meant she was taking a turn for the better. The second doctor supposed that it did not follow from an expression of regret that she knew right from wrong, but did show that she knew the impropriety of her acts when they took place. The third doctor explained that a *general* expression of regret could not show an awareness of wrongful *specific* acts. Four psychiatrists, all interpreted a single act sufficiently differently to confuse the court. No wonder Menninger called it 'antiquated scholasticism' and believes that psychiatrists should shun the courtroom: 'I have seen the most ridiculous, totally senseless appearances of psychiatrists in court'[178]. Szasz, another opponent of forensic psychiatry remarks: 'It is unlikely that toxicologists would be tolerated in courts of law if one would observe that he found a large quantity of arsenic in the body of a deceased person, and another stated that he found by the same operation none. Yet this sorry spectacle is common place in regard to psychiatric findings'[122]. Jury studies have shown that juries tend to vote sane when expert evidence is conflicting and also when no expert evidence is given, so in these instances the only effect of the experts is to prolong the trial and burden the taxpayer. The adversary system demands experts to support each side. To do otherwise is contrary to the basic principle that each side must fight to gain its best advantage. In capital crimes it is literally a matter of life and death, and no man blames someone who, in the shadow of the valley, employs the best and most partisan expert his legal advisors can obtain. But things are different in countries where the law is based substantially upon the inquisitorial system. In Germany the expert is selected by the judge himself. In Switzerland the expert is not even 'a witness', but an expert called by the judge to help him assess the technical issues, although the parties may as an exception call their own experts. In almost all European countries the expert is called by the court independently of the parties. In France the investigating magistrate, and in Holland and Norway the court, selects the expert, but will call an expert nominated jointly by both sides in agreement. In Mexico, Costa Rica, and a number of other countries the procedure is very similar. This has led many legal authorities, e.g. Bib 172 and 178–181, to call for a change of procedure so that experts are called by court and independently of either party, although in discussions there are usually strong objections from practising barristers who insist that the accused party is entitled to present all the evidence which will favour his case. At present there are two departures from the adversary situation: the first is where the court remands the accused person for the purpose of having a medical report furnished for the benefit of the court. Usually the court requests that the accused be seen by a psychiatrist, and it is then at the discretion of the latter whether or not the psychologist is asked to contribute. If the intelligence of the accused is in issue, the psychologist will almost certainly be asked to provide the psychiatrist with a quantitative assessment. In such circumstances the psychologist is acting directly on the court's behalf, and the report, whether tendered in the name of the referring psychiatrist or independently above the psychologist's own name, goes direct to the court and not to either the prosecutor or the accused's legal advisor. In some states of the U.S.A.

staff psychologists attached to the legal administration fulfil this function.

A second example of this departure from the adversary situation occurs under the Rules of the Supreme Court which enable the English Courts to appoint an independent expert, who is thereby authorized to carry out whatever tests and experiments he may deem necessary, and to report back to the court with his findings. Many psychologists object to being asked to operate within an adversary procedure, and would prefer to function in such a way that they can present 'scientific truth'. However laudable this position might be, as Kolasa[170] remarks, it sometimes masks an awkwardness in being challenged to be more precise in their statements than would ever be demanded of them in lecture hall or case conference. 'Good lawyers', he continues, 'are curious, probing, and not content to take easy generalities in support of a position', and he suggests that practitioners need to recognize and admit that there are decided limits to the empirical support they can provide. In the USA, when an *amicus curiae* brief is filed, an independent expert can be called as 'friend of the court', and Zilboorg maintains that this is the only condition under which the expert witness should function[182]. The more sceptical believe this to be an impractical ideal. The logical basis for the independent expert is that the prosecution favours guilt and conviction, and the defence favours innocence and acquittal, while the court itself represents the search for truth and justice. Anyone who has read Mildred Savage's damning indictment of the course of justice in one American Murder case[183], will appreciate that truth is not the essential aim of court proceedings in an adversary system such as ours, but rather the convincing of at least ten uncomprehending souls into believing one argument or at least three souls of an alternative one. As far as the medical witness is concerned, as Glover indicates[184] the court is less interested in the state of mind of the offender than in the lack of social responsibility which ensues from it.

20. Forensic Reports

Psychological Reports
THE EXPERT WITNESS can tender his evidence in one of two forms, testimony or documentary evidence; either answering questions on it from the witness box, or tendering it in the form of a report. Frequently he will be asked to do both, when the report which is also used as the basis for the questioning in the first part of his examination in court becomes known as the 'proof of evidence'. In juvenile courts, or magistrates courts sitting to determine 'domestic' issues, the court may ask for a report but not require the psychologist to attend. In such cases the report itself is likely to be undisputed, and the court will be anxious to save the expert time, trouble and expense. It should be remembered that the report must stand on its own feet in court, be fully comprehensive in giving *all* the relevant facts, opinions (and the reason for them) and recommendations. It must also be fully comprehensible, since the psychologist will not be present in court to explain and amplify any techinical terms. The Children's & Young Persons Act (1933), Section 35(2) imposed a duty on the local authority to carry out an investigation and to render to the court information on the home environment, school record, health and character of the offender. In adult criminal cases, too, the court may be satisfied with a report. Perhaps a patient under treatment by the psychologist has committed an offence and the court will wish to know the likely duration of treatment in order to decide whether or not to adjourn the case until the cessation of treatment, or to guide them when considering a custodial sentence.

Reports to the Court
Among the many recommendations made to the Royal Commission on the Penal System in England and Wales by the British Psychological Society, Sections 34 to 38 concern the provision of information to the courts. It is at the discretion of the court to decide exactly how much information they will receive and take into account in determining the degree of culpability ascribed to the offender and in considering the type of sentence to be awarded. The probation officer's report is

frequently taken into consideration in this way and in certain cases the court is required to consider a medical report. But in the majority of cases courts tend to rely upon impressions gleaned from the behaviour of the offender during his trial and from information contained in the statement of antecedents supplied by the police. The reports presented by medical experts and probation officers, etc. reflect their respective areas of professional competence. They are not intended to be expert assessments of the characteristics of the offender as an individual, including his personality, intelligence, temperament, and abilities. Sometimes of course the physicians providing a report for the court may make use of material which has been prepared by psychologists. For example, psychiatric reports frequently include information provided by the clinical psychologist to whom the offender has been referred for specialized examination, and reports from the prison medical officer commonly include the results of intelligence tests administered by prison psychologists. As a general rule, however, the criminal courts do not, in practice, request written reports or verbal evidence from psychologists although the usefulness of such information has been adequately demonstrated in the juvenile courts. The courts are, at the present time, ignorant of the value of psychological reports or indeed of their differentiation from medical reports. The British Psychological Society argues that expert assessment of the characteristics of the offender are not only necessary when some psychiatric abnormality or social maladjustment is present but that such information be made available to the court wherever this is practicable. They point out that the making of an accurate estimate of psychological characteristics is a task of considerable technical difficulty which demands the application of standardized tests and methods of assessment. Evidence is accumulating from several studies of response to treatment by offenders which indicate that quite subtle personality differences play an important part in determining the effectiveness of different or alternative sentences, in the individual case; thus it is argued that the evidence contained in a psychological report is of value not only in determining the possible effects of different sentences but also in estimating culpability. The British Psychological Society conclude that provisions should be made for psychological assessment (as distinct from psychiatric or social assessments) of all offenders or at least of all those who offend more than once. Such assessments should be furnished as routine information in the courts. Anticipating the criticism that this would be too expensive of resources to be contemplated the BPS points out that it is possible to effect considerable economies elsewhere in the penal system. Indeed the psychological assessments play an important part in allocation procedures and therefore are already being undertaken after sentence has been passed. If psychometric data and other material could be obtained in the pre-trial or pre-sentence phase they could also be used for allocation purposes after the offender had been sentenced, in the way they are today.

Requests for reports may come from a variety of different sources. The court itself is empowered to call for reports and these will come via the clerk to the court. By 1971 the remands in custody for reports exceeded 13,000, and to this must be added an even greater number for non-custody individuals. The probation officer or Social Services Department may also approach the psychologist with a request for a report. The solicitors, if they have had contact with a particular psychologist before, may approach him again. In all cases, the enquiry will be one of two types: either it will merely ask for a report, or it will ask a specific question. In criminal cases the former type is the more usual. The referring authority may suspect that the motives behind the offence are not the obvious ones, as in Case No. 12; or they may suspect that there are mitigating factors, such as mental illness or mental subnormality. Occasionally, however, something of the psychological background of the person involved with the law is already known, for many offenders have been before the courts before, and on this occasion the courts are likely to require more specific information regarding possible changes in mental state, likelihood of being able to profit from one form of correction rather than another, and so on.

In civil cases, the issues themselves are specific, and as one would expect the requests to the psychologist will be more specific too. They may concern testamentary capacity, visual or auditory efficiency (could the plaintiff have seen or heard the warning?), nature of the bonds between children and divorcing parents and so on. See for example, Case No. 24. In civil cases it is usual to put all the expert evidence in the report: the expert is then asked to attend court and asked whether the report before the court is his own. On replying in the affirmative, the report is accepted and the expert released from court. In criminal trials this method cannot be adopted because the jury are usually unable to handle professional reports of this nature.

Proof of Evidence

A clinical psychologist usually has submitted to the psychiatrist who referred the patient a 'clinical' report which stands, as regards confidentiality, in the same category as a medical report. This report may be submitted to the solicitor acting for the patient, or by the psychiatrist, as part of the case material submitted as evidence, which may include reports by consultants in other medical specialties, most frequently the neurologist, radiologist, and pathologist. Sometimes the psychologist may be asked by the solicitor to supply a copy of his clinical report direct to the solicitor. As a matter of policy this should not normally be done without the sanction of the medical practitioner to whom the report was addressed. However, should permission be refused for any reason, the psychologist is entitled to prepare another report for the solicitor unless in doing so he goes beyond the terms of his contract of employment.

Frequently, however, the psychologist will be asked to provide a report direct to the solicitors. If the psychologist has no intention of being called to court to give oral testimony, except under the compulsion of a *subpoena duces tecum*, his report will probably follow the lines of a clinical report except that it will be concluded in simple terminology suitable for a lay readership. If the psychologist has been invited to give evidence in court, however, or believes he may be called, his report to the solicitors should take a different form, and be written in a manner appropriate to oral presentation. The psychologist will not be allowed to read the report from the witness box but he should split up the information into short statements suitable for a question-and-answer type of presentation. In this form the report is called a 'proof of evidence' or 'proof' and represents the basic evidential platform of the expert witness. Proofs are usually prefaced with the words: 'Call Dr Blank who will say as follows:' These proofs are most important documents. The lawyers calling for them will rely on them to determine the strength of their client's case. Evidence concerning disability appearing in the proof will be used in the assessment of any damages to be claimed. Counsel will also make use of proofs in order to prepare for the cross examination of witnesses called by the other side. The psychologist must therefore include every fact which may be relevant, but which nevertheless he can substantiate in open court. It is better, both for the psychologist and his client, to omit statements on which he has only weak convictions, rather than have his opinions about these reversed in public. When part of a witness's evidence is discredited in open court, the effect is to discredit the other part as well. Moreover, if an expert witness, when giving evidence, contradicts statements he has made previously, either in the proof or in the witness box, the counsel, in order to salvage what remains of his case, may treat the expert as a 'hostile witness' and discredit him by cross examining him about the statements in question. Counsel is normally not allowed to cross-examine witnesses called by himself, and before doing so must obtain leave from the court. Cross-examination in order to be discredited is so embarrassing and wounding to the *amour propre* that experienced expert witnesses are exceptionally careful in the preparation of their proofs.

Psychologists who are unwilling to appear in court can nevertheless be compelled to do so by the use of a subpoena. However, they can often avoid an unwanted appearance by their response to a request for proof. A prospective expert witness cannot be compelled to give a proof, and since counsel will be unwilling to examine a witness unless he knows in advance the line the expert will follow, refusal to furnish proof is often effective in preventing a court appearance. Similarly, if the evidence in the proof is damaging to the client's case, the lawyers are unlikely to call the witness who has provided such evidence. However, the psychologist should think very carefully before refusing to give proof, since it may prevent the prospective client from obtaining justice. It is, of course, quite ethical to provide a proof which is hostile to the side requesting it, if indeed the evidence is contrary to what the legal advisors expected. The witness must be, above all, completely honest, and if his examination produces facts unhelpful to his client he must say so (Case No. 25).

The furnishing of proof does not always lead to an appearance in the witness box. In criminal cases, the prosecutor has no access to all the defence proofs, and may decide that there is insufficient evidence to justify prosecution: the expert evidence may provide just enough reasonable doubt to destroy a *prima facie* case. In a civil case, the proof may be accepted at face value by the opposing side, and be read out in court in the absence of the psychologist. It may also be used as a basis for settlement out of court.

There are, however, two cases where it is justifiable to refuse to give proof. The first is where the clinician feels he has a special responsibility to a patient in terms of e.g. medical confidence, or does not wish to divulge clinical secrets unless forced to do so. This problem is dealt with further in the section on privilege. The second case is where the psychologist's own personal or professional interests are involved. For example, the patient's verbalization during the test programme may imply that the psychologist has acted with some impropriety towards the patient either from the effects of some psychotic thought process or as an hysterical embellishment of the truth. The law permits a witness to refuse to answer any question which might incriminate him, and the expert witness, on this principle, is therefore permitted to refuse proof of evidence containing any matter which would possibly render him criminally or tortiously liable. In such cases, the psychologist should seek legal advice from his own solicitor before taking any action in the matter. The same advice applies to those situations where the psychologist has reason to believe his professional competence may be implicated in the evidence he is asked to give.

Psychological reports, whether tendered formally as a letter, a completed printed form or an entry in the case notes of the patient, when entered as evidence in a court of law, require proof of their identity, and according to regulations pertaining to the documents of the particular hospital, may require the issuing of a *subpoena duces tecum* in order to obtain their production in court. The psychologist may, if the court decides, present his report to the court without taking the oath and this is common practice in courts of petty sessions. Such procedure limits the use of the report unless it is accepted by both parties, and it is therefore more desirable for the psychologist to appear in person as an expert witness if his findings are to be challenged by either side.

It is a legal presumption that all reports were made on the date they bear: although *prima facie* evidence, it can be disproved by evidence to the contrary. Sometimes the date on a report is critical to the issue, in cases of testamentary capacity, for example, and if the date is challenged, the psychologist will have to go to court and give evidence on the correctness of otherwise of the date. If the contesting party has any previous documents, or entries in documents, signed by the psychologist, in which the date can be shown to be incorrect, the psychologist is in a difficult position, and it therefore behoves anyone engaged in forensic work to be meticulous when dating letters, reports, entries, and so on.

In civil cases it is very much in the interests of both parties to agree with the expert reports. This will enable them to avoid the expense of calling experts, and will reduce the time spent in court, involving further saving. The psychologist will therefore need to write his report in civil cases with an eye on possible agreement. For this purpose, it is essential to separate each possibly controversial statement so that they can be agreed or possibly modified individually. In *Eachmo v. Leonard*, the defendants admitted negligence and the medical reports tendered by each party respectively were agreed. The medical reports described the nature of the injuries and both gave a prognosis. There was, however, a difference of opinion regarding the date at which the plaintiff was expected to be fit enough to resume work, one suggesting a date six weeks later than the other. At the hearing the plaintiff protested that he could not start work before the later date, and this then complicated the previously smooth and rapid course of the proceedings. The case eventually went to the court of appeal who ruled that prognosis required to be agreed as a special fact, otherwise it had no greater significance than an intelligent medical estimate. Since forensic psychologists with a background in occupational psychology are being used increasingly in compensation cases to advise on working capacity, this problem has relevance to psychological reports. In this case, had the prognosis been entered on the report as a separate numbered paragraph formal agreement on this issue would not have been overlooked. One other danger which attends agreed reports is that they may provide insufficient material for proof when it comes to the hearing, and this problem has been discussed in some detail elsewhere[162].

Forensic Reports to Psychiatrists

A special problem has arisen in some cases where the psychiatrist has been asked to prepare a report for court, and has then referred the patient to a psychologist for assessment as part of his contractual duties. Under the Criminal Justice Act (1948) Courts of Summary Jurisdiction are empowered to send the offender for observation and report on his mental state, so that the clinical psychologist may see him first as an in-patient. In numerous cases the psychologist has not been informed that the information is for judicial purposes, the psychiatrist assuming perhaps that this information is irrelevant or likely to bias the report, and the psychologist therefore tendered a report designed to provide the best possible advice regarding the patient's clinical needs. Such needs are not necessarily congruent with the patient's best interests in connection with his court appearance and immediate future. At best, the psychologist's recommendations may be irrelevant, as when he suggests treatment for a patient likely to incur a custodial sentence where no provision for such treatment could be made; at worst, the information could be of grave disservice to the patient. Even if the psychologist is told that the patient is appearing in court, there is no control which the psychologist can exercise over his report once tendered to the referring psychiatrist, and the contents can, and often are, suitably edited in the form most acceptable to the psychiatrist before being embodied in his own report; this is usually done quite innocently, the psychiatrist believing he has every right to use additional information to supplement his own examination. This problem has been discussed earlier under hearsay: it emphasizes the importance of not carrying out assessments of patients without adequate knowledge of the context of the referral as well as the background of the patient, and all too many psychology departments still work automatically in processing written referrals in this way without further consultation with the referring authority and relevant enquiries of the patient. This unfortunate practice and sometimes even intentional misuse of psycho-logical reports has led some psychologists to refuse absolutely to supply information to psychiatrists for court purposes. Such a reaction, understandable as it is, promotes further interprofessional disharmony, is possibly contrary to the psychologist's contractual obligations, and may not be helping the patient at the centre of it all. One effective method is to have printed on the report form a statement to the effect that the contents of the report are copyright and must not be conveyed to a third party without the permission of the signer. A rubber stamp bearing this message can be used if only selective use is made of this caution. The psychologist should, however, ascertain that his condi-tions of employment do not override his copyright in this respect. Many employing authorities own the copyright of all documents made on their headed notepaper or as part of the duty of the document signer. Another precaution which has been adopted is to have on the report a statement saying that the contents of the report may only be conveyed in toto to third parties and then only with due acknowledgement of the source. This is one that is suitable in those cases where the copyright is not the property of the psychologist.

Psychological Reports

Each psychologist will draw up his report for the court in his own way but it should be both concise, accurate and completely understandable to a lay man. Dr Sir Norwood East's court reports were always regarded as a model of forensic writing. His reports were subdivided under five heads, the first a preamble which gave the general steps adopted to arrive at the opinion, which gave the dates when the accused was seen and the number of interviews and also from whom information concerning the accused had been received. The second section was the family history relevant to the mental state which also stated from where the information had been derived. The third section concerned the personal history and a special note was made of corroboration between the personal history and any material points. Fourthly an account of the physical and mental condition of the accused and the progress of the case and the actual indications of mental state were given. Finally, the last section comprised the considered opinion regarding the mental state and its implications for the case being considered[185]. This layout is probably suitable as the basis for any report, remembering that it really refers to general requests rather than reports on specific problems, but with appropriate modification could serve equally well for the latter. Simpson[136] suggests a not dissimilar style, proposing as contents: (i) mention of the authority for the examination, for instance, 'Acting upon your instructions, I have examined. . .' (ii) name and age of the subject examined, including the age at the time of the occurrence which led to the court proceedings, (iii) place and date of the examinations, and the names of any persons present, (iv) a summary of the relevant history, and any statements made by the subject during the course of the examinations, (v) the present symptoms, and signs observed on clinical examination, (vi) a summary of observed facts and the inferences drawn from them, such as a diagnosis, and (vii) assessment of loss of function and prognosis.

The report will clearly have to be adapted to provide most completely but relevantly the information requested. It will vary slightly depending upon its recipient: if going to a Coroner's Court it will be going to either a medically or legally qualified person. A civil action in the High Court is unlikely to have a jury, so the level of communication can be set higher than a report for the Crown Court where a jury will have to make sense of it, or for the Magistrates' Court, where it may have to be read and understood by an elderly prudish spinster easily embarrassed by references to sexual matters. Apart from the level at which the report should be written, different courts obviously require somewhat different types of information. The problem as posed to oneself should be stated first, since it indicates the main directions of study by the expert and immediately establishes the relevance of the investigation to the issues before the court. The forensic scientist's gambits are models for this type of introductions: 'I examined the bloodstain on exhibit number seven to determine whether or not it was human blood', or 'I compared the markings on the bullet removed from the deceased, exhibit J, with those on three bullets fired from the pistol entered as exhibit L, in order to determine whether the bullet which proved fatal had been fired by the pistol in question'. Notice that the forensic scientist, in his introduction, does not merely state *what* he did but *why* he did it. The forensic psychologist in introducing his proof, should similarly state the reason for his investigation, e.g. 'I measured the intelligence of the plaintiff for the purpose of evaluating his potential earning power'.

A comprehensive psychometric examination, when undertaken, furnishes the psychologist with much of the required information about the client, but not all the information desired by the psychologist will be relevant to the issues before the court. The psychometric data can therefore be grouped into three categories, the first containing information which the psychologist needs as background to the case but which is not relevant to the problems he seeks to solve. It may contain data on personality variables not of immediate concern but which nevertheless assist the psychologist in filling in the picture he is building up of the testee. In this category will also come the protocols of projective tests, such as the Rorschach, Thematic Apperception Test, and the Object Relations Technique, which are often invaluable in revealing thought content, motivation, and other factors of psychological, but not usually of judicial, relevance. One other addition to this first category will be data obtained for research purposes. The psychologist may believe a certain psychometric instrument is of value in providing evidence germane to some particular legal issue, but wishes to validate it on a sample of accused persons or litigants before entering the findings in the proof.

The second category will contain data which are relevant to the case but not directly relevant to the issue on which the forensic psychologist is intending to express opinion. This category will include background psychometric material which will not be used in the preparation of the proof but which may be needed to bolster up the psychologist's case in the cross-examination. This category may also include data from projective material but unlike that in category one, this data may have to be entered as evidence. It must therefore pass the appropriate tests of a scientific datum. When using projective tests for forensic purposes it is important that the need for two levels of test data be kept in mind: usually both quantitative (objective) and qualitative (subjective) data can be obtained from the same test. For example, the author sometimes uses the Rorschach with the free association method to provide background information for category one and then introduces, in the testing limits phase, O'Reilly's Objective Rorschach method which provides numerical data of relevance to category two and occasionally even category three, e.g. *R.* v. *Bouzagio* (1980). The second category will also contain data which will not be introduced by the forensic psychologist but which may be required if the cross-examining counsel widens the area of discussion in order to probe any weakness in the psychologist's case or to demonstrate his professional incompetence. In this category will go details of the client's intelligence, for example, even when this is not relevant to the problem as the psychologist sees it: the medical witnesses called by the other side may well have made some estimate of the intelligence of the person concerned and include this as part of their case. The forensic psychologist's own counsel may then want data in rebuttal—often obtained by *sotto voce* whisperings in the courtroom during his cross examination of the medical witness raising the issue. A prompt concise and authoritative statement on the intelligence of the person concerned may make a substantial difference to the weight assigned to the particular testimony. The psychologist, who in such circumstances, professes ignorance of the facts requested by his counsel, on the grounds that such information was irrelevant to his own investigation, may be acting in a logical and scientific way, but does a disservice to his client and to the course of justice. It is not enough for the forensic psychologist to pursue his investigation in a single-minded way on the basis of terms of reference imposed by himself. He will have been called in to help the court by providing evidence of a psychological nature, and he should therefore anticipate the needs of the court in this respect.

The third category of data will be the facts which fall within the area of the problem to which the psychologist has addressed himself. These are the facts he will present in court and on which his considered opinion will be based. These facts will be entered in the proof, and will be closely scrutinized and probably challenged by the other side. They must be judicially, psychologically and scientifically relevant. They must also be admissible, for however relevant they might be, if they are not admissible they cannot be entered as evidence. The author's first appearance in court as a forensic psychologist was occasioned by the fact that his report on the accused, charged with attempted murder, was tendered by a psychiatrist as part of his own proof, and held to be inadmissible on the grounds of hearsay. The rules of hearsay have been discussed at length earlier, but these are not the only grounds of inadmissibility. For example, the forensic psychologist may enter proof that the accused's behaviour was consistent with an hypoglycaemic attack. He cannot state the logical corollary that the accused was mistakenly deemed to be drunk (if the charge is one involving the concept of drunkenness) since the issue of whether or not the accused was drunk, is for the court to decide. The expert witness should never trespass into the province of the court in this way. Normally, counsel are quick to seize upon any infringement of the rules of admissibility and will immediately raise an objection, but in the lower courts the solicitors may be rather less familiar with the finer points of evidential law and often fail to draw the attention of the magistrates to infringements of this type. Even experienced Q.C.'s are not immune to this failure and in the Oz trial the judge drew attention to this breach in his summing up. This point will be discussed later. Thus although the expert witness, when entering proof for a Crown Court hearing, can usually rely upon one or other of the counsels to question any possible basis for inadmissibility, this will not always be the case, and the forensic psychologist should therefore be sufficiently conversant with the rules of evidence to be able to determine whether or not his own evidence is admissible.

It has been suggested that 'expert evidence would be most useful to the court if it followed the form and sequence of a medical paper for a learned journal but with sufficient explanation and simplicity of language to make it comprehensible to the author's unqualified maiden aunt'[233]. As a general rule this is admirable, but not all psychological evidence can be framed in this way. Where the forensic psychologist is presenting himself as a clinician this principle can certainly be adopted. Technical terms should be avoided wherever possible: if they *have* to be used they should be carefully but simply defined. The most convenient way of doing this is by the use of a subordinate clause, e.g. '. . . is endogenous, by which I mean "originating from inside the person, and unrelated to environmental influences" '. It is always better to use the clausal expression and delete the technical term unless it is necessary to conform to the usage of a supporting or other document. Gibbens gives some good examples of what can be done in simplifying technical language: 'fights against recognizing that' or 'is unable to bring himself to contemplate' is better than saying 'repressed'; 'behaves like a boy of 13' is better than calling him 'immature'[186].

When framing the report it should state at whose instance the clinician is acting, and where and when the examination was carried out. If information from other persons for example police reports, history from the lawyers, or medical case notes, have been supplied it should be stated that these have been supplied before giving details of one's own observations.

The purpose of the examination should also be stated and at the end of the report it should make quite plain the professional status of the report writer. Whenever doubts occur in the presentation these should be clearly expressed as should also one's qualifications of the evidence. It is quite reasonable to talk in terms of probability rather than certainty. On the other hand one's duty to both the client and the court demands that where statements can be made in a qualitative way they should be made in such a manner.

As regards length, reports for judicial purposes should be neither too long nor too short. Obviously their length will reflect the amount of information they have to convey. Reports to the court are always considerably shorter than proofs of evidence, which may contain very many pages. Countries which follow the inquisitorial system usually insist on long reports, since they are interested in collecting *all* information relevant to both crime and to all the suspects. In European countries reports consisting of two dozen closely typed sheets of A4 paper are commonplace. In Magistrates Courts, the justices have to read the report through carefully while the accused is before them. A long report produces an equally long and embarrassing silence whilst it is being read, and the psychological effect is for it to be read hastily. Magistrates can frequently be seen skipping through long reports or going straight to the conclusions and recommendations. Less than one whole side can be considered too short, and more than two sides in general too long. Remembering the circumstances under which it is being read, psychologists can help by breaking the report up into very short paragraphs with subheadings in upper case typeface. Bartholomew argues that the very nature of psychiatric reports and recommendations makes it difficult to be brief[187], but if one looks at the practicalities of the situation which faces the magistrates in considering disposal, a moment's reflection will convince the psychologist that much of what he would like to say really belongs in the context of an ideal world, and probably only one of his recommendations is at all realistic. By narrowing down the field of alternatives in a realistic way he can thus make his report shorter, more meaningful and have greater impact. In making recommendations for disposal, of course, it is worse than useless to counsel the impossible. The court will then correctly surmise that the psychologist knows little about how offenders are dealt with after conviction and assume that the psychologist's appraisal is similarly out of touch with reality. A recommendation for psychotherapy at Grendon Underwood—which is only available to prisoners with two or more years custodial sentence to serve—in a report on an accused person whose offence carries a six months maximum custodial sentence is of no help to the bench and merely weakens their regard for professional advisors. A recommendation made by one psychologist that the female offender should receive behaviour therapy in prison was similarly unrealistic, when not only was this type of therapy not then available in any prison, but negotiations for its introduction had reached an extremely delicate stage which could have been set back substantially had the opposers of behaviour therapy in prison assumed that this meant that the psychologists had taken their victory for granted. Industrial peace has been shattered by considerably less ham-fisted actions. In making recommendations, the psychologists should beware of being hoist by their own petard. In Case No. 12, the author had been called to court in London to explain the treatment he had recommended to the offender who was now in prison. After deciding to allow the prisoner to have treatment, the court ordered the handcuffs to be struck off the prisoner, and that he be placed forthwith in the care of the author—who then had the responsibility of conveying him 70 miles by public transport and getting him admitted as an in-patient.

In preparing reports for criminal courts, there are three things the court needs to know: (1) What practical steps can the court take, i.e., is the accused treatable or not, does he need in-patient or out-patient care and so on. (2) How should disposal be effected?—can the psychologist personally offer treatment and when? Is a bed available in hospital or Part III accommodation? Does the psychologists' hospital or community services offer residential accommodation, temporary or otherwise? Has the psychologist making the recommendation got the backing of a medical colleague qualified as 'responsible medical officer' for the purposes of an observation and treatment order under the Mental Health Act? Does the psychologists' employing authority receive into care patients on Section 60 and Section 65 orders?—not all do. (3) What is the justification for the recommendation? Why does the offender require treatment? Is his treatable condition so closely related to the offence that if untreated he is likely to repeat the offence? How effective will the treatment be in preventing a repetition of the offence?

In the days when aversion therapy, usually using electric shocks, was commonly used to treat offenders, especially sex offenders, many psychologists negotiated for the exclusive use of hospital beds for this purpose, so that it was a relatively simple matter to offer the court immediate in-patient facilities under the appropriate Mental Health Order. Where offenders are considered aggressive or sexual assaultive, the courts are reluctant to allow them at liberty even with directions for treatment as part of their probation, and the aversion therapy bed was a satisfactory compromise between protecting the community and offering the offender some positive form of help. With the reduction in psychiatric beds and the funds which supported them, the position is becoming more difficult and the problems of offering realistic help in reports to the court has been correspondingly reduced. The permanence of a psychological report is not often considered. A copy of it will be in the hospital case notes, waiting to effect the diagnosis on the next admission. Another copy may be in the solicitor's file, perhaps to be offered as evidence in a future offence, for which it is largely irrelevant, on the basis of the Presumption of Continuance. Yet another copy is likely to have accompanied court papers into the prison records, where it may be used, possibly many years later, by the Parole Board to help decide whether the prisoner is still a risk to society. The psychologist who produced the report is not of course responsible for its misuse, and may justifiably argue that it was produced for a particular recipient and for a particular purpose. Nevertheless, it is incumbent upon the report-writer to ensure that his report is understandable to all who might have legitimate access to it, and to qualify any statements which refer to transitory conditions by reference to the possibility of temporal changes. Not without some justification, Rollin, speaking of psychologists, complained that he found 'their bland test results not particularly helpful'. He believes the IQ tests have fallen from grace as a yardstick of anything except what a particular test measures, and 'as for the so-called projective tests the results are so often expressed in jargon as to be incomprehensible'. Psychologists will recognize this as an indictment more of their reporting skills than of the usefulness of psychometric instruments.

21. Pre-trial Preparation

IT HAS been suggested that expert witnesses do better if they know nothing of the legal issues involved, beyond the terms of reference of their own evidence. The suggestion seems to be that witnesses are more likely to remain free from bias if they know nothing of the case beyond their immediate professional horizons. A further argument in favour of this, is that the experimental approach to the problem differs according to the context in which the results are to be set: the less the expert knows of the context, so the argument runs, the more uncontaminated will be the results, and the more 'pure' the experimental design. Furthermore, it is maintained by the protagonists of this theory that the expert is more efficient, more scientific, under examination and cross examination, when he has no prior knowledge of the legal issues outside of his own area of competence.

Simpson[136] regards this theory as completely untenable and points out that a knowledge of the special requirements of the law in a particular case gives an examination and report a special purpose. Indeed, it is truer to say that the more law the psychologist knows, and the more information about the particular case he obtains, the more satisfactorily he can perform his duties in court and hence the better he serves the interests of justice.

The preparation of a case for court requires the fullest possible knowledge relevant to the client, the brief, and the legal issues that can possibly be obtained. This has advantages: (1) It enables the psychologist to anticipate possible questions, and prepare an answer to them in advance: this is obviously very much more effective than giving some off-the-cuff statement which in retrospect one may well regret. (2) It enables the psychologist to assess the possible alternative interpretations which the other side will put upon the client's behaviour or the test results. (3) It provides complete scope for examining possible areas of psychological investigation and experiment which may not have occurred to the client's lawyers.

For this reason, the psychologist asked to appear in court as an expert witness should obtain copies of all relevant documents—the charge or charges, police statements, defendants' statements, witnesses' statements, medical reports from both sides if available, and especially the reports of the Prison Medical Officer and Prison Psychologist if these have been submitted as evidence.

It must be realized that the examination-in-chief will be guided by the report the psychologist will already have submitted. If he has not actually spoken to the solicitor and/or barrister beforehand, their questions will be limited by the report and by what they believe to be relevant. The psychologist may wish to elaborate on some aspects of his report. He may wish to qualify them verbally. He may wish to expound some theory which he believes to be relevant to the facts in issue. But he will not be allowed to do so except in answer to specific questions. His evidence is limited to the document he has submitted and the questions that are put to him and to which the court does not object. It is therefore essential that the report itself includes *all* the main points the psychologist wishes to make, and also that an opportunity is sought to discuss the report with the solicitor or barrister beforehand.

Consultation

It is preferable for the psychologist to make his desire for a consultation clear to the solicitor as soon as his help has been sought, and where possible he should try and accommodate to the convenience of the barrister and see him in his chambers or at home. All too frequently, the consultations take place pacing up and down some draughty corridor outside the court, or wedged into some corner of the barrister's room, shared with other similarly-occupied couples. In the consultation the psychologist should explain simply what he wants to say. It is often helpful if he intimates to the barrister the sort of questions which would enable him to put his evidence in the best way. For example 'why do you believe his behaviour is not the result of the concussion?' (as affirmed by the opposing side) may be easier to answer than 'why do you believe his behaviour to be due to a pre-existing neurosis?' or, of course, the contrary may be true. The selection of the right sort of questions can immeasurably strengthen the case as put forward by the psychologist, and although the expert is appearing for the court, and in the interests of truth and justice, he also has some moral responsibility to the client paying his fees and expenses and is therefore under an obligation to make his evidence as clear and unambiguous as possible.

Consultation with the advocate, whether it is the solicitor acting in this capacity in one of the inferior courts, or the barrister in the superior courts, should be looked upon as an absolute necessity. It should not be foregone due to lack of time on the part of the advocate and, at least in important cases, or where the expert evidence is contentious, consultation should be insisted upon as one of the qualifications of the expert contributing to the case. There are times when, through unpredictable changes in the timing of cases, the advocate finds himself with two cases being heard simultaneously, or when some witnesses unexpectedly withdraw and when experts due to be called later have to be brought forward, but these should be considered exceptional circumstances.

Many forensic scientists complain that consultation with the leading counsel is rare, and that they are usually fobbed off with a quick talk with the junior on the benches outside the court, or even with the solicitor, so that emphases of opinion the expert wishes to convey, or the qualifications he wishes to make, neither of which can be adequately expressed on paper, have to be conveyed to the advocate second, or even third hand. In such an adversary system this clearly places justice at a great disadvantage if the expert cannot do the best with his information.

At the time of telephoning to make the appointment with the advocate, the latter should already have been in receipt of the forensic psychologist's report, or else a proof, provided via the solicitor, and he may even have read it. This should allow the psychologist to indicate the main points he would like to discuss, and also to ascertain from the advocate which special form of attack the other side will use. Sometimes the psychologist can be forearmed by knowing who will be the witness opposed to him. Frequently, at least in London or large provincial courts, he will be of some eminence, probably with an academic appointment, and possibly the author of a relevant textbook. The psychologist can therefore assess in advance his views, and may find advantage in quoting relevant passages from his opponent's previous writings.

At the interview itself, it is useful to provide a list of questions which the expert witness believes would best elicit the information he has to impart. The advocate may not use them all, indeed he may not use any of them, and if he does so they may be in a different order than that originally chosen by the psychologist. Nevertheless, it is helpful in making explicit to the advocate the kinds of questions the psychologist feels qualified to answer. Even barristers and solicitors who have worked with psychologists frequently do not have a very clear idea of the scope of psychology. Their ideas come mainly from their practical experience with psychologists in particular cases, and is therefore likely to be limited to these cases. The questions should be phrased to provide a reasonably comprehensive answer. They should be of the open-ended type rather than eliciting only a 'yes' or 'no'. The advocate will also have questions to ask the witness, some of which are unanswerable, or difficult to answer without considerable explanation or qualification, and the psychologist can help the advocate by suggesting ways in which these can be rephrased. Sometimes the advocate will suggest questions which the psychologist will not wish to answer in the way the advocate obviously wishes, and this should be made clear at the time. Pragmatic arguments will, from time to time, be put forward as to why it is better to come down decisively (on the side favoured by the advocate) rather than confuse the jury by expressing doubt or qualification. Whilst unnecessary indecision helps no one—much less the profession and the status of science, the expert witness should never go beyond the limits of the degree of certainty he places on his facts and inferences. If the advocate wants a clear unequivocal response and the psychologist is unable to provide one in the direction required, then the answer must lie unequivocally the other way. That is, the psychologist can offer to be decisive and say that in his opinion the evidence does not adequately support the client's case.

Apart from discussing the manner of presentation, the consultation should be a fact-getting session from both advocate and expert. The former will want to supplement information already in hand, to have points in the report or proof explained in more detail, to have technical misconceptions cleared up, and to obtain a provisional opinion on the other expert evidence as far as is known. If a psychologist is appearing for the other side, the advocate will want to know his professional reputation, field of expertise, and scope of his technical writing. It is not uncommon for an expert witness to go into the witness box and see the cross-examining counsel with copies of all the witness's publications in front of him, a profusion of bookmarks indicating his own published statements which are going to be used against him. Advocacy, at the Bar, is a game of logical, verbal and thespian skills, at least to the participants, if not to the spectator in the dock, and all being fair in love and war, the psychologist need not feel he is being unprofessional by revealing what he knows of his opponent's Achilles heel. In making photocopies of the relevant papers by the opposition expert, the lawyers will, on request, provide copies for their own experts, so this is of great benefit in making adequate preparation for the cross-examination.

If the case is an important one, and the preparation is going to be attenuated, a number of conferences may be necessary, using these to shape the course of subsequent interviews with the client, providing feedback of the expert's examinations, experiments, or bibliographic researches which he is making during this period. A good conference is always worth while, and although, when time presses, or the client's funds are limited, this has to be fitted in within the purlieus of the court, or over a pre-trial dinner, the forensic psychologist should attempt to have an 'office' conference whenever possible, where papers can be spread over a table, notes made in an easy way, and the milieu is conducive to concentration and serious thought.

Conferences with counsel are necessary, ethical and legal[188]. If the cross-examining counsel asks the expert in the box if he has discussed the case (or his results) beforehand, he should say with great certainty: 'Of course'. Often the witness is surprised at the unexpectedness of the question, and sometimes it is put in such a way that suggests that the expert should not have done so. In these circumstances it is easy to become uncertain and flustered and with a weak and hesitant admission the jury may then think that the expert testimony has been a put-up job. The cross-examining counsel is then on a heads-I-win-tails-you-lose ploy, for if the expert admits to pre-trial discussion in this way, the jury sense a vague discredit and if he denies any pre-trial discussion the cross-examiner will make profit out of his lack of adequate preparation. The only satisfactory response to this gambit is the strong affirmative answer tinged with surprise that the cross-examiner should ask such a question. This again emphasizes the value of being prepared for the question that will be put to the expert in the box. Some of these will be discussed later under cross examination. As Louisell[189] says: 'the prudent psychologist will, before taking the stand, carefully explain to the lawyer of the party invoking his services what he can and what he cannot state under oath. He will be candid in acknowledging the degree of certainty with which he holds his opinions. He will be frank to admit the limitations of his speciality or his own expertise within it. He will be, at once, confident but not cocksure, proud of his profession but humble in his awareness of human limitations.'

22. Forensic Portfolio

As NOTED previously, the forensic psychologist can take with him into court any notes or books relevant to his evidence with which to refresh his memory. The court does not expect the expert to remember every detail of those aspects of the case on which he will be examined, and therefore permits him to refer to original sources. However, the court does expect the expert to be reasonably *au fait* with the general details of the case and the major relevant facts, such as the date of the offence, or accident, the dates on which the client was seen for forensic purposes, and where, and so on. An expert who has to consult his notes to answer every simple question of fact soon gives the impression that he knows little about the case and has even less interest in it.

Documents used to refresh the memory

For many years, the witness has been permitted to refresh his memory from documents, e.g. *Maugham* v. *Hubbard* (1801) and this common law rule was later embodied in the 1938 Evidence Act. The forensic psychologist, when called to the witness box to give evidence, may take with him any document to refresh his memory, even if the document itself is inadmissible as evidence, provided that (1) it was written within his own knowledge and he believes it to be a correct representation of the facts contained therein, or (2) that it was written by himself contemporaneously with or soon after the events recorded (a log book inspected by a superior, one week after the relevant entry, has been accepted for this purpose, Anderson and Wheeley (1852)). Thus, the psychologist when a witness to fact, may refer to his own interview notes and psychometric data, to hospital case notes provided the entries are recent and he knows the medical officer or nurse who made the entries, to notes made by other psychologists in the department at the time, or to letters, diaries or other writings by a patient under his care. The latter are particularly useful as primary evidence in cases of tort since the contents often demonstrate the patient's attitude towards the psychologist and his particular method of treatment.

When the psychologist is appearing as an expert witness, he may, in addition to the above, take with him documents with which to refresh his memory as to scientific facts, as well as documents by accepted authorities to supplement, complement or otherwise substantiate his own opinions.

The expert witness should prepare a portfolio containing all the information he is likely to need to take into the witness box with him. He may need certain original documents, such as the hospital case notes, or a casebook, or a treatment file belonging to the psychology department or community clinic. If he is present under a writ of *subpoena duces tecum* he will have to take all the documents enumerated on the form. This may be in an open form such as 'all medical data relating to the plaintiff' which the forensic psychologist should interpret with care. Since 1824, once taken into court, all documents become available to the other side, so the expert should be *very* circumspect as to what accompanies him into the box. The basic question should be: 'Do I want the cross-examining counsel to see this data in this form?' More often than not, the answer will be 'no', and this suggests that the forensic portfolio should contain *all* the data (because the witness will swear or affirm that he intends to tell *inter alia* the *whole* truth) which has been put in a form which will be most effective for the expert and produce least damage to the client if used by the opposition. The documents should include one sheet bearing all the relevant dates down one side in chronological order, with the relevant occurrence in brief by the side. The sheet, like all the others, should be in large clear script or typed in capitals so that easy reference can be made to the data even when flustered. Note that being chronological, some dates will have been inserted before the file on the client was actually raised by the psychologist. A typical data-sheet is shown in Figure 4.

The importance of having times correct and readily to hand—and knowing the important ones by heart, has been amply demonstrated in a number of cases. Simpson[136] describes a hearing in a Coroner's Court where the witness, a house surgeon, was called to give evidence. He had already been warned that he would be asked only three questions viz. time of admission, action undertaken by himself, and time of death. He arrived in court without any notes or records, and then had to admit he 'couldn't say' at what time the patient was admitted! The Coroner had no such restraints on what *he* could say to the witness for treating the court so casually!

Sometimes the expert witness makes mistakes in dates, not because he is too casual and cannot be bothered to prepare himself adequately, but because he is so concerned to get the essentials right, that he forgets the inessentials. But the court insists on accuracy, and comes to believe that if the witness can make mistakes in minor matters he could do so in major ones as well. Thus in the notorious case of *R. v. Haigh* (1949), the eminent psychiatrist for the defence said he had seen the prisoner five times.

Forensic Portfolio

FOLIO NO.: 1971/63

CASE: REGINA	VERSUS: MICHAEL GEORGE

Other parties joined in pleadings/indictment: NONE

RETAINING SOLICITORS: HOLMES, CAMPBELL & CO.
For the attention of: MR. CAMPBELL
Telephone number: 090.64.4433
Address: ARUNDEL ROAD, LITTLEHAMPTON

CLIENT: M.G.R.
Telephone number: -
Address: CHISWICK, LONDON W.4.

COURT: COURT OF APPEAL (CRIMINAL DIVISION)

JUDICIARY. STEPHENSON, LORD J., THOMPSON, J., BRIDGE, J.

COUNSEL: FOR: R. ANELAY for R. HAYWARD-SMITH
         AGAINST:

LEGAL AID AGREED: YES | HEARING COMMENCED: 26.X.71 | REFERRAL DATE: 6.V.71

FORENSIC PROBLEM PRESENTED:
GROUNDS FOR APPEAL AGAINST SENTENCE (ONE YEAR IMPRISONMENT AND SUSPENDED
SENTENCE OF 3 YRS.)

SUMMARY OF CASE:
SEE FOLIO 1971/24   MAGISTRATES COURT
& FOLIO 1971/30
APPEALING AGAINST SENTENCE ON GROUNDS OF SUITABILITY AND AVAILABILITY OF INPATIENT
                                                    BEHAVIOUR THERAPY

SUMMARY OF INVESTIGATION.
NONE SINCE THOSE FOR TRIAL HEARINGS   SEE FOLIOS 1971/24 & 30

SUMMARY OF REPORT:
NO NEW REPORT.   SEE ORIGINAL D/D 10.V.71

Qualifying Time: 2½
Attendance Time: 6½
Reporting Time: -
Disbursements: FARES £6   LUNCH £1

SOA Sent: 31.X.71 £15 | Reminders sent: - | File closed: 5.XI.71

Figure 4a

Sample data sheet: obverse

PROGRESS SHEET

SUB: R. v.   REF: 1971/63

Date	Action	Date	Action
18.V.71	WEST SUSSEX SENT.^{D} 12/12 HMP FOR DRIVING WHILE DISQUAL. (+ 3 YRS. SUSP. SENT.) 32nd CONVICTION	30.I.72	A.T. TERMINATED
		31.I.72	D/C HOME OP. θ x 1/52 → OCT.
12.VII	SOLIC. REQ. SUPPORT FOR APPEAL	13.II.	"SUNDAY PEOPLE"- FULL REPORT BY LEN ADAMS. NO ADV. KN. OF THIS.
13.VII	DR. B.H. VAWDREY AGREES TO ADMIT TO SUMMERSDALE HOSPITAL	17.III	CAUGHT DRIVING AGAIN! DET. SGT. WILLIAMS VINE ST. POLICE STN. 01 - 734 - 4123
14.VII	LETTER SENT TO APPEALS REGISTRAR		
20.VII.	A.R. ACKNOWLEDGES	20.III	BOW STREET MAGISTRATES CT. REMANDED BRIXTON PRISON. No. 107386.
25.X.	C of A (CD) REQUESTS DIRECT EVIDENCE FROM SELF. 10.30 TUES. 26 OCT. COURT 6 LAW COURTS, STRAND, LONDON.	30.III	LYNN, RELTON & CO. SOLICIT HELP. NEW FOLIO RAISED 1972/12 q.v.
26.X.	ATTEND.^{D} CT. EV. REC'D. SENTENCE QUASHED 3 YRS. PROB.^{N} WITH QUAL:- 12/12 ψ θ I/P S.H. S4. CRIM. JUST. ACT. D/C HMP INTO MY CARE. ADM. S.H. M2 WARD.		
27.X.	A.T. COMMENCED.		

Figure 4b

Sample data sheet: reverse

Attorney-General: You said when you gave your evidence that you had seen the prisoner five times; you had examined him five times. That is not accurate, is it?

Expert Witness: I believe it to be accurate or I should not have said so.

Attorney-General: Look at your notes. When did you see him first?

Expert Witness: I really do not know the dates—between the 1st and 6th July.

The Attorney General then carefully went through all the dates until he finally elicited the fact that the witness had seen the prisoner only three times. He asked the witness if that was correct.

Expert Witness: I am prepared to accept it, and I am sorry to have made a mistake.

Attorney-General: I do not want you to accept anything which is not right. I want you merely to be accurate.

A summary data sheet will similarly show all the data which the psychologist has assembled from which his own inferences and conclusions are drawn and upon which his opinions are based. It is useful to arrange this in three columns, showing source of data, findings, and a measure of the weight the psychologist is prepared to place on these results. In the case of experimental findings these could be in the form of a chance probability value or confidence level; for psychometric test results, a figure derived from the combined co-efficients of validity and reliability could be used. Data from other sources, including symptoms, that is, the patient's own statements about his experiences, could be quantified in terms of how reliable the psychologist believes these statements to be (with reference to malingering, exaggeration, or diffusion over more than one diagnosis for example). The figure may represent no more than the psychologist's honest belief, but by making it both numerate and explicit, it will prevent him from extrapolating his data beyond generally acceptable limits. There will be honest differences of opinion about tests within the profession, and the court will not expect 100% agreement between experts. What the expert needs to possess is positive evidence which is likely to be logically and scientifically superior to any that the opposing experts can offer. Thus opinions are divided about the validity of projective tests, particularly Rorschach Psychodiagnosis.

Very often, however, tests have been shown to have a particular validity with one type of population, or in one type of situation. If this is comparable to the situation in which the forensic psychologist has used the test, then the validating experimental work, when quoted, may be stronger grounds for its use on this special occasion than a long list of experiments invalidating it in more general but less relevant circumstances. When the examination has been extensive, more than one data sheet will be required for this purpose.

Regarding test forms there are two schools of thought. If the documents are to be produced under subpoena, there is little argument, since test forms are usually part of the psychologist's documentation. However, for forensic examinations, many psychologists prefer to use a plain sheet of paper, putting scores or check marks directly down in response to questions given from the appropriate manual, rather than all the verbal responses which could be analyzed in court in possibly irrelevant detail to the discomfiture of both the psychologist and the client. Others use the test form in a conventional way but then transfer the requisite information to a plain sheet and destroy the original by shredding. One of the author's emotionally-disturbed patients had to suffer the trauma of sitting in court while her neighbours in the public gallery, ears like Dumbo, listened to the psychologist being put under a detailed inquisition of why she kept mentioning testicles in a sentence completion test. For what was in all probability a small act of forgetfulness in the supermarket, this woman's psychological punishment of sheer shame and humiliation exceeded anything which the court was empowered to inflict. Needless to say, the author vowed never to take this type of information into court again.

There is, however, an opposite point of view, since some psychologists believe the test data in its entirety should be prepared and available, and that the original test forms, fully completed, should always be taken into the box as part of the psychologist's documentation. From a purely scientific point of view this is a correct and commendable point of view, and in an inquisitorial legal system it could be defended. Even in the accusatorial system, it would still be justified if opposing psychologists were permitted to argue over the interpretations, scoring, conclusions and other judgments which follow the use of a test. But when the test is going to be misused, by being ridiculed rather than criticized on logical or scientific grounds, the former argument is less satisfactory.

The fact that the cross-examining counsel can insist upon the witness explaining how each individual item of the test is scored, and that the whole test then becomes public knowledge and loses its clinical confidentiality, makes one wonder whether the subsequent damage to professional practice is worth the aid to the individual patient.

In *U.S.* v. *Kent*[224], for example, the whole system of scoring the Wechsler was made public, item by item:

Counsel: You asked him: 'What is Winter?' and he stated 'a season of the year'. You gave him a one—why not a two? Isn't winter a season of the year, doctor?

Psychologist: 'Well, again, it is a matter of the norms. A two answer would include 'a cold season of the year'.

Counsel: You asked him: 'What is a slice?' and he said 'to cut'. What is wrong with that? You gave him a one.'
Psychologist: A two answer would include: 'to cut thin' or 'cut into thin pieces'.
and so on . . .

Not only is the test laid bare to the public, but it is made to seem ridiculous, and this would be expected to affect the test-taking attitude of anyone asked subsequently to take the test. For example, a different psychologist being cross-examined on his testing was asked:

Counsel: The fifth question?
Psychologist: 'What does rubber come from?' His answer was 'wood'. I gave him a zero. (He should have said 'trees').
Counsel: Why a zero—aren't trees wood?
Psychologist: Yes, but it doesn't follow that rubber comes from wood!
Counsel: You know where we get wood other than trees?
Psychologist: No.

In one case, (Case No. 29), the author's portfolio was confiscated immediately he entered court by the prosecution. Its contents were photocopied and returned to him, but by lunchtime, further copies were circulating round the Old Bailey and the next day one of the court officials mentioned that half the administrative staff had copies and were busy evaluating their marital state. This was made easier for them by the fact that, as in the Kent case, the prosecuting counsel insisted on going through each item and being told its scoring. In view of the careful control which the National Foundation for Educational Research exercise over the distribution of clinical tests in the UK, the author protested to the judge and pointed out that a professionally confidential test was being publicized needlessly to the detriment of its future use. The judge accepted the author's complaint sympathetically, but said he could do no more than ask the press to exercise their discretion regarding publishing details in their publications. As during the interval that the complaint was being heard, the press had all left for a liquid lunch, the judicial request fell on absent ears. Despite the author's protestations and the reasons given for them, the prosecuting counsel persisted in having all the test scoring, and the author was moved to complain to the Bar Council about this practice and its implications for clinical psychology. However, the view of the Bar Council was that it is quite legitimate and justifiable for an expert witness to be asked in detail about the evidence upon which he bases his opinion, and that any confidentiality, whether it be to protect a person, a psychometric test, or even a profession, must be subordinated to the interests of justice. This is a viewpoint which is arguable on logical, moral and philosophical grounds, but is at least consistent with the other principles of legal practice. It is still a serious and unresolved problem which requires consideration by both lawyers and psychologists. It is only in the adversary system that it arises, and it should not be beyond the wit and goodwill of both professions to come to a code of practice in which some degree of test confidentiality can be preserved yet the test results still critically examined for validity. Both sides have access to psychologists, and the courts can always call on independent psychological assessors, as well as such sources of evaluation as professional test standards committees, independent non-commercial test distributing agencies, and test review publications of the mental measurements yearbook type[190]. Meanwhile, the forensic psychologist must reach a personal decision about the use of tests and test forms, and to what extent he agrees to limit or modify his usual professional psychometric practice to avoid courtroom difficulties. The decision is a difficult one, for by eschewing his usual comprehensive approach, he is avoiding gathering information which he regards as useful to the client and therefore does the client a disservice by making a less complete analysis of the problem than he otherwise would; conversely, if he follows his normal practice of thorough psychometric evaluation, the data may be misused to his client's discomfiture and possible discredit. Steering between such a Scylla and Charybdis is a compromise which spells moderate safety for the client but leaves the psychologist feeling professionally uneasy about such dubious pragmatism. In the long term, personally and professionally satisfying answers may be found, but until they have, the psychologist has to make the best choice the dictates of his conscience will allow. One way he can contribute to the eventual solution, however, is to make manifest to his legal colleagues the nature of the problem and of his ethical and professional dilemmas, and encourage them to consider the problems as inter-disciplinary ones which need a solution.

If the psychologist decides to include the standard test forms in his forensic portfolio, he must then decide whether he will also include the additional qualitative entries usually made, both under 'Remarks' and at the appropriate parts of the scoring sheet. Test administrators commonly pencil in thumbnail sketches of the testee or his behaviour, designed to fix the testee in the mind as an individual, and to remind the tester of facts which are relevant to case. Good quality clothing liberally bespattered with food stains down the front may be a more cogent symptom of early dementia than a particular test pattern, but discussed derisively in court by cross-examining counsel it can disintegrate the patient's *amour propre* and bring a depth of social shame possibly assuaged only by suicide. It would not be the first time that the intolerably shamed individual sought personal release in self destruction.

Another way in which the forensic psychologist's notes can be used against his client is well illustrated by a domestic relations case involving custody of the children. The psychologist who had seen the mother, was asked to provide the court with evidence to show that she was capable of maintaining custody of the children. He brought his records with him to court, in order to quote evidence in favour of her mental stability. However, he had recorded in an earlier interview that the client had fleeting delusional thought that the children were not hers. The records had been perused by counsel for the husband, exercising his legal right to access to documents brought before the court. He made a great play on this delusion. Despite the psychologist's evidence, the woman lost custody of the children. Thus in attempting to help his client the psychologist actually proved detrimental. The fact that all documents known to exist, e.g. hospital case notes, can be brought to court under writ, means that psychologists should be very circumspect in their entries in official documents. In the USA where litigation is prevalent, it is not uncommon for institutions to keep one set of official records, available for subpoena, and another set in the vaults which are unofficial and remain hidden, and which contain all the entries therapeutically necessary but forensically dangerous. The psychologist will therefore need to think carefully what he writes. In certain circumstances the psychologist's notes could be used as a confession by his client, and notes regarding a previous offence may negate his claim to be a first offender of a marginally different offence. During the interview with accused person, it is not unusual for the psychologist to receive confessions of various sorts, and this raises ethical and professional issues which have not received the attention they deserve. Apart from putting the client at risk, for they do not carry the privilege of confidentiality the person expects, they may have longterm implications for justice.

G. M. Gilbert, a clinical psychologist, was engaged by the prosecution in the psychological assessment of Nazi war criminals who were tried at Nurenburg. In the course of his investigation he obtained a documentary confession from Colonel Hoess who was later found guilty and executed. Many years later, Gilbert was called as a prosecution witness for the German Government against another alleged war criminal, Adolf Eichman. Gilbert presented the documentary confession of the deceased Hoess, which implicated Eichman and explicitly negated his plea of innocence.

The author uses a code for descriptive and behavioural analysis, which not only is of value for preserving the confidentiality of test information should unauthorized eyes see it, but it enables the psychologist to interpret the code in a form appropriate to the situation and to the audience. Thus what is 'messy eater' in one context can become in court 'has difficulty in conveying food from plate to mouth', which appears to absolve the patient from responsibility and enables one to expand on, for instance, the possibility of neuropathological tremor in *dementia presenilis*, if this is the diagnosis suggested by other test results.

One expert in forensic medicine wrote all his notes for his forensic portfolio in Latin. This practice had much to commend it. Much residual Latin still exists in the language of medicine—the anatomy one refers to in injuries will be mostly Latin, as will some of the diagnoses. Common Latin abbreviations in hospital casenotes such as *aet.* for age, will already be known to contemporary non-Latin-speaking clinicians. Moreover lawyers of the old school would be as familiar with this dead tongue as their medical counterparts. Yet, although at one time a *franca lingua* of the courtroom, Latin will be unfamiliar enough to the public to enable it to be used as a code, and even when translated by some classical scholar present on the press bench, cannot convey the social nuances which can bring such embarrassment to the person to whom it refers. For clinicians deprived of the benefits of a classical education, there will still be enough Latin words they acquire during their postgraduate training in clinical psychology to enable them to select a suitable number for use as key words on their forensic portfolio sheets. An English-Latin dictionary will supply any additional code words they may require. The code system has the disadvantage of not conveying information to other psychologists, but for forensic purposes this seems to be a reasonable compromise.

Date sheet, data sheets, test forms or their whitewashed equivalents make up the essentials of the forensic portfolio. Added to these will be any additional fact sheets, detailing information which may be relevant. Letters from the patient or client should not normally be included unless special use is to be made of them in the box, neither should the papers in the portfolio contain any mention of statements made to the psychologist by the client, unless these are being used as direct evidence of, for example, hallucinatory or suicidal statements which explained why the psychologist took the action he did or came to the conclusions he reported.

This orderly, clear and precise portfolio enables the forensic psychologist to locate relevant facts quickly and to impress the court that he is efficient in his professional work. It minimizes misuse of information by the opposition while giving the witness all the essentials. The worst possible thing to take into court is the entire file on the patient, consisting of case notes going back to the year dot, masses of letters and reports on every irrelevant matter under the sun, and a mass of odd scraps of paper and backs of envelopes, on which a succession of professional health workers have scratched a few notes at one time or another. The seriousness of taking everything into the box was underlined in the case mentioned above, when notes made by a psychiatrist for the defence while discussing the case by telephone with the author, were confiscated and used in an attempt to discredit the author under cross-examination. This placed the author in a particularly difficult situation, since he was not aware that any record of the conversation existed, much less that it was then in the hands of the prosecution. He could not remember what had actually been said during the telephone discussion, which had lasted for a considerable period of time. Since the psychiatrist could not write shorthand, the notes could only be a precis of the conversation, and in the form obtained by the prosecution were not necessarily exact and certainly not complete in word or phrase with what the author said. The dynamics of auditory perception and the fusion and distortions of memory so well known and understood by experimental psychologists had no doubt played their part between what the author said in Sussex and what the other witness actually noted down later in London. Nevertheless, read out verbatim it gave a very different impression to the one the author was trying to convey to the court; it was a particularly telling and damning ploy by the cross-examining counsel, and any attempt by the author to question its validity in the form as presented must have appeared as a poor and inadequate solution by someone hoist by his own petard. To be actually hoist by someone else's petard is even more frustrating, and the moral is never to discuss the case—by telephone or tête-a-tête—with any other witness without first warning them not to make notes attributable to oneself. Some medical colleagues involved with court work have a dangerous habit of recording their telephone conversations on tape, often without informing the person with whom they are communicating. For this reason, telephone discussions on cases are best avoided, except with lawyers who have long since learnt the art of protecting their information and the sources of it.

The use of a specially prepared forensic portfolio will safeguard the psychologist, his client, and test confidentiality in most cases. There are one or two obnoxious prosecuting counsel, however, who react to sound psychometric evidence proffered by the defence in an emotional rather than rational manner, and who are determined to gain their point regardless of logic. Their two weapons are ridicule and confusion, and generally they prove very effective. To use this approach they require all possible information about the test and its administration, and in such cases, the psychologist's portfolio will be found wanting. They will therefore demand, under writ of subpoena if necessary, *all* documentation pertaining to the psychologist's evidence, including all the original 'working papers' as they are called. These will comprise the completed test forms, scoring keys, informal notes made at the time, together with any additional notes, reports, case records and so on which the psychologist had in his possession while preparing his report.

In *R. v. Bouzaglo* and others (1980), three psychologists were called for the defence, and each was required to provide, during cross-examination, not only all documentation which was remotely relevant, but all the test material as well. Innumerable photocopies were made of such copyright material as the Raven's Professive Matrices, Alice Heim tests, Wechsler Test forms and scoring manual, Schonell scholastic tests, and all other test material. The expert witnesses then had the unedifying spectacle of seeing it all bandied about the court, and the results of many years scientific endeavour belittled and made to appear as some useless and irrelevant parlour game.

If by this time the jury are still not ready to dismiss the psychometric evidence, they are then confused by being taken through the minutiae of each single response to each item of every subtest, until the jury are so overwhelmed with a surfeit of apparently unreliable information that in sheer confusion they are only too thankful to accept the prosecuting counsel's suggestion that they should disregard completely the psychologist's evidence. The author has sometimes spent a whole day in the witness box whilst just one test was being robbed of its confidentiality, dissected and ridiculed. The relevance and validity of the test is thus made an issue to be decided by the jury on the basis of emotional, unscientific, and a highly biased presentation by a lawyer completely ignorant of test theory and construction who distorts the facts to suit his own ends.

In the above case, the author, who had not only reduced his documentation to the minimum, but had purposely avoided using the standard tests of brain damage to prevent loss of confidentiality, was forced to provide all the original documentation as well as the alternative less well-known tests he had used. The latter were retained for court purposes for a considerable period of time, despite the fact that they were the only copies of the test in the whole Region and were in frequent use for clinical and teaching purposes. In this situation the accused also is acutely embarrassed and discomforted, since his responses in what had been a private, clinical interview, are now taken out of context and exposed to public ridicule; to most psychologists these seem to be despicable and unethical tactics, although they are of course a lawful and legitimate part of the adversary system.

23. Attendance at Court

As the executioner said to the doomed prisoner, there are two ways of going to the block—willingly or by force. The same two options are open to the psychologist in going to court. The more usual way is to do it willingly, that is, by arrangement, but sometimes the circumstances are such that the psychologist prefers not to volunteer, and waits for the law to take its course via subpoena. A distinction needs to be made here between common witnesses to fact, who are compellable witnesses, and expert witnesses, who are not compellable. For psychologists anxious to avoid attendance at court, two rules are worth bearing in mind. The first is that 'unco-operative witnesses are rarely called to court'; if they are, it is probably by the other side trying to make capital out of it. The second is that 'the witness who says nothing is never subpoena'd'. One medical practitioner has an infallible method of avoiding court work: he adds to the bottom of every report—'in my opinion you have no case'! It was suggested earlier that psychologists may have a duty to go to court—this may be a legal duty relating to their terms and conditions of employment, or otherwise a moral one in relation to a patient under their care, or merely as a public-spirited citizen recognizing the need to uphold justice.

Compellable witnesses

'Witnesses to fact' are those individuals who possess some direct personal knowledge of the case relevant to the facts in issue. Clinical psychologists are frequently witnesses to fact because they have been responsible for the assessment or treatment of a patient, who is now involved in litigation or is accused of a criminal offence. Sometimes, however, the psychologist is involved because of his presence at a clinical meeting where a patient has been presented, or because he has in his keeping public records (such as psychometric case notes) the contents of which are relevant to the case in hand. Witnesses to fact are said to be compellable witnesses, because, should they decline an invitation to attend court and give evidence, they can be forced to be by means of a witness summons, issued by a lower court, or a writ of subpoena issued by the High Court. In Scotland this is called a 'citation'. The writ of subpoena is delivered personally, to the witness, usually by a police officer, and is accompanied by a sum of money known as 'conduct money' which usually proximates the fare by public transport to the High Court from the witness's address. This is provided to ensure that the witness has no obstacle to his attendance at Court, and originated in the days of the Assize Courts held in the county towns which could have been a considerable distance away from the witnesses' homes. In the case of the witness summons, which normally will request the presence of the witness at his local Police Court, no such conduct money is payable and the summons itself need not necessarily be delivered to the witness personally. Most psychologists feel morally obliged to attend court as a witness to fact when requested to do so, since their role is then a non-controversial one which does not challenge in public their professional abilities. On occasions however, it may be of advantage for the psychologist to ask to be served a witness summons or writ of subpoena. Circumstances when this is appropriate include those where the psychologist has a professional (or personal) relationship with both parties (as in the case of marriage counselling, for example, when he does not want to appear to be taking sides) as well as when he wishes to enforce his intention to go to court against the wishes of a senior colleague or employing authority. By being served with the appropriate instrument the decision to attend court is no longer his but that of the court itself, and he is thus absolved from all responsibility for his appearance in court.

Appearing unwilling also increases the acceptibility of evidence. The expert witness, provides an opinion upon facts before the court (not necessarily furnished by the expert himself), and is therefore not compellable. However, a witness to fact who is coincidentally qualified to be an expert witness, can be asked to give expert opinion whilst still in the witness box as a witness to fact. In many cases the clinical psychologist has seen an individual for psychological assessment before any forensic involvement on the psychologist's part is contemplated: in these circumstances, in the event of the psychologist being reluctant to appear in court to tender expert testimony, it is always possible for the solicitors desirous of introducing this testimony, to make him a compellable witness to fact, on the grounds that he has seen the patient, and then convert him into an expert witness once he is in the witness box.

Normally the legal advisors would not prejudice their case by calling an unwilling witness. If however the opinion of the expert is known in advance, for example, from what the psychologist has written in a textbook or scientific paper, and is likely to materially effect the issue, the solicitor can issue a subpoena to the psychologist as a witness to fact (e.g. that he *is* the author of the relevant publication). Once in the witness box the judge can be asked to admit the witness as an expert, and he could then be asked to endorse the views he has published and given

212

In the High Court of Justice.

1957.— S .—No. 497S

QUEEN'S BENCH   **DIVISION.**

G. 4

Subpoena Duces
Tecum at Assizes

The Solicitors'
Law Stationery Society
Limited
22 Chancery Lane, W.C.2
3 Bucklersbury, E.C.4
49 Bedford Row, W.C.1
6 Victoria Street, S.W.1
15 Hanover Street, W.1
55-59 Newhall Street
Birmingham, 3
19 & 21 North John St.
Liverpool, 2
28-30 John Dalton St.
Manchester, 2
75 St. Mary Street
Cardiff

F3473.22-8-56

Between   ROY GEORGE SCANE (Infant

by his mother and next friend

Her Majesty's   Cinderella Rose Scane)
High Court of
Justice
District Registry   **PLAINTIFF**
Brighton   **AND**
3 Dec 1959
            CHARLES JOHN AINGER

                                            DEFENDANT

Elizabeth the Second, by the Grace of God of the United Kingdom of Great Britain and Northern Ireland and of Our other Realms and Territories Queen, Head of the Commonwealth, Defender of the Faith, To

Dr. Lionel R.C. Haward,
of Summersdale Hospital, Chichester, Sussex,
Senior Clinical Psychologist.

                                            Greeting :

WE COMMAND YOU to attend before Our Justices assigned to take the Assizes in and for the County of Sussex
to be holden at Lewes
on   Tuesday, the   eighth   day of   December,   1959 ,
at the hour of   Ten   in the   forenoon, and so from day to day during the said Assizes until the above Cause is tried, to give evidence on behalf

(1) "Plaintiff" or "Defendant".

(2) Specify documents to be produced.

of the (¹)   Plaintiff
and also to bring with you and produce at the time and place aforesaid (²)
any medical reports or medical data in your possession
relating to the Infant Plaintiff Roy George Scane.

WITNESS,   DAVID VISCOUNT KILMUIR
Lord High Chancellor of Great Britain, the   3rd   day of   December
in the year of Our Lord One thousand nine hundred and fifty-nine.

N.B.—*Notice will be given to you of the day on which your attendance will be required.*

Figure 5

Form of *Subpoena Duces Tecum*

**IN THE SOUTH-EAST LONDON COMMISSION AREA
PETTY SESSIONAL DIVISION OF CROYDON**

To : Lionel Richard Charles HAYWARD

  of 45 Deeside Avenue, Chichester, Kent

      YOU ARE HEREBY ORDERED ~~[if notice is later given to you to that effect]~~*,
to attend and give evidence at the trial of David COLD Cadoline Limited
Goldstar Publications

                               before the [Central Criminal Court,
Old Bailey, London, E.C.4.] ~~[Crown Court at Croydon sitting at the Law Courts,
Barclay Road, Croydon]~~ at the date and time to be notified to you by an officer of the
said Court.

      DATED the   22nd   day of   May   19 72   .

By order of the Court,

          J. D. BERRYMAN,

     Clerk of the Magistrates' Court sitting at the Law Courts, Barclay Road, Croydon.

                      NOTE.—Under section 3(1) of the Criminal Procedure (Attendance of
                      Witnesses) Act, 1965, a person who disobeys a witness order
                      without just excuse may be punished with imprisonment not
                      exceeding 3 months and a fine.

Witness Order.

* *Delete unless the order is a conditional order.*
H.R.G./500/1/72

Figure 6

Form of Witness Order

Attendance at Court

𝕴𝕟 𝖙𝖍𝖊   COUNTY OF DERBY

Petty Sessional Division of ＿＿＿

To DR. L. R. C. HAWARD

of Department of Clinical Psychology, Graylingwell
Hospital, Chichester, Sussex

[Information] [~~Complaint~~] has been [laid] [~~made~~] by
. Harold Adlington of Bakewell Inspector of Police
that
* Alan Morton and Colin Ashley Pick did each drive a
motor cycle in a manner dangerous to the public at
Baslow on the 22nd day of June 1963

AND I, the undersigned Justice of the Peace, being satisfied that you are
likely to be able to [give material evidence] [~~and] [produce the undermentioned
document[s] or thing[s] likely to be of material evidence~~] therein and that
you will not voluntarily attend for that purpose:

YOU ARE THEREFORE HEREBY SUMMONED to appear on
Tues day, the   21st   day of   January , 1964 ,
at the hour of   10.30   in the   fore noon, before the
Magistrates' Court sitting at   the TOWN HALL BAKEWELL
.

to [give evidence therein] [~~and] [produce the following document[s] and
thing[s]~~] :—

Cat. No. M.C. 106.

M.C. Act, 1952, s.77.

Summons to witness.

LONDON :
SHAW & SONS Ltd.,
Fetter Lane, Fleet Street,
E.C.4.

L21   L

DATED the   16th   day of   January   , 1964 .

H. Schofield

Justice of the Peace for the   ~~county~~   *first above mentioned.*

N.B.—Strike out such of the words within the square brackets as are not required.
* State shortly particulars of offence or complaint.

Figure 7

Form of Witness Summons

215

an opinion on the issue before the court relevant to these. To secure the attendance of a witness in this way a *subpoena ad testificandum* is issued, but if the witness is out of the country (even if still in the UK) the permission of a judge must be sought before doing so. The witness is not forced to comply with the subpoena unless the necessary expenses have been paid to him in advance, but once he has accepted payment of expenses he is subject to various penalties should he fail to present himself to the court at the appointed time: these include a fine of up to £100, an attachment for contempt of court, and an action for tort should the party on whose behalf he has been called suffer loss as a result of his non-attendance.

When the judgment expected by the party in a civil action rests substantially upon 'medical' evidence—as it so often does in action in which the clinical psychologist is concerned, the defaulting witness could be exposing himself to a liability of many thousands of pounds by his failure to respond to the subpoena. Witnesses in prison are not issued with a subpoena but are brought to court in custody on an order for attendance issued by a judge or the home secretary, or, if imprisoned on a civil charge, by a writ of *habeas corpus*.

Attendance by Contract

When the psychologist attends court as an expert witness, he normally attends by contract. The contract is between himself and the firm of solicitors, acting for the police or the accused, in a criminal trial, or for the plaintiff or defendant in a civil proceeding. The contract is usually made verbally in the first place, usually by the solicitor telephoning the psychologist and asking if he will appear on behalf of the client. If the psychologist agrees, he will then be asked what his fees will be, and if and when these are agreed, the solicitor will put this into writing. It is important for eventual payment that the psychologist has a written statement from the solicitor acknowledging the responsibility for fees as agreed. Solicitors rarely become bankrupt, but the accused person is more likely to, especially in a case involving business dealings, or in offences contrary to the Obscene Publications Act, when the entire stock belonging to the accused may be seized, forfeited and destroyed. If unforeseen impediments occur in the granting of legal aid, or the Court Taxing Master refuses to accept the expert's claim for expenses, the solicitor will still be liable if under contract to pay the witness the requisite fees and disbursements. This point will be taken up later in the section on fees.

The contract works both ways. If a psychologist contracts with the client's solicitors to give expert testimony for a fee he is under a contractual duty to attend. If he fails to do so he will be liable to the client for any damages which the latter might suffer as a result of the psychologist's failure to give expert evidence. If it should subsequently be proved to the satisfaction of the court, that the client lost his case as a result of the non-attendance of the expert, the psychologist could find himself liable in law for the damages suffered by his client.

The attendance of a witness, expert or otherwise, can be enforced in both the civil and the criminal courts, and also at certain tribunals. It is not customary to do so when the psychologist is being called for the defence in criminal cases, or by either party in a civil proceedings, because he will usually have agreed to attend and give evidence when first approached by the solicitors concerned. If, however, having carried out his investigations, the psychologist feels the results are too equivocal or complicated to discuss in court, he may wish to withdraw his contribution. In such cases, the side engaging him may well agree that there is little to be gained by presenting evidence of a possibly contradictory nature and agree to the psychologist resigning from the case. On the other hand, the defence, especially in a serious criminal offence, may be so short of defence material that they are willing to clutch at any straws and may insist on the psychologist presenting his evidence in court. In such cases, if the psychologist still refuses to attend court, he will be compelled by the use of a summons or subpoena, to attend court as a witness to fact.

In the courts of petty sessions a witness summons is issued, and should this be disregarded the magistrates, in the absence of a medical certificate stating that the witness is prevented from attending by reason of ill-health, may issue a warrant for the arrest of the witness followed by imprisonment for not more than seven days.

Timing Attendance

When agreement between the client's legal advisors and the expert witness is being reached, it is often possible for arrangements to be made for the psychologist to be called at a particular stage of the proceedings to suit the latter's convenience. Because the duration of any trial is unpredictable, cases due to be heard which are well down the list may vary from their expected date of hearing by a week or more, but once the case opens, the solicitors will be able to determine the approximate days on which the various parts of this case will be heard. The least time is wasted when the witness is called early in the proceedings, and the court is usually considerate in granting release from court to professional people giving expert testimony immediately their cross-examination is completed. Where the court is near the psychologist's place of work, it is often possible to arrange to stay at work until warned by telephone that calling is imminent so that undue waste of time is avoided. However, this privilege does place a burden on the solicitors good will and absolute reliance on the psychologist getting there in time. On one occasion the author had prolonged difficulty in getting his car started after receiving the arranged telephone call and was then stopped by the police for speeding. He just made the court in time, but as one of the police officers said: 'next time you'll be changing the box for the dock'. For crown courts outside the psychologist's own area, however, even a short appearance in the witness box may mean a loss of a complete day at work, and for long distances or long trials overnight stay is necessary. Three nights away from home for attendance at court is by no means unusual in the author's experience; on occasions, where the examination of previous experts has been unexpectedly prolonged, the author has experienced delays of as many as three days in getting into the box, and has spent a further three days giving evidence. When the weekend falls in the middle of this period, as not infrequently happens, this means that more or less two weeks have been disorganized by one case. When the forensic psychologist has more than one court case on his books—and on one occasion the author had nine cases in progress concurrently, the problems of timing and attendance increase accordingly. In such circumstances a clash of dates is inevitable at some time or another. The general rule is that the higher court takes precedence, but exceptions are sometimes made depending upon the nature of the case. In Case No. 27 for example, the return of the child to its mother was deemed to deserve the priority of the author over another case scheduled in a higher court for the same day. The counsel in the High Court action obligingly changed the batting order of his witnesses so that the author could attend the Magistrates Court for the 'care and custody' hearing.

The courts regard judicial proceedings as taking priority over all other affairs—except perhaps the convenience of Her Majesty's Judge. However important a particular expert's appointments may seem to be, to himself or others, they must be subordinated to the requirements of the court.

In one case at the Old Bailey the court arranged to call a pathologist from the middle of examining medical students at Oxford University. In another case a surgeon had his operating list interrupted. One medical witness, about to leave for Scandinavia for a medical conference where he was reading a learned paper was telephoned at 6 p.m. just before departure to be told that he was required in court the following morning. But perhaps the prize for inconvenience goes to Professor Keith Simpson, who arrived at Paris for his honeymoon to be greeted by a message summoning him to return to the Old Bailey immediately, where he spent forty minutes giving evidence[136]. Judges are usually considerate enough to extend the afternoon sitting of the court beyond their usual four p.m. termination, if the expert witness in the box is likely to complete his testimony within half an hour or so, but many a witness has had to stay overnight and return the next morning rather than delay the judicial departure.

Sitting In

It was mentioned earlier that the essential difference between a common witness to fact and an expert witness was that the former was required to limit his testimony to the facts perceived by him, whereas the expert is permitted to give an opinion on facts before the court, including both those within his direct knowledge and on facts provided by other witnesses and proved to the court. A second major difference is that the expert witness is normally permitted to 'sit in', that is, to remain in court during the hearing. The witness to fact, whilst waiting to be called to give evidence, must wait outside the court. This is known as the witness exclusion rule. The newer courts usually have a special witness waiting room. After they have been called they are usually required to remain in court, at the back, until they are formally released. The purpose of this is to ensure that the testimony of the witness is not influenced by what he hears other witnesses say. By not returning to the witness waiting room afterwards, the witness is also prevented from telling the following witnesses, who by being close to himself in the sequence of calling, may be testifying on the same point, what questions he was asked and what responses he made. In the case of expert witnesses, the rule excluding witnesses from court before testifying is normally waived, and he can then sit in on the whole case. In Scotland, the rule is that the expert witness may remain in court for the duration of the case, but must leave for the period when other expert witnesses are testifying. The purpose of this is to prevent contamination of opinion. In England, however, the expert has the privilege of hearing other experts give their testimony, including those of the opposite side. This is very helpful, because it may enable the expert to reconcile some of his own ideas with those of the opposing side, and thus reach a more satisfactory measure of agreement—as expected from scientifically based evidence. The importance of the expert hearing the other experts at first hand is also that he may be asked questions about their facts and opinions which differ from his own. It should be stressed that the sitting in of the expert though customary is a privilege bestowed by the court, and not a right which the expert witness can demand. If, for some reason, the presence of the expert witness is objected to by the other side, an application can be made that the expert should withdraw and it is then within the discretion of the judge to grant or to reject the application. This is an extremely rare occurrence; it happened to that great forensic scientist Sir Bernard Spilsbury, in *R.* v. *Barney* (1932), and became something of a milestone in forensic history. However, in Magistrate's Courts set in the more bucolic parts of England, it sometimes happens that some court official, ignorant of the expert's sitting in privilege, will order the expert out of court before the court convenes. This has happened several times to the author, who then has had to get a note to the solicitor, then seated in court, asking him to obtain an explicit waiver from the court so that he could return. It is, of course, essential that one obeys the ushers' orders to leave, although sometimes they will reverse their decision once the expert explains the matter to them. Some ushers, however, are retired regular soldiers who, having made an order, are psychologically incapable of rescinding it. It may be that the solicitor is not available at the critical time, or that the note sent in to court gets delayed because the bearer of the note is suddenly summonsed elsewhere, in which case the expert may lose his privilege at the time he needed it most. In Case No. 9 the author, as expert witness, was asked to leave court by a police officer, even though he was there specifically to give an opinion on the evidence of another police officer who was a witness to fact. The author was later thus asked to report on admissible hearsay rather than upon the direct evidence he should have heard himself. This was one of the points made in the subsequent appeal, although the appellate court rejected this on the grounds that the defence solicitor never asked the court explicitly to waive the witness exclusion rule. In this case, the solicitor was unaware that the expert, who had been placed at the back of the court by himself, had been asked to leave, and the note explaining the situation, given by the witness to the policeman concerned, mysteriously never reached the solicitor. Where the expert is specifically concerned with witness testimony, it is imperative that he remains in court and hears the critical statements as direct evidence, and for this reason, he should ask the solicitor to make a special point of securing the waiver to the witness exclusion rule before the court convenes for the appropriate session.

The value of hearing *all* the relevant evidence is particularly evident to the medical witness.

The Sitting In rule in Scots Law is a compromise between witness exclusion and expert inclusion. It provides the opportunity to assess the entire context of the case and enables the witness to present his own testimony with more meaning. When describing behaviour to illustrate what is meant by certain psychological terms or psychiatric symptoms, it is then possible to refer to actual behaviour which has been reported by other witnesses. For example in Case No. 27 the author was able to support his diagnosis by reference to the evidence of the spouse, given earlier, that her husband, during the critical period, had taken to eating the carpet. This provides a much more satisfactory and telling illustration than to say pica had been reported. The Scots system has some disadvantage in that the expert is likely to be repetitious of other expert evidence, especially when two experts appear to be quoting identical sources and experiments, and this may give the idea of possible collusion. There is perhaps nothing wrong in experts agreeing among themselves before entering court, so that the court receives a consistent picture, and indeed repetition sometimes serves to emphasize the correctness and validity of the experts' point of view. However, it does sometimes suggest that with almost identical facts and viewpoints, one expert could efficiently have replaced all the others, thus saving both the court's time and the taxpayer's money. Forensic psychologists have shown up this aspect of congruence of evidence perhaps more than any other science. This is undoubtedly because of the similarity of their training, and the key sources used in psychology courses. Virtually any psychologist giving an opinion on multiple personality in court is going to quote Morton Prince[191], as well as Thigpen and Cleckley[192]. The trials and tribulations of Miss Beauchamp are as legendary as Eve's three faces, and will be mentioned by all the witnesses in discussing their views on the case concerned. Indeed, the popularization of the latter case in textbook, film and paperback, made the case particularly well-known to most jurors during one decade, a situation the author was able to exploit in one such case.

Even when psychologists do not want to avail themselves of the privilege of sitting-in, either because the evidence they are tendering is too specific and technical to be influenced in any way by the court proceedings, or for other personal reasons, it is professionally worth-while to exercise this option whenever possible, even if only for a short while before being called. Witnesses, even expert witnesses, invariably have to wait their turn in court, at least if they have come to court at the time suggested by the solicitor, and it is usually more interesting than waiting in some cold and less congenial lobby. But it also has a positive aspect. In the first place, the psychologist can acquire some familiarity with the counsel who will be examining and cross-examining, noting their different methods, personalities, and special cognitive styles. This makes it easier to face them when called, than being confronted with them for the first time. It is also a good learning situation in other respects, enabling the psychologist to become familiar with the court layout, with the jury, with the judge and his speed of note-taking, and many other aspects of the environment, advance knowledge of which will be to the psychologist's ultimate advantage. In court one can also learn some relevant aspects of the law of evidence, noting what objections are raised and on what grounds, whether sustained or over-ruled, and so on. One minor, but still important, point is that by exercising the expert witnesses privilege of being in court, one is establishing the fact explicitly to all and sundry that one is there as an expert and this is good for one's own image as well as that of the profession. For this reason, but especially for the learning opportunities if offers, the psychologist is strongly advised to make use of this waiver of the witness exclusion rule.

When the expert witness has finished his testimony, he will normally be expected to go to the back of the court and be seated until the end of the session. The reason for this is that it may be necessary to recall him to the box to explain to the court discrepancies which have become manifest between his evidence and that of the other experts. However, at this point the expert has the benefit of a second privilege, that of being released from the court at the termination of his evidence so that he may return to his duties, although the expert should remember that he is 'on call' until the full hearing is completed. The courts recognize that experts are busy and important men, and will normally release them on request, subject to there being no objection from the counsel on either side. In the inferior courts it is often taken as a matter of course that the expert witness will be released, and many medical witnesses leave automatically when finished with their testimony. As a matter of courtesy to the court, however, the psychologist should obtain explicit release. This is often done by the counsel at the end of the final re-examination; he asks the judge if his witness can now be released to return to his pressing medical duties, or words to that effect. The judge then asks counsel for the other side if they have any objection, and once assured of this, the judge will turn to the witness and inform him he is free to leave court. If the judge actually thanks the witness for coming to court, the witness will know that his evidence has been well received and will be favourably commented upon in the summing-up. Good barristers will make their request spontaneously for release of the expert—John Mortimer, the eminent Q.C. and playwright is meticulous in this respect, and no doubt his famous character Rumpole of the Bailey would be likewise. However, more often than not, counsel will forget, in which case the psychologist should turn to the judge and say: 'May I have your permission to be released from court, My Lord?' Solicitors rarely ask spontaneously, so it is usual to ask the magistrates' permission. There are two schools of thought about whether it is better for the psychologist to remind the solicitor or barrister beforehand to ask for the release of the witness, or for the psychologist to make his own request. In the latter case he is making obvious his courtesy and sense of respect for the court; in the former, the lawyer can frame the request in a way which helps to put his witness in the best possible light, by saying something like: 'Dr Blank has a very busy clinic to run this morning, will your Lordship please release him?' If the cross-examining counsel has tried to convey to the jury that the psychologist is nothing more than an academic dilettante, then the witness's counsel conjuring up the picture of the psychologist hurrying off to don a white coat and administer to the suffering millions may help to redress the balance. Sometimes, of course, the opposing side will object to the release of an expert, or the judge himself will prefer to keep the experts in court. This may happen when the judge has been caught out in a previous case by the absence of expert witnesses just when one was wanted to pronounce on some new or unexpected piece of evidence relevant to their expertise. In one case, for example, the question of whether or not the plaintiff was epileptic was in issue. No one had given evidence of actually seeing him have a fit, and the medical witnesses had all relied on inference from indirect evidence. The Hon. Sir Gerald Thesiger was presiding at the time, and as is customary released the medical witnesses in the afternoon so that they could return to their duties. Later, in their absence, the one thing that was so vital, and which none of them had observed, took place. The plaintiff had what appeared to be an extraordinary fit while giving evidence in the witness box. Was this the *grand mal* that some experts had said had occurred previously or was it some form of hysterical manifestation? Only the laymen present in the court had seen the fit, and the experts who could have made their diagnosis on direct evidence were missing[193]. It is after such experiences that judges become reluctant to release experts from court.

One last point needs to be added in connection with the waiver to the witness exclusion rule. The fact that the psychologist's psychiatric colleague can sit in court, at least in England and Wales, and hear all the psychologist's evidence, before giving his own specialized psychiatric evidence, removes another objection which the psychiatrist may make to the principle of separating the psychologist's evidence from his own report, and further supporting the psychologist's claim to give his own evidence independently, which was discussed earlier under the hearsay rule.

Appearance in Court

Personality, Appearance and Speech, to quote the title of a well-known textbook[194], interact to convey a variety of different pictures about the person. Clothes make the man, but speech contributes no less. Dorian Grey's evil was as effectively concealed by his appearance as Eliza Doolittle's innocence was concealed by her speech. What the jury make of the expert evidence, the cogency the court ascribes to it, the relative weight accorded it, compared with that of the other experts' will often depend more on the *way* the expert presents to them than on *what* he presents.

Thus the appearance of the psychologist in the witness box is an important factor in the acceptance of his evidence by the jury. The law is the most conservative institution in the country and the dress of the witness will determine, whether he is seen by the court as 'one of us' or 'one of them'. Avoidance of bright and flamboyant wearing apparel is to be recommended, the conventional dark suit and tie being a particularly good choice. Some astute counsel, anxious to make the best possible use of their expert witness, go to great lengths in advising him on the most appropriate wear for the occasion. The writer was once admonished for having a fountain pen showing in his breast pocket, and advised to place it out of sight, on the grounds that the judge had, in private, expressed his dislike of people who keep pens and pencils in their breast pocket. Where the balance of evidence is fairly evenly matched, such subtle differences may unconsciously alter the way the judge sums up the expert's testimony.

Sometimes expert witnesses, especially younger ones with a taste for bright clothes, are unwilling to make concessions to the traditions and expectancies of the court, sometimes on the grounds that they wish to appear in their true guise rather than as someone they are not. They insist that they do not want to create a false impression. It should be borne in mind, however, that they are not appearing as themselves, that is, as a person, but as an expert wearing the mantle of his profession. It is the profession which is under scrutiny, as much as the person himself, and in his desire to avoid creating a false impression of himself, he may well be creating a false impression of his profession. In the eyes of the public, even more in the eyes of the law, sobriety of dress goes with conservatism, the upholding of tradition, and a sense of responsibility. Evidence produced in such a context will carry a different weight to that from someone perceived as radical, iconoclastic or otherwise offensive to tradition and irresponsible. The psychologist, more than any other person is aware of the implications of social perception, and it is worth considering whether the best interests of justice are served by being oneself at the cost of the credibility of one's evidence.

As Burke says, in his excellent advice to police witnesses, the court is a setting for a very serious and solemn affair: a man's life, liberty and reputation are at stake. The jury are sensitive to the ethos of the court. They are in a place strange and unfamiliar to almost all of them, and often over-awed by the red-robed judge seated high above them, the wigs, the black robes of counsel and ushers and archaic language which bids the court to 'be-upstanding' and invites 'all persons who have business before Her Majesty the Queen's Justices to assemble at ten of the clock in the forenoon. . .' In this frame of mind, to present as an expert witness dressed, as some lacking social perception, have done, in a garb more suited to a hippie convention in San Francisco, is not only to invite incredulity that the witness has anything serious to say, but arouses feelings of rejection from jurors who generally go to some trouble to dress themselves appropriately to the situation. Judges, justifiably, may well see such flouting of convention as deliberate discourtesy to their court, and make adverse comments in their summing up. Conversely, the witness who arrives in court well-groomed, sober-clad, and with evidence of having taken some trouble to look like the stereotype of the professional person, will win the judge's approbation and is likely to have his evidence more carefully considered. Social psychologists have undertaken a considerable amount of research in this area, and much of the work has direct relevance to witness appearance. For example, other things being equal, the witness who smiles is seen by the jury as being more honest than the one who doesn't: the witness wearing spectacles is judged to be more intelligent than the one who has no aids to vision—or is wearing contact lens! Psychologists will have no need to be reminded of the halo effect. The smiling, bespectacled, soberly clad psychologist, devoid of gew-gews badges and pens, as he steps into the witness box, is already several steps ahead of the experts of the opposition. For the psychologist who rejects the idea of such subtle influences on the jury, and naively believes the true weight of evidence will decide the issue, the case of *Chaplin* v. *Chaplin* (1946) will be instructive. This was a paternity case in which one side produced evidence of blood-grouping which proved conclusively that Party A could not possibly be the father, whereas Party B had compatible bloodgroup with that of the child and could have been. The other side produced evidence that intimacy had taken place between A and the mother, and also alleged that the child resembled A. The jury found in favour of A. In this case the wily counsel won the day with plausible and totally illogical arguments, in which the experts for the other side were denigrated. Had the experts themselves been a little more impressive in the jury's eyes, perhaps the verdict would have accorded with the scientific facts.

The judge, or counsel, may well comment favourably upon the appearance of the expert witnesses in their final speeches, and so reinforce the jury's view of the evidence as they relate it to the individual experts. In case No.30, for example, the defence leader, Mr John Mortimer, Q.C., reminding the jury of the evidence given by the author, said: 'You may remember, perhaps, Dr Haward standing there in the witness box a long time ago, looking less like the idea of any hippy professor, than everybody's friendly neighbourhood bank manager. One of the most conventional and respectable, and in his work, admirable figures of a witness you could hope to see'.

Whatever the merits (or demerits!) of this description, its association with, and influence on, the evidence which was then summarized, was probably different to that which followed another witness, described as wearing 'a T-shirt which bore the picture of a pop-star'. 'Is he the sort of person you would be happy to see married to your daughter?' asked the prosecuting counsel. 'Would you welcome him as the putative father-in-law of yourself or your son?'

Speech in the Witness Box
Clarity of diction and adequate strength of voice are important. It is essential that the court hears the evidence. Simplicity of language is important in making oneself understood, for technical terms are usually unfamiliar to lay people, and often can be misheard and so misunderstood. The jury, when there is one, has the final responsibility of weighing the evidence and reaching a verdict. It is to the jury therefore, that the witness must direct his testimony. When there is no jury, the witness will be required to speak directly to the judge or magistrates.

Since it is counsel who is actually asking the questions, this means overcoming a lifetime's habit of replying direct to the questioner, and in the early experience of giving testimony in court it places the witness under some degree of strain when overcoming the natural tendency to face the person who has just spoken to one. In some courts, for example those at the Old Bailey, the witness box is so placed that the witness stands between the judge and the jury, who are situated in the rear quadrant as the witness faces the court. In speaking directly to the jury, the witness would have to turn his back completely on the judge, which is clearly undesirable, and some compromise has to be effected whereby the witness can speak in such a way as to be seen and heard by both the judge and the jury at the same time. Sometimes magistrates courts are held in public halls normally used as youth clubs or for dances, where the plethora of sports equipment or amplifier apparatus make the acoustics almost impossible. Add to this the situation of an elderly magistrate whose hearing is not as good as it was, and the need for clear loud speaking becomes evident.

Students at teacher training colleges, and others learning to speak in public for the first time, are made aware explicitly of their many mannerisms which are likely to distract or irritate their audiences. It is a very salutary experience to see a videotape playback of oneself speaking before an audience, and most embryo public speakers are astonished at the variety and frequency of their unconscious mannerisms. These same patterns of behaviour are similarly distracting and irritating when seen in the witness box; they tend to be more exaggerated when the witness is nervous through lack of experience, or when anxiety is being generated under hostile cross-examination. Whatever their cause or their nature, they take away the aura of confidence which the expert should exude, and may therefore take away from the jury confidence in the validity of the expert's testimony.

As well as clarity, speed of diction is important. In Superior Courts, although the court shorthand writer is making a verbatim record of everything said in court, this will be kept in the court archives and will not be transcribed unless the case goes to appeal. This means that the judge, in order to provide an adequate summing-up, has to keep a written record of all testimony. Judges, by reason of their seniority, are not fast writers, and it is therefore important that the witness speaks slowly enough for the judge to write down all the relevant details. But as one judge has pointed out[193] it is not enough for him to ensure that he has managed to record everything of substance: he also needs to know what it all means. And he needs to know this at the time, so that he can interrupt the examination to ask the expert to amplify the meaning of what he is saying. With unfamiliar and technical material, the meaning and implication of each fact has to be thought out, and this cannot be done whilst the words themselves are being written down. Accordingly, the judge needs time not only to actually write all the evidence down in longhand, but to actually think about and digest what he hears. With some cases lasting several weeks, and occasionally with a large number of expert witnesses, the judge's summing-up would inevitably show the effects of contamination and distortion so prevalent in memory experiments, unless he copied down all the details as they were given to the court by the witness. In the words of Gladstone's famous dictum: 'The best memory is a note made at the time'[155]. The expert witness should therefore speak in a slow well-modulated voice, pausing after each important statement, and watching the judge's hand writing his notes. Some judges will stop the witness if he speaks too fast, usually in midstream so that he loses his train of thought, so it is better for the speaker to choose the natural breaks. Moreover, it follows that if the expert avoids technical and unfamiliar words, the judge will require less time to absorb the testimony. Simple ideas clothed in simple language make it better for judge and jury alike. Similarly, it helps if the court can be given concrete illustrations of the technical phrases or scientific concepts which the expert is using. 'Aversion' is a good old English word, used to great effect by Thomas Hobbes, tutor to King Charles II, as every philosopher knows, but when applied to 'aversion treatment' it is put into a narrower context which requires explanation. When explaining to the court what can be offered to the offender in the form of treatment, it has often become necessary to explain this form of behaviour therapy. The fact that, from one point of view, it involves a 'punishment' paradigm, often seems to help the court to choose this as an acceptable alternative to the more usual penal measures, and in the inferior courts particularly, offenders who would otherwise be sent to prison are more likely to be offered probation with aversion therapy as a condition of the court order, than they are to be offered one of what the Bench sometimes regards, not without justification, as a 'soft option'. Of course, the use of aversion therapy in this context raises its own ethical problems, especially regarding the nature of the offender's consent, but that is another aspect of the relation between psychology and the law which does not come strictly within the field of forensic psychology as defined earlier. Aversion, in this context, needs explaining to the court, despite the fact that as a word it lies well within the judge's vocabulary. This was brought home to the author when giving evidence in Case No. 30.

The counsel examining the expert witness is asking the questions, but the answers are required by the court in its entirety—by the lawyers of both sides, who are scribbling rapidly the nub of the evidence for use later, the court writer taking the formal record of the hearing, the press for onward transmission to the public, those in the public gallery, who may include embryo barristers learning the art of advocacy or sixth form students taking A level law, and of course the jury, who have to decide the case. It is to them especially that the witness should direct his testimony, attempting, where the design of the court permits, to make eye contact with each member from time to time, and trying to read the degree of comprehension from the expression on their faces. When the expert can actually get jurors nodding their heads in agreement with what he is saying, he knows that his communication is successful.

What used to be called 'the five c's of court address' characterizes one way of addressing the court—candid, courteous, calm, confident, and considerate. To this could be added good humour and dignity—often strained when under attack during cross-examination. Personal disposition counts more with a jury than professional position, and disposition can only be revealed by the way the witness gives his testimony. As one legal writer used to advise medical witnesses: 'Speak to the jury as if you were conversing in a friendly way to your coachman'[155]. Of course, as Aesop remarked, try to please everybody and you please nobody; obviously one cannot easily dictate slowly to the judge while conversing in a friendly way with the jury, but with practice one becomes used to a special courtroom manner which seems to provide a satisfactory blend of the various styles of speech best suited to the occasion. The slow and deliberate pace, with studied assurance and made suitably audible, also helps to reduce the anxiety often attendant upon giving evidence. Even experts can become so nervous they dry up or lose their voice, but this is less likely the more they use everyday vocabulary to avoid speaking, as Carlisle said of Coleridge, 'either oracles or jargon'.

Demeanor, appearance and speech in the courtroom are so important that advice on how to give testimony, both as a common witness to fact and as an expert witness, fills many textbooks (see Bib. 195–98).

24. Privileged Communication and Professional Confidences

THERE are no medical secrets in a criminal court. The medical witness cannot claim privilege for confidences disclosed to him by a prisoner. Counsel for the defence, when putting questions to the witness, will be very careful not to put such questions the reply to which might divulge information which has come to his knowledge but which is adverse to the prisoner. Prosecuting counsel will of course be less concerned. The accused, who will have spent considerable time being interviewed by his legal advisors, will have understood that nothing he has said to them will go further unless it is deemed to be in his best interests. On being confronted by the examining psychologist who has been called by his own legal advisors he may naturally assume that privilege of communication extends to the psychologist also. This is not the case and it is important that the psychologist makes explicit the fact that no privilege exists regarding anything which the prisoner might say to the psychologist. Undoubtedly such an explicit statement will have a dampening effect upon the verbalization of the accused. In his statements to the police when he knows that everything he says will be taken down and may be used in evidence, he will be anxious not to respond in any way which could possibly be construed to his detriment. According to East, the examiner is entitled to note anything that the prisoner might say in connection with the crime and the part he took in it and to ask questions arising out of these statements. But he must avoid asking the prisoner whether he committed the offences and he may not put to him leading questions which assume the crime was committed by him.

In English law, there is no privileged communication between doctor and patient in civil actions either, though some American states recognize this privilege in Civil Courts but not in Criminal Courts. In some states the patient's confidences are protected in Criminal Courts by Statute Law and in Civil Courts by case law[199].

In *Buttall* v. *Buttall and Twine* (1964) counsel for the husband called as a witness a psychiatrist who had been consulted by the wife and the co-respondent. The psychiatrist said he did not wish to give evidence:

Judge: I am sorry. The law is that you must.

Witness: These parties consulted me professionally in my consulting room. They entrusted their confidence to me and I accepted their confidence on the basis that everything said between us would be privileged.

Judge: It is not privileged.

Witness: If you order me to give this evidence it will really strike at the roots of my profession. How can people consult a psychiatrist if they cannot feel sure that their confidence will be protected from disclosure?

Judge: I cannot alter the law, you must go to your MP to do that. The alternative before you is either to give evidence or go to prison.

Witness: It is a very nasty choice.

He chose to give evidence.

Roman Catholic priests are in an unfortunate position, because they are forbidden by their religion to reveal confessional secrets. To be imprisoned for contempt would be a malicious act, but some clinicians feel just as strongly about their own patients' revelations.

At least one doctor in England has chosen to go to prison for 'contempt' of court (an unfortunate and untrue phrase) rather than reveal his patient's confidences. That more have not done so possibly reflects the clinician's judgment that the confidence was probably not serious enough in its possible consequences to justify incurring such a penal sanction. Meerloo, who discusses the conviction for contempt of Congress of Arthur Miller the well-known playwright, who refused to provide information on other people, points out the interesting psychological conflict involved and the moral contradictions implicit in the attitude of the judiciary[200].

The latter was made clear by Judge McLaughlin in his final judgment: 'However *commendable* Mr Miller's action may have been, in refusing to divulge the identity of his associates, he was in contempt for refusing to answer the questions under previous rulings of a Federal Appellate Court'. To protect the state from treason, says Meerloo, the state forces the witness to become a traitor to his own conscience. The paradox here is that by forcing the individual to betray inner things of moral value, we make it easier for him to betray the community at large later. Similarly, many courts regard the clinician's protection of his patient's confidences highly commendable, but nevertheless enforce their legal right to demolish this protection. It is highly debatable whether the interests of justice which are thus served are compensated for by the detrimental effects on the particular clinician, on the patient in the immediate present, and upon future clinical relationships.

If the patient is being seen for the direct purpose of assistance in court by the psychologist the situation is fairly clear. The psychologist can then warn the patient that in giving expert testimony nothing can be retained in confidence. The patient can then enter into the situation with a firm concept of this contract and restrictions. In certain other cases, however, for example, marriage guidance, where a divorce suit may eventually follow and not be anticipated at the time, much of the information given to the psychologist by the client would not be imparted if the client knew that this information may be made public; and, in explaining to the client that whatever he says in a consulting room cannot have absolute confidentiality, he may well be destroying the client's willingness to be honest in his assertions, and both the analysis and the subsequent treatment, if any, may be imperilled.

One of the problems faced by the psychologist is that of whether the information obtained on the patient will do more harm than good if revealed. Evidence given in open court which reveals some personality or psychiatric defect may have marginal value in the settlement of the claim yet can be so threatening to the ego or *amour propre* that it has lasting effect. Levinson[201] made this point when describing the preparation of evidence in the case of a lady injured in a road traffic accident. The medical evidence in regard to physical injury was already substantial, but the husband thought his wife, the plaintiff, had possibly suffered some mental impairment as well, since her memory, he alleged, had been poorer since the accident. Psychometric testing showed her to be functioning intellectually in the low 80's; moreover, the evidence obtainable on her premorbid level suggested it was unlikely to have been higher than this. Taking into account the profession and particular personality of the patient's husband, and the nature of the relationship with his wife, Levinson decided that if knowledge of the patient's low intelligence was made public it could prove extremely embarrassing for her and be detrimental to her best and long-term interests, and this information was therefore excluded from the report. Of course, information of this kind may be elicited from the psychologist under cross examination, and a decision may have to be made prior to the hearing whether in these circumstances the psychologist should be called at all. If the other side suspected that information of this sort was being withheld they could obtain it by issuing the psychologist with a *subpoena duces tecum* forcing him to bring the test forms to court. Information of this sort has a special bargaining value in settling claims out of court, and plaintiffs may be prepared to forego some of the damages they might reasonably have expected to recover in order to avoid public embarrassment of one sort or another. Under English Common Law, however, only the lawyer/client relationship is privileged and in court proceedings both criminal and civil, a psychologist may be subpoena'd and forced to testify concerning a patient involved in litigation. This Common Law principle applies not only in England but in many jurisdictions both State and Federal in the United States.

231

However, in a number of States the importance of the confidential relationship between a physician and patient has been recognized by the passage of special legislation giving to the patient the privilege of preventing a physician who has treated him from being forced to testify against the patient's wishes. The principle benefit is that mentally ill persons are encouraged to seek treatment which would not be sought if privilege did not exist, and the public good which would be achieved is that confidential information could not be compelled to be revealed.

The privilege, where it exists, belongs to the patient not to the physician, and the latter has no right to refuse to testify if the patient waives his privilege. Moreover once the privilege is waived, the physician is obliged to testify as to all knowledge he has acquired in the doctor/patient relationship.

Neustatter[202] says that despite all the improvements in the attitudes of the courts the question of professional confidence remains unsatisfactory. Where the patient has been specially examined for a report and knows that this is so, no question arises; but for patients whose case history has been taken before a criminal act was committed or which was at the time thought to be irrelevant to the criminal act, the case is very different. There is also a big difference between giving objective information such as the physical signs found, which have been recorded in hospital case notes, and revealing matters which the patient thought were being given in strict confidence. It is the more personal details of a man's life which provide the information on which psychiatric diagnosis so often depends. Neustatter regards it as somewhat cynical that the court which can imprison for perjury can also, on the pain of punishment, force a doctor to break his hippocratic oath. One result of this attitude by the courts is that there is a disinclination to enter important details into hospital notes. If the psychologist, in the course of giving evidence is asked a question which cannot be answered without betraying a confidence (or proving detrimental to the defendant or someone present in court to whom the psychologist feels he owes a duty to protect—for example, the defendant's wife in the public gallery) he should explain his difficulty to the court and ask to be excused from answering this question. Sometimes the Court will feel that the question was only marginally relevant and directs that it need not be answered. Usually, however, the Court will feel that it is pertinent to the case and that discretion should not be exercised on this occasion. The psychologist may then ask the court if he may provide a written answer. This is usually much more acceptable, provided the issue raised in the question is capable of a simple and straightforward answer. Very often, however, the very nature of the matter requires some qualification or elaboration, and in such cases a written answer is not deemed practical, for it is then likely to lead to further questions designed to obtain clarification, and the whole question of privilege is continually present. If both of these requests are rejected, the matter becomes one for the psychologist to determine in relation to his own conscience. Since the court recognizes no privilege for the psychologist, if he refuses to answer the question and disobeys the court's direction to do so he commits contempt of court and is then liable to imprisonment. In consulting a psychologist, the client will assume that his disclosures, which, if made public, may expose him to criminal charges, ridicule or embarrassment, will not be passed to others without his knowledge and consent. Such an assumption imposes a confidential relationship between the client and psychologist and raises ethical and legal problems.

The legal concept of privilege communication stems from common law recognition of the relationship between lawyer and client originating in the 16th century. Despite the generally held belief that statements made to priests and physicians (and by implication to clinical psychologists) are privileged at law, lawyers remain the only profession to be accorded this privilege at law. Common law, and later codifications by statute law concerning matrimonial relations have also extended the privilege to the husband-wife relationship. In these circumstances, as with the lawyer, the privileged individual cannot be legally compelled to testify to the content of the confidences they may have received. The privilege protects the client, and the right to exercise the privilege, belongs to the client and not to the professional or spouse. The client may if he wishes, waive his privilege, and then the lawyer or spouse has no legal right to withold his testimony and must testify. The legal theory and justification for privileged communications has been excellently discussed in some detail by Geiser and Rheingold[203].

In the U.S.A., the situation is somewhat different to that in English Court, where no medical privilege regarding communications from the patient is recognized. In America, the privilege of patient's communications to physicians is explicitly recognized by some 33 states. Moreover, at least 11 states have granted the privilege to the clients of psychologists. A sad reflection on the status of the psychologist in that country and of the legal attitude towards the psychologist's clients is that an even larger number of states recognize privileged communications between accountants and their clients and journalists and their informers.

The explicit accordance of this privilege to psychologists has usually been dependent upon state registration, which is now enforced in some third of the States. An example of statutory provision of privileged communications between psychologist and client is that enacted in the certification statute of New York State (*vide* N.Y. Education Law, Section 7611) which states: 'The confidential relationship and communications between a psychologist registered under the provisions of this act and his client are placed on the same basis as those provided by law between attorney and client, and nothing in this article shall be construed to require any such privileged communication to be disclosed'.

The first state to enact a special privilege protecting the confidentiality of psychiatric patients' communications was Georgia in 1959, and it is significant that at least three states which do not have a law recognizing *medical* privilege have passed legislation granting the privilege of confidentiality to patients of registered psychologists. This is on the assumption that psychologists treat patients by psychotherapy. The statutes in each particular state where the privilege exists vary widely—some statutes giving complete privilege others having varying exceptions. For example, when a prisoner is seen privately the examination is privileged but if he is sent to a mental hospital for psychological examination then his examination is not privileged. When privilege is protected by statute the psychologist, if served with a subpoena, may decline to testify. In many jurisdictions where privilege has been enacted only confidential information given in a therapeutic relationship is so privileged and if it is given during a psychiatric examination for other purposes it may not be protected. Conversely, some states have extended the privilege to communication between all in-patients and their doctors; of course, if the patient enters litigation in which his medical state is at issue the patients' privilege, if it exists, is automatically waived. A problem confronting a psychologist, as with other therapists, is whether, how and by what means the patient should be made aware that his confidences are not privileged in law.

Although the psychologist in the USA is accorded greater privileges in law than his English counterpart, he still suffers a variety of limitations in the matter of privileged communications.

In the first place he may be practising in a state which has not enacted explicit jurisdiction on this point. Secondly he may be working in a state which explicitly denies him this privilege. This is a double limitation, since it not only prevents him from claiming any statutory right in the matter, as the New York psychologist can, but it also precludes him from seeking the individual court's discretion in the matter. Thirdly, the law where it exists only protects the clients of those psychologists qualified to be registered under the appropriate Acts, and how the psychologist is defined, and his work delineated, for this purpose, will depend upon the concepts in vogue in a particular state at the particular time the Bill was drafted. Fourthly, even though the psychologist is protected by statute, the latter is open to challenge, as in the cases of *Husband* v. *Cassel* (1961) and *National Psychological Association for Psychoanalysis* v. *New York State University* (1960).

Geiser and Rheingold[202] raise a number of possible issues which may arise from the psychologist-client privilege:

1. What is the position of a client who waives his privilege, but is nevertheless legally incompetent to do so , for instance, by being a minor or insane?
2. What happens to the privilege when the client dies? Does it pass into the possession of his executors, and may his estate be significantly affected by disclosure?
3. What are the responsibilities of the psychologist to ensure the secrecy of the client's confidence in the event of the psychologist's death?
4. Does the privilege extend to the psychologist's secretary, or to a colleague with whom confidential matters have been discussed?
5. If someone, e.g. chaperone or prison officer, overhears a client's confidences to a psychologist, can he be called as a witness?
6. If a psychologist represents himself to be licensed when he is not, does the client who assumes the protection of the privilege in good faith have the privilege?
7. What happens when a psychologist, privileged in one state, is called to testify in a state where no privilege is afforded?
8. When a psychologist is given necessary information by a physician in order to assess the patient for the physician, is he covered by an extension of the physician-patient privilege?

These issues do not exist in the United Kingdom since the psychologist-client privilege they derive from does not exist. They do raise some interesting questions, however, and also point to weaknesses in professional practice which could be strengthened with a little forethought. In particular, the degree of control over confidential matter will be different in forensic work than in normal clinical practice. While medical secretaries usually sign a declaration of confidentiality, most clinicians know that interesting and unusual snippets of personal information do get passed on. In forensic work, information obtained during a clinical session may be of the greatest importance, both to the case, and to the client's immediate future, and it not infrequently becomes necessary for the psychologist to commit such information to memory and to avoid making any record of it whatsoever. A further important aspect of the psychologist's responsibility for preserving the confidentiality of his client, insofar as the law will allow, arises in one of these questions, and that is the one concerned with the death of the psychologist. While we all proceed through life as if fully intending to achieve our expected life span, road accidents and other fatalities reach out into the ranks of the psychology profession, and rarely find the effects of our decease adequately anticipated. Clinical records are often taken over by colleagues, who would deal with their contents as the deceased would wish, but papers of private cases kept at home or in a private office will eventually come under the scrutiny of the executors, who may with misdirected conscientiousness hand them over to improper agencies whose interests are not necessarily those of the client. In one case all the papers pertaining to the defendant in a criminal proceeding were handed over to the police! Similarly, all the documents of the deceased may be scrutinized by officers carrying out the necessary investigation for probate purposes, and so infringe the client's privilege of confidentiality.

As mentioned earlier, the psychologist cannot claim in English law the privilege of confidentiality for his client. However, there are gradations of implicit privilege which the law may accord him. These are purely discretionary, and depend upon the nature of the case and the attitude of the court. It is for the psychologist to put his case, e.g. that testifying to the content of a confidential document would materially damage the therapeutic relationship existing between the client and the clinician, and therefore be detrimental to the mental health of the client. This argument will carry some weight in a civil action, but is less likely to succeed in criminal proceedings. However in *Binder* v. *Buvell* (1952), a trial court in an American state which afforded no physician and patient privileges, the judge distinguished psychiatric treatment from general medical care, and granted privilege from testifying on confidential information to the psychotherapist called as a witness. Similarly, in Canada, where as in the U.K. no physician-patient privilege is recognized, a number of cases are reported in which the court refused to compel a witness to testify on confidential communications. Although these cases generally concerned psychiatrists, one involved a social worker as witness who was granted the court's discretion in this matter *(Kryschnik* v. *Zulynik* (1958)). However, in the interests of justice, criminal courts tend to compel testimony, despite medical witnesses protestations. In the final analysis, the psychologist is left with a moral dilemma which only his own conscience can solve. He must either testify against his patient's interests in order to conform to the needs of an allegedly higher principle—viz. justice or truth, or he can commit perjury and protect his client by misrepresentation of the nature of the confidential communication, or he can commit contempt of court and refuse to testify. The last choice incurs severe penalties and only a professional witness prepared to be martyred for his principles and his patient's good will refuse to testify. The second alternative, while being an apparently easy compromise based on the recognized concept of the 'right to lie' may demand a degree of moral plasticity which one hopes is not found frequently among professional psychologists.

Psychiatrists hold differing views on the subject. Some believe unequivocally that the physician's duty to his patient exceeds that of his duty to the state as a citizen, but others draw the line at some point depending upon their own *weltanschauung*. The case of the airline pilot found to be alcoholic is often cited, since the lives of some hundred or so innocent passengers have to be weighed against the psychiatrist's moral responsibility towards his patient. It could of course be argued that it is in the pilot's own interest for his alcoholism to be made explicit and treated properly, but loss of licence is a major financial—and psychological—catastrophe to a commercial pilot, and his hopes of an adequate cure are probably much less than the psychiatrist seeking an expedient solution to his moral dilemma may suppose. In states of emergency, greater emphasis may be placed upon society's needs, since the risks are so much greater, and one eminent psychiatrist has described how e.g. pro-Nazi sympathies revealed in a soldier being treated for battle neurosis were reported to the military authorities.

One important legal point to be borne in mind by the forensic psychologist is that if any information relating to an undetected crime comes into his possession, whether confidentially or otherwise, he is under a moral obligation to report this to the authorities. Failure to do so originally constituted the offence of misprision of felony and rendered the psychologist liable to prosecution; since 1967 the psychologist in certain circumstances can also be charged with concealing an offence, bearing a two-year prison sentence.

The barristers are of course aware of the moral problem faced by the clinician, and they try to help the latter when he is testifying on oath. Frequently they attempt to soften the clinician's pricks of conscience by making the legal imperative explicit, using the time-honoured sentence: 'I expect you will wish to be commanded by his lordship to testify'.

Psychiatric patients pose a special problem which does not exist in the confidential utterances of other types of patient. This problem occurs when patients' statements are made in circumstances in which their veracity is open to doubt, for example, in emotionally charged situations such as an abreactive session, or in other circumstances when the patient is using conscious or unconscious fantasy. Depressed patients, with their loading of guilt, frequently claim to have committed crimes in the past, or confess to crimes publicized at the time. In such cases, the publication of such statements from the witness box can bring untold misery to the patient, especially after his recovery; moreover, they are extremely difficult to explain away to a lay audience. Frequently, of course, such statements are protected by the Rule of Hearsay, but in Mental Health Tribunals, or indeed in any court of law, such statements may be admitted as evidence that they were in fact made, though not as evidence of their truth. It is this special position of psychiatric communication which has led the American State legislature to treat it differently from that of the physician-patient relationship. Hollander[204] in stating that the legal right to privilege of confidentiality belongs to the patient, points out that the psychotherapist needs a similar right to protect his practice.

The GAP report[205] states that confidentiality is not a hypothetical matter, but one that patients explicitly demand and may refuse treatment without. The special nature of confidentiality in psychological treatment has been recognized by some American states. As one judge remarked, upholding the privilege of confidentiality in the patient-psychotherapist relationship: 'psychotherapy by its very nature is worthless unless the patient feels assured from the outset that whatever he may say will be forever kept confidential. Without the promise of secrecy from the therapist, buttressed by legal privilege, a patient would not be prone to reveal personal data which he fears might evoke special disapproval'.[206] Psychiatrists and psychotherapists have shown differences of opinion regarding patient confidentiality, for some believe that in the patient's interest, confidential matter may sometimes need to be discussed with a helping agency, while others believe that even the physician-patient privilege, where it is legally recognized, is not sufficiently watertight for psychotherapeutic situations. For extended discussions on this subject the reader is referred to other sources.[207-211]

25. Examination-in-Chief

The examination of the expert witness in court occupies three main phases with additional ones inserted when necessary. These are:

1. The examination-in-chief, conducted by the advocate acting on behalf of the client who has engaged the witness.
2. The cross-examination, conducted by the advocate acting for the other party.
3. The re-examination, conducted by the first advocate again.

The judge may interrupt the examinations at any point in order to clarify the witness's testimony, but after the re-examination, the witness must wait to see if the judge wishes to conduct his own examination. If he does so, the counsel acting for the side for whom the witness is appearing, is permitted to re-examine the witness. That is, re-examination, which allows the advocate to clear up misconceptions and correct any bias induced by hostile questioning, always terminates the testimony of the witness. When the evidence is straightforward and brief, the counsel will often forego re-examination as being unnecessary.

Being called
The forensic psychologist will normally be in court already, so that he can move straight into the box when called. If he has been excluded from court, and is waiting outside or in the witnesses room, his name will be called by one of the court attendants and he will make his way into court. It is preferable to be close to the court door near the time one expects to be called, so that no unnecessary time is spent reaching the box. Some witness rooms are a long way from a particular court in some of the older buildings, and a bad impression is created if too long a time elapses before the witness appears. If the psychologist is already in court, his coat, scarf, umbrella and other impedimenta can safely be left on the seat he vacates. If outside the court, they should be brought into court and deposited on some vacant seat *en route* to the witness box. It is never safe to leave possessions unguarded outside of the court, even with the number of policemen coming and going. Some of the larger courts have a cloakroom where garments can be deposited under the care of the cloakroom attendant, but even these safeguards are

inadequate to protect property from the attention of some of the clientele. The author lost a new umbrella in the cloakroom of the Old Bailey within less than an hour, an old but similar one with three broken ribs being left in its place.

One of the merits of the psychologist providing expert evidence in court is that it enables him to replace the views of the 'reasonable man' or that fictional individual so loved by English jurists 'the man on the Clapham Omnibus' with empirical scientific data which more accurately portrays the views of the community. While there is still a long way to go before the findings and techniques of experimental psychology are fully exploited in court proceedings, the acceptance by the court of the social science approach in Brown's case (1954) was a significant development in this direction and stands in marked contrast to the earlier case of *Plessey* v. *Ferguson* (1895).

Taking the Oath

When entering the witness box, the witness remains standing to take the oath, or to affirm, if he has no religious conviction. A copy of the New Testament is usually kept on a shelf in the witness box, and the witness will be asked to take it in his right hand, raise it aloft and repeat the words printed on a card usually handed to him by the usher. Sometimes the usher will dictate the words to him: 'I swear by Almighty God, that the evidence I shall give, will be the truth, the whole truth, and nothing but the truth'. Non-christians are permitted to use their own religious 'bible'. The words of affirmation will be read to those who prefer to affirm. In American courts, witnesses rest their left hand on the book and raise their right hand in the air: habituées to the witness stand often walk into court after being called with one hand in the air, reciting the oath as they walk, and sinking into the witness chair as they reach the final words, touching the Book *en passant* as they do so. This is the so-called 'Travelling Oath', deprecated by the court, but particularly popular with the sort of police witness who comes into court festooned with revolver, handcuffs, jangling keys and a breast pocketful of mammoth cigars looking like Cape Kennedy in miniature.

At one time the oath included the words: 'as I shall answer to God at the Great Day of Judgment' and the witness was required to kiss the book. In the days of stronger religious allegiance the oath was psychologically effective, and indeed there is some evidence that for many witnesses it is still more difficult to lie after taking an oath than without doing so. Nevertheless, as a Scottish soldier in the 1745 Rebellion said: 'There's an uncou' difference atween blawin' on a beuk, an' sennin' awe's soul t'hell'[155]. With Lister and the discovery of sepsis come the realization that when kissing the Book one was exposing the most vulnerable part of the external body surface—the mucosa—to an object handled shortly before by denizens of the underworld and slums.

No wonder it was called 'the insanitary oath'. By the turn of the century writers on forensic medicine were cautioning their readers to take their own copies of the New Testament into court with them, but the many changes in English social life wrought by the Great War of 1914–18 included the disappearance of the 'insanitary' oath.

When the witness has been sworn, his circumstances change in three ways. Psychologically, the probability that his testimony will be truthful has increased, although the differences between individuals will vary enormously in this respect. Secondly, if he is found to have lied to the court he can be convicted of perjury, and thirdly, all his statements made after the oath become privileged so that no action for slander will lie. The affirmation is a logical consequence of an increasingly secular society, but there are good psychological reasons for supposing that justice is the poorer for the diminution in religious faith.

Until the end of the seventeenth century the law was that evidence could only be given upon oath taken on the Gospel, and hence non-Christians, including Jews and heathens, were not able to be witnesses. The Oaths Act 1978 has consolidated the earlier enactments which liberalized the form of oath, and the Law Reform Revision Committee has now advocated the abolition of the oath.

The witness is first examined by the counsel acting for the solicitors who engaged his services. The first part of the examination consists of questions designed to establish the 'credit' of the witness and his competency to give expert testimony. Under the Rules of Evidence, counsel may not ask leading questions, but this Rule is usually waived in the introductory phase of the Examination-in-Chief, since the matters to be elicited are not in dispute. The psychologist will first be asked to give his name, which he must do in full, and his place of residence. Next he will be asked his qualifications. This does not mean merely his academic degrees, but the training and experience which 'qualify' him to give an expert *opinion* as distinct from the facts to which the ordinary witness is confined. The counsel usually wishes to make this an impressive gambit, since it may be used as a piece of one-up-manship in order to counteract the allegations of the opposing counsel that the witness is less competent, and thereby his evidence is of less value, than that of the witnesses called by the other side. Degrees, together with the names of the universities awarding them should be given in full, together with any other affiliations to learned bodies relevant to the nature of the case. Thus 'Master of Arts and Bachelor of Science of the University of Bristol, Fellow of the British Psychology Society' would always be appropriate, whereas more specialized qualifications may not be. For example, an ophthalmic qualification would be relevant if the facts in issue concerned vision, but not if the controversy was whether the plaintiff's deafness was of hysterical or organic origin. Sometimes counsel wishes to create a special impact and makes full use of everything the witness has to offer in the way of qualifications, but irrelevant ones leave an opening for opposing counsel to criticize, belittle, or otherwise cloud the issue and are therefore best avoided. The qualifications will usually include statements about relevant experience, e.g. working in a psychiatric hospital for so many years, or having special responsibilities in a specialized unit such as a drug addiction clinic, alcoholic ward, and so on. There will also be questions asked about published work, where again a compromise is necessary between the impression of learning given by an extensive personal bibliography and the relevance of the titles to the present case. A Parkinsonian type rule in these matters, and a corollary of Murphy's Law, is that if any statement can be misunderstood then it no doubt will be: even a list of published books is open to misinterpretation as to the writer's degree of expertise, as when Professor H.J. Eysenck, having had a list of his many publications read out in court, was asked whether he did more than just collect statistics or record facts, (*R.* v. *Anderson* (1971)).

Sometimes the qualifications of an expert brought to court by the other side are daunting:

Counsel: Would you state your qualifications, please, Doctor?

Witness: I am a Bachelor of Science, and a Bachelor of Medicine, and a Bachelor of Surgery, and a Bachelor of Law, and a Master of Arts. I hold the Diploma in Public Administration and I am a Fellow of the College of Pathologists. I am a consultant psychiatrist specializing in forensic psychiatry and London lecturer in Forensic Medicine in the London Hospital Medical College. I am a Physician Superintendent and was formerly senior lecturer in Forensic Medicine at the University of Leeds for eight years. Before that I was Fellow in Forensic Medicine at Harvard University.

Counsel: And so Doctor, you are a qualified lawyer, a qualified pathologist, and a qualified psychiatrist?

Witness: I have qualifications in them all!

Despite this impressive array, the witness was described in court, by his own counsel would you believe, as a man with 'a strange and esoteric science, which is not a recognized brand of science, but rather a matter for the library shelf or discussion between medical gentlemen'.(*Att. Gen.* v. *Norton*, (1966)). If the courts still see psychiatry in that way, what hope is there for psychology?

More than once the present writer has had his evidence interrupted by the judge who has asked him to define the difference between a psychologist and a psychiatrist, and it is sometimes helpful if this distinction is brought out at the beginning. Sometimes, however, the counsel purposely wishes to avoid making the distinction explicit, in the hope that the other side will not make an issue of it, and that the jury will assume that the psychologist is a medical doctor and therefore

242

competent to discuss medical matters. This is an unfortunate situation to which the psychologist may well take exception. It occurs because psychology as a profession has not fulfilled its responsibility in educating the public as to its nature, role and purpose in contemporary society.

Sometimes a good counsel will use the difference between the non-medically qualified psychologist and the medical practitioner to his client's advantage. This can often be done by first, establishing the essential psychological nature of the fact in issue, then by expanding the psychologist's training, qualifications and experience in psychology, and finally by exposing the paucity of psychological training or experience of the medical practitioner during the cross-examination of the latter. In the interests of justice it may be better that the jury should be misled about the psychologist's medical competence in order that they should give equal weight to the evidence itself, but this is a controversial matter which will only be solved when the public become more enlightened about modern professional psychology. In *R. v. Ranson* (1975) Maurice Yaffe, a psychologist from the York Clinic, London, appearing as an expert witness for the defence and asked to describe the differences between a psychologist and psychiatrist, pointedly emphasized the number of hours of taught psychology each received.

Frequently counsel himself will not be very clear about the difference, and sometimes has been surprised to find in court that his witness is not the medical expert he understood him to be: this likelihood makes it essential for the psychologist to clarify the situation during the pre-trial briefing. Medical witnesses are not always what they purport to be. One medical expert[212] called on a psychiatric issue described himself as an army psychiatrist. His so-called expert qualifications were shown up under cross examination to be completely irrelevant and/or inadequate:

Counsel: Doctor, have you had any psychiatric experience since the war?

Witness: No

Counsel: Have you been associated with any psychiatric clinics?

Witness: No

Counsel: Are you a member of any psychiatric medical societies?

Witness: No, Sir

Counsel: A Diplomate of Psychiatry?

Witness: No. I emphasized that initially. I said qualified army psychiatrist.

Counsel: Your principal experience, then, is in paediatrics?

Witness: Yes the greater emphasis today, I might add, in paediatrics is on mental health.

Counsel: Your chief concern with mental health, then, is with the mental health of children?

Witness: As a paediatrician, yes, as a paediatrician.

Counsel: Apart from being a paediatrician, your concerns are those of a layman rather than of a physician?

Witness: (floundering) I don't consider myself actually as an ordinary layman. I feel I am a little bit better qualified than the average physician in the field of psychiatry. I have done this on and off in my own practice with young people of 13, 14 or 15. I have advised considerably young people ready to get married.

Readers working in paediatrics might consider marriage guidance to be an unfamiliar activity in their own clinics. Even the court seemed a little astonished by this evidence.

The expert's pretensions on other aspects of his knowledge are also quickly revealed. A medical witness was called to give an opinion in court of an allegedly obscene book:

Counsel: You testified on direct examination, Doctor, that you are familiar with contemporary literature?

Witness: Within reason as an educated man, I would say, not a literary expert.

Counsel: Are you familiar with the writings of James Baldwin, Doctor?

Witness: Within reason. He is considered to be a contemporary good writer, a well-known writer.

Counsel: Did you read his novel *Giovanni's Room?*

Witness: No

Counsel: Did you read his novel called *Another Country?*

Witness: I perused it. I would not be considered an authority on the subject.

Counsel: The answer is, you did not read it well enough to tell us what was in it?

Witness: The answer is, I did not read it well enough to discuss it intelligently, yes.

Counsel: Are you familiar with the works of John Updike?

Witness: No

Counsel: Are you familiar with the works of Mary McCarthy?

Witness: I haven't read her book. I have just read reviews of it. I don't know it intelligently enough to discuss it.

Counsel: Have you read *Ulysses* by James Joyce?

Witness: No

Counsel: What contemporary novels have you read?

Opposing Counsel: I object to the question.

Counsel: He testified he was familiar with contemporary literature.

Witness: Yes

Counsel: I want to know what he has read.

Judge: We don't want to go through every book he has read!

Counsel: But he has not mentioned one yet that he has read.

Judge (to witness): Just answer the question.

Witness: I keep myself in good contact by reading of course all the book review sections. I grant you that does not give me the right to discuss a book. I have read *The Carpetbaggers*.

Counsel: Other than *The Carpetbaggers*, is there any novel that has been published in the last ten years that you have read?

Witness: Of course. I can't recall all those things. I am not prepared to discuss the articles.

Counsel: Can you name a few that you have read?

Witness: This is silly.

At this point the judge felt that counsel had made the point that the witness, contrary to what he had testified earlier, was not directly familiar with contemporary literature, and suggested counsel should continue his cross-examination on a different point.[212]

The credibility of the witness is important in determining the weight which can be attached to his evidence, and for this reason, the opposing counsel will often go to some length to discredit the witness in the eyes of the jury. In the case of the ordinary witness to fact, this procedure can go to extreme lengths; his morals can be impugned, and his intelligence denigrated: in the case of the expert witness, the procedure may be more subtle but is often no less painful and humiliating. A psychologist with a doctorate may be told: 'of course you are not a proper doctor, you have had no medical training whatsoever'. Although the witness may then protest that his doctorate indicates academic distinction in his subject and that medical training is irrelevant to his evidence, the damage has been done and in the eyes of the jury his credit has been considerably diminished. Another ploy is for the counsel to emphasize his title by saying: 'of course, you are only a Doctor of *Philosophy*' in such a way as to make the jury wonder what philosophy has got to do with brain damage—to them a clearly medical matter. In this respect a Bachelor of Science is a little better served by the title of his degree. The psychologist obviously labours under some professional disadvantages in this way compared to his medically qualified colleagues, whose status is explicit and easily understood by the lay jury: and the disparity is often pointed out by the opposing counsel, especially when, as often happens, the psychologist appears on opposite sides to a medical practitioner. It is often helpful to make one's area of competence clear to the counsel beforehand, and in the opening stages of his examination he can then effectively explain the precise status of psychology and the psychologist, relevant to the issues before the court, at the time he established the credit of the witness.

Foreign degrees are often made to sound *infradig.*, or even beyond the pale. Sometimes counsel will studiously ignore one's doctorate title as if to belittle one's status, as if to emphasize that one is not a 'proper doctor'. Sometimes, emphasis is placed upon the institution awarding the degree, enabling the cross-examining counsel to exercise his thespian talents with appropriate looks of disbelief or incredulity, 'Stretchford?' he will ask. 'Did you say the University of *Stretchford?*' He will then shake his head commiseratingly with an 'Oh! well!' as much as to say: 'well, we can't expect much help from *this* witness'. If the expert is of foreign extraction, this is sometimes insistently pointed out in the final speech, and sometimes, even in the summing up. As the judge reminded one particular jury, the psychologist was 'a lady of *Dutch* birth'. Many of our most eminent and senior professional colleagues were refugees from the Nazi anti-semitic activity before the war or from wartime invasions of their own country, so there is plenty of scope for this form of belittlement.

The expert witness may be asked by the opposing counsel whether the expert on the other side is not a greater authority or in possession of wider experience than the witness himself. In such circumstances it is tactful and frequently diplomatic to admit that the other experts are senior in experience or status to the witness giving evidence. But it is also fair for him to say that this is a question which is bound to have a degree of personal bias and he would prefer this to be answered by a third party.

This was made more explicit in *Attorney General* v. *Parker and Hulme:*

Prosecuter: How many patients have you?

Witness: We only have 74 at a time but we have a large admission rate.

Prosecuter: How long have you been there?

Witness: I have been there seven years with the exception of one year in the United States.

Prosecuter: You will agree that Dr Hunter, Dr Saville, and Dr Stallworthy are psychiatrists of good experience and considerable standing?

Witness: Yes

Prosecuter: And they have examined thousands of mental cases?

Witness: Yes

Prosecuter: Do you know that when a witness is convicted of murder he or she is examined by a psychiatrist before being executed?

Witness: Yes

Prosecuter: And the persons who examine them are the doctors I mentioned?

Witness: Yes

Prosecuter: So that their medicolegal experience is very great?

Witness: Yes

Prosecuter: And if I may say so without offence, greater than yours?

Witness: I was at Porirua for eight years where there was provision for 1500 patients.
Prosecuter: They must have had considerably more experience of this work than you?
Witness: Yes
Prosecuter: Have you ever examined a convicted murderer?
Witness: No!

Despite being outnumbered on all flanks—qualifications, years of experience, kinds of experience and numbers of patients, the witness holds his own:

Prosecuter: Does it disconcert you that three experienced psychiatrists disagree with you?
Witness: No. I have held different opinions many times with colleagues. Sometimes I have been right.

The expert witness himself will not normally be allowed to speak spontaneously but will be expected to answer questions as simply and as briefly as possible. The purpose of this is to enable the opposing side to object to any question, the answer to which would be legally inadmissible. If the expert witness is giving his views at length it is not always possible for the opposing counsel to prevent statements which should not be made in the court. However in order to enable the court to understand the specialized concepts and terms appropriate to the profession of the expert, considerable latitude is normally extended when asked to give some account of these concepts. However not all judges are patient with expert witnesses. In one trial a professor was stopped in his testimony by an angry judge and told he was not there to lecture the court (*R. v. Anderson et al.* (1971)).

The forensic psychologist will be expected to present, in his evidence, the data on which his opinion is based, the reasoning by which he linked fact with conclusion, and any qualifications which may be pertinent. The weight given to this evidence will depend upon the status and authority of the witness established by counsel at the commencement of his proof, on the presentation of the evidence and the weight explicitly ascribed by the judge in his summing up.

As far as the first factor is concerned, there is an increasing tendency by juries to over-value qualifications and undervalue experience. This is possibly due in part to the increasingly important role which paper qualifications play in everyday life, but the expert who acquires his knowledge by practising his speciality over many years is more vulnerable to apparently simple questions on technical theory. The manner in which an expert witness can be discredited is well shown in the case of *R v. Rouse* (1931). In this case the judge, Norman Birkett, discredited an engineer as an expert witness who gave testimony concerning the effect of fire on nuts and bolts. The witness, Mr Arthur Isaacs, was managing director of the Bramber Engineering Company in Cricklewood, who were specialists in the heat treatment of metals. Isaacs himself had 18 years experience as a fire assessor for an insurance company and volunteered some information after reading the case two days before the trial. Mr Isaacs gave evidence during the examination-in-chief that fire always loosened nuts. Despite his considerable experience as a fire assessing engineer, Birkett suspected that his theoretical background was poor and that his status as an expert could be discredited on this basis:

Birkett: What is the co-efficient of the expansion of brass?
Isaacs: I am afraid I cannot answer that question.
Birkett: If you do not know, say so. What do I mean by the term?
Isaacs: You want to know what is the expansion of metal under heat?
Birkett: I asked you what is the co-efficient of expansion of brass. Do you know what it means?
Isaacs: Put that way, I probably do not.
Birkett: You are an engineer?
Isaacs: I dare say I am. I am not a doctor, nor a crime investigator.

Although persisting in saying he was qualified by experience and not by academic degrees the damage had been done. As an 'expert' he was discredited. The defence called a second fire assessor, a Mr A. J. Cotton, who supported Isaac's evidence that fire loosened nuts. Under cross examination he also failed to define the co-efficient of brass. The prosecution called a Colonel Cuthbert Buckle, who admitted he had carried out no experiments, but nevertheless believed Isaacs and Cotton were both wrong. In his summing up the Judge devoted 700 words to this point, pointing out the contradiction between Colonel Buckle and the so-called 'experts' and reminding the jury of their status. After conviction, Sir Patrick Hastings on appeal asked for evidence from a Dr H.S. Rowell to be admitted who would confirm that nuts loosened with heat. The Lord Chief Justice refused. An interesting sequel—too late to help the prisoner—came 32 years later, with a scientific report by R.V. Jones on an experiment carried out, which showed that a temperature of 600°C, that is, a dull red heat, would loosen nuts in a few seconds[213]. Isaacs and Cotton were vindicated. However Jones found that no amount of heat would rotate a nut 360 degrees, as found in Rouse's car, so that perhaps in the final analysis justice was done, even though it was not seen to be done.

In such cases as Rouse the qualifications of the expert witness have little standing; indeed they may only serve to point out the contrast between the status claimed and the type of evidence given. Psychologists in court are not normally considered poor representatives of their profession since in the words of one prosecuting lawyer they are men 'with more degrees than a thermometer'. On one occasion following a poor testimony by a psychologist the presiding judge literally threw a set of projective test cards on to the floor. The defence lawyer then requested that the court records show that the judge had expressed his feelings towards the testimony of this expert witness, to which the judge replied that the records would also show that he, the judge, was going even further in that he was throwing out all the testimony of this psychologist. Obviously testimony which can arouse such a negative reaction in a court of law must be of great concern to psychologists interested in the contribution they can make to society and to the law in particular. The situation is made even more difficult when psychologists on the same side disagree among themselves. It is difficult enough for the court to reach decisions based on psychological data when disagreement is expressed between psychologists appearing for the defence and prosecution respectively but when the psychologists are both on the same side and unable to agree the court can have little confidence in the overall psychological evidence. In the case of *United States* v. *Kent* (1964) the first psychologist, appearing as expert witness for the defence, administered the Szondi test and reported the results in court in the following way:

Psychologist: This showed a passive depressed person who withdrew from the world of reality with an inability to relate to others.

Attorney: Was not the Szondi test made up about 1900 and wasn't it made up of a number of pictures of Europeans who were acutely psychotic?

Psychologist: Yes, this is true.

Attorney: And this tells you something about his personality?

Psychologist: Yes, you can tell something about the person from his responses to the photos.

Attorney: Why did you use photographs of mentally ill persons, why not normal persons?

Psychologist: Because photographs of mentally ill persons are supposed to accentuate the needs or drives or deprivations or frustrations which human beings experience. Normal people have managed to resolve their frustrations. I don't know why it works. It is something underneath. It is difficult to explain and understand. Doctors use digitalis for heart disease without knowing why it acts as it does. A psychologist can diagnose illness by the pictures a subject selected as those he liked or disliked.

The second psychologist for the defence was called:

Attorney: Did you administer the Szondi test, doctor?

Psychologist: No, I don't happen to think much of it. The test assumes that a schizophrenic looks a certain way and we have evidence that this is not so.

Undermining the evidence of a professional colleague on the same side points to inadequate pre-trial conference. The defence attorney should have discovered this discrepancy in opinion about the validity of the Szondi test before the trial and either brought about a unanimity of views by professional discussion or suggested that the evidence be withdrawn on the grounds of inadequate validity.

When the attorney asked the psychologist how the Rorschach test was scored, the situation became ludicrous. A reference to cars and guns as power or phallic symbols was questioned and a discussion of the feelings and fantasies of the accused, in particular his fear of impotence, which was manifested in promiscuity in order to prove his masculinity, brought an interruption from the court.

Judge: You mean, the way to prove you are adequate sexually is to keep having sexual intercourse.

Psychologist: No, in order to keep proving that he is not inadequate to himself he continues to have sexual relations because . . .

Judge: Don't you think that would satisfy him that he was adequate.

Psychologist: Unfortunately these things don't happen that way, if the feeling is very deep within a person.

Judge: Have you had any personal experience?

One of the problems of using depth interpretations of this sort, apart from the obvious one of proving the validity of them is that some of the jury may have had a passion for guns and big cars and they may well fear a psychologist's similar verdict about themselves. They might feel because it could not be true of themselves it could not be true of the accused. The jury is no more prepared to accept deep psychological interpretations than any other unprepared group or individual including the judge or magistrate. As one justice said pointedly after a most lucid explanation of the effects of early trauma in the family environment: 'Of course I am taking no notice of all that nonsense about the accused's childhood!'[202]

Subject to any rules of court made in pursuance of Part 1 of the Civil Evidence Act (1968), the Civil Evidence Act (1972) provides that a person who is qualified to give expert evidence and is called as witness in any civil proceedings may also give opinions on any relevant matter, even if this includes an issue in the proceedings in question. Moreover, even if he is not qualified to give expert evidence on a particular matter, he may, under Section 3(2) of this Act, still give an opinion on matters outside his own expert qualification if made as a way of conveying relevant facts personally perceived by him. This makes it very much easier for the clinical psychologist, giving evidence for the plaintiff in a brain injury case, to describe the behaviour of the plaintiff in medical terms. Formerly, it was not generally admissible for the psychologist to use specialized medical terms, and on occasions psychologists referring to their patient as being e.g. comatose have been rebuked for going beyond their professional competence in giving an 'opinion diagnosis' on a neurological state. He can, by virtue of the 1972 Act, now describe the patient's state in scientific terminology of another profession, if by doing so he conveys to the court the facts *as perceived by him*. It is important to remember, however, that the provisions of these two Civil Evidence Acts do not apply to Scotland or Northern Ireland.

Computer Evidence
The Rules of Evidence in civil proceedings have always been wider than those in criminal trials, but the Civil Evidence Act (1972) widened further the rules relating to expert testimony. It provides for the acceptance of statements of opinion where under the Civil Evidence Act (1968) only statements of fact would apply, although an exception of importance to the psychologist is that Section 5 of the latter Act is not amended. The effect of this is that opinions produced by computers are not admissable even under the liberalizing 1972 Act, and this rules out the use of computerized reports, such as those commercially provided for clinicians by the MMPI Computer Diagnosis Service. However, it should be noted that this refers only to the verbal report from the computer. The quantitative data, as facts, are still admissible, so that the clinical psychologist is still free to submit as evidence the computorized MMPI psychogram and his *own opinion* based on the data embodied therein. The same considerations apply to the computerized diagnostic opinions based on any other psychometric instrument.

Medical witnesses are often criticized for their presentation as expert witnesses. The reason for this is partly due to the expectations of the court. The expert witness is well educated, possessing a scientific background and is assumed to be versed in the arts of both logic and argument. Like all witnesses however he will be nervous in a strange atmosphere and will be emotionally prevented from doing himself justice. The performance of a psychologist in court is always very different from that of the same person teaching in a university lecture, or at a clinical meeting.

Simpson recommends that no attempt should be made to memorize the records, reports, details of observations and other data which one wishes to quote in the box.[136] Simpson also recommends certain stock phrases which cannot be bettered in court conditions, for example, 'I form the opinion or view that . . .' or 'The findings or observations were consistent with . . .' Opposing counsel might say 'that is only an opinion, doctor' but this is all that has been asked for and a psychologist will disarm the counsel by saying so.

Forms of Address
Knowing the correct form of address is important, for some members of

the judiciary are touchy about this. A Colonel would object to being called 'Corporal' and an Admiral 'Midshipman'. Similarly, so would a judge being addressed in a way appropriate to the chairman of an inferior court. As always, the rule is when in doubt, choose the higher of possible titles. People rarely complain of being promoted in status. However, the expert witness displays courtesy and evidence that he has gone to the trouble of ascertaining the right form of address when using it correctly in Court.

Judges of the High Court are addressed as 'My Lord' or 'Your Lordship'. This title is also given to the Law Lords, including the Lord Chief Justice, and the Lord Justices in Appeal. High Court Judges who are not peers can be identified on the lists outside the Courtroom by their title: the Honorable Mr Justice ————. High Court Judges also attend certain Crown Courts when serious crimes are to be heard, so they will be encountered from time to time in the provinces. Mostly in the Crown Court will be seen the Circuit Judges, named on the court lists as: His Honour Judge ————. These judges are addressed as 'Your Honour'. County Court judges are referred to and addressed similarly. In the inferior courts, the Justices of the Peace are addressed as 'Your Worship', and the stipendiary magistrates as 'Sir'. Recorders and Coroners are also addressed as 'Sir' although some prefer to be called 'Mr Coroner'. Chairmen of Tribunals, Presidents of Court Martial and of Courts of Enquiry are also addressed as 'Sir'.

The psychologist will often be asked what appears on the face of it to be a simple question requiring a yes or no answer but which carries implications relevant to the issue before the court. The more expert in a subject one is, the more aware is one of the ramifications and complexities. This makes the real expert cautious in his replies, which tend to be limited by a wide variety of qualifications. Such a learned and scientific approach is applauded in academic circles but is discouraged in court, and the expert may find himself sharply rebuked. On one occasion the Lord Chief Justice, Mr Justice Goddard said: 'Jurymen are not college professors . . . it would only confuse them to go into metaphysical and philosophical distinctions'. To psychologists the distinctions are sometimes of profound importance. In one case, the witness had described the accused as suffering from a 'paranoid reaction following brain damage'. In cross-examination this was interpreted by counsel as meaning the accused was a paranoic, a diagnosis carrying significantly different implications. On this occasion the witness was permitted to clarify the distinction but this is not always possible. In such circumstances the author has usually adopted the form: 'I cannot answer the question as asked without misleading the court'.

The medical witness faces the problem of providing expert testimony in a foreign milieu, and on the basis of criteria set by law[214]. Such criteria often appear ambiguous, and in some cases are satisfied in such a manner that the clinician may believe injustice is being done.

The psychologist is required to answer any questions put to him, even if it fails to make sense or is scientifically meaningless. Frequently the author has been asked by the court, after he has attempted to provide a scientific explanation of a mental condition, couched in lay terms: 'let me put it to you simply—is this man suffering from a mental disease, yes or no?' Even after explaining that 'mental disease' is not a meaningful concept, or one used by clinical psychology, the court has repeated the question and insisted upon a dichotomous answer. Sometimes an understanding judge will give guidance in such a way that one can swallow one's scientific qualms and give the kind of answer the court requires. To refuse to answer the court leaves one open to a charge of 'contempt of court', and more than one witness has been imprisoned on this charge. One medical witness, Dr J.L. Gilbert, by his courageous refusal to answer with a 'yes' or 'no' the traditional questions, set in motion a chain of judicial events which led to the Durham Decision and effected a major advance in forensic psychiatry by revising the M'Naghton Rules in many American jurisdictions.

The use of technical terms should be avoided as much as possible. It is necessary that the expert testimony should be understood by those in the court who are completely ignorant of scientific terminology, not just psychological terminology. The prisoner is entitled to understand what is being said in connection with his own case as well as the court. As part of his clinical training the psychologist will of course have learnt to make good use of ordinary language in describing technical facts, and this training will stand him in good stead when he is giving expert testimony in a court of law. Court officials are not unreasonably suspicious that unfamiliar polysyllabic terms are merely disguising ignorance. There is a special danger in the use of complicated technical terms in that they may be mistranscribed by the official court shorthand writer or by the court typist and this could well mislead a higher court of appeal on some important point.

Lord Devlin once remarked that clinicians appear to talk to the judge as if he was a fellow expert. This is quite unreasonable for only a small proportion of the criminal cases which they hear contain any medical evidence whatsoever. Some judges have a short way with witnesses who are too 'technical' as the following example shows:

Judge: I want you to deal with something of the fundamentals of the matter from the point of view of psychiatry, let us start with the word 'amnesia'.

Witness: Memory occurs at three levels: the basic vegatative level of the personality—

Judge (interrupting): That probably means a lot to you, but it means 'cabbages' to me!

Wiseman discusses the problems of medical testimony and says: 'psychiatry is a branch of medicine which like others is constantly tackling and solving problems in human behaviour and it has been shown that much of what has been regarded as criminal conduct is overt evidence of disease. Studies on epilepsy by chemical and structural changes in the brain and psychological influences may provide just as reliable evidence of disease as a solid lung does of pneumonia but it might not be quite so easy to explain these things to a jury who tend to choose the testimony they can best understand and which corresponds to their own sentiments. The explanation of a crime to a jury by a confident psychiatrist may be too complex both intellectually and emotionally for a jury to understand or act upon.'[215]

Because medical and psychological concepts have to be translated into legal concepts before they are fully accepted in court, expert witnesses may often appear to be differing in opinion when there is no basic disagreement of fact. What they are disagreeing about is the translation of concepts from one profession to another. Thus one expert may confine his use of the term 'disease of the mind' to psychotic conditions only, while another will be prepared to include any psychiatric condition including neurosis and psychopathy. On one occasion the author had told the court that the probability that the accused was schizophrenic was 95%. He was then asked whether or not this meant that the accused was suffering from a disease of the mind. Uncertain of whether this transition of concept was valid, he looked to the judge for assistance, and received an encouraging nod. On the basis of this unverbalized direction, he then stated that the accused was suffering from a disease of the mind (Case No. 31). On another occasion, when a man accused of murder had pleaded 'diminished responsibility' the author presented qualitative evidence to the court to show that the man exhibited approximately 25% deterioration from his estimated pre-morbid state. The judge, unwilling to create a precedent in which a legal term like 'diminished responsibility' became linked to a concrete figure, guided the author into interpreting this deterioration as 'a disease of the mind' (Case No. 32).

Sometimes a particular concept is in dispute. One of the most common is that of concussion, which is not always easy to establish unequivocally. Although the question of whether the plaintiff did or did not suffer concussion may be quite irrelevant to the forensic psychologist's own evidence, he may well be asked questions about this condition. Where such questions are strictly of a medical and non-psychological nature, the psychologist should state explicitly that they are outside his special field of competence. On no account should he be drawn into a discussion on such medical topics as fractures, unless he has had some special training and experience which justifies his encroaching upon the physician's professional ground. Some topics, however, are borderline between medicine and clinical psychology and the problem of a fractured skull may be inseparable from the problem of the presence and degree of brain damage. Concussion similarly falls into this overlap of disciplines, and the psychologist can hardly expect to have his opinions on brain damage given due weight if he refuses to comment upon the inter-related condition of concussion. However, although it is sometimes expedient for the clinical psychologist to answer questions on such a topic, his statements may and probably will be challenged, by medical experts on the other side. In these circumstances, it is judicious to refer to medical dictionaries and textbooks by recognized authorities to confirm support or supplement one's statements. For this purpose, it is not acceptable to take copies of the appropriate entry or paragraph, for this would offend the Best Evidence Rule. The original volume must be used. The relevant entries should be clearly marked by numbered bookmarks and line-indicators so that the witness can refer to them expeditiously. Leave must be obtained from the court before doing so.

In paranoid cases, when the M'Naghton rules are being applied, an appropriate textbook quotation is usually helpful. In contested diagnoses even more so. The problem here is that the seriously psychotic patient has all his primary delusions well-encapsulated and is in all other respects in good contact with reality. It is difficult for the lay person to believe the patient *is* seriously ill, even more difficult for him to believe that although the M'Naghton Rules are inapplicable, the patient's moral attitudes are set within a frame of reference of delusional belief which distorts any cognitive judgments and decisions he makes. In one murder trial, faced with medical colleagues holding opposite opinions on diagnosis, one psychiatrist read this excerpt from a textbook of forensic psychiatry:

> Perhaps no evidence concerning the insanity of an accused person is so convincing in a court of law as that of systematized delusional insanity; but it may fail to satisfy the requirements of the legal definition of insanity. For the offender often knows both what he is doing, and that what he is doing is punishable by law. He may however be convinced that his act is morally right.[217]

This exactly recounted the point the expert witness was trying to establish.

The process of *textbook referral* in the witness box is of course a two-edged weapon. On the one hand it enables the witness to make a concise and authoritative statement which can be impressive in its own right and have additional value if the authority one is quoting is relatively well known: on the other hand it may convey to the jury that the expert is not conversant with his own subject. It is generally better if the expert goes into court well prepared beforehand, with all the relevant points well memorized. Good preparation is in any case essential, since the counsel for the opposite side is likely to be armed with reference books and may cross-examine the forensic psychologist on relevant pasages which appear to put forward a contrary view to that advised by the witness. In one case where visual acuity and perception were involved, for example, the writer was examined on large extracts from Wright's *Physiology*, in another on Cunningham's *Neuro-anatomy*. Unfortunately, the passages hurled at the witness for explanation and comment, while superficially germane to the point at issue may, through either ignorance or design on the part of the cross-examining counsel, be completely irrelevant. In such cases they can become a useful red herring to the other side, clouding the issue and immersing the expert's telling points in a sea of irrelevancies; more often they are used deliberately to expose the weaknesses of the witness and so damage his reputation as an expert. Although as we have seen, the expert may refresh his memory from books, he should not rely on the work of others to support his own case when the essential facts are missing. The general rule for textbooks is *cite*, but do not *quote*.

The Hypothetical Question

The hypothetical question is used for two purposes: viz. to supplement the information gained from the witness, and to counteract points made by the other side. During the examination-in-chief counsel may use it to bring out the strength of the psychologist's opinion, and at the same time anticipate a criticism likely to be made by the cross-examining counsel. This not only weakens or nullifies the point which the opposing counsel would wish to make, but also alerts the witness to possible lines of attack being prepared against him. For example:

Counsel: Let me put it this way, doctor. Supposing you agreed with the neurologist who stated on oath that in his opinion Mr .... had suffered no concussion, would you still feel as confident about your own belief that brain damage was in fact present?

This hypothetical question enabled the writer to refer to his earlier evidence about test results and point out that the diagnosis he had formulated rested on psychometric data and was made independently of the presence or absence of concussion. Since the validity of the psychometric evidence of brain damage was not in question, whereas the existence of concussion in this case was, the opposing counsel would be less likely to raise this question during the cross-examination. An obvious line of attack would be to ask the court to weigh the relative merits of the opinions of a London neurologist and a provincial psychologist, but by explicitly excluding the controversial basis or the neurological opinion from that used by his own witness, the counsel had cleverly removed the justification for a confrontation. The value of this technique is that an astute counsel can raise possible criticisms, but put them in a non-ego-threatening way, and so encourage the expert witness to work out his defences, in the sympathetic atmosphere of the examination-in-chief. The same points would otherwise be presented without warning in a question form, aimed at assaulting the *amour propre* of the witness; the response made in an intrapersonal setting of stress and dysphoria, and an external atmosphere of disbelief and hostility, would probably be inadequate and possibly damaging to the forensic psychologist's own case.

In civil actions including contests of will and personal injury suits, the psychologist may be asked to give an opinion in respect of an individual whom he has never examined. In these circumstances he may commonly be presented with the so-called hypothetical question. He will often be obliged to give his opinion on the basis of information presented to him on the witness stand in the form of the hypothetical question. This question usually commences with the phrase 'assuming that': for example, the examining counsel or the judge could say 'assuming that the plaintiff was subnormal before the accident (which is the conclusion the psychologist is arguing against) would you expect to find any difference in your post-injury examination?' Since the counsels on each side will include information from the evidence favourable to their cases when putting the hypothetical question, it can be seen that the psychologist may have to give two different opinions on what was originally the same evidence. If the hypothetical question is framed by the counsel, he may, prior to the trial, obtain the necessary data from the psychologist, and wish to ensure that this information is introduced into evidence. Opposing counsel may attempt on cross-examination to unsettle the psychologist as an expert witness by asking questions implying a prior collusional conference with the counsel to ask the hypothetical question. This may be done in such a way that the inexperienced psychologist then feels that he has presented his evidence in an improper way, and may be inclined to withdraw it, which is what the cross-examining counsel wants. It must therefore be emphasized that pre-trial conference between the counsel and the expert witness engaged by his own side is part of the ordinary and proper preparation of the witness.

In one compensation case, the psychologist, while in the witness box, was asked to comment upon (1) the behaviour of the plaintiff, who, when taking the oath, threw the copy of the Holy Bible at the Court, and (2) the interpretation of this behaviour, given by a psychiatrist appearing as expert witness for the defendant, to the effect that it clearly confirmed the diagnosis of hysteria which he had put forward in his proof. She was able to provide a detailed and logical explanation of why this behaviour was more in keeping with her own assessment of brain damage than with an hysterical condition.[216]

Committal Proceedings

A special problem arises in connection with committal proceedings. Here the question to be decided by the court is whether the accused is to be committed for trial at a higher court. For this purpose all the oral evidence, or parole evidence as it is called, is taken down verbatim by a typist. The typescript is read back to the witness before he leaves the witness box, and if he agrees that it is a reasonable record of what was said, he is asked to sign it. These affidavits are then passed on to the Higher Court in the event of the accused being committed for trial. There are a number of difficulties confronting the witness which emanate from the method of recording the parole evidence. The first is that all spontaneity of verbal expression is lost by the necessity of replying by slow dictation. Obviously typing takes longer than writing shorthand, and the response to questions has to be in short phrases which make it difficult to keep a cohesive line of thought in mind. Also, the noise made by the machine often causes the typist to miss something of what was said, and he has to interrupt the response to ask the witness to repeat an earlier phrase. By this time one is in the middle of the next phrase and formulating mentally what is to follow, and this disruption of the thought processes often produces a blocking which leads to statements which are worded rather differently than the one intended. Unless the statement is actually untrue the courts are unwilling to amend individual statements in what they would regard as the interests of literacy rather than of justice. To retype a multipaged document in order to correct the actual wording or to modify an impression would slow down the progress of the case beyond all limits of reasonableness. Thus it is, that the final form of the testimony in committal proceedings, and the information it conveys, depends very much on how the questions are asked and how the typist rephrases the question into a response statement. For this reason it is important to give a clear, explicit and emphatic Yes or No at the beginning of the response where appropriate. Sometimes the counsel will make incidental remarks which are typed into the statement and which are not easily expunged from the testimony. For example in *R.* v. *Gold* (1972):

Counsel: Now, doctor, you have had a lot of experience in this type of case and must know as much about the obscenity laws as anyone. Do you really believe. . . .

In reply, the writer explicitly denied knowing as much about the law as anyone else (pointing out tactfully, that both the bench and counsel were well versed in this aspect of law) and gave a qualified response to the remainder of the question. The final version read, however: 'I know as much about the obscenity laws as anyone and I really believe. . . .' which offended the writer's natural modesty and implied a strength of belief regarding the matter in question which was the reverse of what was intended. The court were reluctant to amend this statement since it was not exactly a factual contradiction of a truth, but eventually consented to do so when the writer remained adamant and refused to sign until the emendation had been made.

These difficulties do not normally occur with witnesses to fact, since the testimony itself comprises statements of fact. With the expert witness the situation is very different, for his evidence may be largely opinion and belief, presented with qualification and nuances of meaning which are vulnerable to gross distortion by this method of recording.

One court stenographer told a lawyer that he customarily left certain things out of the trial transcript, things he thought were not seriously intended. As the lawyer commented: 'censorship is everywhere!'[212]

Fortunately for the expert witness, the examination-in-chief, which comes first, is the easiest part of the testimony, and gives him time to adapt to the milieu of the court. The questions will be expected, because they flow naturally from his report or proof, and he may have already gone through them with the advocate in the pre-trial conference. The problems he faces at this stage are not so much in answering questions about the psychological evidence, but in putting them within the framework of the law. Forensic psychologists and psychiatrists are at a grave disadvantage to their forensic scientist colleagues in this respect. The latter have clear hard facts which are instantly translatable to everyday language. The fact that a nut unscrews in the heat can be conveyed at any level of communication. But those concerned with the facts of mental life are dealing not in direct observations but in inferences. Moreover these inferences are converted into concepts, or purely imaginary constructs, like mind. The mental expert is then asked by the court to contaminate two levels of concept, such as disease and the mind, and finally give an opinion on a purely legal concept, like insanity. To make life even more difficult, he must do so within certain rules of evidence, many of which owe their authority to case law. In the case of insanity, for example, the psychologist who has examined the accused may wish to give his opinion on

(i)   whether or not the accused was insane
(ii) whether his insanity, if present, was of a kind that usually prevents people from judging between right and wrong.

The psychologist cannot be asked whether the accused *was* capable of judging between right and wrong. *R*. v. *Layton* (1850) & *R*. v. *Richards* (1855). Having heard the witness's evidence, he can be asked to take particular facts so given, and assuming these to be true, give his opinion as to the sanity of the accused. *R*. v. *Francis* (1850) & *R*. v. *Mason* (1911).

He cannot be asked whether, having heard the evidence, he considers the accused to be insane or not. *R. v. M'Naghten* (1843) & *R. v. Francis* (1850). He may, however, be asked to give his opinion upon the question of whether the behaviour of the accused is commonly seen in people of unsound mind. *R. v. Dove* (1856). In forensic science the methods are not peculiar to forensic problems but to general science. The analysis of alcoholic content is basically the same whether blood or beverages are being examined. But in forensic psychology the problems are not the same. The psychologist is not doing a diagnostic analysis to help his medical colleagues, because the court is not interested in medical labels, only legal ones. A schizophrenic patient may be perfectly sane or completely insane in law, and this will depend upon the nature of his condition, not the particular diagnosis. Similarly, when a psychologist carries out a behavioural analysis he does so with an eye to choosing the appropriate therapy, not to decide on the patient's insight into moral principles.

Even when the psychologist has something relevant to say, he may not be able to say it adequately. Some psychologists are poor clinicians or scientists but have a good flair for communicating their opinions in court. Some are good clinicians or scientists but have no flair and may be a menace to their client. In the superior courts, the psychologist may help his potential client better by refusing the case than by fumbling out his results in the court and then getting discredited during cross-examination. This all points to the need for good preparation and adequate training. Police officers, who number giving evidence as witnesses to fact as one of their professional duties, have special training for this purpose, and some basic elements of forensic psychology should be *de rigeur* in any course of professional psychological training.

When the forensic psychologist gives testimony there is a tendency for him to be over-inclusive. This occurs in two ways. First, because in his attempts to be thorough and comprehensive in the examination of the client, he tends to accumulate more data than is necessary and bearing differing degrees of relevance. Although the expert has sworn to tell the *whole* truth, this refers to the whole of the *relevant* truth, therefore much of the data, after initial analysis, may be put on one side. The temptation to bring in obvious psychopathology is often very strong, especially when the expert believes this to have a strongly mitigating factor, but unless it is relevant to the facts in issue it must be discarded at this stage. If the accused person is found guilty, then the counsel may make a plea in mitigation, and may, at that time, call the psychologist into the witness box to describe to the court what the counsel believes are mitigating features. The advocate is always a better judge of this matter than the psychologist because he knows from long experience what the court regards as mitigating. In a sex offence, the factor which the psychologist regards as the most mitigating feature may be the one which prompted the judge to add another year to the prison sentence.

The other way in which over-inclusion occurs stems from the first. Having used a broad spectrum of assessment methods, and at the same time gathered information from external sources, the psychologist, in thinking over the case as a whole, will be attempting to put all the pieces together to make a logical and complete picture, like solving a jigsaw puzzle. The problem here is to disentangle the picture when giving evidence, for it is easy to confuse previous information for real recollection of fact. Having read several medical reports on the party at the time the case first started, it is easy to come to believe that some of the behaviour described in the report was seen by the psychologist. It is not uncommon for one or two years to elapse between the first examination of a patient and the subsequent court hearing, and in that time, the fusions of memory can be quite considerable. In particular, where there are gaps in the evidence, it would be expected that these would be filled in over the passage of time, in a way which conforms to the psychologist's *expectancies*. Psychologists are not quite as bad as the chambermaid in Martin Chuzzlewit, who 'made out as much of the letter as she could, and invented the rest, believing it all from that time forth as a positive piece of evidence'; nevertheless they, more than most experts, know the distortions of memory produced by lapse of time[148]. Juvenal's *sit pro ratione volumtas* is a fallacy to be guarded against.

Not only is giving too much information to the court likely to make the whole testimony less relevant, but it clouds the issue. Lay people can take only so much of a new subject at one time. The fewer the technical ideas and concepts they are introduced to, the easier it is for them to absorb the implications of what they have been given. Even the lawyers themselves can be blinded by too much science, however well they have studied the case and discussed the technical issues with their own experts.

A good plan is to work through all the material and reach a conclusion relevant to the problem posed by the court. Then list all the steps supporting that conclusion which are drawn from the psychologist's own data. Would the conclusion stand up on the basis of this information alone? Are there any facts which go against the conclusion? Deduct these and examine what is left. *That* is the expert's case when stripped of all support. How well will it stand up in cross-examination? Note that it is not merely a collection of facts which are being looked at here, but a process of reasoning. As the court said in *Carter* v. *U.S.*[234] 'unexplained medical labels are not enough. Description and explanation of the origin, development, and manifestations of the alleged disease are the direct functions of the expert witness. The chief value of the expert's testimony in this field, as in all other fields, rests upon the material from which his opinion is fashioned and the reasoning by which he progresses from his material to his conclusion'.

26. Cross-examination

THE PURPOSE of cross-examination is for the expert witness to be truly examined—it is the *raison d'etre* of the forensic psychologist. Without cross-examination, the experts could present their own opinions on the evidence, and the court would be no further forward. In such circumstances the jury would need the services of yet another expert in order to weigh up the respective merits of the two presentations. Such a need would be contrary to the basic principles of English law and British justice which affirm that, in the final analysis, the question of guilt or liability should be judged, with special exception, by representative members of the community. The cross-examination is the judicial way of testing the merits of opposing arguments. At best it may be merely a polite probing for possible weaknesses or inconsistencies, an attempt to obtain some acceptable degree of rapprochement between two apparently different sets of opinion. At worst the cross-examination can be a rude, emotional, overbearing and personal attack on the witness as well as a devious, subtle and biased critique of his methods, findings, conclusions and opinions: which end of this continuum any particular cross-examination falls will depend upon the personality, skill, and experience of the cross-examining counsel and the nature of the evidence being given by the expert. Sometimes when the expert testimony is unopposed or when there are no acceptable grounds for defence, and conviction is a foregone conclusion, the cross-examining counsel may be content to accept the essence of evidence and decline to cross-examine. But this is a rare happening, and any psychologist tendering a forensic report must expect to end up under cross-examination.

The courtroom is unfamiliar territory to most witnesses and provides an atmosphere of strangeness, awe and apprehension which is not conducive to clear thinking. In this situation and under the influence of such mixed emotions, even the most intelligent witnesses may find themselves behaving stupidly and making statements they would afterwards wish they could retract. Under cross-examination, the opposing counsel will work on these emotions in order to impair clarity of thought even further, hoping that the witness will so tie himself up with inconsistencies and far-fetched and easily controvertible statements that his evidence will be discredited.

As Mr Justice Donovan once said: 'To make a so-called expert look a fool appears on occasions to be the sole object of counsel conducting the cross-examination'. The arousal of affect in legal negotiations, even in a substantially less threatening milieu has been amply demonstrated in psychiatric studies forming part of a law course[11].

Sometimes the protection of the witness against undue pressure from the cross-examining counsel is written into the legal code, as in the state of California where 'it is the right of the witness to be protected from irrelevant, improper or insulting questions, and from harsh and insulting demeanour'. In English law, irrelevant improper questions can be objected to by the counsel calling the witness on the grounds that such questions are inadmissable under the rules of evidence. Other aspects of the behaviour of the cross-examining counsel are not covered by these rules. The duration of testimony in the witness box also has its effect upon the mental state of the witness. On two occasions, the author has spent three consecutive days in the witness box.

One of the most damaging methods of the cross-examiner is to confront the witness with an incontrovertible fact which is inconsistent with what the witness has just said or has put in his written report. This confrontation may be supplied by a letter or report the witness has written, or by some entry in the patient's case notes made either by the witness himself or by some other professional person, such as the admitting doctor, the casualty officer or ward sister. Sometimes the expert witness will be confronted, not by some admissible fact, but by some authoritative opinion. The cross-examiner will usually seek to establish the authority of the citation: he will prefer to do this if possible through some independent witness, often through the preceding medical witness who perhaps has nothing to be defensive about in this particular area. For example, counsel may be cross-examining the casualty officer who admitted the patient after the accident. He will perhaps signify that his cross examination has come to an end and remark casually 'Before you go, Doctor, will you tell the court whether you have ever consulted the works of Henry Head' (or whoever the authority to be cited might be). The doctor, usually fresh from his recent medical training, will agree that he has. He may then be asked whether the author is well known as a neurologist, which will generally be answered in the affirmative, and then will be asked about the author's reputation. Young doctors tend to give writers of standard non-controversial textbooks rather more prestige than would consultants with more academic experience, and the reply of a casualty officer to this question is usually sufficient for the cross-examining counsel's purpose. If the witness is feeling a little uncertain of where this line of enquiry is leading, he may attempt to hedge, and will then be verbally reassured by counsel. If his answers do not appear to be establishing the authority of the textbook writer, the counsel will either drop the subject or allow the witness to leave the box, or renew his attack by asking the witness to name other neurologists of equal eminence. He may confront him by reviews from leading medical journals, written by medical practitioners of professional status, proving that his opinion is not held by more senior members of the witness's own profession. Once having established, to his own satisfaction, that the writer of the textbook is an accepted authority on the subject he will then use this to undermine the 'credit' of the forensic psychologist. The exchange goes something like this:

Counsel: Now, Doctor, have you heard of Henry Head?

Witness: Yes, he was a well-known neurologist.

Counsel: The previous witness, an experienced medical practitioner, said he himself had consulted the works of Henry Head. He said that he was considered an authority on aphasia, and was cited as one of the standard authors on the subject. In the opinion of this doctor, Henry Head is one of the leading authorities on aphasia. Do you agree with his opinion?

At this point the witness is in a quandary. He knows by this time that this is going to be quoted against him although he may not know in what respect or in what context. If he undervalues the status of the author, he will be confronted by evidence of opinion to the contrary and may be shown to be out of touch with other members of his profession. If the author is not contemporaneous the most useful ploy is to admit that he *was* indeed an eminent authority *in his time*, but that increasing knowledge in the subject has brought more up-to-date authorities to the fore. It is of course important that the psychologist can himself cite alternative and more recent authors of recognized merit. Counsel will then brush aside this temporal qualification and ask the psychologist 'to listen to what this eminent authority has to say on. . . .' He will then read an appropriate paragraph which would have been supplied by one of the medical specialists acting for his own side, and which contradicts something the psychologist has said. For example, here is Sir Hartley Shawcross cross-examining an extremely experienced forensic psychiatrist[10].

Counsel: Is paranoia a mental disease at all?

Witness: Yes, paranoia is a profound mental disease.

Counsel: I am reading from page 746 of Professor Tansey's *Textbook on Mental Diseases*. He says: 'Paranoia is not a true disease. It is an intellectual anomaly'. Now do you agree with that?

Witness: No. It is simply a matter of words. It is really very easy. All mental diseases, if they do not recover, pass into a stage of mental enfeeblement which is called dementia and which is shown by alteration in the brain as an organ. The exception is paranoia. A man may be a profound paranoiac for 50 years, and at death, an examination will show no changes or alterations whatsoever. For that reason many rather strict purists in medicine decline to call it a mental disease. What they should do is to decline to call it a brain disease. It is not a disease of the brain in that sense. That is how the misunderstanding, if it is one, has arisen. It is a most profound mental disease.

Here the witness has not only given the court a clear picture of what paranoia is. He has successfully explained the reason for the discrepancy between his statements and those of a professor and textbook-author, and for good measure has implied that the latter has been semantically inaccurate. A little later, when a contrary textbook statement is again quoted at him:

Counsel: You do not agree with that?

Witness: I do not agree with any sentence taken out of its context applying to anyone 30 years after the writer has died.

The cross-examining counsel does not always have written or published material with which to confront the expert witness, especially if the latter has taken special care over the preparation of his proof and has attempted to avoid any possible inconsistencies. In such circumstances the counsel of the opposing side will be listening attentively during the examination-in-chief, making note of any possible inconsistencies occurring in the parole evidence. In the event that none are forthcoming, he may spend some time during the cross-examination attempting to elicit information which can be used in this way. Some material for the purposes of confrontation (of this and other witnesses) may be obtained by leading the enquiry into areas which to the psychologist are not obviously relevant to the matter in issue. The witness is often caught off guard in this way, and may make statements which he otherwise might be inhibited from making. The admission of error by the witness obviously lowers his apparent competence. Another ploy of the cross-examining counsel is the use of flattery, which may induce the witness to relax his caution and express opinions which he would normally inhibit. In this respect, the cross-examining counsel, having acknowledged the eminence of the witness and his long experience in professional problems, will use the 'exception' ploy. This is to force the witness to admit that exceptions exist in most of the rules of diagnosis, or in the relationship between treatment and response. The witness cannot but admit the existence of exception in almost any matter of human behaviour. The presence of recognized signs or symptoms do not always lead to an unequivocal diagnosis. Patients do respond differently to the same type of treatment. Effects do not always follow some well-defined cause. Once having forced the witness to admit that exceptions exist, the cross-examiner will then suggest that the present findings produced by the psychologist could similarly be an exception to the general rule which forms the basis of the psychologist's opinion. This puts the forensic psychologist in an extremely difficult position. He knows all too well that his conclusions rest on statistical inference, that the norms on which his opinion is based are means of a standardizing population, some of whose members behaviour may have run contrary to the group majority. If 99% of the patients who achieve a specified score on a certain test are shown to be brain-damaged there is still a one per cent minority for whom no evidence of brain damage exists. With his back to the wall on a particular issue, the psychologist cannot but accept the hypothesis that the client or accused could be this exception to the rule. The best defence to these lines of attack is to remember that it is the expert opinion which is being questioned, not real scientific facts. The patient's test behaviour, if necessary to be presented to the court, is a matter of fact and should be incontrovertible. Psychologists for the other side cannot challenge the actual test data—the quantitative psychometric scores, description of overt behaviour, psychophysiological records, and so on, without impeaching the professional integrity of the psychologist presenting them. It is the inferences and conclusions drawn from these data which may be challenged. The correct response of the forensic psychologist confronted by the opinions of experts, which differ from his own, is to admit clearly that everyone has a right to his own opinion, and although his opinion may be different to those of other people, it does not follow that his opinion is the wrong one. Galileo, Copernicus, Keppler, and other men of science all held minority opinions which later proved to be closer to the truth than did those held by the so-called 'authorities' of their day.

Apart from the foregoing ploys, cross-examining counsel will also make effective use of the hypothetical question. If the psychologist is giving an opinion that brain damage was incurred following a road traffic accident, he may be asked whether or not it was possible for some preexisting organic condition to produce similar evidence as that in question. Usually, of course, the honest answer is that it could. Unless there has been an open head injury or focal signs are reasonably unequivocal (in which case the neurologist's evidence alone is usually sufficient and may not require psychometric evidence to supplement it) the typical brain damage sign from a closed head injury could have predated the injury. It is unusual for there to be sufficiently detailed evidence of the plaintiff's pre-morbid mental efficiency to enable a psychologist to be completely positive in excluding a pre-traumatic cause. Yet on the face of it, admission to this possibility destroys the essential basis of the psychologist's opinion. It is therefore important to insist on providing the necessary qualifications to any answer central to the opinion, by saying that while the possibility does exist, it is extremely remote, and then explain why. Having obtained a damaging admission the cross-examiner will not want to have it qualified anyway, and may try various devices to prevent the court hearing the qualification. The most successful tactic is to interrupt the witness with a simple innocuous question which may or may not have relevance to the preceding answer though of course it must be relevant to some aspect of the evidence.

Counsel: I put it to you, that in the absence of evidence to the contrary, it is possible for this defect you speak of to have been present before the accident?
Witness: Yes, it is possible but. . . .
Counsel: And you are certain that there was memory loss?
Witness: Yes, there was clear psychometric evidence of a memory deficit.

In this instance, the psychologist had given up qualifying his first answer in order to answer the second, about which he felt confident and had a ready reply. The cross-examining counsel, when addressing members of the jury will then be able to remind them that the witness admitted that the memory loss could have preceded the accident. More importantly he cannot be criticised or corrected by the judge for failing to mention any qualifications, for the psychologist has not made any. Nor will the judge be able to include any qualifying statements when the time comes for him to sum up.

Some advocates are known for their effective use of hypothetical questions. This is how the technique of one Treasury Q.C. and particularly able prosecutor is related by a defendant in his book[219].

Counsel started all sweetness and light:
'Thank you, professor, for talking in terms we all understand, not like yesterday!' (referring to Haward). 'You would agree your opinion is based on some information, and if you had more information about the case your opinion could be amended?'
'Yes', the rot was already setting in.
'May I put a hypothetical question?' said the advocate cunningly. 'Supposing the prisoner had chosen another identity to take money, escape from his responsibilities and set up a new life with his lover, would that influence your view?'
'Yes'. (how could he reply otherwise, but he should have added a qualification as Haward, a firmer character, would have done!).

Gradually, the cross-examining counsel persuaded this eminent professor of medicine to undermine his own evidence, even to the point of agreeing with the prosecutor, and admitting that his previous statements were too categorical.

Another way of dealing with the hypothetical question is shown by the following expert witness[203]:

Counsel: Do you think it's a good idea that children should indulge in sexual intercourse all over the streets of London?

Witness: People could not lie down in the streets of London and, in the technical word, copulate. I think we are discussing something which is impossible.

Counsel: I'm afraid it is not impossible. Is it a good idea or a bad idea? Is it or isn't it?

Witness: It is a completely hypothetical question!

Counsel: What is the answer.

Witness: I don't think I can give an answer to a hypothetical question.

Counsel: Or won't.

Witness: No. Any answer I give is just not the truth, and I said I would speak the truth.

Another form of discrediting the witness is by 'mistranslation'. The expert makes a statement, which the cross-examining counsel translates into everyday speech for the benefit of the jury. In doing so, however, he deliberately distorts the meaning in such a way that the expert's statement sounds ridiculous or unbelievable. Sometimes the distortion is not so much a change of meaning as an exaggeration which has the same effect. In one case,[220] the clinical psychologist was trying to make the point that the defendant lacked the capacity to entertain murder—that whereas the person committing murder 'with malice aforethought' would be entertaining the wish to encompass the death of the victim, the defendant in this case was too grossly disturbed to formulate these thoughts clearly enough. This careful exposition of psychological insight was translated by the prosecutor as 'If you hate a guy a little, and kill him, its murder. If you hate a guy a lot and kill him you're sick'. Another example of exaggeration comes from the Solberg murder trial[183], where the witness, denying that she is in any way afraid of the mentally-ill woman, nevertheless confesses that she makes her feel nervous. This is mistranslated by the cross-examining attorney as 'feeling scared to death'. Exaggeration converted the true nervousness at the strangeness of the psychotic (which was probably outside the experience of all of the jury), to being 'scared to death', which was a highly emotional and understandable feeling to them. The same prosecutor could also tone down the evidence of defence witnesses when contrary to his own case. Notice how he minimizes the importance of a psychiatrist's very comprehensive examination, which occupied a session lasting two-and-a-half hours:

Attorney: And did you make a diagnosis of amnesia, or of memory gap?

Witness: I didn't make a diagnosis at all. I prefer not to make a diagnosis of any kind on the basis of a two-and-one-half-hour examination.

Attorney: (ponderously) In other words you recognize the very definite limitation of a mere two-and-one-half-hour examination?

Witness: I think I am the first one to recognize that.

Attorney: And you recognize that, without making a diagnosis, opinions relating to the motives and thoughts and truthfulness or nontruthfulness of the individual are difficult for you to evaluate? (The witness recognized no such thing. Such a conclusion could not possibly have followed from the earlier statement. The attorney cross-examining the expert witness is beginning the *cul-de-sac* ploy, explained below, in the hope that the witness, lulled into a sense of false security, might be prepared to take the easy way out and acquiesce to the above portmanteau question. The witness, however, had got lost in the ramifications of the question, and wanted it repeated. The attorney realizes that the witness is too careful to admit to questions without thinking, and so he goes back to diminish the adequacy of the psychiatric interview).

Attorney: Well, you made no diagnosis, and your examination was so short that a diagnosis was impractical if not impossible?

Witness: Yes.

So what started out as a very comprehensive interview which the witness regarded as sufficiently long to thoroughly evaluate the amnesia, becomes, in the cross-examining attorney's words, first a *'mere'* $2\frac{1}{2}$ hours examination, and then *'so short'* that a diagnosis was impossible. He now has ample testimony on record to discredit the doctor's opinion on the grounds of insufficient opportunity to obtain the requisite medical evidence to support such opinion.

One potent method of attacking the witness by cross-examining counsel is known as the *cul-de-sac*, rather akin to the chess player's 'fools mate'. The counsel leads the witness in a certain direction with questions which seem only marginally relevant and which the witness is only too happy to agree with, being grateful for the relief from the more critical questioning. Gradually he finds himself, in order to be consistent, agreeing with questions he is not too sure about, but is not too worried since these do not appear to effect the main issue. Eventually he finds himself committed to a particular point of view. Abraham Lincoln is credited with inventing the *cul-de-sac* attack. In a murder trial he conducted he induced the alleged eye-witness into a position in which he could only account for his significant observation by saying there was a moon. Lincoln then produced an almanac showing there was no moon, and the witness was discredited. In the Illinois circuit where Lincoln practised, the story goes that the almanac was not even of the year of the murder[195]. The author has also fallen victim to the *cul-de-sac* attack. In a compensation case (Case No. 33) involving a questionable head injury, the psychometric evidence all favoured the presence of organic pathology. The author had made much of the evidence of dysmnesia he had found, together with some retrograde amnesia, which the medical experts for the defendant claimed was hysterical in origin. The author guilelessly followed the cross-examiner down the *cul-de-sac* discussing concussion and was gradually led round to the relationship between post-traumatic amnesia and duration of concussion. Finally the author was led to the position of having to conclude, from what he had been led to say previously, that if retrograde amnesia was present the patient must have been concussed. The cross-examining counsel then produced the hospital record in which the casualty officer had written, unequivocally, 'No Concussion'.

The author was invited into the *cul-de-sac denouement* because he had been too emphatic over the psychometric findings on the memory disturbances. It is seldom good to over-emphasize some particular part of the evidence—the counsel for one's own side will do this adequately, anyway. Overemphasis tends to make the opposing counsel consider the evidence more deeply than he otherwise might, and sometimes leads him to ask other experts for advice on where to look for chinks in the armour of the witness. Probably the best example of this occurred in the murder trial of *R. v. Seddon* (1912). Dr William Willcox, the pathologist called for the crown, was cross-examined by Sir Edward Marshall Hall, and forced to admit that arsenic at the distal end of the hair of the victim was compatible with chronic administration over a year or more. This negated an acute homicidal dose. If Marshall Hall had sat down at that point, Seddon would have been acquitted. Instead, he kept emphasizing the fact that this conclusion was the only one applicable to the facts, as admitted by the prosecution, and this set Willcox considering whether there were any alternative possibilities. Later, after much thought, he arrived at one, and after confirmatory tests, was recalled by the Crown and testified that arsenic could reach the distal ends of the hair by absorbing it from body fluid in the coffin, and this would be compatible with a large acute dose of the poison. As a result, Seddon was convicted and hanged.

The witness is expected to answer questions put to him, briefly and succintly. He is not expected to go beyond the precise limits of the question, and he may justifiably be interrupted if he does so. Nevertheless, he has a responsibility to the court to communicate meaningfully as well as truthfully, and for this reason the expert witness should insist on his right to complete his answer. He has sworn on oath to tell not only the truth but the whole truth, and he must therefore ensure that necessary qualifying statements are clearly linked to the simple affirmative or negative response which the cross-examining counsel really wants. The forensic psychologist should not fall into the trap of being side-tracked on to easier questions. Qualifying statements are sometimes not very easy to formulate in a way in which they can be understood by the lay members of the jury, especially if the question is one the witness is unprepared for, and under the tensions of the occasion, it is all too tempting to escape from the situation by accepting the lure of safe *terra cognita*. The temptation should be resisted, however, and the expert witness should refuse to answer the following question until he has completed what he wanted to say in answer to the first.

If the witness is calm, careful, and concise, the cross-examining counsel may be unable to find any weakness in the testimony by which he can devalue it in the eyes of the court. His last means of attack may then be against the source of the evidence rather than against the evidence itself. It is perhaps fair to say that the majority of counsel will not choose this course against an expert witness, although it is a common way of dealing with the witness to fact. When the forensic psychologist is in the position of having his qualifications and experience impeached, he may suffer acute embarrassment unless he has been completely truthful and modest about his competency as an expert. His degree may be sneeringly referred to as 'second class'; having boasted of ten years experience in clinical work he may be asked to enumerate the number of true aphasics (or whatever the case may be) he has studied in depth—usually a pitifully small number for those psychologists working in psychiatric rather than neurological departments. His two year's intensive post-graduate study of some closely relevant diagnostic group may be studiously ignored and much will be made of the time which has elapsed since he last saw such a case, the implication being conveyed that his experience is limited to the infrequent case seen in his present department. If the witness cannot be satisfactorily deflected by this attack on his professional standards and competence, the cross-examining counsel may, as a last resort, attack the character of the witness. He may ask him about past convictions, especially where the offence itself, or the statements made to the police can be used as evidence of dishonesty. One expert witness was asked if he had ever been treated for venereal disease. Unfortunately he had; his moral standard was thus impugned. This is a legitimate way of attacking the witness though with experts, fortunately infrequent. Obviously, since both sides are proffering contradictory evidence, it follows inevitably that one part or the other are either mistaken, or are lying. If the cross-examining counsel cannot find any mistakes in the evidence, it is logical for him to question the veracity of the witness. The author has found that the best way of answering such an allegation is to refer to the oath which he swore on taking the stand:

Counsel: Doctor, may I ask you if that's really so.
Psychologist: Yes, indeed. I was very serious when I took the oath on entering the box. (*R. v. Anderson et al.* (1971)).

Sometimes, the cross-examination is quite perfunctory. The cross-examining counsel may appreciate the fact that the evidence of the forensic psychologist is watertight. For example, the expert testimony may be confined to a statement for the defence on the intellectual level of the accused. If the accused had already been assessed by the prison psychologist, the prosecution will have the details of both examinations, which can be expected to tally within acceptable limits. In such circumstances counsel will not really doubt the evidence given by the defence psychologist. Nevertheless, unless this evidence is challenged, the court will assume that the evidence is fully accepted. This assumption stems from the more general *presumptio juris* of English Common Law that it is natural for a man explicitly to deny an accusation made against him. Silence implies assent. So, if the counsel wishes later to cast doubt on any aspect of the psychologist's testimony, it is necessary for him to challenge the evidence in cross-examination. In such circumstances the counsel will ask a few straightforward questions about the psychologist's evidence, which, while not necessarily yielding him any useful ammunition, will at least ensure his right to criticise it later.

Sometimes in order to upset the expert witness the counsel may ask the witness if he realizes the serious consequences his evidence may have for the prisoner. Since the abolition of the death penalty and the shorter duration of detention in Broadmoor Hospital, this question is unlikely to be asked, but the psychologist should remember the reply given to a similar question by a famous toxicologist who replied that he was not concerned with consequences. So too the concern of the psychologist for the accused would seem to end when he has give his evidence honestly and to the best of his ability. The result such evidence may have ultimately on the prisoner is the concern of others.

Barristers are, of course, only human, and after a number of frustrating hours fruitlessly spent in trying to find loopholes in the evidence of an expert witness, some of them not unexpectedly lose their temper particularly if the witness himself has been less than courteous in his replies. It is, however, a breach of professional conduct under a Ruling of Bar Council (1950) for counsel to put questions intended only to insult the witness. Moreover, under Rule 38 of the Supreme Court (Order No. 36) the Court may object to questions which, while impugning the witness's character, do so by reference to events which are so long ago, or so irrelevant to the issue in hand, that the court believes they are unlikely to effect significantly his credibility at the present time.

For example:

Prosecutor: Adolescence is a difficult period, isn't it?

Witness: Yes.

Prosecutor: I take it you were an adolescent once?

Defence Counsel (interjecting): We can all agree with that. So were you.

Prosecutor: Did you have a difficult adolescence, Doctor?

Witness: I refuse to answer questions about myself!
(At this stage there was laughter and ribald comments from the public gallery, which were eventually stopped by cries of 'Silence!' from the Court Usher and the constables).
Judge: I think, Doctor, you need not answer that question.
Later, the prosecutor again descended to personal reference.
Prosecutor: They said you were an irritating fool and displeasing to look at. Do you think they were mad when they said that?
(Laughter in court, quickly silenced).
(*Attorney General* v. *Parker & Hulme*).

The experience of being cross-examined by a counsel of top-calibre; quick-witted, keen, incisive, penetrating and very much at home in his familiar professional surroundings can be a traumatic one for most psychologists, and the prospect is so daunting that others take pains to avoid involvement. Very often, however, ethical considerations force the psychologist to believe that he has a moral duty to give evidence, sometimes because he is the only witness a patient can call on, sometimes because he believes an injustice would result if psychological evidence was not tendered in court, and sometimes because his conscience leads him to defend some social principle of moral importance to him. Nevertheless, those psychologists with an introverted, tender-minded, ultra-sensitive personality who suffer so deeply under public onslaught in the witness box, may do their client's cause more harm than good, and may justifiably decline from participating in such a potentially ego-shattering experience. As the late Harry S. Truman said 'If you faint in the heat, don't go in the kitchen'.

It seems unlikely that psychologists will ever engage in a 'battle of the experts' as humiliating as that produced by psychiatrists, if only because the former deal in possibly more objective and certainly more quantitative data than the latter. The shifting sands upon which psychiatric nosology has been erected provide strikingly contrasting interpretations and lawyers have gone on record as saying that they can always find a psychiatrist who, in the witness box, will take a diametrically opposite view to that given by another psychiatrist[221].

It should be remembered that the prepared lawyer may well have read up details of psychological tests with which he will confront the psychologist in the box. For example in one case where the psychologist had used the House Tree Person Test, the cross-examining counsel said 'Are you familiar with the occasion upon which a psychologist gave this test to 50 psychotics and then gave 50 normal subjects the same test and then had a group of psychologists rate them?' The psychologist answered that he was not familiar with this research and was then told that the findings of the research invalidated the test as a diagnostic instrument. One rather subtle way of undermining the confidence of a psychologist is to present him with a statement which the psychologist may feel has been drawn from an authoritative textbook. In one case the cross-examiner said: 'Doctor do you agree with this statement: "it is well established that psychiatrists and psychologists freely concede there is no absolute accuracy and reliability of tests in the measurement of intelligence"?' The psychologist answered 'I do not agree'. The cross examining counsel then made a second foray in the following way. 'How about this statement. "Two persons of substantially the same mental capacity may test with materially different scores or rating depending upon education, training, environment etc".' Answer: 'Well, environment includes so much that I would think that this would affect the performance on intelligence tests.'

In this case the psychologist was holding his own but it is very easy when offered an apparently authoritative statement to be unprepared to be dogmatic and to begin to hedge one's earlier conclusions. At other times the psychologist may be led into areas of controversy where again his confidence can be undermined unless he is careful in his reply. For example:

Cross-examiner: Do you believe in free will?

Psychologist: I believe it means complete control over one's actions and thoughts. I believe one's environment and heredity affect one's ability to exercise choice, Man has ability to make choices but this is affected by other factors.

Cross-examiner: Do you come from the so called behaviouristic school?

Psychologist: No, I am an eclectic.

Cross-examiner: Do you believe all crime is a product of mental illness?

Psychologist: No.

Cross-examiner: Any category of crime.

Psychologist: I would expect bizarre crimes to be the product of mental illness.

Compare this with another psychologist asked the same question:

Cross-examining counsel: Do you believe in free will?

Psychologist: That is a philosophical not a psychological problem. Freewill is an arbitrary sudden explosion without cause. I don't believe that. If I am free to choose, why is it I choose one thing and you choose another? It is because of the structure of the nervous system and the influence of the environment.

Cross-examiner: Do you believe in God?

Psychologist: Yes. Certainly.

The judge interjects: You believe in free will, don't you?

Psychologist: I believe I can make a free choice based on what I am.

Judge: Any individual is free to make a choice isn't he?

Psychologist: Yes.

Despite the persistence of the cross-examining counsel in trying to elicit the answer he wants, the witness can be equally persistent. In the notorious Irish Arms Trial[222] Mr Finlay, defence counsel, cross-examining Mr Gibbons, a witness for the prosecution, repeatedly asked him whether the rifles were despatched to the North for distribution to non-Army personnel.

Gibbons: I think counsel is trying to put words in my mouth.
Finlay: I have asked you that question five times and I only want a yes or no answer.
Gibbons: One cannot give a yes or no answer to such a complicated question.

Sometimes the witness actually defeats the inquisitor, as in this exchange between the cross-examiner and expert witness in *Attorney General* v. *Parker & Hulme* (1954):

Counsel: Have not many persons been calm and callous right up to committing the crime?
Witness: I doubt if any sane person would approach murder with a completely calm mind.
Counsel: Was not Judas Iscariot cool and calm when he took bread and wine to our Lord?
Judge: (interposing) Mr Brown, Mr Brown. Whatever the temptation I think it would be inadvisable to continue that topic.
Counsel: I will not take it further, Your Honour.
Witness: I am sorry we did not continue with it for it would lead us to where Judas hanged himself.

Even psychologists who believe they have been treated with scrupulous fairness in court like McKellar[223] seldom wish to repeat the experience. Jeffreys reports a number of cases in which psychologists have been subjected to what he calls 'a technique of selective demolition', and provides examples of psychologists being cross-examined about individual items on intelligence tests and the answers given to them by the defendant[224]. Lifted out of context, and presented to the jury in isolation, they can be made to look ridiculous as a basis on which to support a professional opinion on the mental state of the examinee.

Counsel: (examining the psychologist's test forms) You gave him the Wechsler Adult Scale?
Psychologist: Yes.
Counsel: On the word information part of the test, the word 'temperature' appears. What question did you ask the defendant?
Psychologist: At what temperature does water boil?
Counsel: You gave him a zero. Why?

Psychologist: Because he answered 190° and that is the wrong answer. The right answer is 212°F.

Counsel: What question did you ask about the Iliad?

Psychologist: I am not sure; I believe I asked him to identify the Iliad or who wrote the Iliad. (The psychologist is here exhibiting a lack of familiarity with the test administration).

Counsel: And he answered 'Aristotle'?

Psychologist: Yes.

Counsel: And you scored him zero?

Psychologist: That's correct.

Counsel: Now you asked the defendant to define blood vessels, did you not?

Psychologist: Yes. (The test item calls for the test administrator to ask for the names of three types of blood vessel, not a definition).

Counsel: And his answer was capillaries and veins. You scored him zero. Why? Aren't capillaries and veins blood vessels?

Psychologist: I don't know. (Can one believe a psychologist doesn't know this elementary anatomy? More likely the psychologist is showing cognitive impairment under the stress of cross-examination, which is what the cross-examiner wants since his expert witness is then particularly vulnerable.) The norms don't consider that answer acceptable.

Counsel: What norms?

Psychologist: You see, these tests are scored on the basis of norms secured by administering the test to thousands of people. (There is no need to revert to this level of excuse: the subject was scored zero because he failed to answer the question completely.) Later:

Counsel: You asked him: 'What is winter?' and he stated 'a season of the year'. You gave him a one—why not a two? Isn't winter a season of the year, Doctor?

Psychologist: Well again it is a matter of the norms. A two answer would include a 'cold season of the year'.

Counsel: You asked him to define 'calamity' and he said 'a bad thing'. You gave him a zero. Isn't a calamity a bad thing, Doctor?

Psychologist: Bad is not an acceptable answer in terms of the norms.

Much of this expert's explanations were with reference to 'norms'. The court does not really understand the concept of norms neither has it been adequately explained. The court would, however, have understood that responses can be graded, and the logic behind the Wechsler grading, if that had been explained. As it is, the test itself has been belittled, and with it the status of this psychologist's evidence, since any simple-minded juror, unfamiliar with psychometric theory, would have sided with the cross-examining counsel during the above exchange. Even more devastating is when the cross-examining counsel tempts the psychologist into making speculative interpretations of projective test material.

For example:

Counsel: And the House-Tree-Person Test—you handed the defendant a pencil and blank piece of paper. Is that right, Doctor?

Psychologist: That is correct.

Counsel: And you asked him to draw a house?

Psychologist: Yes.

Counsel: And what did this tell you?

Psychologist: The absence of a door and the bars on the window, indicated he saw the house as a jail, not a home. Also you will notice that it is the side view of the house; he was making it inaccessible.

Counsel: Isn't it normal to draw a side view? You didn't ask him to draw a *front* view did you?

Psychologist: No.

Counsel: And those bars on the window—could they have been Venetian blinds and not bars. Who called them bars, you or the defendant?

Psychologist: I did.

Counsel: Did you ask him what they were?

Psychologist: No.

Counsel: What else did the drawing reveal?

Psychologist: The line in the front runs from left to right. This indicates a need for security.

Counsel: This line indicates insecurity? Could it also indicate the contour of the landscape, like a lawn or something?

Psychologist: That is not the interpretation I gave it.

Counsel: And the chimney—what does *it* indicate?

Psychologist: You will note the chimney is dark. This indicates disturbed sexual feelings. The smoke indicates inner day dreaming.

Counsel: Did I understand you correctly? Did you say dark chimneys indicate disturbed sexual feelings?

Psychologist: Yes.

Such a miserable performance in the witness box by a trained clinical psychologist has led many academic psychologists to question the value of clinical training and the competence of those responsible for providing it[245]. On the other hand, many psychologists provide expert testimony and are cross-examined without it appearing that the psychologist and his technique are on trial as much as the defendant, if not more so. They are often subjected to unsuccessful attempts to discredit them as expert witnesses, and to attempt to discredit the evaluative techniques upon which their testimony was based, but it is not usual for them to be forced to defend in detail every aspect of the procedure involved in the administration scoring and interpretation of psychological tests. Shearn suggests that 'it is a naive error for a psychologist to go into court armed with his testing materials and protocols as though he were going to present his findings at a clinical case conference attended by sophisticated and sympathetic colleagues'. He argues that to do so places him immediately in a defensive position, tends to convey the impression that the psychologist feels insecure in his role as expert witness. However, what the psychologist takes into court is not necessarily what he intends to talk about. He may expect every opinion he gives to be challenged, and so feel that he must stand ready to offer proof of everything he says. But such an overt attitude is not a necessary concomitant of going into the witness box well prepared.

As a general rule, the cross-examining counsel is allowed to ask questions only about testimony elicited in the direct examination. If therefore the psychologist carefully avoids a detailed discussion of the tests administered during his initial testimony, and provided he has not gone into psychometric detail in his previously submitted 'proof' there is no reason why the cross-examining counsel should ask destructively critical questions about test materials and test interpretations.

While it is no doubt a salutory experience to justify one's psychometric expertise at such a bar, the psychologist is there to provide an expert *opinion* not statements of fact concerning the defendant's or plaintiff's test behaviour. Moreover the court has neither the time, nor the inclination, to allow the psychologist to formally educate a body of uninformed laymen into the theories and practice of psychometrics. A useful ploy, in this respect, is for the psychologist to emphasize that his opinion is based upon a complete examination of the patient (including behaviour other than test responses) in the context of all that is known about him. Under critical and detailed cross-examination he can then fall back upon this statement, and so ward off questions about individual responses on the grounds that it is inappropriate and meaningless to discuss them out of context. He has every right to insist that his opinion is based upon a totality of data—past history and present behaviour as well as psychometric techniques.

Of course, the court has every right to insist that the expert provides the facts upon which his opinion is based. The expert is not there merely to give an opinion. He is there to provide for the court first and foremost facts relevant to the issues of the case. He is there as an expert only for the purpose of giving an opinion on those facts which the court cannot fully understand without his help. When psychologists are brought in for both sides, the situation is often easier, since the psychometric findings from both sides will have much in common. This means first, that the cross-examining counsel will already have the information he wants from his own expert and will know that a substantial amount of it (though by no means all) is valid and possibly incontrovertible; second, that if he discredits the psychometric evidence of his opponent, he probably will be discrediting that of his own expert as well. When psychologists are appearing for only one side, however, these restraints no longer apply. When it is clear to the psychologist under cross-examination that the psychometric basis of his examination is going to be brought out in great detail, the fall-back hierarchical defence is the best one to adopt. This is based upon the fact that evidence can be given, and may be accepted, at various levels of complexity. The expert will try, at the start, to keep his evidence at the most comprehensive (i.e. complex) level, and under pressure will yield to the next stage, hoping that by doing so the cross-examining counsel will be satisfied. For example, if the issue is one of intelligence, the psychologist will give a statement during the examination-in-chief which reports his findings in a qualitative way. The competent experienced psychologist will appreciate the fact that any test of intelligence is not a test of *complete* intelligence, but only a selective assay, that any score is likely to alter within limits on retesting, especially with differences in the environment, the situation or the state of the testee. His verbal description of intelligence will therefore refer to a bandwidth on the scale of intelligence defined by the expert's own subjective confidence limits. If the expert qualifies his answer efficiently, as indeed he should, the cross-examiner may not find any weakness in which to probe. If he does demand to know the basis for the expert's opinion regarding the intelligence of the party concerned, the psychologist moves down to the first level of description, by explaining that it is based on a complex assessment of the behaviour of the subject, supported by information from additional sources. If this does not satisfy the counsel, then the psychologist falls back to the next level, enumerating the sources in detail—test scores, interview behaviour, spontaneous vocabulary, scholastic record, vocational level reached, developmental history (infancy milestones) and so on. If the cross-examining counsel persists in requesting yet more detail, the psychologist falls back to discussing individual sources, hopefully being able to select the less contentious and more easily understood ones first. If the counsel insists on dealing with the test or tests first, generally signifying that he has had experience of demolishing psychologists on test before, the psychologist falls back on the individual test scores (e.g. Wechsler IQ 80; Terman-Merill IQ 85), emphasizing that these figures are approximations and represent the mid-point of a probable bandwidth of x IQ points. In one case, the counsel in his closing address asked the jury to disregard the psychologist's evidence on intelligence on the grounds that since his tests gave different scores, no reliance could be placed on them. He invited the jury to believe rather, the testimony of the boy's mother, who had testified that her son was quite normal. If the counsel still persists, the psychologist falls back to details of the subtests, describing them in general terms of how many words the subject knows, how many numbers he can remember, etc. If the counsel is still not satisfied, the psychologist finally has to capitulate and go through the individual items, as in the notorious Kent case. It will be seen, however, that by falling back to one general level after another, the expert witness is delaying the final denouement, and there is every hope that the judge will question the relevance of the repeated questions concerning the same things and save the psychologist from his final reluctant revelations.

East reminds us that it is only by the intensive study of cases and of modern concepts that the medical witness can hope to withstand frequent examinations in the witness box with success[164]. It is, therefore, instructive to examine the cross-examination of other expert witnesses because the psychologist will find himself, at one time or another, being asked almost identical questions. In the cold light of day outside the court, the expert will always be able to think of how he could have handled his own evidence under cross-examination to better affect. By studying examples, the forensic psychologist may be able to learn those lessons in advance. In addition to quotations from court records already given, the following excerpts from cases will give some additional examples which the reader may care to use as the basis for an improved version.

Solicitor-General: You said yesterday that he had 63% of average intelligence.

Witness: Yes.

Solicitor-General: Do I also gather that, when you reach the age of 16, you attain, if you are a normal person, 100%.

Witness: I did say the age of 15.

Solicitor-General: And you can never get more than that, under this system of calculation.

Witness: What I said was—

Solicitor-General: I am not asking you what you said. Is it right that 100 is the maximum at the age of 15.

Witness: That does not summarize it.

In this part of the interrogation, the witness has used the concept of 'percentage of average' intelligence instead of the better known, but more mis-used IQ. Psychologists frequently get into difficulties in court because they produce an IQ based on one test, for example the WISC, while an expert on the other side produces a substantially different one based on a different test, for example the Stanford-Binet revision. This is especially the case when children are involved, since school medical officers were at one time trained exclusively on the Binet-type test, at a time when most psychologists were switching over to the Wechsler-type tests. Another way of expressing intelligence which produces its own difficulties is the Mental Age. One psychologist was laughed out of court by describing the adult in the dock as having the mental age of a child when it was later shown that he was running a thriving black market business and enjoyed a considerably higher income than the psychologist concerned. In the above case of Straffen, the triple-child murderer, who was examined in the author's hospital, Dr Leitch has chosen an easily comprehended way of describing intelligence but has not managed to convey to the court the full implications of the arithmetic involved. Of course, the cross-examining counsel may pretend to be obtuse or deliberately misunderstand what the expert says in order to depreciate his evidence. The Solicitor-General, an advocate of considerable skill and experience, also uses the method of wearing his witness down until he no longer bothers to qualify his statements. For example, the witness in direct examination had explained that the quality of the prisoner's 'knowing' was inferior to that of the average person.

Judge: You agree that he knew that stealing was contrary to the law?

Witness: Yes, within the limits of his low intelligence.

Solicitor-General: Do not we all know things within the limits of our intelligence?

Witness: There are degrees of understanding.

Solicitor-General: But we cannot know something if it is outside our degree of intelligence?

Witness: We can lack appreciation.

Solicitor-General: I was asking about knowing. Whatever the limits of his intelligence may or may not have been in your opinion, when he told you that he thought it was clever to steal and not be caught, did he know that stealing was contrary to the law and that the police might catch him for it?

Witness: He did, in his own confused illogical way.

Solicitor-General: Is the answer that he did know it?

Witness: If I am not allowed to give my answer fully, then I must answer 'yes'.

Solicitor-General: A person either knows a thing or he does not know it, whatever his intelligence may be. I am putting to you: did Straffen know that, in your opinion?

Witness: To me, that question is like a similar question: all things are either black or white, ignoring that there are intermediate shades of grey.

Solicitor-General: I will come back to the question and give you one further opportunity of answering it.

The prosecutor did so. The witness, now in his second day in the box, unconsciously realizes that he will be subjected to persistent reiteration of this question until he responds with a 'yes'. For virtually all of the following questions he responds with a simple affirmative. The cross-examining counsel has now got the witness into a pattern of response borne of fatigue and frustration. He administers the *coup de grace* with some telling short crisp questions which emphasize both the *actus reus* and the fact that Straffen possessed *mens rea*—he *knew* what he was doing: the witness is psychologically no longer able to qualify the nature of his knowing—it has become a dichotomous thing—either he knows or he doesn't know:

Solicitor-General: He would have known it when he put his hands upon her throat?
Witness: Yes.
Solicitor-General: And he would have known it when he squeezed her throat?
Witness: Yes.
Solicitor-General: And he would have known it when he destroyed her life?
Witness: Yes.

Throughout this part of the testimony, the witness has been prevented from explaining the quality of cognition. His opportunity to recover lost ground should have occurred in re-examination, but he cannot take this opportunity unless the defence counsel asks him about this point, which does not happen. Exceptionally, he is given another opportunity in the further examination by the judge, but the pattern of single word response is now set:

Judge: I think the jury would like to know a little more about this intelligence test. You say that this man knew the nature and quality of his act—within the limits of his intelligence, I know you would want to add?
Witness: Yes.
Judge: Did he know he was squeezing a little girl's throat?
Witness: Yes.
Judge: He was under no delusion as to that?
Witness: No.
Judge: Did he know that if you squeezed a little girl's throat for long enough, life would become extinct?
Witness: Yes.

The importance of having relevant facts at one's fingertips, if not in one's head, is demonstrated by the closing questions of the judge:

Judge: In an average sample of 100 persons, how many would you expect to have an intelligence not greater than 63%?
Witness: I cannot give the exact figures, but speaking from memory I should say much less than 10%.

Judge: I should have thought so. You must not leave us with the impression that out of every 100 people we see ten of them are feeble minded?

Witness: I can put it this way: there are about 200,000 mental defectives in the country out of a population of almost 50 million. If one assumes that all those mental defectives are less than 63% that gives one in 250, which is a ¼%.

The difficulties of communicating a measure of intelligence are well demonstrated by this case, in which the defence expert describes the intelligence of the prisoner as being '63% of normal intelligence' and 'having a mental age of 9 years'. A prosecution expert, brought in to give evidence in rebuttal, assessed the prisoner as having a mental age of 12 years, although agreed that he was mentally defective. This was based upon the prisoner passing 5½ of the seven tests for year 12, although the psychiatrist giving evidence *did not administer* any tests of the lower age range, which the prisoner may well have failed. A second prosecution psychiatrist also assessed the prisoner as highgrade feeble minded, without any tests, but on the basis of an interview, including a discussion of Contract Bridge, which the prisoner had learnt during his sojourn in Broadmoor. The judge was much impressed by the latter as a sign of intelligence and went into detail in his summing up of how the prisoner knew the number of cards in the pack, the number of suits, and how many tricks would be made by a bid of four hearts. So much for the science of psychometrics.

The forensic psychologist is continually finding difficulties in communication. Psychologists often use words intending them to convey a technical meaning, although the lay public usually mean something more general. Depression, as a psychiatric diagnosis, is one example of this. Sometimes, a word means three different things, to the medical expert, the court and the jury, representing the public point of view. Insanity is an example of this. To the English lawyer it means only one thing, a condition of mind defined by the M'Naghton Rules. To the layman, insanity is a synonym for madness; for the psychologist, except when he is actually in court and has to conform to contemporary legal definitions, it is a state of mind negating *mens rea*, which is arbitrarily defined by law in different ways, at different times and in different sovreignties, and which he sees as lying at the extreme of a continuum of a decreasing ability to be morally aware of one's own actions.

Unfortunately, the court is not always helpful in permitting the expert witness to establish agreed definitions or terminology. Here is a psychologist and college principal trying to clarify meanings:

Counsel: Have you any experience with pornography?

Psychologist: Would you like to give me some examples—

Counsel (interrupting): I'm asking YOU. Have you any experience of pornography?

Psychologist: Would you like to define for me what—

Counsel: (cutting her short): I'm asking you a simple question, Doctor.

Psychologist: (at last getting a word in edgeways) I do really need a little bit of information as to what is meant in this court by the word pornography. It's not a concept which I use in my daily life. I don't divide things up into 'this is pornography' and 'this is not pornography'. I think most people don't. I can see that it may be important in a court of law. In fact, I can't think of anywhere else that it is important. So you must explain to me what you mean.

(Despite this clearly understandable plea and explanation, the cross-examining counsel ignores both and continues)

Counsel: Would you try, please, to answer my question. Have you any experience of pornography?

Psychologist: (persistently holding her ground despite the fact that the question has now been put to her four times) I think I must ask you what the definition is, in this court, of pornography. I think I'm entitled to ask that.

Counsel: The answer to your question is either YES or NO. Or, I don't know.

Psychologist: That IS my answer!

Judge: (intervening) She doesn't know because she doesn't understand the question.

One way out of the impasse here would have been for counsel to ask the psychologist what *her* definition of pornography would be, and then ask her to answer the original question based on her definition. This is a common practice both in the examination-in-chief and in the cross-examination, although one often feels that the cross-examining counsel prefers it as above, so that he can later discredit the witness by implying that she was testifying about pornography without even knowing what it was. However, it pays to be firm. The judge in his summing up can restore some of the witness's credit—if he has a mind to (in this case he had not!)—and the witness could have lost more credit had she gone into detail about her reading habits in the field of pornography. As it was the court remained in ignorance of whether she was an avid and extensive reader of this type of literature or had encountered it for the first time in this case. This particular psychologist retained complete control throughout her cross-examination: it ended when counsel drew attention to a cartoon of three schoolmasters caning each other:

Counsel: One of them is having his bare bottom beaten with a cane and the other has a cane pushed up his rectum, hasn't he?

Psychologist: Well, or between his legs. It is quite hard to judge.

Counsel: (in tones of sheer disbelief) Now, Doctor, please—

Psychologist: Don't you 'Doctor, please' me. It could be either, couldn't it?

So biter becomes bit, inquisitee becomes inquisitor, and counsel gives up. Compare this conflict on definitions with one where the same counsel is cross-examining a different witness, an eminent social psychologist:

Counsel: What do you understand by the phrase 'speed freak?'

Psychologist: What would *I* understand, or what the average child who reads it would understand?

Counsel: (feeling more magnanimous towards this witness) Well, if you think there's a distinction, by all means draw it, and let us hear two different definitions.

Psychologist: I understand the word speed to be a slang term for taking a drug.

Counsel: Freak?

Psychologist: I would have thought it simply meant a person.

Counsel: So speed freak is a person who indulges in the use of methadrine or any amphetamine drug? (this is not how the witness defined it).

Psychologist: It originally meant that. But you must understand, and you must accept, that words like these are so over-used in society, that their meaning becomes wider and wider.

Counsel: But it hasn't so changed its meaning that it means somebody who exceeds the 30 mph limit on the road, does it?

Psychologist: No, but a freak usually means somebody in the Youth Culture.

Counsel: (Raising his voice and making his point) Yes! But when it's used in the phrase 'speed freak' it means somebody indulging in the so called youth culture who uses that particular drug, 'speed', doesn't it?

Psychologist: (shouting back) It does not. And you are trying to make me say some things which simply are not true: it's a simple phrase. It's an everyday phrase used in the underground. It doesn't mean all these incredible things you want me to say. What do you think you are doing by analyzing every single word?

Counsel: Well what does it mean if it doesn't mean what I suggested?

Psychologist: It's a headline—a catch headline. It means nothing.

Counsel: It must mean *something*.

The psychologist is now lost to all logic. Having started by giving a meaning to the words, he ends up denying that they have meaning. It was, as one observer put it 'a complete demolition job'. Although it is difficult to be at all objective about one's own performance in the witness box, because even the court transcript loses much of the meta-communication that takes place in testimony and examination, the author lost to counsel in at least one exchange, according to one writer. Overwhelmed on this occasion, not by logic, but by repetition of the sheer vulgarity which characterized the magazine in question, as Palmer noted, the use of emotional and perjorative language seemed to preclude any rational reply or even any simple and direct answer. He says: 'The witness appears to be reduced to a state of confusion; not wishing to sound evasive, he is forced to be so unless he accepts the moral assumptions of the question. It was no good Dr Haward insisting that a lot of the material in the magazine was unnecessary but not necessarily undesirable. With Leary flinging around words like sadism, filth, bare bottoms, and fucking in the streets, Dr Haward could have said anything he liked and it wouldn't have made that much difference to the level of debate'[140].

The earlier psychologist's firm stand on the matter of definitions was echoed by another expert on the child mind, a Cambridge don whose keen intelligence more than matched that of his Oxonian cross-examiner:

Counsel: Do you agree that it is a disgusting drawing?
Witness: I personally think that it is very unpleasant drawing.
Counsel: Do you think it is *disgusting*?
Witness: It's not a word that I use.
Counsel: (Banging his desk) I am asking you to consider it as a word appropriate to this drawing.
Witness: As a word in *your* vocabulary, I would accept that you could use the word disgusting.
Counsel: Do you agree or disagree that it is a disgusting picture?
Witness: I will not use words that I myself do not use, and I cannot agree to use them.
Counsel: Have you never used the word disgusting?
Witness: No.
Counsel: I thought you were here to assist us.
Witness: If sir, you want my opinion, I shall give it. If you want to put words into my mouth, then that must be your responsibility.

This was an Oxbridge Trial by Battle, where the weapons were words and where the witness, for every thrust, had a riposte and counterthrust:

Counsel: What do you suppose is the effect intended to be of equipping Rupert Bear with such a large sized organ?
Witness: I don't know enough about bears to know their exact proportions. I imagine their organs are hidden in their fur.
Counsel: Why is Rupert Bear equipped with a large organ?
Witness: What size do you think would be natural?
Judge: (Interrupting) Well! Forgive me but you mustn't ask counsel questions.

27. Fees for Forensic Services

Introduction

THE FEES paid to the forensic psychologist for his professional services in relation to legal proceedings will depend upon a number of factors. These include (i) the nature of the proceedings themselves, that is, whether they concern the High Court in London, a Provincial Crown Court or County Court, a local Magistrates' Court, a Coroners' Court, or one of the quasijudicial tribunals; (ii) the circumstances in which the psychologist became involved, for example, by referral from a medical practitioner with whom he has a contract of service, by request from a police detective, probation officer or social worker, by agreement and contract with a solicitor, as by a writ or subpoena from the Court; (iii) the existence of any statutory direction as to the amount of fee or allowance payable in relation to (i) and (ii) above, such as those embodied in the Witnesses Allowances (Amendment) Regulations 1971, Coroners (Fees & Allowances) Rules 1971 etc.; (iv) the professional status of the psychologist, both in terms of his present appointment, such as Professor, Consultant, Research Fellow and so on, his qualifications, his overall professional experience, and his specialized experience relevant to the problem for which he has been called. If he is the only person available to have adequate experience in some highly specialized professional skill, his fee will naturally reflect his market value. When, in 1978 a Professor of Mining demanded a fee of £200 per diem plus expenses for a three month research into a town's gas leak, it was pointed out to the protesting ratepayers on whose shoulders the financial burden would fall, that there was simply no one else available with this particular skill. The Council finally negotiated an all-in figure of £13,000 to cover the fees and expenses of the whole research, their spokesman pointing out that 'the fee may seem high to the layman but the professor is an expert and his fee must be looked at against those of top barristers and surgeons, where they compare very favourably[221]. Clearly, if one is wanted badly enough, one can demand five times one's normal remuneration, although the occasions when one's forensic services are of this order are necessarily limited.

Primary and Secondary Sources

Forensic work originates from two types of source, which might be labelled primary and secondary. Primary sources are those where the person requesting the report has a direct interest in receiving the information. Primary sources are usually the judiciary, who normally seek psychological information for the purposes of reaching decisions on the disposal of the case via the sentence, but may seek help in a High Court civil action where neither side wants, or possibly cannot afford, a particular piece of expert evidence; the solicitors acting on behalf of a party or the accused, who approach the psychologist either at the instigation of their client, or of the counsel whom they have retained, or more likely, on their own initiative; and the client himself who may come to the psychologist direct because his legal advisors have been sceptical of the relevance or potential value of the psychologist, or, more frequently, do not wish to add to the costs of the case when the available funds are limited. Direct requests from clients are surprisingly frequent. They often originate during professional contact with patients when the psychologist is seeing them as part of his Health Service duties, but often intelligent prisoners trying to muster their forces for an appeal, will write to the 'chief psychologist' at any psychiatric hospital they may know, or perhaps to a university department. Some are received by the British Psychological Society and forwarded on to members known to be competent in the particular forensic problem concerned and geographically convenient to the address of the enquirer. The *cri d'coeur* emanating from one of Her Majestys' Prisons is often a non-starter: indeed one only has to visit such an establishment to carry out, say, a lie-detection test, than one is bombarded with requests from fellow prisoners looking for any means of changing their circumstances, however long the odds. However, the genuine cases often produce interesting and realistic problems.

Once the forensic psychologist has shown himself to be useful in court, he can expect to be asked for help by an increasing number and diversity of workers in the community. Not all of these are in a position to offer or negotiate fees, however, or even to authorize the psychologists' involvement in the case. In court proceedings, the request for forensic help should be funnelled through one of the parties, or their legal advisors, as far as the question of remuneration is concerned. Of course, the psychologist will normally be anxious to help colleagues in other professions in providing psychological facts and expert opinion, but this will normally be undertaken as part of his normal appointment in the NHS or Local Government. In this way, a wide range of problems can be examined on behalf of those concerned with law enforcement or community health and welfare, and these provide a useful way of acquiring forensic experience. They rarely lead to expert testimony in court, and frequently the advice given in the report to whoever requested the information is conveyed to the court in the context of other information provided by a social worker, probation officer, policeman, or community nurse. These people are experienced in detecting evidence of psychological factors, while recognizing that they lack the professional training by which such factors could be uncovered. The forensic psychologist can often make a unique contribution behind the scenes in this way so that the court has, at the time of their hearing, more relevant and pertinent evidence on the accused or complainant than it would otherwise have. The police have discretionary powers regarding prosecution and once a relationship with a forensic psychologist is established, will often make use of his services to help them reach a decision. Many cases of children showing physical injury are referred to them for investigation, following the alerting of the appropriate services by a casualty officer or family doctor. The evidence is rarely other than circumstantial, the injuries more often than not are appropriate to the accident alleged to account for them, and only the nature of the family, its past social history, and the psychology of the parents, can give any extra weighting on the question of whether this is another case of baby-battering or merely inadequacy of parental care. Sometimes the forensic psychologist will be able to provide evidence which supports the latter, and so saves police time, public expense, and personal distress. At other times the evidence is suggestive of assault, and the constabulary can then act with the extra confidence of the psychologist's report behind them.

At this stage the discussion has centred upon the forensic work which the psychologist undertakes as part of his normal duties as an applied psychologist. For forensic work undertaken privately for remuneration, it is essential that a contract is made with one of the interested parties. These will be, in civil proceedings, one of the two parties to the suit or their legal agents, and in criminal proceedings, the prosecutor or the accused, or his solicitors. The prosecuter may be either the office of the Director of Public Prosecutions, the local Constabulary, or a private person. Private prosecutors have made little use of psychologists so far, although one New Zealand psychologist has come to the UK to give evidence for the prosecution in a case brought under the Obscene Publications Act, this being virtually the only kind of criminal proceeding prosecuted privately in England these days.

Nineteen out of every 20 prosecutions take place in the magistrates court, so the constabulary are the most frequent prosecuters. While many police forces, once they realize the potential value of forensic psychology, are only too pleased to seek the psychologists' help, their funds are extremely limited and this fact puts considerable restraints on their freedom to engage the professional services of the psychologist. The author has adopted the principle of giving his services without fee to the police, and charging only out of pocket expenses. This seems to provide a number of benefits. It provides experience of a variety of

forensic problems which otherwise would not come his way; it provides
the constabulary with professional assistance which they otherwise
could not generally afford; it provides a psychologically beneficial
balance to the forensic psychologist himself, who otherwise would be
appearing only for the defence all the time and thus easily become
unduly biased; it enables him to make a positive contribution to the
maintenance of law and order and to accept in this way one of the
responsibilities of the good citizen; and it enables him to get a better and
more detailed understanding of the difficulties of a hard-working and
often-maligned body of men charged with the protection of his
community. The latter benefit is a double one, since it also enables him
to serve the interests of the accused person better, by knowing more
about the opposition, and indeed by having friendly personal relations
with them.

However, it should be appreciated that work with the police can by
its very nature, be very demanding upon time. The police, when
working on a serious case, devote every minute of their waking life to it.
They are therefore likely to make demands upon the forensic psychologist appropriate to their own standards of dedication rather than his.
Thus on one occasion the author received a telephone call from one
detective-superintendent asking him to 'fly up and interrogate 17
witnesses under hypnosis'. In fact, he did so continuously over the next
three days, but lacking the policeman's stamina, was not good for much
else for sometime afterwards. For this reason, even if a fee is not being
charged, the forensic psychologist should have a written record of
contract of what he agrees to do and how much time he can spare for the
endeavour. Where the disbursements are likely to be heavy, such as
airfares and hotel accommodation, it is administratively easier for the
police to arrange the payment of these themselves. The Department of
the D.P.P. employs its own solicitors, so there is no problem here in
respect of fees and the arrangements will be made in the same way as
with the solicitors for other parties, as described below.

Medical Fees System

Before considering the question of fees for work for the courts it is
instructive to examine the fee-paying system in which the psychiatrist
employed in N.H.S. hospitals operates. The purpose of doing this is
threefold: first, the psychiatrist represents the model to which the
clinical psychologist, for this purpose, most closely approximates.
Secondly, experience of current practice indicates that the psychologist
is unlikely to receive fees higher than those payable to medical
practitioners of equivalent professional status for similar types of work;
the fees paid to medical practitioners may therefore usually represent
the upper limit of the fees payable to the psychologist under similar
circumstances. Thirdly, the profession of clinical psychology will

eventually be recognized by legislators for the purpose of formalizing
the payments to psychologists for duties performed under the terms of
various acts of parliament, and it is very much in the best interests of
the profession that it adopts a system as readily acceptable as that of the,
British Medical Association. This system evolved with the introduction
of the National Health Service Act (1946) and has been subsequently
modified from time to time as experience over the past quarter century
has indicated possible improvements. However, it must be recognized,
and the fact made explicit, that a psychological examination is not the
same as a medical one. It is considerably more time consuming, both in
time spent with the patient, and in the analysis of the psychometric data,
and this additional temporal burden needs to be taken into account
when assessing the size of fee payable for these services. Payments to
medical practitioners for examining the mental state of patients became
authorized by statute during the 19th century and were put on a formal
and explicit basis by Section 285(1) of the Lunacy Act (1890), which
empowered local authorities to provide reasonable remuneration to
physicians in respect of 'all reasonable expenses in and about the
examination and enquiry relating to persons of unsound mind'.
Successive Acts maintained this principle until the N.H.S. Act (1946),
which introduced, in Section 3, explicit limitations on payment for
duties undertaken as part of the contract of service and led to the
recognition of two distinct categories of duty.

Categories of Supplementary Duties

Duties supplementary to those incorporated into the contract fall into
two categories: Category I contains those medical duties considered to
be within the scope of the services provided by the Act, and Category II
contains those duties which are not deemed to be within the scope of
those services. The principle underlying this dichotomy of medical
duties is that those examinations conducted primarily for the preven-
tion of illness are considered to lie in Category I, while those conducted
in the pursuance of other objectives (for example, in the interests of an
employer) are placed in Category II. Doubts occasionally arise concerning the appropriate category into which a certain type of work falls, and
these doubts are normally resolved by the Regional Hospital Board
under which the medical practitioner operates. In cases of dispute the
matter is referred to the DHSS. The schedule of duties in the two
categories is revised occasionally by a joint working party of representatives of the medical and dental professions and of the Health
Department, and approved under Regulation 3 of the National Health
Services (Remuneration and Conditions of Service) Regulations, 1951
(SI 1951 No. 1373). The schedule is published by the DHSS as an
appendix to the memorandum entitled 'Terms and Conditions of
Hospital Medical and Dental Staff Private Practice and Retention of

Fees', and a copy of this memorandum should be held by the Administrative Department of each hospital and is available for inspection by any member of the staff.

Basic Principles

In considering those cases in which fees may reasonably be claimed, it is important to appreciate that the memorandum stresses two fundamental principles, namely (1) that whole-time practitioners shall not be entitled to undertake private practice and (2) that where a whole-time hospital doctor has hospital duties which would normally fall into Category II (for example, screening prospective hospital employees) the employing authority should have those duties *written into his contract of service* so that they no longer remain supplementary duties and the question of categories no longer applies. With legislative cognisance of NHS psychologists it would not be unreasonable for this first principle to be enforced as part of the psychologists' contract of service: until it is, clinical psychologists are in the fortunate position of being able to undertake private practice in addition to a full time employment with the NHS, and it is thus sometimes possible for forensic work to be included as part of the private practice of the psychologist and so justify the retention of fees when this would not otherwise be possible. Regarding the second principle, there are signs that contracts of service are gradually becoming more explicit, and it is important for Heads of Psychology Departments to safeguard the interests of their newly appointed junior staff by vetting, possibly through the staff side representative, the form of contract being offered to the new entrant. It would seem fair to oppose the inclusion, in a clinical psychologist's contract of service, of duties comparable to those which are supplementary in the case of psychiatrists and for which the latter obtain additional remuneration.

Unpaid Forensic Duties

With respect to duties relating to court work, para. 167 of the Memorandum places in Category I(f) reports on patients 'under observation or treatment at the time when the referral is made, to interested third parties with the patient's consent, when the information required is reasonably incidental to such observation and treatment and can be given without special examination of the patient by reference to hospital records or from knowledge acquired in the course of attendance on the patient'. A psychiatrist, furnishing a report to the Court on the basis of case-note entries, or on psychologists' reports previously supplied to him, would thus not be eligible to receive a fee, since the provision of a report under these circumstances is held to be a duty falling within his terms of employment within the N.H.S.

Similarly, Category I(g) includes the attendance at court hearings as a witness giving evidence either on his own behalf or on behalf of his employing authority, in relation to patients involved in legal proceedings with whom he is professionally concerned. Attendance at Coroners' Courts is specifically excluded from this category.

Paid Forensic Duties

Work for courts for which fees may be requested and retained comprises all those duties and professional activities which are not included in the Contract of Service or enumerated in Category I of the Memorandum. For psychologists, they would fall into two subgroups (i) the examination of patients, provision of reports, and attendance at Court in those cases where the psychologist as an employee of the hospital, has a duty, parallel to that of the medical practitioner implied or made explicit within the terms of the Memorandum, which is supplementary to those in his contract of service; and (ii) psychological work in connection with forensic problems which are unrelated to the duties of the psychologist within the N.H.S.

The Memorandum stipulates for subgroup A four subcategories, namely: II(i) Reports on patients not under observation or treatment at the hospital at the time the report is asked for, or a report involving special examination of the patient other than in the circumstances referred to in Category I.

II(x) Examinations of and reports on persons in connection with legal actions other than reports which can be given under category I(f) and reports associated with cases referred to in Category I(g).

II(xii) Examinations and reports for coroners, and attendance at Coroners' courts as a medical witness and

II(xiii) Examinations and reports requested by the Courts on the medical condition of an offender or defendant, and attendance at court hearings as medical witnesses otherwise than in the circumstances referred to in Category I(g).

Into Subgroup B would fall those classes of forensic work in which the clinical psychologist assumes the role of the *forensic scientist* as distinct from that of the *medical witness* (69). It would include those laboratory and field studies and experimental programmes in which the clinician is acting as an experimental psychologist and in which his client's mental status is not in issue. It would also include, for example, the preparation of evidence in relation to proceedings under the Obscenity Acts.

Distinction between categories

The principle implicit in the distinction made between clinical duties in Category I and II respectively seems to be this: if the individual concerned is a N.H.S. patient with whom the practitioner is already concerned prior to the legal proceedings the duties in connection with the preparation and presentation of evidence for court will normally fall into Category I, for which no fees are payable. However, if such a patient requires a special examination for this purpose, and not as part of his investigation or treatment, this examination will be a supplementary duty in Category II, for which a fee may be claimed. In addition, if the practitioner is asked to prepare or present evidence on a patient with whom he has not been concerned as part of his clinical duties, this forensic work will also fall into Category II, for which a fee is payable. A second exception to the rule concerning forensic work in connection with the practitioner's own patient also occurs in the case of attendance at Coroners' Courts, which are also in Category II and eligible for remuneration.

Statutory Provision for Psychologists' fees

Because clinical psychology as a profession was not sufficiently recognized by the medical profession at the time the Beveridge Report and subsequent National Health Service Bill were being prepared, the legislators and their draughtsmen were unable to foresee the precise role of the psychologist within the structure of the N.H.S. and therefore omitted to impose upon them any explicit statutory obligations or to make any statutory provision of fees. The obligations at present imposed upon psychologists are thus confined to those written into their own contracts of service by the employing authority. These are usually expressed in such general terms as, for example, 'to perform such duties as may be required of him', but various duties are sometimes expressly stated and described in the contract and may include specific reference to the preparation and presentation of evidence for judicial purposes.

The situation at present regarding fees for forensic services provided by clinical psychologists would therefore seem to be as follows: If the examination of, and reporting or giving evidence on, a NHS patient is clearly within the terms of employment, no fee is payable in respect of these services. In all other cases, the psychologist is legally entitled to charge a fee for his services, since these then become part of his *private* professional activities. However, the situation is not quite as simple as the foregoing principle would suggest; firstly, because considerable doubt can arise as to whether or not a particular duty (for example, attending court to give evidence on a patient whom the psychologist has previously tested as part of his clinical duties) is, in fact, an essential part of his N.H.S. employment. Not all clinical psychologists are interested in pursuing forensic work, and may indeed ask for this to be excluded from their contract of service. In such circumstances they would be entitled to refuse to attend court for this purpose, unless they were either reimbursed or issued with a subpoena. This would then create an undesirable professional anomaly of a psychologist receiving fees for

Category I duties for which medical practitioners could not be remunerated. More commonly, psychologists are asked by the psychiatrist to examine and report on a person as part of their hospital duty, and the psychologist's report is used in the preparation of the psychiatrist's medical report for which he will be remunerated as a Category II duty. This introduces another anomaly, in that two professional colleagues may be sharing a supplementary duty for which only one is being remunerated. These far from infrequent situations are generally resolved amicably with a measure of good will and understanding, often by adopting a fee-splitting basis, but where interpersonal relationships are unsatisfactory the situation may engender ill feeling and impair interprofessional relations.

Until such times as national agreement is reached regarding forensic services by clinical psychologists, the onus is on each individual psychologist to have these made explicit, both in his terms of contract of employment, and in his relations with medical practitioners who refer 'patients' to him for judicial purposes. A formal circular, drawn up with the co-operation of the hospital secretary and medical administrator, and circulated to the medical staff and to legal sources of primary referral, is the most satisfactory way of making the psychologist's position regarding forensic services explicit.

For legal administrative purposes, however, the clinical psychologist is not on a par with his medical colleagues. This is because the law recognizes as a separate category the 'professional witness', who may be either a qualified lawyer, physician, dentist, or veterinary surgeon. These professions are eligible by statute to receive fees for 'professional evidence', which administratively makes no distinction between *expert witnesses* and *witnesses to fact*. The explicit recognition of the particular value of evidence from the two senior professions of law and medicine has been extended to dentistry and veterinary science because of their obvious relationship to the medical profession. Clinical psychologists might not unreasonably argue that the level and duration of this professional training and its relationship to the medical profession justifies the inclusion of their profession in this category, but this is a matter for parliamentary decision and it is not within the power of court administrators to vary these statutory conditions.

One misunderstanding which has frequently arisen in the past is the payment of fees by the court to psychologists under the Witnesses Allowances Regulations. The relevant legislation, namely, the Mental Health Act (1959) Section 62, and the Powers of Criminal Courts Act (1973) Section 3 make it clear that for the purposes detailed in the Acts the courts are only authorized to receive and take into account a written report made by a qualified medical practitioner: consequently, the allowance regulations provide for the payment of a fee only to a person thus qualified. The psychologists who on many occasions have received such a fee have been paid in error because the person responsible for applying the regulations has incorrectly assumed that, because it is, in essence, a medical report, the writer has been suitably qualified under the above acts. Psychologists on other occasions who have been refused payment for reports to the court have naturally complained, and this has caused considerable embarrassment to the court officials and disappointment and frustration to the psychologists concerned. At all levels, the courts are subject to audit by the Lord Chancellors' Department, and failure to comply with the regulations calls down censure upon the court staff long after the case is no more than a distant memory to the psychologist. Eventually of course, it produces aggravation and impairs the harmonious relations which normally exist between the courts and the professions.

The psychologist therefore finds himself involved in forensic activities in which the situation regarding fees is either:

(i) One in which the work forms part of the psychologist's implied duties or is within his terms of contract of appointment, and for which no fees are receivable.

(ii) One in which his forensic work is carried out in co-operation with a medical practitioner or colleague of another profession, for whom a fee is payable, and who may, or may not, make some arrangements for the psychologist to receive part of it.

(iii) One where the psychologist works independently of and outside his contract of appointment, for a fee agreed with his client in advance. The following notes refer to this situation.

Fees paid by Prosecutors

In criminal proceedings as mentioned earlier there are three classes of prosecutors. The most common prosecutor is the police who normally bring charges against persons accused of non-indictable offences. For indictable offences, the prosecutor is usually the Director of Public Prosecutions: most rarely, prosecutions are brought by private individuals. In each type of prosecution, the scale of fees will be different. For the non-indictable offences, the fees for providing evidence for the prosecution are decided by the police authority concerned, since the provisions of the Witnesses Allowances (Amendment) Regulations (1971) do not apply in this case. However, the police authorities tend to use these regulations as a basic guide to fees payable, using their discretion on how much below the recommended maximum they are prepared to pay.

For indictable offences, the fees for prosecution witnesses to fact are prescribed in England and Wales by the above regulations and by the Costs in Criminal Cases Acts (1908) and (1952) and by the 'Schedules of

Rates of Payment to Witnesses, Interpreters and Shorthand Writers' in Scotland. Prosecution fees are paid by the Taxing Master, Court Paymaster or other court official and normally have to be collected immediately after the hearing. As with the coroner's scale of fees, prescribed under the Coroners (Fees and Allowances) Rules, the fees paid to prosecution witnesses are defrayed out of public funds and therefore payable below the stated maximum at the discretion of Court.

Fees for expert witnesses for the prosecution are generally a little higher than those for witnesses to fact, but vary considerably. In addition to attendance, overnight and travelling allowances, payable at the court's discretion, out of pocket expenses are more readily reimbursed, but note that the attendance fee includes all meals; thus overnight expenses can not include the breakfast portion of the hotel bill.

Fees paid by the Accused

The highest fees for court work undoubtedly come from the defendant in criminal proceedings. With liberty, or in some instances, life at risk, defendants are not unnaturally prepared to invest a substantial proportion of their wealth to safeguard their interests. The death penalty is still in force in England for persons convicted of treason, and psychologists may be involved in appeals from prisoners overseas in jurisdictions where the penalty for murder is still a capital one. Fees for expert witnesses are paid in respect of the four separate services:

(1) the report.
(2) 'qualifying', that is, the preparatory work undertaken before giving evidence; this will include laboratory, field and bibliographic research, and the preparation of both the written and the oral testimony.
(3) attendance at court, on a per diem basis
(4) 'holding in readiness', that is, subjecting daily work schedules to the constraints necessary to enable the witness to attend court at short notice. Fees paid out of legal aid do not recognize this service for payment.

The fees paid by the defendant or his legal advisors are negotiable, and it is important that the psychologist should reach agreement on the fees before the case is heard. It is open to both the witness to fact and the expert witness to fix defence fees for the above services at any figure capable of being agreed by the party calling them. Obviously, there are limits to which the fee can be set—if too high the defendant will call someone else, so that economic considerations have over the years enabled a reasonable and acceptable level of fees to be charged and met. In addition, if the accused has been granted legal aid, and the payment of fees is coming from public funds, the Court officials responsible for 'taxing', that is, assessing the defence costs, will not agree to an unreasonable amount charged in respect of witness fees. Useful guidance can be obtained from the Medical Defence Union pamphlet 'Medical Witnesses Fees and Allowances'. Once the fees have been agreed, they are legally due on completion of the service. Moreover, the agreed fee for attendance at court is payable even if, as often happens, the witness is not called to give evidence. Legal aid fees are payable by the appropriate court official immediately after the witness has been discharged from the court. Often fees are payable on receipt of a statement of account. If the solicitor makes himself explicitly liable for the fees, they are recoverable from the solicitor, otherwise they are recoverable from the party on whose behalf the witness is called. It is preferable that in all cases the psychologist should obtain from the solicitor a statement of liability for the fees, since payment of the fees in due course is then assured. When the client is of doubtful credit worthiness the solicitor will be unwilling to accept liability for witness fees, being more than a little concerned to recover his own expenses. In such cases, the psychologist has to take his chance with the rest of the creditors. Sometimes the client loses his case and is sentenced to pay a heavy fine, and may therefore be both reluctant and unable to pay the costs of his defence. At other times, when the defendant is not convicted, he may disappear from his known address into the underworld, leaving his unpaid fees behind him. In any event, it is seldom financially worthwhile to attempt to recover fees by civil action, however satisfying it may be in other ways. It should also be noted that in Legal Aid cases the payment of fees for expert evidence is entirely at the discretion of the Taxing Master. If he disagrees that expert evidence was necessary he can refuse payment to the expert of both fees and expenses. The solicitor then becomes liable for these under the laws of contract and for this reason it may prove helpful to have had the fees agreed in writing beforehand. To do so does not imply any lack of trust in the solicitors; on the contrary it is a businesslike arrangement which enables them to assess their clients' overall expenses and helps them in deciding to what extent, if any, expert evidence is justifiable if supporting the clients' case. Solicitors are normally extremely helpful in obtaining for psychologists a reasonable remuneration and are always willing to advise on these matters. Occasionally the solicitors are unable to agree on the fee but nevertheless require the psychologist to give evidence. This is especially the case when he is a witness to fact—e.g. having examined, as part of his N.H.S. duties, the accused prior to the commission of the alleged offence. In such circumstances, the solicitors will issue a subpoena, or if they require the psychologist's report entered as evidence as well, a subpoena *duces lecum*. It is then open to the psychologist, when he is called to the witness box, but before taking the oath, to declare that he does not wish to give evidence because no fee has been agreed. At this juncture the court may inquire of the defence solicitor or counsel for their justification in calling this particular witness. If the defence lawyers justify their action to the satisfaction of the court, the judge will direct the witness to give evidence, and instruct the Taxing Master or equivalent court official to fix the witness's fee at an appropriate level. When a subpoena is issued the police constable delivering the document will also pay over 'conduct money' to cover public transport fare from the witness's home to the court. Conduct money is usually rounded up to the nearest pound but adjustments are made when the attendance fees are being 'taxed'.

The size of the actual fee negotiated will obviously depend upon the status of the witness, the level of the court, and the amount of work involved. Generally speaking, the latter is reflected almost entirely in the qualifying fee, while the status of the witness is related more to the attendance and holding in readiness fees. The reports themselves show least variation between witnesses of different status. In addition to the fees for the actual services performed, the witness will also incur certain expenses in connection with travelling, overnight accommodation, subsistence and other related disbursements. A major item may be payment for a locum tenens; the writer, for example, has frequently been required to pay for substitute lecturers to cover WEA and other lecture courses interrupted by sessions spent at court—in one case which required attendance at court for more than a week, the cost of various locum tenens approximated a full-time salary. Because the range of fees for the preparation and presentation of evidence for the defence is so great, and inflation makes any figure outdated within months it is difficult to provide adequate guide lines; moreover, it is becoming customary for composite fees to be charged which includes all services as well as disbursements.

Fees in Civil Actions

The attendance fees allowable under County Court Rules are stipulated, but since most of the psychologist's civil forensic work will be in the High Courts, the remarks concerning the accused above are relevant. The qualifying fees are the most difficult to assess as far as expert witnesses are concerned, since it is almost impossible to estimate the time required for extensive laboratory or field research. It is not unusual for research time to occupy as much as 150 hours, and it would be a fortunate psychologist who found himself adequately rewarded for time spent in this way. Few litigants will be prepared to give the experimental psychologist *carte blanche* in this respect, although in some cases involving large companies this is not unknown. Frequently, however, the psychologist will be asked to provide an estimate of the upper limit of the research costs, or more usually, asked to submit a statement of fee for agreement, which would cover all the expected costs. Experimentalists usually have some experience of the time spent on different types of experiment, and it is not unreasonable to expect them to be able to estimate costs within acceptable limits. Where the fee is fixed on an hourly basis, this should not be less than the sessional rate appropriate to the psychologist's grade.

Discretionary Reduction of Fees

Some expert witnesses, especially those regularly retained by insurance companies defending compensation cases arising from road traffic acts or industrial acts of negligence demand, and usually obtain, the highest level of fees that can be negotiable. More frequently, professional witnesses adjust their fees to the circumstances of the client. Medical practitioners, especially those outside the metropolis, rarely demand the fees recommended by the BMA and frequently perform forensic services for no fee at all, even when one might justifiably be claimed. Psychologists are expected to emulate this practice: contributing to the work of the court is, after all, a social service, and although it would be unreasonable to expect psychologists to incur expenses without reimbursement, many cases arise in which the psychologist can participate as part of his normal duties. Hospital management committees are usually prepared to accept this function as a necessary part of the psychologist's professional activities, and in these circumstances both the preparation of the evidence and attendance at court can be undertaken in the psychologist's normal working hours. Whilst psychologists would be expected to waive their fees in cases of undoubted poverty, obviously there will be cases where no concessions need, or should, be made. Large companies can usually be expected to protect their own interests, and psychological evidence which favours their case may save them damages running into four figures. The solicitors approaching the psychologist for forensic help will often intimate that their client is in straitened circumstances and will ask if the fee could be kept to a modest level; in other cases it is left to the psychologist to inquire into the client's ability to meet his fees. Where a good relationship develops between the forensic psychologist and the solicitors the latter will sometimes advise when they believe the fee requested could reasonably be increased, but in general, lawyers naturally prefer to keep their costs (including witness fees) as low as possible since their first duty is to protect their client's interests.

Overheads

Apart from psychologists who practise privately and have no official appointment in the National Health Service or other central or local government organization, or indeed with any Commercial company, the question will arise whether, and in what conditions, the psychologist can make use of his employer's facilities in the pursuance of his forensic undertakings. When these form part of his recognized duties, the answer is clear, for he can, and should, carry out these duties in his appointed place of work and using the equipment and other facilities and back-up services upon which he normally draws. When he is undertaking forensic work on a private basis, however, he is no longer able to do this without prior consent and agreement with his employing authority. If he does, he will be making himself liable to tort for one or more actions of trespass. While engaged in private work, the psychologist is also deprived of the legal protection normally available to him under the National Health Service Act (1946), or other statutes referring to his own particular employing authority. Preferably then, he should be using his own time, premises, tests and apparatus for his forensic activities, and should certainly have professional indemnity cover on which the British Psychological Society will always be pleased to advise. Where, however, there are good reasons for using some or all of the facilities belonging to his employer, the psychologist should enter into an agreement with the former to enable him to undertake forensic work using the facilities required, and for which he will be required to pay part of the remuneration from forensic work, usually in the form of a fixed percentage. This will obviously vary depending upon the extent of the services provided by the employer. If they include use of a consulting room together with heating, lighting, and possibly reception and secretarial services the percentage will be substantial and can normally be costed from the figures already computed for cost-accounting purposes; it may be considerably greater than the cost of hiring a consulting room in the locality. In universities the 'Overheads', as this fixed percentage is generally known, ranges from zero to 80% of the total remuneration, but this takes into account the fact that the work being undertaken occupies the normal working time of the staff member concerned. In 1970, the Division of Clinical Psychology of the British Psychological Society set up a working party to look into the question of clinical psychologists undertaking private work, including forensic activities, and circulated a code of conduct in connection with the receiving of fees in the universities and in the National Health Service, and details can be obtained from the Society's Head Office.

Delays in Payment

The forensic psychologist must expect considerable delay in the payment of his fees, especially in the case of civil actions in the High Court. In some criminal cases, the expert witness can go to the Taxing Master, as he is called, in the courts administration offices, and receive payment for his services under Legal Aid, as soon as his charges have been agreed. Witnesses to fact usually receive their loss of earnings and travelling expenses at the conclusion of their service to the court. Generally, however, the payment of fees has to go through a long bureaucratic process before completion. In compensation cases, the time between accepting the commission to act in the case and the hearing itself, may be almost a year: there may then be negotiations out of court which occupy some months, and a delayed judgement extending the time. The solicitor may then wait until all hope of an appeal is exhausted before submitting the experts' account to the court for 'taxing'. Depending upon the size and nature of the court, the staffing situation and the backlog of work, the taxing may occupy three months more, and if the solicitor working for the other party, objects to the costs claimed by the expert, on the grounds that he is protecting the interests of his own client (who may have to pay all or a proportion of the costs) there is an additional delay. Finally there is a wait while the other side pay their share of the costs, these are submitted to the Law Society and finally forwarded to the solicitor who engaged the witness in the first place. One doctor writing to a national newspaper complained that he had been waiting for two years for payment of his fees and expenses. Importuning the solicitor is rarely effective since the delay is usually, though admittedly not always, due to circumstances beyond his immediate control, and this only impairs interprofessional relations. However, it should also be noted that because of the passage of time, solicitors do on occasions forget completely about the expert's unpaid account, so that an occasional 'to a/c rendered' reminder, perhaps on a six-monthly basis, serves to keep the file open at their office.

Summary

The fees payable to psychologists for forensic services are dependent upon a number of factors:

(1) No fees are payable if the services come within the explicit terms of the psychologist's contract of employment. It is unlikely that fees will be payable for services which come into Category I of Circular H.M. (71) 2 if, where and when the provisions of this document are construed as applying to psychologists equally with the medical practitioners. Fees for forensic reports to medical practitioners who themselves receive a fee are solely at the discretion of the medical practitioner.

(2) Statutory upper limits are imposed on witnesses allowances (both fees and expenses) paid out of public funds, either as Legal Aid or as prosecution or inquest costs. Precise information on the particular case can be obtained from the Registrar or Taxing Master of the court concerned.

(3) There are no prescribed limits to fees incurred on their own responsibility by a defendant in a criminal trial or a litigant in a civil suit. Such fees are contractual and decided by agreement with the person concerned or his solicitor. Liability for payment of fees is

held by the former unless explicitly offered by the solicitors. The fees agreed upon will reflect (i) the type of court receiving the evidence, (ii) the status of the witness, (iii) the nature of the services offered.

(4) Fees, when payable, cover (i) reports to court (ii) daily attendance at court (iii) 'holding in readiness' to attend court (except in Legal Aid cases) and, in the case of expert witnesses (iv) 'qualifying' by the preparation of expert testimony. In addition, allowances for travelling to court, cost of overnight accommodation, out of pocket disbursements, and such expenses as paying for locum tenens, etc.

(5) Apart from the additional qualifying fee, expert witnesses usually receive higher fees than witnesses to fact, unless they are 'professional witnesses'; when no such distinction is made. Psychologists are not professional witnesses as defined by statute.

(6) Psychologists charging fees for forensic services should not use their employers time, premises or facilities without prior consent and agreement on the payment of overheads and arranging adequate cover of professional indemnity.

(7) Further information can be obtained from the office of the Clerk to the Court (where details of fees payable under statutory regulations may be consulted), from the N.H.S. circular H.M. (71) 2 entitled 'Terms and conditions of service of Hospital Medical and Dental staff Private Practice and Retention of Fees' available in hospital administrators offices, from the British Medical Association's Publication 'Fees for Part-time Medical Services' and from the Medical Defence Union's Booklet 'Medical Witnesses: Fees and Allowances'. Although some of the medical fees are applicable only to medical practitioners, they provide a useful guide to the appropriate size of fees for different purposes.

List of Journals

Acta Psychiatrica
Acta Psychiatrica Scandinavia
American Bibliographic Association
American Journal of Clinical
  Pathology
American Journal of
  Orthopsychiatry
American Journal of Psychiatry
American Journal of Psychotherapy
American Psychiatry
American Psychologist
American Law Reports
Archiv für Kriminologie
Archives of General Psychiatry
Archives of Neurology and Psychiatry
British Journal of Criminology
British Journal of Delinquency
British Journal of Hospital Medicine
British Journal of Law and Society
British Journal Medical Psychology
British Journal of Psychiatry
British Journal of Psychology
British Journal of Social and
  Clinical Psychology
British Medical Journal
British Psychological Society
Bulletin of the British Psychological
  Society
Bulletin of the British Society for
  Experimental and Clinical
  Hypnosis
Canadian Behaviour Review
Canadian Psychology
Criminal Justice and Behaviour
Criminal Law Review

Delcague Journal
Diseases of the Nervous System
International Journal of Forensic
  Psychology
International Criminal Police Review
Journal of Criminal Law,
  Criminology and Police Science
Journal of Forensic Medicine
Journal of Forensic Science
Journal of the Forensic Science
  Society
Journal of Legal Education
Journal of Mental Science
Journal of Science Issues
Journal of Social Therapy
Louisiana Law Review
Man
Maquette Law Review
Medical Press
Medical Science and Law
Medical Tribune
Minnesota Law Review
Modern Law Review
Nordske Medizin
Occupational Psychology
Ohio State Law Journal
Portsmouth Journal of Psychology
Proceedings of the 82nd Annual
  Convention of the American
  Psychological Association
Professional Psychology
Psychological Reports
Scandinavian Studies in Criminology
Scientific American
Sociologia y Psicologia Juridicas

Bibliography

1. Higham, T.M. (1957) 'Basic Psychological Factors in Communication,' *Occup. Psychol. 31* 1–10.
2. Cowan, T.A. (1963) 'Decision theory in law, science & technology.' *Science 140* 1065–1075.
3. Plato (1935) *Republic*. Trans. A.D. Lindsay, London: Dent.
4. *Chaplin* v. *Chaplin* (1946) 74 Co. App. 652. 169 Proc. 2d. 442.
5. Allen, R.C., Ferster, E.Z. & Rubin, J.G. (1968) *Readings in Law and Psychiatry*, Baltimore Hopkins UP.
6. Szasz, T. (1972) *Myth of Mental Illness*, Paladin, London.
7. Bazelon, D. (1972) 'Psychologists in corrections' in Brodsky below (9).
8. Clinard, M.B. (1956) 'Research frontiers in criminology'. *Brit. J. Delinq. 7* 110–122.
9. Brodsky, S.L. (1972) Psychologists in the Criminal Justice System. A.A.C.P. Marysville.
10. Connolly, K. & McKeller, P. (1963) 'Forensic psychology', *Bull. Brit. Psychol. Soc. 16* 16–24.
11. Pattison, E.M. (1960) 'Teaching human relations in legal negotiation'. *Amer. Psychiat. 126* 525–531.
12. Brown, L. (1966) 'Experimental preventive law course'. *J. Legal Educ. 18* 212–220.
13. Haward, L.R.C. (1974) 'Investigation of torture allegations by the forensic psychologist' *J. For. Sci. Soc. 14* 299–309.
14. Clifford, B.C. & Bull, R. (1978) *Psychology of Person Identification*, London: Routledge & Kegan Paul.
15. Ellis, H., Shepherd, J. & Davies, G. (1975) 'An investigation of the use of the photofit technique for recalling faces', *Brit. J. Psychol. 66* 29–37.
16. Simon, R. (Ed.) (1975) *The Jury System, A Critical Analysis*. Beverley Hills: Sage Publications.
17. Haward, L.R.C. (1963) 'Some psychological aspects of parole evidence', *Brit. J. Criminol. 3* 342–360.
18. Haward, L.R.C. (1964) 'Psychologists contribution to legal procedure', *Mod. Law Review 27* 656–668.
19. Healy, W. (1915) *Honesty: A study of the Causes & Treatment of Dishonesty among Children*, Bobbs-Merrill, Indianapolis, U.S.A.

20. Healy, W. & M.T. (1915) *Pathological Lying, Accusation and Swindling*, Little, Brown: Boston.
21. Karpman, B. (1933) *Case Studies in the Psychopathology of Crime*, Mental Science Pub. New York.
22. East, W.N. (1942) *The Adolescent Criminal*, Churchill, London.
23. Goddard, H.H. (1915) *The Criminal Imbecile*, London: Macmillan Co.
24. Haward, L.R.C. (1964) 'Thematic apperception analysis as a forensic technique', *J. Forensic Sci. Soc. 4* 209–216.
25. Barnes, H.E. & Tecters, N.K. (1959) *New Horizons in Criminology*, Prentice-Hall, New Jersey.
26. Grygier, T. (1964) 'The teaching of criminology as part of the curriculum of a department of psychology', *Canad. Psychol. 5* 35–40.
27. Green, E. (1961) *Judicial Attitudes to Sentencing*, Macmillan, London.
28. Marshall, J. (1966) *Law and Psychology in Conflict*, Bobbs-Merrill, New York.
29. Diamond, S. Zeisel, H. (1974) 'Courtroom experiment on juror selection and decision-making', Proc. 82nd Ann. Conv. APA New Orleans.
30. Shapley, D. (1974) 'Jury selection'. *Science 185* 1033–34.
31. Sealy, A.P. & Cornish, W.R. (1973) 'Juries and the rules of evidence', *Crim. Law Rev.* 208–223.
32. James, Rita M. (1960) 'Jurors' evaluation of expert psychiatric testimony', *Ohio State L.J. 21* 75.
33. Broader, D.W. (1958) 'The University of Chicago jury project', *Nebraska Law Rev. 38* 744–760.
34. Hopwood, J.S. & Snell, J.K. (1933) 'Amnesia in relation to crime', *J. Ment. Sci. 79* 27.
35. Leitch, A. (1948) 'Notes on amnesia in crime for the general practitioner', *Med. Press 219* 459.
36. Gudjonsson, G.H. (1979) 'Use of electrodermal responses in a case of amnesia', *Med. Sci. Law 19* 138–140.
37. Hopwood, J.S. & Snell, H.K. (1933) 'Amnesia in relation to crime', *J. Ment. Sci. 79* 27.
38. Kiersch, T.A., (1962) 'Amnesia: a clinical study of 98 cases', *Am. J. Psychiat. 119* 57–60.
39. Glueck, S. & T.E. (1930) *Five Hundred Criminal Careers*, Knopf, New York.
40. Hammond, W.H. & Chayer, E. (1963) *Persistent Criminals*, H.M.S.O. London.
41. Argyle, M.A. (1961) 'A new approach to the classification of delinquents', Board of Corrections, Sacramento.

42. Watson, A.J. (1963) 'Teaching mental health concepts in law school', *Amer. J. Orthopsychiat.* 33 115–122.
43. Smedley, T. (1963) 'A pervasive approach on a large Scale', *J. Legal Educ.* 15 435–443.
44. Loria, D.W. (1959) 'Recognizing and handling a traumatic neurosis case', *J. For. Med.* 6 64.
45. Miers, D. (1979) 'Responses to victimization: compensation for acts of criminal violence', Farrington *et al.* (eds.) *Psychology Law and Legal Processes*, London, Macmillan.
46. Corsini, R.J. & Miller, G.A. (1954) 'Psychology in prisons', *Amer. Psychol.* 9 184–185.
47. Haward, L.R.C. (1976) 'Experimentation in forensic psychology', *Crim. Just. Behav.* 3 301–314.
48. Ohlin, L.E. (1951) 'Selection for parole', Russell Sage Foundation, New York.
49. Glueck, S. (1961) 'A comparative criminology', *Jurist* 1961 Feb. 21.
50. Haward, L.R.C. (1968) 'Assessment of criminal behaviour for judicial purposes', *Bull. Brit. Psychol. Soc.* 21 87A (Abstract).
51. Toch, H. (1969) *Violent Men; an enquiry into the Psychology of Violence*, Aldine, Chicago.
52. Bard, M. (1969) 'Family intervention police teams as a community mental health resource', *J. Crim. Law, Criminol. Pol. Sci.* 60 247–250.
53. Bard, M. (1970) 'Training police as specialists in family crisis intervention', U.S. Govt. Printing Office, Washington, D.C.
54. Danish, S.J. & Brodsky, S.C. (1970) 'Training policemen in emotional control and awareness', *Amer. Psychol.* 25 368–369.
55. Blum, R.H. (1964) *Police Selection*, Thomas, Springfield.
56. Kubis, J.F. (1974) 'Comparison of voice analysis and polygraph as lie detection procedures', *Polygraph* 3 1–47.
57. Gudjonsson, G.H. (1979) 'Electrodermal responsivity in Icelandic criminals, clergymen and policemen', *Brit. J. Soc. Clin. Psychol.* 18 351–353.
58. Haward, L.R.C. (1963) 'Reliability of corroborated police evidence', *J. Forens. Sci. Soc.* 3 71–78.
59. Glaser, D. (1964) *Effectiveness of a Prison and Parole System*, Bobbs-Merrill: Indianapolis.
60. Black, D., Blackler, C., Blackman, R. & Haward, L.R.C. (1973) 'Memorandum of evidence to the Butler Committee in the law relating to the mentally abnormal offender', *Bull. Brit. Psychol. Soc.* 26 331–341.
61. Black, D., Blackler, C., Blackman, R. & Haward, L.R.C. (1975) 'Evidence to the Butler Committee on the law relating to

the mentally abnormal offender: a reply to Saunders', *Bull. Brit. Psychol. Soc. 28* 395–402.

62. Haward, L.R.C. (1976) 'What Lord Butler said', *Psychology Today 2* 50–51.

63. Roebuck, J. (1967) *Criminal Typology*, Thomas, Springfield.

64. Haward, L.R.C. (1973) 'Test colour usage by indecent exposers', *Mann 2* 19.

65. Rutter, I. (1961) 'A jurisprudence of lawyer operations', *J. Legal Educ. 13* 301–309.

66. Fahrmann, R. (1962) 'Psychological speech analysis and the technique of interrogation', *Arch. furKriminol. 130* 72.

67. Gall, J.C. (1962) 'The case against narco-interrogation', *J. For. Sci. 7* 29.

68. Haward, L.R.C. (1961) 'Psychological evidence', *J. For. Sci. Soc. 2* 8–18.

69. Brodsky, S.L. & Robey, A. (1972) 'On becoming an expert witness', *Professional Psychol. 3* 173–176.

70. Ziskin, J. (1970) *Coping with Psychiatric and Psychology Testimony*. Law and Psychology Press, Beverley Hills.

71. Gough, H.G. (1956) *Predicting Job Effectiveness among Correctional Officers*, Univ. Calif. Berkeley.

72. Mannheim, H. & Wilkings, L.T. (1955) *Prediction Methods in relation to Borstal Training*, H.M.S.O. London.

73. Fineman, K. (1968) 'An operant conditioning program in a juvenile detention facility. *Psychol. Rep. 22* 119–120.

74. Sacks, H. (1967) 'Talking with clients', *Student Lawyer 13* 14–18.

75. Nicholson, J. (1965) 'Psychology and law', *Portsmouth J. Psychol. 7* 5–8.

76. Cunningham, C. (1969) 'Recollections of a forensic psychologist', *Portsmouth J. Psychol.*

77. Haward, L.R.C. (1961) 'Forensic psychology', *Bull. Brit. Psychol. Soc. 43* 1–5.

78. Onions, C.T. (1933) *Shorter Oxford English Dictionary*, Vol. I. Oxford: Clarendon.

79. Haward, L.R.C. (1973) 'Forensic psychology' in Haward & McGann: *Psychiatry, Psychology and the Law Courts*, Dublin.

80. Gunn. J. (1974) 'Disasters, asylums and plans: forensic psychiatry today', *Brit. Med. J.* (iii) 611–613.

81. Robitscher, J.B. (1966) *Pursuits of Agreement: Psychiatry and the Law*, Lippincott, Philadelphia.

82. Moller, T. & Thorsteinsson (1977) 'Present status of forensic psychiatry in Iceland' *Acta Psychiat. Scand. 55* 183–186.

83. Kinberg, O. (1935) *Basic Problems of Criminology*, Munksgaard, Copenhagen.

84. Nycander, S. (1970) *Avskaffa Rattspsykiatrum* Aldus, Stockholm.

85. Svendsen, B.B. (1977) 'On Forensic Psychiatry in the Scandinavian Countries', *Acta Psychiat. Scand.* 55 161–164.

86. Anthila, I. (1971) 'Conservative and radical criminal policy in the Nordic Countries', *Scand. Stud. Criminol. 3* 9–21.

87. Christie, N. (1972) 'Rettspsykiateren; strid med. legerollen' (The role of the forensic psychiatrist in conflict with the physicians role) *Nord. Med.* 87 307–308.

88. Anchersen, P. & Noreik, K. (1977) 'Present status of forensic psychiatry in Norway', *Acta Psychiatry* 55 187–193.

89. Meyerson, A. & Torngrist, K.E. (1977) 'Present status of forensic psychiatry in Sweden', *Acta Psychiatry* 55 194–198.

90. Svendsen, B.B. (1977) 'Present status of forensic psychiatry in Denmark', *Acta Psychiatry* 55 176–180.

91. Tuovinen, M. (1977) 'Present status of forensic psychiatry in Finland', *Acta Psychiatry* 55 181–182.

92. Gibben, T.C.N. (1968) 'The task of forensic psychiatry', *Med. Sci. Law 9* 3–10.

93. Szasz, T.S. (1956) 'Some observations on the relationship between psychiatry and the law', *Arch. Neurol. Psychiat.* 75 297–315.

94. Cuclemaare, A. (1959) 'A tentative definition of criminalistics as forensic science', *Laboratory Digest 23* 4.

95. Nagle, R. (1970) 'Medico-legalism', *Med. Sci. Law 10* 158.

96. Nagle, R. (1975) 'A national medical-legal service for Scotland'. *J. Forens. Sci. Soc.*

97. Guthrie, D. (1958) *History of Medicine*, Edinburgh: Nelson.

98. Haward, L.R.C. (1976) 'Forensic Psychology' (letter) *Bull. Brit. Psychol. Soc.* 29 86–87.

99. *National Register of Scientific and Technical Personnel* (1970), U.S.A. Washington.

100. Castell, J.H.F. (1966) 'The court work of educational and clinical psychologists', *Brit. Psychol. Soc.* (EDPP) London.

101. Castell, J.H.F. (1968) 'Introduction', to Proceedings of the Conference 'The Psychologists Contribution to the work of the Courts' N.I.S.W.T. Tavistock Square, London, November 1968.

102. Haward, L.R.C. (1959) 'The psychologist in a court of law', *Bull. Brit. Psychol. Soc. 39* 1–8.

103. Haward, L.R.C. (1960) 'Scane versus Ainger', *Bull. Brit. Psychol. Soc. 41* 26A (Abstract).

104. Haward, L.R.C. (1961) 'Psychological evidence', *J. Forensic Sci. Soc. 2* 8–18.

105. Haward, L.R.C. (1963) 'Reliability of corroborated police evidence', *J. Forensic Sci. Soc. 3* 71–78.

106. Haward, L.R.C. (1964) 'Professional psychology in the Magistrates Court', Part I, *Law Times 235* 491.
107. Haward, L.R.C. (1964) 'Professional psychology in the Magistrates Court, Part II, *Law Times 235* 511.
108. Haward, L.R.C. (1964) 'Psychological experiments and judicial doubt', *Bull. Brit. Psychol. Soc. 17* 23A (Abstract).
109. Haward, L.R.C. (1964) 'Psychology in the Magistrates Court', *Bull. Brit. Soc. 17* 23A (Abstract).
110. Haward, L.R.C. (1969) 'Role of the psychologist in English criminal law', *Int. J. Forensic Psychol. 1* 11–22.
111. Haward, L.R.C. (1971) 'Forensic psychology and road traffic accidents', *Int. J. Forensic Psychol. 3* 4–11.
112. Haward, L.R.C. (1972) 'Role of the forensic psychologist', *Prison Medical Journal*, April, 53–57.
113. Haward, L.R.C. (1972) 'Forensic psychology in the Court of Criminal Appeal', *Bull. Brit. Psychol. Soc. 25* 152A (Abstract).
114. Haward, L.R.C. (1974) 'Investigation of torture allegations by the forensic psychologist', *J. Forensic Sci. Soc. 14* 299–309.
115. Haward, L.R.C. (1975) 'Psycologia forense ye accidentes de trafico' *Soc. Psy. Juridicas 3* 41–47.
116. Haward, L.R.C. (1975) 'Admissibility of psychological evidence in obscenity cases', Bull. Brit. Psychol. Soc. 28 466–469.
117. Allport, G.W. (1937) *Personality*, New York: Holt.
118. Haward, L.R.C. (1976) *Forensic Psychology*, London: Home Office (Restricted).
119. Eddy, P., Potter, E. & Page, B. (1976) *Destination Disaster*, London: Hart-Davis.
120. Haward, L.R.C. (1977) 'Forensic hypnosis', *Hypnosis: Bull. Brit. Soc. Exp. Clin. Hyp. 1* 4–5.
121. Laing, R.D. (1967) *The Politics of Experience and the Bird of Paradise*, Harmondsworth: Penguin.
122. Szasz, T.S. (1957) 'Psychiatric expert testimony: its covert meaning & social function, *Psychiatry 20* 313.
123. Munsterberg, H. (1907) *On the Witness Stand*, New York: McClure.
124. Haward, L.R.C. (1967) 'Subjective variables in electrophysiological recording', *Acta Biotheoretica 17* 195–204.
125. Haward, L.R.C. (1960) 'Subjective meaning of stress'. *Brit. J. Med. Psychol. 33* 185–194.
126. Eggleston, R. (1978) 'Evidence, Proof and Probability', London: Seminar at Institure of Advanced Legal Studies.
127. Cunningham, C. (1964) 'Forensic psychology', *Bull. Brit. Psychol. Soc. 54* 7.
128. Harding, A. (1966) *Social History of English Law*, Harmondsworth: Penguin.

129. Burford, E.S. (1973) *The 'Orrible Synne*, London: Calder & Boyars.

130. Fennel, P.W.H. (1977) 'The Mental Health Review Tribunal: a question of inbalance', *Brit. J. Law Soc.* 4 186–219.

131. Greenland, C. (1968) *Mental Illness and Civil Rights*, Univ. of Wales. M.Sc. Thesis.

132. Giles, F.T. (1949) *The Magistrates' Courts*, Harmondsworth: Penguin.

133. Mellor, J.C. (1959) *The Law*, English Univ. Press.

134. Morecroft, J. Coughlin, C., Glenton, G. Spring, E. & Gerelli, R. (1971) *The Old Bailey*, Corporation of London.

135. Archer, P. (1963) *The Queen's Courts*, Harmondsworth: Penguin.

136. Simpson, K. (1962) *A Doctor's Guide to Court*, London: Butterworth.

137. Padfield, C.F. (1975) *Law made Simple*, Fourth Edition. London: W.H. Allen.

138. Haward, L.R.C. (1975) 'Obscenity and the forensic psychologist', *New Behaviour* 2 4–6.

139. Haward, L.R.C. (1976) 'Porn: the thin blue line', *Psychology Today* 2 38–39.

140. Palmer, T. (1971) *Trials of OZ*, London: Blond and Briggs.

141. Justice of the Peace. *136* (1972).

142. Barber, D. & Gordon, G. (eds.) (1976) *Members of the Jury*, London: Wildwood House.

143. Ryan, G. (1959) *Evidence*, London: Sweet & Maxwell.

144. Taylor, A.S. (1956) *Principles & Practice of Medical Jurisprudence*, 11th Edn., London: Churchill.

145. Phipson, S.C. (1923) *Best's Principles of Evidence*, London: Sweet & Maxwell.

146. Trankell, A. (1965) *Witness Psychology*, (Vittnes Psykologin) Stockholm, Liber.

147. Haward, L.R.C. (1964) 'Rule of hearsay & psychological reports', *Bull. Brit. Psychol. Soc. 18* 21–26.

148. Bartlett, F. (1932) *Remembering*, Cambridge University Press.

149. Altavilla, E. (1961) 'Value of a dying person's accusations', *Int. Crim. Police Rev. 16* 170.

150. Ryle, A. & Lunghi M.E. (1969) 'Measurement of relevant change after psychotherapy', *Brit. J. Psychiat. 115* 1297–1304.

151. Hamilton, M. (1973) 'Psychology in Society: ends or end?' *Bull. Brit. Psychol. Soc. 26* 185–190.

152. Cross, R. (1963) *Evidence*, London: Butterworth.

153. Phipson, S.L. (1952) *Law of Evidence*, London: Sweet & Maxwell.

154. Ward, E.S. (1978) 'A Point of evidence', *Bull. Brit. Psychol. Soc. 31* 8–10.

155. Atkinson, S. (1908) *The Law in General Practice*, London: Hodder & Stoughton.

156. Stephen, Sir H.L. & Sturge, L.F. (1936) *Digest of the Laws of Evidence*, London: Macmillan.

157. Burrows, R., (1943) *Phipson's Manual of Evidence*, London: Sweet & Maxwell.

158. McCormick, C.T. (1945) 'Some Observations on the Opinion Rule and Expert Testimony', *Texas Law Review 23* 109–136.

159. Braverman, S. (1962) 'Procedure and the expert witness', *J. For Sci. 7* 371.

160. Moore, C.C. (1908) 'Yellow psychology', *Law Notes 11* 125–127.

161. Moore C.C. (1908) 'Psychology in the courts', *Law Notes 11* 185–187.

162. Louisell, D.W. (1955) 'The psychologist in today's legal world', *Minnesota Law Rev. 39* 235–272.

163. Gaines, I.D. (1956) 'The psychologist as expert witness in a personal injury case', *Marquette Law Rev. 39* 239–244.

164. Arbit, N. (1960) 'The psychologist as expert witness', *Amer. Psychol. 15* 721–724.

165. Schulman, R.E. (1966) 'The psychologist as expert witness', *Kansas Law Review 15* 88–97.

166. Hochel & Darley, J.G. (1962) 'A case at law', *Amer. Psychol. 17* 623–654.

167. Lassen, G. (1964) The Psychologist as an Expert Witness in assessing mental disease or defect. *Amer. Bib. Assoc. J. 50* 239–242.

168. Bock, J.A. (1961) 'Annotation: qualification of non-medical psychologist to testify as to mental condition or competency', *Amer. Law Rep.* (2nd) *78* 919–927.

169. Haward, L.R.C. (1980) 'Psychology, law and legal processes: review', *Literary Review 1* (9) 31–32.

170. Kolasa, B.J. (1972) *Psychology and Law*, Pittsburgh: Duquesne University Press.

171. Brodsky, S.L. & Robey, A. (1972) 'On becoming an expert witness: issues of orientation and effectiveness', *Prof. Psychol. 3* 173–176.

172. Lund, Sir Thomas (1962) 'Expert evidence', *Med. Sci. Law 3* 401–410.

173. Schwartz, U.S. (1960) 'Expert medical testimony', *Decalgue J. 10* 13.

174. Ormerod, R. (1962) 'Doctor in the witness box', *Practitioner 189* 5.

175. Adelson, L. (1964) 'Pathologist takes the witness stand', *Amer. J. Clin. Pathol. 41* 4841.

176. Diamond, B.L. (1966) *N.Y. Times* 28 March p. 19.

177. Bazelon, D.L. (1974) 'Psychiatrists and the adversary process', *Sci. Amer. 230* 18.

178. Menninger, K.A. (1969) 'Psychiatrists should shun courtroom', *Med. Tribune* 27 Feb.

179. Moenssens, J.D. (1974) 'The "impartial" medical expert: a new look at an old issue', *Scalpel & Quill 8* 1.

180. Schiff, S.A. (1963) 'The use of out of court information in fact determination at trial', *Canad. Bev. Rev.* Sept.

181. Camps F. (1968) *Gradwohl's Legal Medicine* Bristol: Wright.

182. Zilboorg, G. (1954) *The Psychology of the Criminal Act & Punishment*, N.Y. Harcourt Brace.

183. Savage, M. (1970) *A Great Fall: A Murder and its Consequences*, London: Cassell.

184. Glover, E. (1961) *Roots of Crime*, London: Imago.

185. East, W.N. (1927) *An Introduction to Forensic Psychiatry in the Criminal Courts*, London: Churchill.

186. Gibbens, T.C.N. (1974) 'Preparing psychiatric report for court', *Brit. J. Hosp. Med. 12* 278–284.

187. Bartholomew, A.A. (1962) The Psychiatric Report for the Court. *Crim. Law Rev. 19* 491.

188. Burke, J.J. (1975) 'Testifying in court', *F.B.I. Law Enforcement Bull. 44* 8–13.

189. Louisell, D.W. (1955) 'The psychologist in today's legal world', *Minn. Law Rev. 39* 235–272.

190. Buros, O.K. (1972) *7th Mental Measurements Yearbook* New Jersey, Highland Park: Gryphon Press.

191. Prince, M. (1906) *The Dissociation of a Personality*, New York: Longmans Green.

192. Thigpen, C.H. & Cleckley, H.M. (1957) *Three Faces of Eve*, London: Secker & Warburg.

193. Thesinger, Hon. Sir G. (1975) The Judge and the Expert. *Med. Sci. Law 15* 3–8.

194. Pear, T.H. *Personality, Appearance and Speech*, London: West 1957.

195. Bailey, F.L. & Rothblatt, H.B. (1971) *Successful Techniques for Criminal Trials*, Rochester: Barcroft-Whitney.

196. Cusumano, C.L. (1942) *Laugh at the Lawyer who Cross-examines you*, N.Y. Old Faithful Pub. Co.

197. Heffron, F.N. (1955) *Officer in the Court Room*, Springfield: Charles C. Thomas.

198. Pantalconi, C.A. (1971) *Handbook of Courtroom Demeaner*, Eaglewood Cliffs, N.J.: Prentice Hall.

199. Schiff, L.J. (1952) 'Doctor patient privilege in civil cases in Lousiana', *Lousisian Law Rev. 20* 418.
200. Meerloo J.A.M. (1962) in *Criminal Psychology*, R.W. Nice (Ed.) New York: Philosophical Lib.
201. Levinson, F. (1972) *Personal Communication*.
202. Neustatter, W.L. (1970) 'Personal view', *Brit. Med. J.* ii 240 (24 Oct.).
203. Geiser, R.L. & Rheingold, P.D. (1964) 'Testimonial privileged communications', *Amer. Psychol. 19* 831–837.
204. Hollender, M.H. (1965) 'Privileged communication & confidentiality', *Dis. Nerv. Syst. 26* 169–175.
205. GAP (1960) Group for the Advancement of Psychiatry, *Report No. 45*.
206. Alverson Judge (1958) in Hollender M.H. (1965).
207. Hollender, M.H. (1960) 'The psychiatrist and the release of patient information', *Am. J. Psychiat. 116828*.
208. Lovenkor & Usdin, G.L. (1961) 'Psychiatrist and privileged communication', *Arch. Gen. Psychiat. 4* 31.
209. Stern, H.R. (1959) 'Problem of privilege: historial and juridical sidelights', *Am.J. Psychiat. 115* 1071.
210. Goldstein & Katz (1962) Psychiatrist—patient privilege *118* 733.
211. Diamond, B.L. (1959) 'Discussion of papers on privilege', *Am. J. Psychiat. 115* 1078.
212. Rembar, C. (1969) *The End of Obscenity*, London: Deutsch.
213. Jones, R.V. (1963) 'Nuts & bolts: a reflection on *R. v. Rouse*', *Med. Sci. Law 3* 289.
214. McCartney, J.L. & J.R. (1959) Psychiatric Testimony in Military & Civilian Courts. *J. Soc. Ther. 5*.
215. Wiseman, S. (1961) 'Psychiatry & law: use and abuse of psychiatry in a murder case', *Amer. J. Psychiat. 118* 289.
216. Rastall, M.L. (1973) *Personal Communication*.
217. (1954) The Press Christchurch, N.Z. Aug. 25.
218. Haward, L.R.C. (1979) 'The Psychologist as Expert Witness', In: *Psychology Law & Legal Processes*, London: Macmillan.
219. Stonehouse, J. (1976) *My Trial*, London: Wyndham.
220. (1966) N.Y. Times, March 12 p. 24.
221. Lesse, S. (1964) 'Psychiatry and the law: a *danse macabre*', *Amer. J. Psychotherapy 18* 184–186.
222. Kelly, J. (1972) *Orders for the Captain*, Dublin: Kelly.
223. McKellar, P. (1968) *Experience and Behaviour*, Harmondsworth: Penguin Books.
224. Jeffrey, R. (1964) 'Psychologist as an expert witness on the issue of insanity', *Amer. Psychol. 19* 838–843.
225. Teaham, J.E. (1964) 'Clinical training and expert testimony', *Amer. Psychol. 19*

226. Daily Telegraph 25 Nov. p. 17. (1978).

227. Fransella, F. & Bannister, D. (1979) *Manual for Repertory Grid Technique*, London: Academic Press.

228. Osgood, C.E. (1957) *Measurement of Meaning*, Illinois: University of Illinois Press.

229. Cross, Sir R. (1979) *Evidence*, 5th Edition. London: Butterworth.

230. Blom-Cooper, L. (1963) '*A-6 Murder: Regina v. James Hanratty*', Harmondsworth: Penguin.

231. Kutchinsky, B. (1973) 'Effect of easy availability of pornography on the incidence of sex crimes', *J. Soc. Issues* 29 163–181.

232. McGillis, D. & Mullen, J. (1977) *Neighbourhood Justice Centers*, Washington, DC. U.S. Govt. Printing Office.

233. Legal Correspondent (1964) Doctor as a Witness, London: B.M.A.

234. Wiley, H.J. & Stallworthy, K.B. (1962) *Mental Abnormality and the Law*, N.Z.: Peryer.

235. Eggleston, Sir R.E. *Evidence Proof and Probability*, London: Weidenfeld & Nicholson.

Index of Statutes Cited

in chronological order

Index of Statutes Cited

317

Index of Cases Cited

Index of Cases Cited

Index of Persons Cited

This index *excludes* authors already cited in the bibliography, and also excludes parties to an action cited in the Index to Cases. In the latter, plaintiffs and appellants are listed alphabetically; accused persons will be found with the Crown cases and arranged alphabetically under 'R. v.'. Defendants in civil actions are cited with the name of the plaintiff/appellant preceding them.

Subject Index